CONSUMER ECONOMICS AND PERSONAL MONEY MANAGEMENT

CONSUMER ECONOMICS AND PERSONAL MONEY MANAGEMENT

SECOND EDITION

FRANCIS M. ALBIN

Highline Community College
Midway, Washington

PRENTICE HALL, Englewood Cliffs, N.J. 07632

Library of Congress Cataloging in Publication Data

Albin, Francis M.
    Consumer economics and personal money management / Francis M.
Albin.—2nd ed.
      p. cm.
    Bibliography: p.
    Includes index.
    ISBN 0-13-168048-X
    1. Finance, Personal. 2. Home economics—Accounting. I. Title.
HG179.A42 1989
332.024—dc19

Editorial/production supervision and interior design: *Madelaine Cooke*
Cover design: *Lundgren Graphics*
Manufacturing buyer: *Ed O'Dougherty*

© 1989 by Prentice-Hall, Inc.
A Division of Simon and Schuster
Englewood Cliffs, New Jersey 07632

Printed in the United States of America

10 9 8 7 6 5 4 3 2 1

ISBN 0-13-168048-X

Prentice-Hall International (UK) Limited, *London*
Prentice-Hall of Australia Pty. Limited, *Sydney*
Prentice-Hall Canada Inc., *Toronto*
Prentice-Hall Hispanoamericana, S.A., *Mexico*
Prentice-Hall of India Private Limited, *New Delhi*
Prentice-Hall of Japan, Inc., *Tokyo*
Simon & Schuster Asia Pte. Ltd, *Singapore*
Editora Prentice-Hall do Brasil, Ltda., *Rio de Janeiro*

To my wife Hideko

Contents

11   Income Taxes   319

Preface

I want a textbook that will help me to become a better money manager, yet this text must not be too bookish or so encyclopedic that I am constantly awash in technical detail. My job and other responsibilities prevent my spending vast amounts of time either learning the subject matter or maintaining a sophisticated system that neither I nor my family will ever comprehend.

This statement seems to summarize the needs of today's busy adult student who wants to enroll in a course on personal money management. It is a constant challenge for instructors of consumer finance courses to develop new and relevant material continually for their classes in a rapidly changing consumer world.

Today's personal finance class is much more complex and diverse and therefore more difficult for both the instructor and the student for several reasons:

1. The classroom is no longer the province of a homogeneous group of students of similar ages and backgrounds. A typical community college class of 30 or 40 students consists of the young and older adult student, the veteran, the housewife, the career changeover person, the foreign and immigrant student, the divorced and the displaced, the well-off, and those on welfare.
2. Rapidly changing life-styles are making it more difficult to draw upon past "rules-of-thumb" for gauging progress or success.

3. America is rapidly changing from an industrial society to one based on information. For the consumer, the U.S. economy has changed vastly over the past decade. Inflation, conversion to alternative energy resources, an aging population, greater interdependence with other nations, and rising world population are all affecting each individual and his or her pocketbook.

4. Instant communications and rapid transportation are creating a one-world economy and a growing interdependence among all nations.

The material in this text will cover the basics of sound money management with the topics of food, shelter, transportation, insurance, budgeting, banking, saving, investing, and the inevitable death and taxes included. There are brief exposures to what I call "shirt-sleeve economics" to provide essential background about our economy. There are many illustrations, basic worksheets, tables, and lists of data for organizational purposes and for "mind-jogging." The worksheets assist the reader on the "how-to" aspect of accomplishing his or her money-related objectives. Furthermore, the illustrated worksheets can be easily revised by the reader to meet individual needs and life-styles.

Last, the approach or system illustrated throughout this text is one that this author has used rather successfully for almost 30 years. The adult student will not have to spend very much time with these basic budgets, records, and files, although they are essential and universal starting points. After reading this text, the student will be able to spend much more time on those activities that are probably far more interesting. If this book emphasizes a show-and-tell approach, it is to give the student the basic information necessary to be in control of personal financial affairs for a lifetime.

Francis M. Albin

Acknowledgments

Several years ago Prentice Hall representative David Garrison stopped by my office and suggested that my personal money management course handouts should be made into a book so others could learn my approaches to handling the basics relating to money management. And, with the assistance of other P H staff such as Steven E. Cline, John Duhring, and Barbara Grasso, this book was made possible. Since then, after this book entered its third printing, my editors, Read Wickham and Susan Jacob, suggested it was time to make a thorough revision for the benefit of the many individuals, service agency personnel, and thousands of students in high schools, technical schools, and colleges who have used this book.

As in the first edition, business corporations, newspaper services, and non-profit associations have been most kind and generous in allowing my use of their materials for examples.

Special acknowledgment is made to the *Northwestern Endicott-Lindquist Report*, Pillsbury Company, and Standard & Poor's Corporation, as well as to the Dow Jones Company Incorporated and the *Seattle Times*; others contributing materials include the Concern for Dying, National Garden Bureau, and the Washington Education Association.

I owe a special word of thanks to Theresa A. Hanlon, a long-time consultant to me on financial problems relating to the displaced, divorced, minority, and elderly. Her background in human services and community work has made her an able spokesperson in calling attention to the financial concerns of these groups. Many topics included in this book are approached with these groups in mind.

The typing of the basic manuscript and initial proofreading were done by my wife, Hideko K. Albin, an executive secretary and former journalist, who helped me to keep the book production schedule. Last, there are hundreds of students of every age and background who have attended my classes and made the topic of consumer economics and personal money management an ever-fascinating and provocative one.

ADOPTIONS

The author extends appreciation and thanks to the following people, school districts, technical schools, community colleges, universities, corporations, and social agencies who have used the first edition for instruction and in-service training: Carol Matich of American River College; Augusta Area Technical School; Baker & Taylor Co. of Momence, Ill.; Beaufort Technical College; Bessemer State Technical College; Bladen Technical College; Bristol Community College; Carman Ainsworth Community Schools; Carroll County Georgia Area Vocational Technical Schools; Charles Dunham of Centralia College; Charles County, Maryland, Board of Education; Christopher, Illinois, Board of Education; Coker College; College of the Redwoods; Columbia Christian College; Crandell College; Daytona Beach Community College; Downers Grove, Illinois, High School District 99; Endicott Junior College; Erie Community College, North Campus; Follets Varsity Bookstore; Grand Rapids Baptist College, Harrisburg, Illinois.

Among the community schools are Richard H. Gradwohl of Highline Community College; Hill Junior College, Housatonic Regional Community College; Beth Blair, Laura Carnie, and Michael Miller of Idaho Junior College; Indiana Vocational-Technical College; J. H. Dubois Bookstore; Johnson County, North Carolina, Department of Social Services; Knoxville, Illinois, Community Unit Schools; Hiroshi Yoshida of Kobe University of Commerce; Mary Hardin of Baylor College; Midlands Technical College, Northern Michigan University; Old Salem Enterprises, Inc., of North Carolina; Ottumwa, Iowa, Community School District; Ross Maloney of Peninsula College; Pierce College of Los Angeles; Richmond County, Georgia; Board of Education, Salesisnum School of Delaware; Dolores Washington of San Joaquin Delta College; Savannah Area Vocational-Technical College; Ronald Leverett of Seattle Central Community College; Southwest Baptist University; Ronald A. Siltzer of Spartanburg Technical College; State of Illinois Board of Education; The College Store of Oakland; Troup County, Georgia, Area Vocational Technical Schools; University of Cincinnati; University of Connecticut; University of Salt Lake City; Utica Michigan Community Schools; Wayne Westland, Michigan, Community Schools; Heinz Pruss of Wenatchee Valley Community College; Western New Mexico University; and Western Oregon State University.

How to Use This Book

TO THE GENERAL READER

This book is designed to serve as a consumer survival kit for managing your money today and in the future. It may be read from cover to cover or used as a reference book. The basics are covered—food, clothing, shelter, transportation, insurance, banking, saving, investing, taxes, retirement, and estate planning. In addition, this book will help you learn how to plan, to become better organized, to approach budgeting in a businesslike way, and to control spending. More than 400 useful consumer economics–related terms are listed in Appendix B for ready reference. The section called Tips found at the end of each chapter provides additional suggestions and perspectives on personal money management. Many illustrations and completed worksheets help the reader to grasp key ideas at a glance. For example, if you are planning to buy a house, the glossary in Chapter 8 will help you brush up on essential real estate terms, and material in the chapter will show you how to calculate what you can afford for a house and review other costs of home ownership. For other topics, a similar approach has been taken. You are encouraged to modify, revise, condense, or omit resource materials to fit *your* own particular life-style.

TO THE INSTRUCTOR

The instructor may use this textbook in any of the following types of courses.

1. As a first-year course in personal finance offered by a department of business at a college or community college.
2. As a first-year course in a family finance and household budgeting course offered by a home economics department or similar curriculum at a college, community college, or technical school.
3. In special seminars or courses directed toward the "woman in transition" or "expanding horizons for women" where the emphasis is on sound practical money management.
4. In high school courses, predischarge or prerelease programs, alternative and community education programs in which the emphasis is on consumer survival skills, or similar popular short courses.

The Instructor's Manual for this textbook includes suggested lecture outlines and test material.

TO THE STUDENT

The student will find that the material can be comprehended easily if the following approach is used.

1. Read the Learning Objectives at the beginning of each chapter.
2. Skim the chapter, looking at the various topics and captions, tables, figures, worksheets, and so on.
3. Read the Summary at the end of the chapter. The summary highlights the major points covered in the chapter in concise sentences.
4. Read the chapter for meaning and underline key terms, concepts, and ideas.
5. Reread the Summary. Close the book and try to remember the key ideas in the chapter.
6. Review the Glossary of Useful Terms at the end of the chapter. The glossary is supplemental to the material covered in the book. The chapter glossaries cover more than 400 basic terms and current "buzzwords" related to the chapter topics. Some of the terms covered in the chapter may be repeated in the glossary.

1

Personal Money
Management and Planning

LEARNING OBJECTIVES

Upon completion of Chapter 1, you should be able to identify and remember

- Many of the basic facts and factors that summarize the U.S. economy today.
- The impact of continued inflation, population growth, and scarce economic resources on one's personal money management goals.
- The importance of choosing a career and preparing for it as well as that career's importance in reaching your financial goals.
- How to assess your own strengths and weaknesses of your own personal attributes or assets.
- How to prepare a balance sheet or net worth statement.
- The money management model for attaining your personal and financial objectives.
- The four elements of planning.

THEME OF THIS TEXTBOOK

This book offers a practical approach for managing your personal financial affairs in an organized and uncomplicated manner. The material covered is designed to provide sufficient relevant and useful information to make you a prudent money manager for the rest of your life.

This lifetime program of personal money management should be viewed in light of the following important areas:

1. A basic understanding of the U.S. economic system.
2. Your career(s) as well as your lifetime goals and objectives.
3. The ever-present threat of inflation.
4. The population growth in the United States and worldwide.
5. The shift to alternative energy resources.

OVERVIEW

Your are about to embark on a most necessary but often neglected phase of learning—that of successfully gaining control over your financial affairs for the rest of your life. Many of the topics discussed in these pages are so basic, yet so essential, that you may wonder why we all did not think of using many of the concepts and approaches years ago. Other techniques to be discussed are well known, but most people simply have not found the time to make use of them.

Many individuals spend much of their time on learning "how to earn a living," but only a few seem to know "how to spend a living." Still others, who have spent much of their life raising and managing a family, have not learned some good, basic job skills. Since most people are cast in various roles at one time or another during their lifetimes, one of your goals might be to learn about some of those areas in which you are weakest. Every adult should be prepared both to earn a living and to spend a living. With the rise in the divorce rate among married couples, one should be prepared to find one's self "being single again." Given that women live longer than men, many women can expect to have to deal with widowhood, facing major financial and legal considerations at an emotional time in their lives. It is hoped that these chapters will provide essential financial guidance in this important area.

While some people can set aside money for minor emergencies and others are able to save for certain major household appliances, only a small number are successful in accumulating sufficient money and investments for a life of financial independence.

You may have heard the following lines before, but they are worth repeating:

Out of 100 Americans reaching the age of 65, 84 people will have no savings and therefore must look to such programs as Social Security as their sole source of income or continue with some employment, 8 persons will have a little income, 6 will live comfortably, and 2 persons will be considered well-off.

This is not a very optimistic forecast, particularly when Americans can expect to spend approximately 25 percent of their normal life span in retirement. Recent changes in mandatory retirement laws will permit many people to work until they are 70 years of age and older, which will help those older employees to maintain their purchasing power through their job and provide time for additional saving and investment for their postworking years. But, with the rate of inflation averaging around 6 percent the past few years, unless one's income increases proportionately, the individual's purchasing power will be cut in half in 12 years. Should inflation average 10 percent a year, purchasing power would be cut in half in just over 7 years. This factor should be considered by those approaching retirement.

Let us return to the quotation. For people to spend nearly half their total life in the world of work and to end up with little or nothing to show for it cannot all be the result of bad luck or fate. The real problem appears to be that many

Herman

"Got any books for about a dollar on financial planning?"

people have unrealistic ideas and goals or no goals at all and therefore seem to drift through life. It is true that younger people do not think seriously about their eventual retirement when it appears to be so far distant. But retirement does have a way of sneaking up on one, and, when one does seriously begin to establish investment programs for those postworking years, the effort is often too little and too late. We should also note that retirement is popularly referred to as a condition affecting those career men and women whose activities were at workstations outside their homes. Yet consider the millions of women who have been homemakers and are not included in current retirement programs. While they do not "retire," they have made a substantial contribution to the economy. We will return to the topic of retirement in Chapter 12. At this time, we will review some other important factors included in the subject of personal money management.

In planning a lifetime money management program, one must consider the prospects of:

1. Continued inflation.
2. Prolonged human life span.
3. Continued high unemployment.
4. Increasing world population and world economy.
5. Energy shortages and conservation of resources.
6. The role of big business, government, and labor.

This is not to say that other factors will not affect your financial planning. The career you choose, the state of your health, the person you marry, the place in which you live, and the number of children you have will greatly affect your income and spending. However, it is very likely that people will continue to focus on these six issues, with one or another gaining particular interest from time to time. It is beyond the scope of this text to touch upon all these matters or on certain others, such as the threat of war or natural disasters. Nevertheless, the six issues will be discussed briefly to permit the reader some perspective for better planning of a money management program.

To be successful as a money manager, one must know something about the U.S. economy as it exists today. (The glossary at the end of this chapter contains additional basic economic terms included to expand your understanding.) Let us begin by reviewing some of the business and economic data about the United States in the late 1980s.

A SKETCH OF THE U.S. ECONOMY TODAY

As we look at the nation approaching the 1990s, the U.S. population is at the 250 million mark, or about 5 percent of the earth's total. The gross national product

(GNP) is rising from $5 trillion a year toward $6 trillion. Using the 1967 consumer price index with a base of 100 as a benchmark, prices are now four times higher today. Yet, wages and salaries of men and women during this same period have not kept pace when adjusted for inflation. (Exhibit 1-1 illustrates the trend of consumer prices in the 1960–1987 period.) Of our total population in 1990, approximately 120 million men and women will be employed, up from 99 million in 1980, with the work force nearly equally divided between women and men. Moreover, many are having to work at two jobs and at longer hours to maintain their standard of living in this world economy. The United States is losing many of its industrial firms, and displaced skilled and white-collar workers and their families are starting new businesses at the rate of 600,000 to 700,000

EXHIBIT 1-1 Consumer Price Index, 1960–1987 (1967 = 100)

Year	Index
1960	88.7
1961	89.6
1962	90.6
1963	91.7
1964	92.9
1965	94.5
1966	97.2
1967	**100.0**
1968	104.2
1969	109.8
1970	116.3
1971	121.3
1972	125.3
1973	133.1
1974	147.7
1975	161.2
1976	170.5
1977	181.5
1978	195.4
1979	217.4
1980	246.8
1981	272.4
1982	289.1
1983	298.4
1984	311.1
1985	322.2
1986	325.7*
1987	340.8†

Consumer Prices

In percent (1967=100).

[Graph showing Consumer Prices from 350% down to 300%, with years 1986, 1987, 1988]

* Preliminary

† Through July 1987

Graph reprinted by permission of *The Wall Street Journal,* © Dow Jones & Company, Inc. (1988). All rights reserved. Data are from U.S. Bureau of Labor Statistics, *Monthly Labor Review.*

per year. Savings by individuals is very low, causing businesses and government to borrow money from overseas. Poverty in America still runs at 12 to 15 percent, with from 30 to 40 million facing a harsh and uncertain future.

The United States is part of a growing and interdependent world economy: one in six jobs is related to world trade activity, and two of every five acres cultivated are devoted to crops destined to other countries. Canada, Japan, Mexico, and China are among America's largest and culturally diverse trading partners.

Total U.S. trade with underdeveloped and emerging nations exceeds its combined trade with Europe, Japan, and Russia, and we lead the world in high-tech, information, and service areas. However, large U.S. budget deficits and our failure to study foreign customers' needs and cultures have caused many American firms to lose export opportunities.

The nation's capitalistic or "free enterprise" economic system is undergoing rapid change. Businesspeople will say that it is not what it used to be and that the free enterprise system is in danger. They say that there are too many regulations, too many taxes, and too much government paperwork. No doubt, much of the criticism is true, but the trend will probably continue, with local, state and federal government maintaining its role in the marketplace as a sort of referee or arbitrator for both business and consumers in the years to come. On the other hand, taxes have become a major burden, and many Americans are demanding more equity in taxation. Symbolic of a growing taxpayer's revolt are California's Proposition 13, which called for a limitation on property taxes, and President Reagan's income tax reforms.

Even with these obvious difficulties, however, there are many opportunities that you as consumer can take advantage of to improve your economic well-being, namely, to change jobs, start your own business, move to another city or across town, work as many hours as you want, follow a life-style of your own choosing, and so on.

While much could be written concerning the consumer movement in the United States, our discussions will focus on those areas in which consumer protection laws help relate to personal money management. Let us carry our discussion on the American economic system a step farther by spending some time with the very basics of economic philosophy as it works to shape the activities of the marketplace.

Scarcity of Economic Resources

It is difficult for the average individual living in a modern society not to have some understanding of fundamental economics. A hundred years ago an educated person may have had to understand Latin. Today, an educated person should have some economics and maybe some accounting to function in a modern economy. Economists have long talked about the fact that human beings have unlimited desires or wants. They say that when one want has been satisfied, another want takes it place and so on. Some of the things we want are free or almost free. The economist will usually offer such things as air and water as *free goods* because those items are in relatively great abundance and require little or no effort to obtain them. On the other hand, some of the goods we desire to satisfy one of those unlimited wants will require a greater degree of effort to obtain them.

People's demands for things must be accompanied by (1) a real desire for something and (2) the ability to pay for it. Those things that are called *economic goods* by the economist are much more scarce than are air and water. The more scarce the good or service, the more a person may have to pay for it. Here we come to an interesting term, *value*. Individuals and groups of individuals today attach some estimate of worth to most all goods and services. Therefore, values (prices) are attached to everything offered in the marketplace. The value of goods and services is set by a combination of the relative scarcity of the actual goods and services and the number of people wanting those goods or services. It is the *supply* of goods and services available and the *demand* for those goods and services that basically establishes the value of their sales prices.

In simpler economic systems and in earlier times, there seemed to have been a built-in regulatory function. People who might make a substantial profit from selling a particular item or rendering some special service would soon find themselves attracting imitators or competitors. Then there would be a leveling off of prices and profits. The number of competitors coming into the marketplace would slow when they could no longer earn sufficient income from that activity. However, this self-regulatory function could only work when there were many businesses and each of those businesses was rather small. Today, when there is a worldwide demand for some goods, such as gasoline, and huge multinational corporations supplying these goods, the basic economic theories or models no longer work. Since resources, education, enlightened governments, and so on are not equally distributed throughout the world, many segments of today's marketplace lack competition or at least price competition. The term that describes this situation is *monopolistic competition,* as when there are few sellers and many buyers in the marketplace. Earlier in this century, for example, there were between 1,500 and 2,000 automobile makers in the United States; today, there are only 3 major U.S. manufacturers.

Another important condition of the U.S. economic system is the amount of *interdependence* that exists among business firms. For example, a shutdown of activities in the steel industry can create substantial difficulties in, say, the automobile industry. Lost automobile production will soon have an impact on railroad freight car loadings; deliveries of cars and parts to dealers and repair shops decline. Because of a shutdown caused by a severe winter in the Northeast, an auto loan clerk in Southern California could soon be on a reduced work schedule or temporarily out of a job. In planning your financial future, you should determine how directly or indirectly your job is affected by such things as strikes, weather, and government action. Today's government regulatory agencies will act as an arbitrator to prevent what might otherwise result in a rapid deterioration of the public welfare or the nation's defense.

One more economic concept at work in the United States that should be mentioned is the *principle of substitution*. At present, there is a shortage of adequate housing. Single-family dwelling homes that could be bought for $25,000 just 15 years ago now sell for $95,000 or more. As prices go up, many people will no longer seek a private detached dwelling and will look for alternate forms of homes such as row houses, condominiums, and mobile homes. Some of the substitutions have not come as a result of higher prices but as a result of major technological advances. One of the best examples is the small hand-held calculator or computer, which has all but replaced the older bulky metal adding machines and has made the engineer's slide rule obsolete. Incidentally, an inexpensive pocket calculator will be an essential tool in your money management program.

Inflation, One's Lifelong Adversary

There is probably no greater threat to your financial planning and financial security than that of inflation. Many people who retired only five or six years ago are finding that their retirement income is already insufficient to meet their needs. Dreams of traveling and living a more carefree life are being modified because the costs of basics such as food, shelter, medical care, and transportation have all risen faster than most people had anticipated. Since inflation affects government costs as well, many state and local taxes, particularly property taxes, have risen. Table 1-1 shows the general rate of inflation for the United States over the past four decades.

Several conclusions can be drawn from this table. First, the inflation rate remained at around 2 percent a year from 1948 to 1966, with the exception of 1950 and 1951, which were influenced by war in Korea. This 18-year period of relatively modest inflation was also a period when a worker's real productivity and take-home pay greatly exceeded the 2 percent inflation rate.

Second, from 1966 and to the present, there has been an alarming increase in the inflation rate, with the 1966–1973 inflation rate averaging well over 6 percent a year, which has served to erode the purchasing power of business and workers. A declining productivity rate of goods and services is a major cause of U.S. inflation.

Third, since we are no longer experiencing inflation at the double-digit levels of 1974, 1979, and 1980, many public officeholders and news writers convey the notion that any lower inflation rate is almost normal.

Consider, however, that 6 percent inflation is still 300 percent higher than that when the rate was only 2 percent ($6\% \div 2\% = 3X$, for a 300% increase).

TABLE 1-1 Changes in the Consumer Price Index, 1948–1987

Year	CPI rise	Year	CPI rise
1948	2.7%	1968	4.7%
1949	−1.8	1969	6.1
1950	5.8	1970	5.5
1951	5.9	1971	3.4
1952	0.9	1972	3.4
1953	0.6	1973	8.8
1954	−0.5	1974	12.2
1955	0.4	1975	7.0
1956	2.9	1976	6.0
1957	3.0	1977	6.8
1958	1.8	1978	9.0
1959	1.5	1979	13.3
1960	1.5	1980	12.4
1961	0.7	1981	8.9
1962	1.2	1982	3.9
1963	1.6	1983	3.8
1964	1.2	1984	4.0
1965	1.9	1985	3.8
1966	3.4	1986	1.1
1967	3.0	1987 est.	4.7

Data were derived from the Bureau of Labor Statistics, *Monthly Labor Review.*

Table 1-2 presents selected information about the American family and how it has changed since the mid-1960s.

Inflation in the past has caused many people to turn to less expensive cuts of meat to reduce their grocery bills, keep their automobiles a little longer, or buy smaller cars. Inflation has caused others to postpone buying new clothing or to perform more of their home and car maintenance. However, to restore a more tolerable inflation rate of, say, 2 percent or even 3 percent a year, consumer activity must become more assertive and on a broader front. Major efforts toward reducing the importation of oil, achieving a balanced federal budget, developing greater cooperation between labor and management to increase productivity in business, and achieving more equitable state and local taxation will be necessary.

Fourth, to stay "even" by the year 2010, see Table 1-3, which projects the required annual gross salaries or wages that a person would need at three arbitrarily selected levels of inflation with a $10,000 assumed salary being earned in the base year of 1988. (These figures ignore the impact of the graduated federal income tax and its impact on reducing real purchasing power.) One can well understand that a 2 percent national inflation rate is certainly a goal to strive for.

TABLE 1-2　The Changed American Family

	1965	1980	1985
Working women (percentage of all women 16 and over)	36.7	51.1	54.7
Fertility rate (number of children the average woman will have at the end of her childbearing years)[1]	2.9	1.8	1.8
Marriage rate (number of marriages per 1,000 population)[2]	9.3	10.6	10.2
Median age at first marriage			
Men	22.8	24.7	25.5
Women	20.6	22.0	23.3
Divorce rate (number of couples divorcing per 1,000 population)	2.5	5.2	5.0
Single-parent families (percentage of all families with children under 18)	10.1	19.5	22.2
Pre-marital births (percentage of all births)	7.7	18.4	21.5[3]
Living alone (percentage of all households occupied by single person)	15.0	22.6	23.7

[1] A 2.1 rate is needed for the natural replacement of the population.
[2] Remarriages account for about one-third of the recent totals.
[3] Estimated

Sources: Census Bureau; National Center for Health Statistics; Department of Labor

Otten, Alan L., "Deceptive Picture: If You See Families Staging a Comeback, It's Probably a Mirage," *The Wall Street Journal,* September 25, 1986, p. 1. Reprinted by permission of *The Wall Street Journal,* © Dow Jones & Company, Inc. (1986). All rights reserved.

One final comment concerning inflation is in order. Suppose that a person is 25 years of age in the year 1988, expects to have a career extending over the next 40 years, and then retires at the age of 65. The retirement year will be 2028. Let us also assume that this person is earning $10,000 in the base year of 1988. Table 1-4 shows the required annual income in year 40, the last career year (2028), at inflation rates of 2, 6, and 10 percent.

A person is entirely in his or her right to question this presentation. Perhaps, you say, the government will step in and put a stop to this inflationary spiral. But it is doubtful that any government will effectively halt rising prices or rising price trends. One has only to look back or read about life in America just 40 years ago. At that time a factory worker earning $2,000 a year probably wondered if the family could really afford that $700 car or buy that dream home advertised for sale at $2,800. In 1938 a 12-oz bottle of cola was 5 cents, a loaf of bread was 10 cents, and a quart of fresh milk delivered to your door was only 10

TABLE 1-3 Annual Gross Salaries at Various Inflation Rates to Maintain a $10,000 Base, 1988–2010

Year	2% Inflation	6% Inflation	10% Inflation
1988	$10,000	$10,000	$10,000
1989	10,200	10,600	11,000
1990	10,404	11,236	12,100
1991	10,612	11,910	13,310
1992	10,824	12,625	14,641
1993	11,041	13,382	16,105
1994	11,261	14,185	17,716
1995	11,487	15,036	19,487
1996	11,172	15,939	21,435
1997	11,951	16,895	23,580
1998	12,190	17,909	25,937
1999	12,434	18,983	28,531
2000	12,682	20,122	31,384
2001	12,936	21,329	34,384
2002	13,195	22,609	37,975
2003	13,459	23,966	41,773
2004	13,728	25,404	45,950
2005	14,002	26,928	50,545
2006	14,283	28,543	55,599
2007	14,568	30,256	61,159
2008	14,860	32,071	67,275
2009	15,157	33,995	74,003
2010	15,459	36,035	81,403

cents. Fortunately, and looking at things in another perspective, 40 years is a long time and people still live each year one day at a time. Forty years, or 14,600 days, is plenty of time to make up a list of life goals and plan just how to accomplish them despite the current rate of inflation. Later, we will see why some people today can think of buying a $90,000 home and a $7,000 automobile without too much hesitation. However, let us continue our review of the current

TABLE 1-4 Required Annual Income Calculations at Various Rates of Inflation

Inflation rate	Required annual salary for year 2028
2%	$ 22,080
6%	102,857
10%	452,593

setting for planning a lifetime money management strategy by looking at the prospects of population growth and how it may affect you in the future.

Population, the Crowded Future

Others in history developed theories of population growth, but this is the first generation of people to have to deal actually with the situation on a global basis. Regardless of where you stand on this issue, rising U.S. and world populations must be understood as they affect the availability of land, foodstuffs, and other natural resources such as oil, gas, and basic metals.

As was stated, the United States constitutes about 5 percent of the world's total population. At the same time, the United States currently produces about 40 percent of the goods and services for the world and consumes around one-third of those same goods and services. Table 1-5 projects the U.S. population through the year 2025. Table 1-6 outlines past, present, and future world population figures. After you have looked at these tables, consider the following questions:

1. What is likely to happen to the price of land in the future?
2. Will neighboring states or countries continue to sell to the United States those basic raw materials that have made American life enjoyable?
3. Will the gap between the have and have-not nations create more hostile relationships in the future?
4. Will there be more social democratic or social welfare governmental structures in the future to determine the distribution of scarce and expensive resources?

TABLE 1-5 Projected U.S. Population Growth, 1985–2025

Year	U.S. population (millions)
1985	237
1990	246
1995	253
2000	258
2005	263
2010	267
2015	271
2020	274
2025	275

Data are from *Statistical Abstract of the United States, 1985*, p. 8.

TABLE 1-6 Estimated World Population, 1800–2050

Year	World population (billions)
1800	1
1930	2
1960	3
1976	4
2000	7
2050	14

Source: United Nations

YOUR OWN FUTURE: HALF THE FUN IS GETTING THERE

Americans born today have a life expectancy of approximately 71 years for a man and 78 for a woman. These figures apply to all races in America, according to the National Center for Health Statistics. Is it really possible to project what life will be like in the future and list the impact of future events on you, the nation, and the world? Making predictions into the distant future on how men and women will live their lives can be a harmless and amusing pastime. So why not draw up your own list of things to come? The areas of inflation and population could serve as basic guideposts that may well continue to have an impact on your future. The past 100 years produced such inventions as the electric light, telephone, automobile, airplane, radio, TV, and X ray. Add your own expectations of major breakthroughs for sewage disposal, computers and microcircuits, a cure for cancer, cheap solar energy, and so on, and you may have as good an idea about what the future holds as any expert around. Marketing experts know that many of the items that we will be using in everyday life just 10 years from now have not been invented as yet. If you were around 25 years of age in 1988, you could live to see the year 2030. A few hearty souls will still be celebrating birthdays in the year 2050, and a few will see the year 2060 ushered in. How we will earn and spend our money in the future will certainly be influenced by other factors such as the ability to perceive and take advantage of career and investment opportunities as they arise. Let us move on to the topics of careers, lifetime goals, and objectives.

Careers, the Means to the End

The U.S. economic system is the one that should cause each person to give substantial consideration to a career goal at an early age. A competitive economic environment tends to cause people to work in the field of their highest skill level. Therefore, one's ability to be successful in a career may well depend closely on how well a person prepares himself or herself for a specific career.

Most readers of this book will have a large block of years ahead of them in which to master the fundamentals of a specific career or a group of allied careers providing that the individual knows what it is he or she wants to do. Unfortunately, many people do not spend much time thinking about what they would really like to do and hold jobs that are not meaningful to them. Others view their jobs as dead ends and are unable to see the potentials that lie ahead. Nevertheless, accumulated job experience—even at a low level—plus appropriate training and education, being observant, having the desire or motivation to be successful—all can assist a person to work into the higher echelons of management. Many senior executives and administrative officers of corporations retiring today were first hired some 30 years ago in one of the entry-level positions in the firm.

Affirmative action programs are now helping many people in entry-level positions to apply for other paying jobs. If you are in this situation, you should think "nontraditional." Driving a truck, learning to be an electrician, selling cars and real estate, working for the state highway system, or becoming a police officer, firefighter, or welder are still nontraditional career areas for women to explore, for example, and the income is good. The rising divorce rate of recent years should make women in particular consider long and hard about stopping their education upon marriage.

People put off thinking about their career goals because other things seem more important at the time. Career planning requires considerable thought, reading, and research. When one is younger, there always seems to be plenty of time to pursue such important matters. The most important critical factor associated with career planning is that *only you* can make the final decision. People around you can be of valuable assistance in finding the right career or career area for you. But nothing in itself is interesting; you have to bring your interest to something.

Your true *interest* in a particular job or career area should also be separated from your current *ability* to do certain kinds of tasks well. For example, you may have grown up in your parents' hardware store business. You have learned a lot about tools, paints, dealing with customers, handling money, writing sales invoices, and so on. However, you may really want to be a research chemist, even though it may take years of study before you can earn a decent paycheck as a chemist. Nevertheless, this has become an overwhelming desire. You give up the opportunity to stay in the hardware business. You even give up the chances to take over the family business. If you begin to feel this way about a specific career area, then you are probably on the right track about where your true interests lie. The fact that you could have been a reasonably good hardware business expert probably would have proved very unrewarding in the long run, and unhappily somewhere in middle age, you would have found it almost impossible to change careers.

If your goal is to make a lot of money, be prepared to put in very long working hours. And in the beginning it may be necessary to work at two jobs. If you are not willing to put in long hours and live rather frugally during the earlier years to reach this challenging goal, then your goal of becoming a millionaire is wishful thinking.

If your goal is to have your own business (probably still one of the best ways to become a millionaire), then you should gain all the information and experience you can by obtaining the relevant education and training as well as work experience as an employee with some business firm already established in the field. To be successful in your own business you must wear many hats. In addition to knowing your product or service, you need to know something about keeping a set of books for tax purposes, personnel and customer relations, basic marketing, and economics and enough about law to know when to call an attorney. Many small businesses fail because the owner was unable to deal with cash flow problems, personnel problems, budgeting, and inventory control.

Perhaps your career goal is not to make a bundle of money but, rather, to have a comfortable income and seek intangible rewards such as respect, recognition, and influence in your community. There seems to be no other way to learn this field other than by on-the-job experience. And local nonprofit civic, cultural, education, and community health agencies are always looking for people who are genuinely interested in helping the community.

A final point regarding careers should be made. No longer can people rely on the basic education gained in high school or college to carry them through their working years to retirement. Most people will be returning periodically to some form of education to upgrade their skills or learn some new ones because of new developments in technology, the workplace, and so on.

Lifetime Goals, Yours for the Thinking

We all think of the things we want to do over our lifetime. Many of these goals and objectives will require money to accomplish. Others will require time, and others will take both. A simple but useful technique is to write down your goals on a piece of paper. Next, review your goals each day. Make additions, revi-

© 1980. Reprinted by permission:
Tribune Media Services.

TABLE 1-7   Goals: Financial and Nonfinancial

Financial goals	Nonfinancial goals
Finish my education	Maintain good health
Have financial independence in retirement	Enjoy marriage and family
Own my own home	Develop good speaking voice
Own a sports car	Have many friends
Travel around the world	Set a world's record
Send children through college	Improve my memory
Own my own business	Have influence in the workplace
Possess a valuable antique collection	Develop good vocabulary
Own vacation property	Enjoy respect of others
Give money to a favorite cause	Learn a foreign language
Become a major stockholder in a company	Read 1,000 great books
	Play a musical instrument
	Write a book
	Play tennis

sions, and deletions to your list of goals as necessary. By keeping your goals in mind each day, they may help you plan how you might earn and spend your income. This is particularly important when most Americans will spend 95 cents of each dollar they earn. Note the two lists in Table 1-7 with the simple headings Financial Goals and Nonfinancial Goals. While many of the nonfinancial goals may require mostly time and self-discipline, they could be helpful in enhancing your career income.

Well, as you can see, this list may or may not include the goals that you see as wanting to accomplish. However, they are some that are on the minds of your peers. If one is very serious about wanting to accomplish those financially oriented goals, then it is important to select a career that will best help one to reach those goals. If what you want to accomplish is going to require $40,000-a-year salary or net income, then be sure that you prepare yourself for that level of job skill and responsibility. Otherwise, your goals are examples of wishful thinking. In the next section we will look at some of the accumulated skills and talents that you may already have and how these can be most helpful in accomplishing your lifetime goals.

Assessing Your Personal Talents or Assets

Each of us has a vast reservoir of untapped talents or personal assets. Exhibit 1-2 presents a list of personal talents, abilities, and accumulated skills that you may possess but do not use or think of as being relevant tools for success in your job or in reaching some of your money management objectives.

To complete the assessment, rank each item on a scale of 1 for the *lowest* to 7 for the *highest* rating. Make as honest an appraisal as possible.

EXHIBIT 1-2 Personal Asset Assessment Sheet

Personal Asset Category	High						Low
	7	6	5	4	3	2	1
1. Accuracy							
2. Adaptability							
3. Alertness							
4. Appearance							
5. Assertiveness							
6. Athletic ability							
7. Cheerfulness							
8. Color perception							
9. Concentration							
10. Cooperativeness							
11. Creativeness							
12. Dependability							
13. Drive							
14. Calmness							
15. Enterprise							
16. Enthusiasm							
17. Forcefulness							
18. Geniality							
19. Good health							
20. Good sport							
21. Guided by reality							
22. Honesty							
23. Imagination							
24. Impartiality							
25. Industriousness							
26. Listening ability							

EXHIBIT 1-2 (*continued*)

Personal Asset Assessment Sheet

27. Logic							
28. Loyalty							
29. Memory							
30. Meticulousness							
31. Moral courage							
32. Muscle coordination							
33. Native intelligence							
34. Persistence							
35. Physical strength							
36. Pleasant voice							
37. Poise							
38. Prudence							
39. Openmindedness							
40. Reading ability							
41. Responsibility							
42. Resourcefulness							
43. Self-confidence							
44. Self-discipline							
45. Sensitivity							
46. Sincerity							
47. Stamina							
48. Sympathy							
49. Tact/Graciousness							
50. Thrift							
51. Thoughtfulness							
52. Tolerance							
53. Visual perception							
54. Vocabulary							

Assessing Your Financial Assets and Net Worth

Having looked at personal talents or assets that can be of major use to us, let us now compile a list of our financial assets into a basic and very useful financial document called the *balance sheet*. While some people can pile all their worldly belongings into their automobile, others would need a large moving van and a Brink's armored truck.

The balance sheet is essentially a listing at a moment in time of all those things (*assets*) presently owned or being purchased in some form of installment plan by an individual or family. This listing includes the present money value or what these items could be sold for in today's marketplace. Another section of this balance sheet consists of a list of creditors (*liabilities*) or debts owed to other people or businesses. This would include amounts owed to department stores, finance companies, mortgage companies, banks, relatives, and friends. The difference between the total dollar value of assets owned or being purchased on time and the total amount of debts owed will result in a final figure called *net worth*. This is your residual interest or *equity* in all the things that you own. The net worth, or equity, is approximately what you might receive in cash if you were to sell everything that you owned and paid off all your creditors. The balance sheet for individuals is often expressed as follows:

$$\text{Assets} - \text{liabilities} = \text{net worth}$$

$$\text{Assets} - \text{debts} \quad\;\; = \text{equity or net worth}$$

If a person were to buy a $4,000 used automobile and give the dealer $1,000 as a down payment and a set of installment notes for $3,000, the buyer's equity in the car at the time of purchase would be $1,000 (asset of $4,000 minus debt of $3,000).

If you are making progress with your financial management program, then your net worth (equity) should increase each time you prepare your balance sheet. It is a good idea to prepare a balance sheet at least once a year. It is hoped that the size of your increase in equity is going to exceed by a considerable degree the rate of inflation that is taking place. Exhibit 1-3 is a simple illustration of a balance sheet. The balance sheet is very much like a snapshot of one's financial picture. It is a good idea, in addition to preparing a balance sheet each year, to draw up some balance sheets to indicate where you would like to be 5 years from now, 10 years from now, and so on. In Exhibit 1-3, Ruth Jones has a net worth of $7,865.00 on December 31, 19X1.

Your Money Management Model

The personal money manager may never regard himself or herself as a business world executive; however, the money manager must follow essentially the same fundamental management process or functions. First and foremost, always keep

EXHIBIT 1-3   Sample Balance Sheet

Ruth Jones
Balance Sheet
December 31, 19X1

Assets

Cash in bank	$ 350.00
Cash on hand	50.00
Credit union savings account	900.00
Two months rent paid in advance	500.00
Antique collectibles	700.00
Fifty shares of AT&T common stock	2,500.00
Automobile (current market value)	1,750.00
Clothing and jewelry	1,200.00
Furniture, typewriter, books, stereo	2,200.00
Total assets	$10,150.00

Liabilities

Department store charge accounts	$ 175.00
Telephone bill payable	10.00
Highline College loan payable	750.00
Payments owed on automobile	1,350.00
Total liabilities	$ 2,285.00
Ruth Jones, net worth	$ 7,865.00

goals or objectives in mind at all times. Your financial goals may be similar to those listed earlier in this chapter, and all may seem easy to keep in mind. However, people can become so bogged down in day-to-day problems and minor crises that they forget about where they are headed financially. Again, try to spend a few moments each day reviewing your long-term financial objectives and make revisions if necessary. Second, set up plans on how to accomplish these objectives. Organizing one's self so as to accomplish those financial objectives is a matter of arranging some degree of orderliness into some of the many everyday things that people do. The goal here will be to find batches of time that are presently being wasted or simply lost because of the way in which we are doing basic routines. This function of organizing will be taken up in Chapter 2; the control function (budgeting) will be taken up in Chapter 3. The money management model, which is common to management in any field, is as follows:

Planning for Your Objectives: Personal and Financial

As a student, people may have said to you, "You must plan for your future." The problem with this advice is that no one ever tells you how to plan. Probably it is because few people themselves really ever learn how to go about planning. Good leaders and managers know how to plan and spend much to their time in the planning process. There is nothing that says that you cannot use the same process to accomplish your financial objectives. Planning is simply the process of

1. Determining *what* is to be accomplished.
2. Determining *how* it will be accomplished.
3. Determining *when* it will be accomplished.
4. Determining *who* will do the accomplishing.

Only by spending much time reflecting on these financial and personal goals will you be able really to sort out which ones must be accomplished first, second, third, and so on. Some of your objectives will require money; others will require large blocks of time; some will require both. This is probably the best way to determine whether some of those objectives are realistic or are merely wishful thinking.

You may find that setting up your goals into short- and long-range categories will be very helpful. Setting up five-year plans or benchmarks for measuring progress may be of some assistance. There will be many revisions to an initial detailed plan, and it may take longer or shorter to attain that goal. But, by setting out a plan in writing, many activities can be fitted into logical and sequential time frames.

SUMMARY

A lifetime program of personal money management will be influenced by one's career, lifetime goals and objectives, an understanding of the economic system of the United States, inflation, population growth, and future energy resources. Most people end their working careers with little or no savings. The U.S. economic system requires that a person give strong consideration to career objectives at an earlier age. Lifetime objectives may be viewed as financial goals and nonfinancial goals. Each person has a vast reservoir of talents or personal assets that can be helpful in accomplishing his or her lifetime objectives. A balance sheet is a useful tool to measure the growth of one's personal net worth. The money management model for accomplishing objectives is through a three-part process of planning, organizing, and controlling. The four steps in planning are (1) what is to be accomplished, (2) how it is to be accomplished, (3) when it is to be accomplished, and (4) who is to do the accomplishing. Writing out one's lifetime goals and objectives and using benchmarks of five-year intervals will help to keep one's objectives continually in mind and to determine whether or not your objectives can be accomplished realistically.

TIPS

Contacting Your Elected Representatives

Many of the topics presented in this chapter relate to politics, and it is important that people let their elected representatives know their feelings about specific public issues. The letter shown in Exhibit 1-4 can be adapted to write to a city, county, or state official as well as to a representative, a senator, or even the president.

The Basics of Job Hunting

A second area of importance is that of career planning. Only you can decide what it is that you want to do in life. Your career is the means for accomplishing most of all the financially oriented lifetime goals. Learning about jobs through friends, relatives, co-workers, and business association contacts is very helpful.

However, some well-established rituals must be followed to ensure greater success in landing a job. The failure to do well at any one of the following steps may jeopardize your chances.

The Resume. A resume is a one- or two-page summary of information that identifies you, your address, and telephone. It includes a statement of your objectives and abilities, past work experience, education and training, and some personal data. It is brief, it states facts, and it is a professionally done piece of work.

People who hire others have come to expect to receive resumes that conform to a specific *style, format,* and *neatness.* Resumes are typed on 8 ½" × 11"

EXHIBIT 1-4   Sample Letter to an Elected Official

Your Address
City, State, Zip Code
Date of Letter

The Honorable ——————————
Title of Office
Building Name, Street Address
City, State, Zip Code

Dear (Title) Last Name:

In writing to an elected official, keep your letter brief but courteous. The letter should be no longer than this sample letter format of one paragraph. Write your letter in pen and ink or ball point pen. Use plain white stationery without any letterhead, designs, or symbols. *Do not type the letter.* Hand-written letters will always carry more weight with elected officials than will typed or form letters. List the items that you want supported or voted against or the issue that you are raising. Do not say that you are associated with a specific association or organization. If you do, it may be viewed as a bloc vote tactic. You do not have to say how old your are. Close the letter as follows:

Sincerely,
Your Signature

quality bond white paper, have good margins, and have no misspelled words, smudges, eraser marks, and so on. Many business communication textbooks will help you put together a good resume. Photocopies may be used if they are of excellent quality. In mailing, use quality business letter-sized envelopes and regular postage stamps. If you are answering an ad and it requires certified mail and a postmark, be sure to follow those requirements. Be prepared to make the appropriate investment both in time and dollars for this activity.

References. In the course of job hunting, a person needs to have three to five personal references. References are another required ritual. Most personnel people know that references will usually say only good things about a person. Their true value in actually securing a job is probably minimal. However, if a person cannot supply references, it may tell much about the job applicant to the personnel officer. Rather than including the references' names and addresses on a resume, however, state on the resume that "References will be furnished upon request." Be sure that you spell your references' names correctly and know their current addresses, zip codes, and telephone numbers. Have this information with you so that you do not spend time looking for it while completing an employment application or while in an interview. A personnel officer will mentally note your ability to handle this material. In summary, references are a necessary hurdle to jump over in the employment process.

Application Forms. Keep in mind here too that a good application form for employment is half ritual and half psychological. Even if a company is not hiring people, it will probably give you an application form to fill out. If you fill out an application form on the business firms' premises and are to be interviewed shortly afterward, try to fill in the application form in 20 minutes or less. All parts must be completed neatly and accurately and with correct spelling. If you enter the incorrect date on the application form or leave it blank, for example, it is telling the personnel people that your are not sensitive to details or are careless. If you take too long to fill out an application form, it may imply that you have difficulty reading instructions or that you are slow or unprepared. Complete all parts of the work history section and leave no gaps in your work history. Neatness and accuracy here will give good first impressions. A "crowded," messy, smudged, eraser-marked application form will send negative impressions to any reader, and you may not be taken seriously. As a suggestion, practice filling in application forms rapidly and accurately.

Interviews. The interview is a 20- to 30 minute period in which to sell the company on the idea that you should be hired over all the other applicants for the position. Interviews are part ritual, part psychological, and they are critical. The professional interviewer will know this and so should you. Again, first impressions are very important. What one says, how one says it, how one is dressed, and what one does in this short period will be remembered by the interviewer. A man or a woman who has been actively seeking work and has gone to 20 to 30 interviews should be proficient at handling such interviews. By then they know the right kind of clothes to wear, they overcome any negative mannerisms, they have learned many of the typical questions to be raised at an interview, and they learn to answer them forthrightly and positively.

Legally, the interviewer can only ask questions that are called "bona fide occupational qualifications" (BFOQs). It is now illegal for prospective employers to ask questions relating to your age, sex, race, color, national origins, religious affiliation, credit rating, educational level, marital status, cohabitation arrangement, and family situation or arrangements. Questions asked must be relevant to the job. All questions asked by an interviewer should be applicable to both men and women unless the BFOQ requires it. This should theoretically eliminate questions asked of women about children to be born, present number of children, provisions for day care, and children's illness arrangements. The key to all questions is relevancy to the job. If the question is an illegal one, try to be as tactful as you can so that those matters, whatever they are, are already taken care of or arranged for and will not pose any difficulty with your work activities.

Negative Factors Evaluated During the Employment Interview Which Frequently Lead to Rejection of the Applicant*

1. Poor personal appearance.
2. Overbearing, overaggressive attitude, "superiority complex," "know-it-all."
3. Inability to express one's self clearly.
4. Lack of career planning.
5. Lack of interest and enthusiasm.
6. Lack of confidence and poise.
7. Failure to participate in activities.
8. Overemphasis on money—interest only in best dollar offer.
9. Poor scholastic record.
10. Unwilling to start at the bottom—expects too much too soon.
11. Makes excuses—hedges on unfavorable factors in record.
12. Lack of tact.
13. Lack of maturity.
14. Lack of courtesy.
15. Unfavorable references from past employers.
16. Lack of social understanding.
17. Marked dislike for schoolwork.
18. Lack of vitality.
19. Failure to took interviewer in the eye.
20. Limp handshake.
21. Indecision.
22. Sloppy application blank.
23. Merely "shopping around."
24. Wants job only for short time.
25. Lack of knowledge in field of specialization.
26. No interest in company or in industry.
27. Emphasis on who one knows.
28. Unwillingness to go where company may send one.
29. Cynicism.
30. Laziness.

* As reported by 153 companies surveyed in the *Northwestern Endicott-Lindquist Report,* The Placement Center, Northwestern University. Reprinted by permission.

31. Intolerant—strong prejudices.
32. Narrow interests.
33. Poor handling of personal finances.
34. No interest in community activities.
35. Inability to accept criticism.
36. Lack of appreciation of the value of experience.
37. Late to interview without good reason.
38. Never heard of company.
39. Failure to express appreciation for interviewer's time.
40. Asks no questions about the job.
41. Seems to be under stress.
42. Indefinite response to questions.

ADDITIONAL READINGS

From time to time, this text will include a listing of books and magazines that may be of assistance in personal money management and may be helpful as additional background for material covered.

Bolles, Richard N., *What Color Is Your Parachute? A Practical Manual for Job Hunters and Career Changers,* rev. ed. Berkeley, Calif.: Ten Speed Press, 1987.

Dusky, Lorraine, "Career Workshop," *Working Woman,* June 1986, pp. 91—93.

Heilbroner, Robert L., and Lester C. Thurow, *Economics Explained.* Englewood Cliffs, N.J.: Prentice-Hall, 1982.

Irish, Richard K., *Go Hire Yourself an Employer.* New York: Anchor, 1978.

"Keys to a Successful Job Hunt," *Changing Times.* September 1985, pp. 71—72.

LaFevre, John L., *How Do You Really Get Hired?* New York: Arco—Prentice Hall Press, 1986.

Levering, Robert, Milton Moskowitz, and Michael Katz, *The 100 Best Companies to Work for in America.* Reading, Mass.: Addison-Wesley, 1985.

Naisbitt, John, *Megatrends.* New York: Warner, 1984.

Shepherd, Shirley, "How to Get That Job in 60 Minutes or Less," *Working Woman,* March 1986, pp. 118—20.

Siverd, Bonnie, *The Working Woman Financial Advisor.* New York: Warner, 1987.

Webster's Ninth New Collegiate Dictionary or similar desk copy.

GLOSSARY OF USEFUL TERMS

Assets Items of value owned by an individual or family, such as cash, land, houses, furniture, stocks and bonds.

Balance Sheet A financial statement that measures the assets, debts, and net worth of an individual or family at a specific time.

Capital The wealth (money, property, equipment, etc.) owned by an individual, business, or corporation. The term has many vague uses as in money capital and capital assets.

Capitalism A vague concept used to describe an economic system. In theory the U.S. economy is capitalistic, as the bulk of the nation's resources is owned by people directly or by business firms. Concepts such as free enterprise, the right to own property, and freedom of movement are closely identified with capitalism. Government does have a key role in capitalism today as a referee or regulator. Capitalism will mean different things to a businessperson, a labor leader, and a political scientist.

Consumer Price Index An economic index prepared by the U.S. Department of Labor to indicate the relative change in prices of a selected group of consumer goods.

Ecology The study of human populations in terms of their environment.

Economic System An arrangement of rules under which production, distribution, and consumption of goods and services take place.

Economics The science that investigates production, distribution, and consumption of goods and services to satisfy human wants.

Gross National Product The total of all the goods and services produced by a nation.

Index Number A ratio of two numbers expressed as a percentage.

Inflation An overall, generally upward price trend for all goods and services that results in the decline in the value of the dollar.

Labor Force All persons over 16 years of age who are willing and able to work and who are employed or are seeking work.

Liabilities Debts owed to creditors.

Liquidity Cash or the ability to convert other assets into cash with ease.

Money A medium of exchange.

Money Income The amount of money earned by a worker in a given period.

Private Enterprise A system that exists when the private citizens rather than governments own businesses.

Real Income Purchasing power measured by the quality of goods and services that money will buy.

Recession A decline in business activity.

Standard of Living A measure of wealth of a nation expressed as the total production of a nation (GNP) divided by the total population.

Wealth All property that is useful and therefore has value.

2

Organizing

Upon completion of Chapter 2, you should be able to identify and remember

- Your lifetime goals and objectives and be able to find the time to review and revise them periodically.
- Steps in constructing and completing a time analysis worksheet to assess your present utilization of time.
- Techniques that will help you save time.
- How to plan and implement a simple functional records management system to maintain control over both financially and nonfinancially related documents.
- The importance of preparing an inventory of your personal and household property.

OVERVIEW

Chapter 1 provided brief discussions on a broad range of matters that a student of personal money management will need to be aware of to make better long-range financial decisions (the U.S. economic system, inflation, population growth, changing energy resources and usages) as well as individual concerns (individual life goals, life-styles, personal talents, balance sheets, and the manner in which planning is undertaken).

Chapter 2 focuses on organizing skills and techniques for the individual or individual family unit. This chapter asks us to reflect on where it is we are in life, that is, what we have accomplished so far, what are our responsibilities and obligations, what possessions do we own, what are our daily routines, where is our time spent, and how wisely is our time being spent? Few people will admit to having too much leisure time these days. It seems the day is over before we really get started, and we stand in awe of those people who seem to be able to put their talents to many areas as well as accomplishing much. We feel the pressures of our jobs, our family responsibilities, and our daily chores, and the home tends to leave precious little time for ourselves and the things that we truly want to do. Sometimes we feel that our time is really not productive, rewarding, or fulfilling. Most people decry being "straight-jacketed" into rigid time structures or laden with boring routines. However, it is a fact that most of our days or at least several days in a week do follow rather definite patterns or routines. Patterns and routines are a lot like habits; that is, they can be good habits or bad habits. We will want to hold onto those good routines and cast off those that are not helping us. Let's be realistic and admit that much of our day is one of reacting to someone else's agenda—our job, our spouses and children, the upkeep and care of our home or apartment and cars. We never seem to have a minute to ourselves. Actually, life is not all that bad. Most of the things that we pursue were willingly taken on, and only a few were unwittingly entered into.

What we want to do is learn how to find the valuable few minutes in each day that seem to be lost or presently unavailable to us, recapture them, and put them to our own use for those things that we really want to do. It is the making use of those few minutes each day that separates those people who seem to get much accomplished from those who seem never to get control of themselves or their lives. Those are the minutes that can be used to develop and work on a hobby, read a few pages in a novel, improve our job skills, improve our vocabulary, for example, or just plain loaf for 10 minutes without interruption. Yes, many people must even learn to loaf. Ulcers, hypertension, and other illnesses are brought on because some people cannot find time to take it easy for a few minutes. We call them workaholics.

HOW WE SPEND OUR TIME

Whether or not one's future will be spent in a rewarding and personally satisfying career will for the most part be determined by how one plans the use of one's time in the future. Notice how successful and highly motivated persons are very much aware of their time. You will not find them wasting time over petty and idle activities that do not benefit either themselves or those around them. They strive to spend their time on those activities that interest them and utilize the services of others to fill in those necessary areas in which they themselves are either not qualified or not interested. The U.S. economic system, as we mentioned in Chapter 1, with its accepted concept of competition, will tend to cause people to concentrate much of the working careers in those areas in which they do them best and in which those efforts are in demand by the public. Going to college, for example, is a reasonably efficient means of absorbing a tremendous amount of useful knowledge as well as enriching present knowledge in a brief span of time.

Every person has 24 hours, or 1,440 minutes, available each day. The material presented in Table 2-1 is adjusted so that Saturdays, Sundays, holidays, vacations, and rest periods are integrated into the year. You may find that the categories of sleeping, main job, eating, personal care, and cooking are reasonable estimates for basic living; the other categories can be reviewed and adjusted to reflect your present personal life-style.

In connection with the main job category in Table 2-1, let us review just how many days are actually spent in what might be considered a normal working year:

Number of days in a year	365
Less: Saturdays	52
	313
Sundays	52
	261
Average holidays	10
	251
Vacation	10
Actual employee workdays per year	241

The calculation of 241 days or 1,928 hours (241 × 8-hour business day) should be reduced farther to allow for authorized rest pauses and absences due to sickness or injury. Two 15-minute rest pauses of coffee breaks each day will in effect amount to an equivalent of 15 8-hour days over the course of the 241-day business year. We might even assume a few days off for illness during the year. In summary, an average employee's time spent on the job is somewhere between 220 and 230 days (or from 1,760 to 1,840 hours per year).

TABLE 2-1 A Day in the Life of Alec Smart

	Activities	Time (minutes)
1.	Sleeping (7 hours)	420
2.	Personal grooming, showering and dressing	30
3.	Meal preparation, eating, cleanup at home	120
4.	Commuting to work or school for 5 days (5 days × 60 minutes per day ÷ 7 days)	43
5.	Part-time job (4 hours per day × 5 days ÷ 7 days)	171
6.	Routine shopping, errands, and bill paying	20
7.	Home entertainment viewing and listening	210
8.	Light reading of newspapers and magazines	30
9.	Household chores, laundry, yard work, etc.	20
10.	Vacation (2 weeks a year)	10
11.	Socializing, conversation, telephone calls, etc.	20
	Subtotal	1,094
12.	Alec Smart's unallocated time per day	346
	Total minutes in one day	1,440

Notice that your employer is paying you for 30 minutes each day in the form of coffee breaks or rest pauses. Here are 30 minutes that could be spent on trying to accomplish your own personal goals, such as reading a few pages in a relevant business or trade journal for career enhancement. You could also use a portion of your lunch hour for reading and study or, as many more employees are doing, to work on physical fitness.

ESSENTIAL TOOLS FOR ORGANIZING ONE'S TIME

The Time Analysis Sheet

The simple time analysis worksheet in Exhibit 2-1 is designed to show all 24 hours of the day, to permit for the allocation of appropriate restful sleep. This analysis of present time, in a written or charted form, forces one to come to grips with what one is actually doing in a typical week. Begin by blocking in routine activities, say, those things that you normally do from Monday through Friday. For example, if it takes you a half-hour to shower and get dressed in the morning, then block in that time and label it. If it takes you 30 minutes from the time you leave your home to the time you arrive at your work bench or desk, then block in that time and label it "commuting time." Be sure to do the same for your commute home. Fill in employment work periods, authorized coffee breaks or rest pauses, and authorized lunch periods and evening activities such as prepar-

EXHIBIT 2-1   Time Analysis Worksheet

Hour of Day	Sunday	Monday	Tuesday	Wednesday	Thursday	Friday	Saturday
6 A.M.							
7 A.M.							
8 A.M.							
9 A.M.							
10 A.M.							
11 A.M.							
12 noon							
1 P.M.							
2 P.M.							
3 P.M.							
4 P.M.							
5 P.M.							
6 P.M.							
7 P.M.							
8 P.M.							
9 P.M.							
10 P.M.							
11 P.M.							
12 midnight							
1 A.M.							
2 A.M.							
3 A.M.							
4 A.M.							
5 A.M.							

ing and eating the evening meal, cleaning up after meals, newspaper reading, specific TV programs, hobby and craft activity, or self-improvement activity. As for TV watching, label those programs during the week that mean very much, watch the program, and then turn the set off. TV watching is a great time thief.

After blocking in the hours that you normally sleep, you will have completed your routine weekday activity commitments. Blank spaces on your worksheet represent intervals of time that are apparently not being used and can be put to profitable use. You can read a few pages in a book, work on a hobby, do some exercises, take a walk, work on vocabulary, work crossword puzzles, and the like. Do the same sort of blocking in of time for your Saturdays and Sundays. Your weekends will often provide large blocks of uncommitted time. Students in college should block in the times for class lectures and study. College courses generally require a minimum of two hours of outside preparation for each hour in the classroom. Students should also be realistic in balancing jobs with school work. Students who work at a full-time job should enroll in only one or two college classes at first.

Now that you have identified all your activities for a normal week, you can take positive steps to prepare yourself for those things that you really want to do in your life. Even if you have family responsibilities, try to obtain a few minutes of time for yourself. Remember that all family members should plan for some uninterrupted time.

Keeping Life Goals in Sight

From your time analysis worksheet you have found those areas of the day when some time is not being utilized. Make up that list of goals *now* and write them down. Such goals as replacing the old car, getting new carpeting for the living room, or expanding a stock portfolio should be reviewed and eventually ranked in some order, undertaken or discarded, reconsidered, and so on. If you have certain specific goals clearly formed in your mind, you will develop a much clearer picture of what to do with those blank spaces on your time analysis worksheet.

ESTABLISHING A SIMPLE RECORDS SYSTEM

"Planned paperhood" is a term used by records managers of business firms to establish some control over the mountains of paper created by government and businesses. Because we are concerned with our personal record keeping, let us begin the "planned paperhood" of our home records management system by examining what should be kept on our person in a wallet or purse.

Essential Items to Be Carried in Wallet or Purse

Personal identification card, current address, and current telephone number

Names of persons and their telephone numbers and addresses to be notified in case of emergency

Drivers license, auto insurance, I.D. card (if not a driver)

Hospitalization insurance I.D. card

Blood type card

Medical problems and allergies card

Coins to operate public pay telephone

Spare car key (if a driver)

Bank credit card

Cash (not an excessive amount)

Organization membership cards

Important Documents, Names, Numbers

Important documents (personal, financial, and property related) are listed in the following pages. The first list concerns vital personal papers, many of which may have only intrinsic value or are irreplaceable items for which attaching a financial value is extremely difficult. Individual items are *not* in any priority.

Vital Personal Papers

Birth certificates

Social Security cards/records

Family medical records

Marriage certificate

Insurance policies:

Medical, hospitalization, disability income protection, life insurance, auto insurance, homeowner, tenants property, special property coverage policies, title insurance, fire insurance

School transcripts and diplomas

Citizenship papers

Alien registration documents and identification

Divorce and annulment documents

Retirement program documents

Wills and codicils

Community property agreements

Passports/vaccination records

Adoption papers

Military discharge records

Veterans Administration education and disability records

Employee handbook of company benefits

Family history records

Special family photographs

List of property owned

List of property with serial numbers and special photographs of property items

The following items are primarily financially oriented records.

General Financial Records

Bank statements

Credit card statements

Unused personal checks

Canceled checks and stubs

Savings account statements

Credit union savings/borrowing records

Federal income tax records, past years

Federal income tax records, current year

Safe deposit box contents list

Personal balance sheets

Personal income statements

Household/family budget worksheets

Mortgage payments record

Property tax records

Apartment/house rental agreement

Stock certificates and records

Alimony payments/receipts records

Child support records

Copyrights and patents

Contracts, leases, partnership agreements

Warranties and instructions

Bills of sale of property

The following is a much narrower list of documents representing things that people own today and may be important when it becomes time to sell an item of personal property, transfer title, seek an adjustment, or obtain insurance coverage.

Specific Property Documents

Automobile papers:

  Title

  Bill of sale

Warranty book/maintenance history
Owner's manual
Battery warranty
Tire warranty
License plates/tabs payment receipts
Television set sales slip/warranty
Instruction booklets:
    Appliances, kitchen and laundry
    Cameras, stereos, calculators
    Carpet and clothing care
Pets:
    Pedigrees
    Medical/shot records
    License tag serial number/receipts
Title and registration records of:
    Guns and rifles
    Bicycles, motorcycles, mopeds
    Boats and trailers
Home improvement expenditures
Real estate:
    Titles to land and building
    Leases
    Easements

The final list presented is designed to provide an added measure of security for the things that one may own. In the case of theft, for example, serial numbers are an important factor in recovering one's property. The following items are examples of many that carry serial numbers.

Items Normally Carrying Serial Numbers

Bank credit cards
Department store credit cards
Cameras, light meters, lenses
Typewriters, adding machines
Automobile/body/engine block
Automobile tires
Bicycles
Major household appliances:
    Refrigerators, washers, dryers, dishwashers, microwave ovens, stoves/ranges, sewing machines, carpet sweepers, air conditioners, fans

Television sets/VCRs
Stereo equipment
Tape recorder/player sets
CB radios
Automobile tape players
Pocket calculators/personal computers
Electric motors
Electrical power tools
Gasoline engines
Rifles and shotguns
Handguns
Fishing reels
Binoculars and scopes
Pocket and wristwatches/watch cases, clockworks

COMPONENTS OF A BASIC RECORDS SYSTEM

Basic Equipment Needs

Once you have located all those papers and other important financial documents, you must arrange this material in a readily retrievable fashion and thereby bring an end to long and frustrating searches. The particular records system that we want to emphasize for now is one that involves activities closely related to earning and income, household expenses, property owned, and estate planning. You may want to establish a second records system to handle school material, correspondence with family and friends, news clippings, and so on.

File Box. Essential to even the most modest financial records system is a standard-sized portable file box, preferably plastic, with a carrying handle. This file box should hold file folders that will handle 8½″ × 11″ standard papers and documents. The file box is not to serve as a vault or a substitute for a safe deposit box, which will be discussed later. Because the file box may not have any file folders, or because those that do are flimsy, invest a couple of dollars in one or two dozen standard 8½″ × 11″ manila file folders, three-cut headings. Exhibit 2-2 contains a sample of captions, starting with the first file folder in the front entitled "Personal Information Sheet" and concluding with the last file entitled "Will, Copy."

The purpose of the personal information sheet file folder is to have the names, addresses, and telephone numbers of the banks, credit union, attorney, stockbroker, insurance agent, accountant, and the like in the event that a

EXHIBIT 2-2 Sample Captions for a Standard File

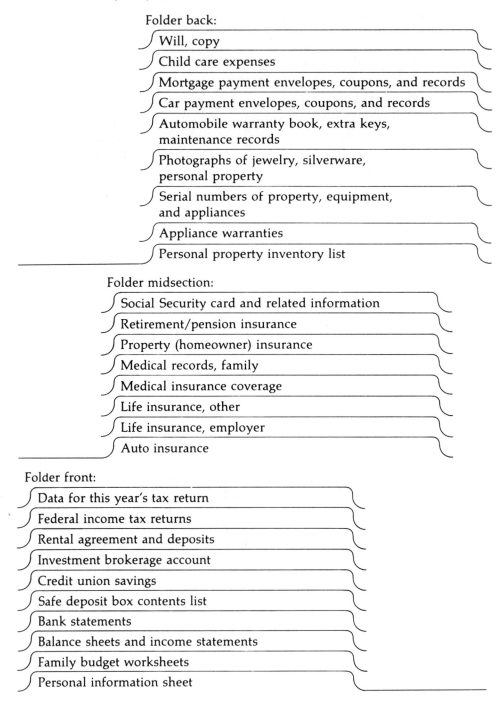

Folder back:

Will, copy

Child care expenses

Mortgage payment envelopes, coupons, and records

Car payment envelopes, coupons, and records

Automobile warranty book, extra keys, maintenance records

Photographs of jewelry, silverware, personal property

Serial numbers of property, equipment, and appliances

Appliance warranties

Personal property inventory list

Folder midsection:

Social Security card and related information

Retirement/pension insurance

Property (homeowner) insurance

Medical records, family

Medical insurance coverage

Life insurance, other

Life insurance, employer

Auto insurance

Folder front:

Data for this year's tax return

Federal income tax returns

Rental agreement and deposits

Investment brokerage account

Credit union savings

Safe deposit box contents list

Bank statements

Balance sheets and income statements

Family budget worksheets

Personal information sheet

spouse, child, or attorney has to step in and manage your affairs. This sheet should also indicate the location of vital documents such as the original copy of your will, where safe deposit boxes are located, and addresses of specific real estate owned. A sample personal information sheet appears in Exhibit 2-3. The reader may wish to modify the particular example to conform to his or her particular needs.

File folders should be reviewed each year and statements of materials just completed removed to a large envelope to be boxed for permanent storage. You will probably never need these materials again, but the amount of space that these permanent or "dead" records take is minimal.

Canceled checks and check stubs should be kept separately as their odd sizes do not lend themselves to fitting neatly in file folders. Here again, instead of saving only those checks that you think will be needed in the future, simply arrange all canceled checks by their serial numbers and store them. If you have two checking accounts, you will need a second box for permanent storage.

Federal income tax returns more than three years old should also be transferred to a permanent storage box. If possible, place these in the large envelope

EXHIBIT 2-3 Personal Information Sheet

Name	Date
Attorney's Name	Phone
Attorney's Address	
Location of Will	
Name of Executor(s)	

ACCOUNTS	ACCOUNT NUMBER	NAME OF FIRM, BANK, ETC.
Checking Account		
Savings Account		
Safe Deposit Box		
Key Location		
Investment Broker		
Insurance Agent (life)		
(medical)		
(auto)		
(home)		

Miscellaneous (accountants, other brokers, credit card numbers, etc.)

for the specific year. As an alternative, you may want to keep all your income tax returns in separate envelopes. The reason for this, as will be covered in more detail in Chapter 3, is that tax returns will provide you with data to prepare or reconstruct some personal income statements.

How long should you keep your income tax records? Forever and a day seems to be the most practical advice. While the Internal Revenue Service must perform one of its audits within three years, it still has authority to review your tax return many years later. It is a good idea not to use some vague statute of limitations as a convenience for throwing out old financial, particularly income tax, records.

A final aspect of establishing a basic financial record system is to have a notebook, preferably a spiral notebook, in which to jot down daily expenses (to be discussed in greater detail in Chapter 3), some letter-sized envelopes, and a spindle or similar device on which to place sales slips and other proofs of purchases. This system can be used for the rest of your life, it will be simple to use by all members of the family, and it can be revised for individual needs. The best thing about it is that it will save you time for more important things.

Safe Deposit Box. As you are thinking about gathering together your personal property and certain documents, no doubt the need for security of certain items is crossing your mind. A safe deposit box is a realistic place in which to put certain important papers and other valuable items. A small-sized box measures 2″ × 5″ × 24″ and rents for around $20 a year. This is one of the many services provided by commercial banks (discussed in more detail in Chapter 5).

It is easy enough to obtain a safe deposit box. The major consideration is, who is to have access to the box? Husband and wife should each have a key. This would require both signatures to appear on the bank's authorization card. Should you die, the bank will seal your safe deposit box and prevent entry until the necessary legal procedures are completed for an authorized person to open it. This could take weeks or months. With this in mind, never put items in a safe deposit box that you need in a hurry or that you might need on a weekend or at night. For example, resident aliens should not keep passports in a safe deposit box. Since tax authorities will probably have access to your safe deposit box at its authorized opening should you die, do not put cash in such box. Your estate may have to pay income taxes on it again since the tax authorities might assume illegal activity. Rare coins and bills and gold and silver bars are appropriate monetary items to be kept in such box. Other items might include birth, marriage, and death certificates; stock and bond certificates, titles to property; deeds; bills of sale; important contracts, patents, copyrights; military service records; citizenship papers; household inventory records; serial numbers list; and family history records and rare family photographs. As for your will, your attorney might be the best person to keep this document so as to reduce delays in probating your estate (see Chapter 13), though you might want to have a copy or your will at home in your files. Family heirlooms such as grandfather's gold pocket watch might be placed in the safe deposit box, but jewelry for daily or dress-up occasions should be kept at home. However, you are exercising appropriate care if you were to place some of the items in your safety deposit box before going on a vacation or extended business trip. You are of course in the best position to determine the relative security of your valuables. No place is entirely secure, and the safe deposit boxes of some banks (though rarely) have been broken into and the contents stolen.

The final section of this chapter, which concerns taking an inventory of your personal property items, may give you additional clues for items to be placed in a safe deposit box by determining the relative security of items in your home, as well as seeing that valuable items are not too concentrated in one or two rooms of the home but are reasonably distributed throughout the home in the event of fire or burglary.

HOUSEHOLD INVENTORY

The purpose for drawing up an inventory of personal property is to determine what insurance coverage is needed in the event of the financial loss of these items. The total value of these items will become an important figure in your personal balance sheet as illustrated in Chapter 1. Preparing an inventory list of personal property will not require a lot of time for those just starting out in life. On the other hand, a long-established family will need substantial insurance coverage to hedge against possible losses. The major concern of this latter group will be to determine the current adequacy of their insurance coverage. And the only way to be sure you have adequate coverage is to compile that inventory list.

It takes a lot of motivation to undertake an inventory. For some family units, it will require many hours to do a proper job, and, once completed, there is the chore of keeping it up to date.

Most insurance companies will want to make a quick settlement when you experience a property loss. When the settlement check is in hand, just endorse and deposit it in your bank account and start making purchases to replace the lost, damaged, or stolen property. The insurance settlement is determined from statistical samples of various population groupings by compiling age, education, economic status, and average of property owned, its depreciation through use, and so on. Once you have accepted the check and endorsed it, it is most likely that the insurance company is freed from any additional settlement liability even though you determine months later that you forgot about a piece of personal property that was also a part of the loss. The only way to avoid the possibility of not overlooking items that might be lost due to fire, theft, or whatever is to compile this inventory list. It will also provide you with negotiating leverage in obtaining a better settlement from the insurance company.

To begin this task of inventory taking, set up a separate sheet of paper for each room in your home and label it across the top (see Exhibit 2-4). Next, enter the quantity and the name of item with a brief description. Descriptions should include manufacturer's name, color, size, serial number, distinguishing characteristics, and so on.

Ideally *all* items should be listed. One solution is to invest in several rolls of color film and take pictures of specific items. Take pictures of books lined up in

EXHIBIT 2-4 Household Inventory Sheet

QUANTITY	DESCRIPTION OF PROPERTY	ORIGINAL COST
		TOTAL FOR PAGE $

their bookcase or shelves. Spread jewelry out on a table and take pictures. Placing a ruler in with some of the pictures of jewelry will help gain a perspective as to their size. Open the doors of kitchen cabinets and take pictures. Spread silverware and pieces of fine china on the kitchen counter and take pictures of these. Be sure that you can pick up patterns and designs in your shots.

The most difficult part of inventory taking is assigning the date of purchase and the price paid for the items. Here you will have to do your detective work by sorting through old check stubs, canceled checks, installment contracts, and sales slips. You will also need your pocket calculator for tallying all this information. The age of your furnishings will have some impact on the amount of insurance recovery. For example, your color TV set is stolen from your home. The set originally cost you $500 6 years ago. If your insurance company considers the estimates that the normal life of your particular TV set is 10 years, then you might expect a claim settlement of $200. Let's figure this calculation: Subtracting the used life of six years from the 10-year total life will leave 4 years of estimated remaining life: $4 \div 10 \times \$500 = \$200$. However, due to inflation, a similar set may sell for $600 now. Then the present replacement value depreciated for 6 years may give you a closer estimate of the monetary loss of your TV set. The insurance company then may settle for around $240: $4 \div 10 \times \$600 = \$240$. As you can see, adjusting all your possessions to their present replacement value and then depreciating them is no easy task. Therefore, at the least (1) prepare the room-by-room list of possessions listing the quantity and description; (2) assign the original purchase price to each of the items (this should be fairly easy for those big-ticket household appliances, furniture, and jewelry); and (3) try to establish the approximate or actual date of the items purchased. Then make photocopies of your inventory lists and place a copy, along with photographs of your property, in your safe deposit box.

SUMMARY

This chapter has covered some of the basic methods of how to gain control over your time by looking at the available time allotted to each of us, in days and in hours on and off the job. The time analysis worksheet is a tool to find where time may be slipping away from us during typical routine weeks of activity. Finding the lost time then allows each of us to begin to apply that time to the things that we really want to do, to really accomplish in a lifetime. Establishing a basic filing system helps us to manage our time better and to bring us up to date on the financial responsibilities we have incurred as well as an idea of the things we own. This "taking stock" of ourselves provides the starting point. Taking an inventory of the things we own will reveal past spending and shopping habits, the ability to purchase good products, the distribution of valuables throughout the home, the need for an off-premise safe deposit box, and the need for insurance coverage in the event of loss.

TIPS

The following are techniques that you might apply to make better use of your time without much disruption to your present life-style. Select the ones that appear right for your situation. If you are living alone, you will have more flexibility in setting your time goals. If you are part of a family, you should discuss the ideas with other members to gain support for the idea that each member should have some time for themselves. Additional time-saving tips will be found in other chapters.

1. Arrange your study or office desk in such a way that it does not invite people to stop by for a chat or cause you to look up when people pass by.
2. Combine shopping trips with your coming to or from work or school.
3. Use your driving time to catch up on the news by using the radio; if you commute to and from school or work, carry something to read.
4. Carry 3" × 5" cards and a pencil to jot down ideas, thoughts, and lists of things to do. List your goals and review them periodically.
5. Establish a quiet hour at home where all members of the family may have a time when they are not to be interrupted. Do not answer the telephone during this hour. Remember, the telephone is for your convenience, not for someone else's.
6. Use an egg timer to limit the length of your telephone calls.
7. Establish a file cabinet in your home to keep news clippings, letters, pamphlets, and the like.
8. Control TV watching.
9. Do not spend time dwelling on the past or how things might have been different.
10. Get your plans and ideas established on paper.

ADDITIONAL READINGS

McCullough, Bonnie, *Totally Organized.* New York: St. Martin's, 1983.
McNatt, Robert, "What Every Spouse Should Know," *Money,* February 1985, pp. 99–104.
Winston, Stephanie, *Getting Organized.* New York: Warner, 1979.

3

Budgeting

Upon completion of Chapter 3, you should be able to identify and remember

- How budgeting is helpful in accomplishing your financial objectives.
- How to develop basic worksheets for
  1. Estimating annual disposable income by month.
  2. Estimating family or household expenses for a year.
  3. Establishing categories and estimating ordinary expenses.
  4. Estimating unusual and extraordinary household expenditures.
- How to determine the amount of money to be saved for the year.
- How to determine the elements of and prepare a family income and expense statement for the year based on budgeted expectations.

OVERVIEW

Chapter 2 has provided an understanding of just how the reader stands at present with respect to possessions, important business documents, and commitments or responsibilities. Chapter 3, Budgeting, is a natural continuation of organizing. This chapter is perhaps the most critical in the text because, without being reasonably organized financially, most of one's financial goals will never be accomplished.

Why budget? Well, if you (or a household unit) seem to have little money left over at the end of the month, postpone certain ordinary and necessary purchases, or have to borrow or use credit to take a vacation or buy groceries and clothing, then budgeting can be of great assistance to you.

WHO NEEDS BUDGETING? "A FAMILY AFFAIR"

As noted in Chapter 1, every person has unlimited wants. When one want is satisfied, a new one takes its place. Only a few people in the world can buy all the things that they want. Therefore, we must reconcile ourselves to the fact that at any one time, we must do with less. In other words, each person must establish priorities for those things he or she needs most, such as food, shelter, clothing, transportation, health care, and the like. Even within these categories, planning is needed and impulse buying must be reduced to a minimum.

If you live by yourself, the matter of financial planning and budgeting is pretty much the product of your own best efforts. For others, those with families, budgeting should be made a family affair.

A good time to start a budget program for a family is at the beginning of the new year or perhaps when there is a change in life-style, such as just after a recent move, upon graduation, after a job or career change, upon divorce, at retirement, and so on, as these changes are often accompanied by substantial changes in the amount of money available for spending. Look for the first opportunity to initiate the idea of financial planning and budgeting. Be comforted in the fact that your first efforts may not be all that satisfactory. Keep in mind too that, once a budget, say, for one year, has been prepared, it is not to be rigidly followed. If, after a couple of routine months, you notice that certain actual expenditures are exceeding your budget, make an appropriate correction. You should of course study the reasons why your original estimate is wrong. If you find a change is in order on certain categories, then make it. However, once you have made this "midcourse correction," resolve to live within the budget for the balance of the budget period. If you find that your life-style is very erratic, then compromise and make a series of three-month budgets. This will increase the time being spent on preparing your budget, but it may be necessary if you are to take control of your financial life as you pursue your career.

Encourage all members of the family to participate in the development of the budget. The first session might consider the following questions: Where shall the family spend the vacation for the coming year? How much should be allocated for vacation? What clothing is needed by each member for school, for work, for dress-up occasions? What are the younger children's needs for toys and clothes? And so on.

Older children should prepare a list of requirements for special school clothing, school supplies, books, sporting and recreational equipment, and lunch money. Parents should prepare a list of things needed for the home, automobiles, entertainment, clothing, insurance coverages, home maintenance and repairs, and emergency reserves. These lists of requests should include all items solicited from each member regardless of how unreasonable some of the wants might appear to other members of the family.

Some consensus will usually emerge of those items that have merit. While the "around-the-world vacation cruise" may be utterly out of the question for now, it could be a major target for the family to rally around.

A second, less exciting, list of the day-to-day expenses that go to provide the family's basic needs should then be reviewed. These expenses will include the rent or mortgage payments, food items, insurance coverages on certain members of the family, and home and automobile expenses. Estimates will have to be presented so that there will be money available to cover these areas. The family automobile is usually the second largest expenditure after a home purchase; these subjects are treated extensively in Chapters 8 and 9.

Other areas that the family will need to consider are personal improvement and medical care. Make some realistic estimates of money that should be spent for education, career, and social improvement and personal hygienic care, dental checkups, and grooming aids. Today, an informed citizen and consumer should subscribe to a daily newspaper at the very least. Most newspapers carry good shopping ads for comparison shopping for the basics, food, personal health care, grooming items, and automobile care needs. By reading the newspaper routinely, you will recognize the new items coming to the marketplace, bargains versus nonbargains, and sales of certain items. This is one of the best ways to win the battle of inflation as a consumer.

While the purse strings may still be held mainly by the adult members of a household, all members living in the home should be informed about the real cost of running a home. It may be that the spouse with the most *money sense* should take on the duty of being the "chief budget director" in the home to carry out this major function. Children should be taught the concept of money sense by developing an allowance system for each child as soon as they learn about the function of money. Even "live-in" friends and relatives should be expected to contribute to their out-of-pocket costs if their stay exceeds some reasonable period of time. Children of elderly parents feel obliged to do much to make their parents' life more comfortable in their twilight years. These costs often pose financial and emotional strains on members. The recent increase in Social Security is at best only a partial solution to one of the major problems of the future of taking care of the elderly. Parents who stay with their children should recognize the time and financial costs of that stay. If the parent has income from pensions, Social Security, or a trust, some of this income should be turned over to pay for food, laundry, and transportation at the minimum.

To begin our study of household budgeting, let us look at some national figures for families and households. The data in Table 3-1, the most recent available, indicate the relationship of family income to education. Clearly each additional day spent in school results in several hundred additional dollars of lifetime income.

Table 3-2 presents information about U.S. households, incomes, population, and poverty. The dramatic changes occurring within households in this country are obvious. There are fewer persons per household, for example. Poverty remains at persistently high levels despite enormous efforts in the past 30 years to reduce it. In the future, increases in population will mean higher costs and use of land, housing, and the nation's infrastructure—schools, roads, government services, and so on.

Table 3-3 gives some approximation by categories where families spend their money. The percentage of spending for housing and energy are beginning to reach the 50 percent range.

As stated earlier, almost everyone has a different life-style, and this will be affected by such things as the amount of gross income, number of members in the household, age levels, education, geographic location, individual interests,

TABLE 3-1   U.S. Family Incomes by Age and Education, 1983

		Family income ($)	
Categories	% of Families	Mean	Median
Age of family head			
Under 25	8%	$13,385	$12,003
25–34	23	23,963	20,097
35–44	19	32,449	27,114
45–54	16	32,935	25,535
55–64	15	32,292	21,855
65–74	12	21,818	12,538
75 and over	7	11,334	7,176
Education of family head			
0–8 grades	14%	$11,718	$ 8,870
9–11 grades	13	17,146	13,755
High school diploma	32	23,830	20,000
Some college	20	27,412	22,000
College degree	19	46,443	35,000

Data are from "Survey of Consumer Finances, 1983," *Federal Reserve Bulletin,* September 1984, p. 682.

TABLE 3-2 Comparisons by Selected Years of U.S. Population, Households, Family Incomes, and Persons at Poverty Level, 1960-–1990 est.

Year	Total households (millions)	Median family income	U.S. population (millions)	Persons in poverty (millions)
1990 est.	90.0	$30,000	247	37.0
1985 est.	86.0	26,000	240	35.0
1980	80.8	21,023	226	29.3
1975	71.1	13,719	214	25.9
1970	63.4	9,867	204	25.4
1960	53.0	5,620	179	39.9

Data are from *Statistical Abstract of the United States, 1979* and *1985*, and author's projections.

TABLE 3-3 Percentages of Consumer Spending by Category (rounded)

Food	18.5%
Housing	37.4
Energy/utilities	11.4
Transportation	21.4
Medical care	6.2
Appearance and upkeep	5.1
Total	100.0%

Data are from Department of Labor, Bureau of Labor Statistics, 1984.

and so on. Indeed, America is changing. Erosion of the blue-collar middle class, the movement to a service-information society, changing social values, and the emerging global economy provides both great opportunities and uncertainties for the balance of this century. (When reviewing Tables 3-1, 3-2, and 3-3, remember that government statistics about the family of four and its spending habits apply to about only 10 percent of the total households in the United States.)

SOURCES OF INCOME

Usually this phase of budget construction is the easiest, as most family or household units can determine their total income quickly. The following list, which is representative of the major sources of family income, should serve as a reminder so as not to overlook certain income in preparing an income budget for a year.

1. Salaries, commissions, wages, tips, and bonuses earned from all jobs.
2. Interest earned on savings and credit union accounts and bond interest.
3. Alimony and child support income.
4. Public assistance cash income, food, and food stamps.
5. Veterans education benefits: cash, books, tuition.
6. Veterans and workers disability income, dependent's allowance compensation.
7. Social Security and supplemental income.
8. Education scholarships and fellowships.
9. Retirement income and insurance annuity income.
10. Rental income from property owned.
11. Income from garage sales.
12. Income from parents, guardians, and friends.
13. Dividends from corporation stock.
14. Royalties from patents, copyrights, licenses.
15. Income from inheritances and trusts.

A majority of household income will be confined to three or four sources, and the amounts are reasonably predictable. Those individuals and households whose income is largely derived from commissions or whose work is irregular or affected by the weather must take additional steps to save and allocate their income evenly over those months when income is low. In household budgeting, the total amount or gross income of salaries and wages is really not available for spending. Therefore, it is necessary to look at the income remaining after deductions are made, that is, one's disposable income.

DISPOSABLE INCOME

It is more realistic in personal money management to focus one's attention on disposable income rather than on the gross income received from salaries, wages, and bonuses, as disposable income is the amount of money available for spending after federal income taxes and Social Security taxes are deducted or withheld. For employees of a business firm, the terms disposable income and take-home pay are interchangeable. When inflation rates are running at 6 to 8 percent per year, a person must mentally adjust the disposable income additionally downward to reflect the actual purchasing power of those disposable dollars in the coming year.

A simple example will illustrate some of these key concepts. Assume that the wages earned by an individual in the year 19X1 were $10,000, federal income taxes withheld were $810, and Social Security taxes deducted were $585. For the year 19X2 this person is to receive a 10 percent raise, for a total gross wage of $11,000 upon which federal income taxes will be $1,000 and Social Security taxes will be $644. Assume that the year 19X2 is expected to have an inflation rate of 6 percent.

While the wage earner's income in dollars actually increased by $1,000 in the second year, this person's effective increase in purchasing power over the past year is only $190 for the whole year in 19X2, or less than $16 a month. This

"We've done it again. We've disposed of all our disposable income."

Reprinted by permission *The Wall Street Journal*

From *The Wall Street Journal*—
Permission, Cartoon Features Syndicate.

$190 is determined by taking the final figure at the bottom of the column of the year 19X2, or $8,795, and subtracting the disposable income in the base year 19X1, or $8,605.

	19X1	19X2
Gross wages	$10,000	$11,000
Less: Federal income taxes	810	1,000
Social Security taxes	585	644
Total taxes	$ 1,395	$ 1,644
Disposable income	$ 8,605	$ 9,356
Less: Impact of inflation in 19X2 (.06 × $9,356)		561
Real purchasing power in 19X2		$ 8,795
Less: 19X1 base-year income		8,605
Net purchasing power increase		$ 190

An alternative calculation of the $190 worth of net additional purchasing power can be made:

Amount of pay raise	$1,000
Less: Net additional income taxes	190
	$ 810
Net increase in Social Security taxes	59
	$ 751
Erosion from inflation	561
Net increase in purchasing power	$ 190

Had our wage earner spent just half the raise for the year, say, $500 toward a stereo set or some new clothing, he or she would have found those expenditures acting as a major strain on the budget. Had the inflation rate been 8 percent instead of 6 percent, the wage earner would have had no increase in purchasing power for the year 19X2. In summary, wage earners must consider both federal income and Social Security taxes when determining a disposable income and further adjust the disposable income downward by the estimated inflation rate to plan expenditures effectively for the coming year. It is easy to see why wage demands of employees are reaching rates of 10 to 15 percent, which still only allows for modest increases in purchasing power. With the higher wage demands, employers will be concerned about increased productivity to absorb the increases and maintain their competitive position or raise the prices of the products they sell. There should be ample incentive to reduce inflation, as every dollar saved in this area is a dollar of pure profit recovered to the individual or a business. Before going into the detailed study of worksheets, a few words are in

TABLE 3-4 Impact of Taxes on Earned Income

Tax rate	Married, filing joint returns, and surviving spouses	Heads of households	Single individuals
15%	$0–29,750	$0–23,900	$0–17,850
28%	Above $29,750	Above $23,900	Above $17,850

order regarding the impact of the federal income tax and Social Security tax on planning and budgeting.

Federal Income Taxes and Budgeting

Our purpose here is to assist the reader in establishing a rough estimate of disposable income. (Chapter 11 covers in more detail the topic of federal income taxes.) The U.S. income tax structure is a *progressive tax system.* That is, as one's income goes up, both the amount of levied tax against specific income and the percentage rate of the tax levied increases. Table 3-4 illustrates the impact of actual taxes levied on earned income.

"Here's your loot less withholding tax, Social Security, medical insurance and savings bond deduction."

From *The Wall Street Journal*—
Permission, Cartoon Features Syndicate.

TABLE 3-5   Social Security Taxes, 1979–1990P

Year	Taxable wage	Tax rate	Maximum tax
1979	$22,900	6.13%	$1,404
1980	25,900	6.13	1,588
1981	29,700	6.65	1,975
1982	32,400	6.70	2,171
1983	35,700	6.70	2,392
1984	37,800	7.00	2,533
1985	39,600	7.05	2,792
1986	42,000	7.15	3,003
1987	43,800	7.15	3,132
1988	45,000	7.51	3,380
1989	–	7.51	–
1990 and after	–	7.65	–

P–Projected.

Social Security Taxes and Budgeting

As noted, federal income and Social Security taxes are withheld from employees' salaries and wages. The remainder is usually the take-home pay or disposable income. Since 1977, presidents of the United States signed important legislation for financing the Social Security system into the year 2030. The Social Security tax, which is levied against both the employer and employee, is rapidly becoming one of the fastest growing taxes paid by the public and may well exceed the property and federal taxes paid by many families. Attempts to repeal the recent federal legislation have failed. One has only to think about the year 2030 and calculate that this will be the time when the post–World War II baby boom will be retiring. Earlier funding of the Social Security program was based on the concept that there would be a continually growing work force in the country. The declines in the birth rate of the past several years will mean fewer people working in relation to the number of people retiring. These are only a couple of the factors that led to revising the Social Security tax rates. Table 3-5 illustrates the growth trend of this tax. You will note that in the years 1979–1988 both the maximum amount of salaries and wages subject to the tax as well as the percentage rate increase with successive years. For budgeting purposes, it is a good idea to know what percentages of salary and wages is going for Social Security. Keeping an estimate of 7 percent in mind will be convenient in budgeting the amount being withheld from a paycheck.

WORKSHEET FOR BUDGETING HOUSEHOLD INCOME

While the income of a household is usually limited to three or four regular sources, it is still a good idea to draw up a worksheet similar to the one shown in

EXHIBIT 3-1 John & Kay Adams
Worksheet for Budgeted Household Income

Income Sources	JAN	FEB	MAR	APR	MAY	JUN	JUL	AUG	SEP	OCT	NOV	DEC	Total
J&K 's take–home pay	1,500	1,500	1,500	1,600	1,600	1,600	1,600	1,600	2,100	2,100	2,100	2,100	20,900
Interest income			80			95			105			120	400
Tips, commissions, and bonuses													
Alimony income													
Child support													
VA benefits													
Social Security													
Retirement													
CETA grants, WIN													
Unemployment													
SSI, ADC, etc.													
Food stamps													
Dividends	50			50			50			50			200
Total estimate	1,550	1,500	1,580	1,650	1,600	1,695	1,650	1,600	2,205	2,150	2,100	2,220	21,500

Exhibit 3-1. The worksheet illustrated sets out information spaces for one full year and provides for totals. A person can easily modify this worksheet to meet his or her own special needs. The left-hand margin shows several examples of income for illustrative purposes only. An individual or household need only enter the sources of income that are relevant to them.

As for salaries and wages, enter only the take-home pay to be received. Enter the amount of interest earned or to be earned on bank savings accounts when it becomes available even though you do not plan to withdraw the money. Enter amounts to be received in checks from retirement, welfare, dividends, or other sources. Money to be received from various training grants such as the Veterans Administration and Work Incentive Program (WIN) should be entered in those months in which funds are expected to be received. If you receive free food stamps, enter the total retail value for each month's allotment. If you pay for a portion of your food stamps, enter only the net additional purchasing power in the food stamps line of your worksheet.

A THICKET OF EXPENDITURES AND HOW TO KEEP TRACK

Whereas individuals or households can determine their total income for the year with some degree of certainty, determining expenses is something else. Expenses reflect the unique aspect and the personality of individuals, families, and households. Although income is derived from a few sources, expenses are extremely varied. Expenses occur almost on a daily basis, whereas incomes are received on a weekly, semimonthly, or monthly basis. Some expenses are only pennies; others seem to descend upon us in big chunks and without warning. A paycheck, on the other hand, may be for exactly the same amount for each pay period for a whole year.

Because of the difficulty in finding statistical norms for the ways in which individuals, families, and other household units spend their money, it may be just as well to keep track of your expenditures for a period of time by writing them in some sort of notebook. Include *all* expenditures whether made by cash, check, or credit card. Include pay telephone and parking meter money. Write down your spending for coffee breaks and vending machine snacks and minor impulse spending for gum and cigarettes. Here are some things that may result from this 60-day record: (1) You will notice that certain definite spending patterns exist. (2) You will have a complete record of where your money was spent. (3) Chances are that there will be fewer than 100 transactions for each month or about 3 a day on average. (4) You may experience days in which no money was spent. (5) After keeping such record for 60 days, you may want to continue keeping such a record.

If, after reading this text, you still find that developing a formal budget or budgeting in general is not possible under present circumstances, then try to maintain this simple expense journal-diary. It is better than no record at all, and you may resume your attempts at budgeting later on.

Because of a *lack of thoroughness at the outset,* many budgeting attempts falter when one large unplanned expenditure has occurred and thrown the budget out of balance for the next several months. We often call these expenditures *emergencies.* But most financial emergencies are really expenditures that we had forgotten about (such as license plate renewals, an insurance policy to be paid, or taxes owed). To do a better job in allowing for potential expenditures, we will begin looking at expenses by categories.

Developing Expense Categories

Summarizing the many and varied expenses in today's modern household is not always easy. The following categories, however, will provide a basic framework for most household units from the modest to the very affluent.

1. Food	Food to be prepared and eaten at home, school lunches, office lunches and coffee break money, bread and milk shopping money, basic human consumption groceries, simple meals eaten in modest cafés or fast-food outlets. (Party foods for home entertainment, home bar replenishings, special dinners, and pet food belong in the Entertainment category.) Exclude paper towels and soaps from foods.
2. Housing, furniture, and fixtures	Mortgage payments and property taxes, rent or lease payments, indoor and outdoor maintenance and repairs; chairs, lamps, kitchen and laundry room appliances, clocks, radios, stereos, dishes, fix-it tools; yard and garden tools and supplies; furniture, carpets, paint; kitchen and bathroom cleansers, etc.
3. Utilities	Electricity, telephone; garbage and trash hauling fees and assessments, trash liner bags; water, home heating oil or other energy, natural or bottled gas; septic tank expenses and inspection fees, sewage; cable TV, mass transit utility tax, long-distance phone and public pay phone.
4. Transportation	Automobile payments, license plates or tab renewal fees, driver's license, vehicle inspection fees, auto insurance, gasoline, oil, lubrication, minor maintenance, major maintenance, tires, snow tires, mufflers, exhaust pipes, batteries; antifreeze, major repairs fund, washing and polishing materials, parking meter money, parking stall fees; bus tokens and passes, taxi money; car rentals; plane, train, and bus tickets. (The portion of transportation cost and lodging devoted solely to vacations should be placed in the entertainment category.)
5. Clothing and care	Basic clothing needs for work, school, office, special gym clothing and shoes, underwear, socks, shoes, jackets, coats, billfolds, hand bags, accessories; sewing patterns, yardgoods, notions; dry cleaning and laundry soaps, bleach, softeners, coin-operated washer and dryer money. (Special work safety equipment and shoes, uniforms should be placed in work-

	related expenses; ski boots, golf shoes, etc., should be under recreation.)
6. Health and life	Hospital, medical, major surgery, and dental insurance; life insurance, long-term disability policy; salary insurance, accidental death insurance. (Property insurance, tenant's property insurance, and auto insurance should be listed under Housing and Transportation, respectively.)
7. Personal grooming, self-medications	Bath soaps, shampoos, water softeners, hair preparations, combs, brushes, shaving items, dental care (pastes, powder, floss), deodorants, makeup preparations, nail care, pain relievers; prescription refills, cold medicines, and allergy relief, cut and burn medicines and dressings; female hygiene and family planning; tissue and toilet paper, infant care items; appliances (hair dryers), mirrors; suntan lotions, orthopedic assists, batteries.
8. Recreation, entertainment, vacations	Vacation budget, hobby supplies and tools, amusement entrance tickets and parking; special dinners, drinks, tips, parking, baby-sitter fees; pet care; stereo tapes and records; golfing, fishing, camping, hunting equipment and supplies; recreational clothing, running clothes; home bar and beverage supplies, gourmet goods, snacks, nuts, TV munchies; candles, specialty wines; camera film and processing; club memberships.
9. Personal improvement, education	Newspaper and magazine subscriptions; tuition, books, and supplies; conference and workshop fees; professional journals, home office equipment and supplies, files, reference books, dictionary, personal library, book shelves.
10. Work related	Union dues, special clothing and cleaning costs, safety goggles and gloves, safety shoes, tools and toolbox, retirement and gift donations, pot luck office parties, physicals, license renewals, special training, child care.
11. Gifts, contributions	Church pledges, United Way and other charitable organizations, charity cake bakes and donated foodstuffs; birthday, anniversary, wed-

	ding, graduation gifts; holiday and other greeting cards; gift wrapping paper, postage stamps, cards, stationery.
12. Contingencies	Amounts of cash not covered by insurance policies such as the deductible portion of auto and medical claims; legal advice, emergency telephone and telegram expenses; emergency storm repairs; unexpected travel and lodging; hassle money for resolving auto repair cost, stranded traveler expenses, unexpected guests.
13. Allowances, allotments, mad money	Portions of adults' and children's allowances that do not need to be accounted for. The individual is free to spend these monies without question (these small sums are often the price paid to obtain family cooperation in developing a budget program).
14. Miscellaneous	Small infrequent expenditures that do not warrant spending time classifying in one or more categories: notary fees, bank service fees, flashlight batteries, padlock, duplicate keys, postage due, cost of job hunting; photocopying, etc. This expense category requires accountability, but total expenses should not exceed 1 or 2 percent of the total of all expenses by a household unit.

These examples are designed to address the many questions frequently raised when this section of budgeting is discussed. The reader may wish to revise some of the material into other expense categories or to expand, reduce, or even omit one or two of the categories. However, if you have not previously been actively attempting to budget your expenses before now, you will probably find that these categories will indeed work rather well and that they will never have to be revised in the future. This material may seem extremely detailed, but in reading you may have been reminded of a certain important expense item temporarily overlooked. The key to budgeting for expenses is to reduce the chance of a major expenditure's not being accounted for. Something as rare as a class reunion or a very dear relative's wedding anniversary are also enjoyable occasions that can make life more interesting if we can plan ahead and share in those activities. It should be noted that several small expenses can add up and place a strain on the budget. Finally, your expenses should reflect to some degree, if not now at least in the future, your long-term financial goals.

Planning for Unusual Expenditures—"Budget Busters"

One reason why so many well-intended budget plans fail is that budget makers have not been sufficient in drawing up their original budgets. Thoroughness is important, but you should not confuse it with flexibility or rigidity. You may have planned to see 12 movies this year and have earmarked $75 or this. You may have set aside $25 for camera film and processing for the year. This is an example of thoroughness. Later you may decide not to attend the movies or buy film but to use the money to enroll in a course in furniture refinishing. That is flexibility. Rigidity might mean that the cost of the refinishing course should not exceed the money that you originally set aside for movies and film. Rigidity should be pursued insofar as making sure that you have the money to pay the rent or the mortgage, utilities, and insurance. In this section we want to look at those expenses that can be called "budget busters" or "emergencies." Again these are expenses that have been forgotten but normally occur, or they are expenses that may come without reasonable forewarning or expectation.

No budget will ever be completely accurate, and actual expenditures will not always coincide with every budget category established. But, if you come within 5 percent of your original estimates at the end of the year, consider yourself a true expert or very lucky. If you come within 10 to 15 percent of your estimates for the year, you are doing a commendable job. Governments regularly use budgets because legislation is often very explicit as to how money shall be spent. Many public school and city budgets are not allowed to incur a deficit. Because most businesses face uncertainty in the marketplace, budgeting is not an exact art. Even so, many successful business managers feel that the time and money spent on budgeting is well worth it because budgeting does help to sharpen managerial skills. You can sharpen your skills in budgeting by reviewing the following two lists and making some reasonable estimates of their likelihood of occurrence. Just as preparing a budget for the second year is much easier than preparing for the first, a planning sheet such as the one shown in Exhibit 3-2 will help you search for infrequent and unanticipated expenses for the second year.

Group One: Expenses Often Overlooked

Automobile and trailer license renewal tabs
Automobile insurance premiums
Utility bills
Magazine subscription renewals
Membership dues to clubs and associations
Medical insurance premiums
Life insurance premiums
Child support payments

EXHIBIT 3-2 Planning Worksheet for Estimating Irregular and Infrequent Expenditures

John & Kay Adams family

JAN	FEB	MAR	APR	MAY	JUN	JUL	AUG	SEP	OCT	NOV	DEC
$150 Auto License		$300 Auto Insurance 1 yr.	$400 Property Tax ½ year $275 Home Insurance 1 yr.		$1,500 new furniture	$1,630 family vacation	$800 Clothing for family		$400 Property Tax ½ yr. $120 new snow tires	$200 Holiday gifts	
150		300	675		1,500	1,630	800		520	200	

Total estimate of expenses for year $5,775 ÷ 12 months = $481.25 monthly estimate to be set aside in actual cash in a special savings program.

Snow tire mounting and balancing costs
Property taxes
Automobile servicing
Automobile mufflers and shock absorbers
School tuition, books, and supplies
Graduation gifts
Installment payments on new purchases made
Dental checkup bills
Income tax payments to the IRS
Church and charity pledges.

The following items are "budget busters" that often give little or no fore-warning prior to their occurrence.

Group Two: Unanticipated Types of Expenses

Automobile battery failure
Tire blowout

Sudden illness or accident

Veterinary costs for sick or injured pets

Travel and lodging due to illness or death of close relative or friend

Financial losses not normally covered by insurance

Automobile timing chain failure

Automobile transmission failure

Alternative transportation needs

Extended electrical power failure

Damages caused by other members of the family

Legal advice

Unexpected visits by relatives and friends

Another way to help determine most irregular and infrequent expenses is to review canceled checks for clues as to when such things as insurance, licenses, and subscriptions come due. Once you made a good effort to account for these groups of expenses, you may notice something important. Are these expenses tending to pile up in certain months? If so, you might try to have some of the payments charged to other months. Or you might try to adjust certain expenditures to months in which cash commitments are not so large.

To complete the worksheet in Exhibit 3-2, total the amounts for each month and make another total for the whole year's estimate of these two groups of expenses. There is one simple and reasonable way to try to meet such expenses: (1) Take the total for the entire year and divide that total by 12 months. The answer will be the amount that must be set aside each month to have the money available for these expenditures. (2) Do your best to set this money aside even if you have to set up a separate bank account, savings account, credit union account, or the like. Chapter 5 introduces techniques for saving actual cash.

Sample Master Budget Format for Students. If you are a full-time student and are living at home, at a college facility, at a military base, or at a state institution and if your food and living costs are being paid by your parents or a government agency, then you need a very simple budget program. Exhibit 3-3 shows a student's budget in summary form. In planning for student needs, remember that the school year is only nine months long and that the other three months, usually in the summer, may well reflect a completely different life-style and different expenditure patterns. A separate three-month budget just may have to be prepared on a separate sheet of paper. Student travel will usually be heavier in the months of September, December, and May or June. It is a good idea to do all the work in developing budgets in *pencil*.

Budget for the Divorced, the Widowed, the Displaced, and Others. Among the people who need budgeting assistance are the young divorced woman with

EXHIBIT 3-3   Student's Master Budget Format Year: Estimated Income

Estimated Income		
Savings from summer and part-time job	$ _____	
Money received from parents	_____	
Scholarship, grants, student loan, etc.	_____	
Veterans and Social Security benefits	_____	
Total income from all sources		$ _____
Estimated Expenses		
Food	$ _____	
Rent	_____	
Transportation and parking	_____	
Registration, tuition, lab fees	_____	
Textbooks, supplies	_____	
Refreshments	_____	
Personal care	_____	
School medical insurance	_____	
Recreation	_____	
Contributions and club dues	_____	
Laundry and cleaning	_____	
Clothing	_____	
Other	_____	
Total estimated expenses		$ _____
Estimated savings or (deficit)		$ _____

children, the older divorced woman with children, the displaced older woman homemaker, the recently widowed woman, those new to the United States, foreign-born spouses of military personnel, persons released from correctional and other institutions, those who have changed careers, veterans, and the newly retired. Many of these people are undergoing major emotional and psychological adjustments, but their problems can often be relieved or aggravated by the way in which they handle their financial affairs.

Some of the problems that these people experience are as follows:

1. A radically different change in life-style and usually a material drop in their standard of living.
2. A substantial drop in gross income and disposable income, with little or no discretionary income remaining.
3. A complete break with former social contacts and friends.
4. Very little effort to manage money in the past beyond immediate needs or until the next source of income arrives; no concept of money.

5. Readjustment period that includes periods of extreme loneliness, which can trigger irrational financial or other decisions.

It appears that some people tend to work through the financially related problems of a divorce or widowhood better than others. Those who have jobs or at least currently salable skills will still have their contacts with co-workers and business associates and will probably still have credit ratings (to permit borrowing, if necessary). Job skills make people mobile in the job market and enable them to move from unpleasant situations. They may still have a portion or all of their retirement programs intact and may receive health care protection under their firm's group insurance plan. Such people have learned to be competitive and to suppress their emotions at work.

On the other hand, there are those whose background skills and education do not equip them to gain control over their financial affairs quickly and efficiently. Many have been sheltered from major financial decisions concerning the family and must try to learn almost overnight about these matters when they become widowed or divorced. Some with careers gave up those careers or interrupted their education at the time of marriage, and their job or career skills may be dated. Then there is the investment to be made in suitable clothes for work and reliable transportation to and from the work place.

The automobile is perhaps the weakest link in gaining control over one's finances. A nonfunctioning automobile often affects one's ability to get to school or work on time and to do necessary shopping; alternate transportation needs are usually more time consuming, and auto repair costs soon deplete any savings.

In the case of ownership of the home, even if the house is fully paid for, maintenance and upkeep, utility bills, and property taxes will often be more than a single person can realistically afford to pay from immediate sources of income. For example, the widow who is without dependents and who has a house but no job skills may find that the house is considered "wealth," which makes her ineligible for public assistance.

Finally, it appears that divorce or widowhood has a greater emotional impact on some than on others, particularly when there is no discretionary income to offset emotional trauma.

In summary, people who find themselves on an extremely confining source of income need to become very realistic and adopt financial budgeting as their plan to bring them into a controlling situation instead of being controlled by their immediate circumstances. The budget illustrated in Exhibit 3-4 is designed for a person who might be pursuing education and training under a Job Training Partnership ACT (JTPA) or Work Incentive program.

This particular budget is designed for a displaced homemaker presumed to be divorced or widowed with no or grown children. This person is not eligible for Social Security benefits and does not qualify for public assistance such as welfare. She has not worked outside the home and therefore does not qualify for

EXHIBIT 3-4 Budget for Displaced Homemaker on One-Year Training Grant

Income estimate (rounded)	Week	Month	Year
Basic training grant income	$ 86	$373	$4,472
Plus: Commuting allowance	16	69	832
Income supplement	23	100	1,196
Total estimated income	$125	$542	$6,500
Estimated expenses (rounded)			
1. Food (home meals/carried lunches)	20	87	1,040
2. Housing (assume home is paid)	0	0	0
3. Utilities (phone, heat, light, water, trash)	20	87	1,040
4. Transportation (commuting allowances)	20	87	1,040
5. Clothing and cleaning	3	13	156
6. Health insurance and prescriptions	18	77	936
7. Personal care and grooming aids	3	13	156
8. Recreation, social	4	17	208
9. Personal improvement (newspapers/magazines)	6	26	312
10. Work related (tools, uniforms)	4	17	208
11. Gifts, contributions, postage	1	4	52
12. Contingency/property taxes	20	87	1,040
13. Personal allowance	4	17	208
14. Miscellaneous	2	10	104
Total estimated expenses	$125	$542	$6,500
Balance remaining	0	0	0

unemployment compensation. This person owns her home, has applied for a training grant under WIN, and has received a transportation allowance and supplemental grant for payment for training materials, books, and supplies. The basic training grant income for a 40-hour-per-week program is $86, based upon the federal minimum hourly wage. Her total weekly income is $125.

The budget emphasizes four major areas of spending: food, utilities, transportation, and the contingency/property tax. If the person did not own her home, then a rent allocation would have to be made. It would mean that this person may have to seek public housing if she does not own her home outright. The fifth major category is health insurance. This person will have to purchase a private plan since she would no longer qualify under her former husband's group medical plan if he had one. The other areas shown on the budget are of modest amounts but should be budgeted for. Clothing and cleaning may have to be increased if the woman is working in an office where public contact is expected. The same might be true for personal care and grooming aids. At any rate, be sure to allocate actual cash to the smaller areas even if you have to set up special little envelopes marked with the category on the outside. The contingency fund should actually be placed in a checking or savings account. (Chapter 5 discusses banking in greater detail; the areas of food, clothing, and automobile costs are discussed in more detail in Chapters 7 and 9.)

A final word for those on a temporary subsistence-level budget. To have money at the end of the week or month or whatever the pay period, keep a daily diary of your expenditures. Do so for at least 60 days. Know what your fixed and variable living expenses are. In our budget illustration, the individual is receiving $125 per week. Food, utilities, transportation, health insurance, and contingencies add up to $98 per week to be earmarked and spent for those items. This leaves $27 remaining for the week that can be spent on nonessentials or $3.85 (27 ÷ 7 days) per day as the outside limit for all other items in the budget.

WORKSHEET FOR BUDGETING FAMILY EXPENSES

Having become more aware of the varied expenses of even the most modest of household units, now we will develop the basic budgeting approach for the well-established family unit. We want to look at a household that has a gross income of over $15,000 per year, where there are both parents and some children, one or two cars, a house, and emotional stability.

Some may feel that a family earing $15,000, $25,000, or $40,000 a year really does not have to engage in budgeting. As a matter of fact it is precisely this group of people who needs budgeting most. Many families in this income range are middle-aged parents with teenaged children. Federal income and Social Security taxes and state sales and property taxes are taking big chunks of money right off the top of these incomes. These families are also subject to the impact of inflation. It may well be that the husband's real purchasing power from his work has remained unchanged for the past four or five years. If this family is getting ahead financially, it is probably due to the wife's taking a job. But, then, that second job often puts the family into a higher tax bracket. Moreover, there are expenditures for better grooming, an upgraded wardrobe, transportation, and often child care. Still, a wife's income will allow the family to spend money for categories of activity as they have over the past four or five years rather than having to retrench. In brief, the family's income will follow the trend established long ago in *Engel's law* as noted in the glossary.

It is the family budget that provides the essentials to study when developing a realistic and useful budget of our own. A family that has been long established is usually in the midst of accomplishing goals set by the adults many years ago. Many of the *goals in process* are the marriage, having a family, buying a home, providing for the children's education, increasing the awareness and enriching the lives of the family members, having adequate insurance protection, and setting money aside for savings and emergencies.

Let us establish a budget for a middle-class family, the John and Kay Adams family and their teenage daughter Jill. John and Kay were married 16 years ago and both are working. While it would be difficult to construct what might be called a "typical American family" budget of income and expenses, the emphasis here will be to review the details of one of their annual budgets as they relate to *expenditures*. Keep in mind that it is the unlimited variety of expenditures that causes the difficulty in budgeting and the forgotten big expenditure that creates panic and jeopardizes successful budgeting. For our purposes the family income is portrayed and summarized in Exhibit 3-1; a detailed worksheet of the family master expense budget in the 14 established categories is shown in Exhibit 3-5; the complete summary of the family's gross income, taxes, expenses, and savings is in Exhibit 3-6. As you will notice, expenditures have been broken down into roughly their fixed and variable components. The fixed expense portion alerts the family to its cash needs under the most austere conditions.

While most budgets for families stop at this point, we will want to analyze each of the 14 expenditure categories by setting up several "mini" worksheets that show in detail areas of proposed spending. These worksheets are designed to accomplish the *thoroughness in the planning stage of budgeting*. This is again the key to budgeting. If you have carefully thought through your expenditures for the coming year, then any unforeseen expenditure, emergency, or event not covered by insurance may well be covered by the contingency reserve fund. These supplemental worksheets supporting the 14 major categories are shown in this and other chapters in the text. *They are primarily designed to assist the reader in recalling common expenditures or simply for "mind jogging."* If you wish to draft some of your own expenditures using these or modified planning worksheets, your time will be well spent. This is particularly true for those people with very well-established routines. Keep in mind that the second year of budgeting and thereafter is always much easier and may require only an hour or so to prepare. In fact you may want to turn over the budgeting activities to other members of the family in the following years to help them learn about this important but neglected area of controlling one's financial affairs.

The worksheets of expenditures for the 14 expense categories as well as the exhibit references are given in Table 3-6.

In the Adams family, John is a skilled artisan in a supervisory capacity at work. Kay is managing a small service-related firm. John's income is estimated to be $18,000 in the coming year and Kay's income will be $10,000. They estimate that $1,600 will be deducted in Social Security and that $5,500 will be paid in federal income taxes. They will earn about $400 in interest on savings and $200 in dividends on some stock they own. In addition to the equity buildup in their home, they have a goal to save around $2,000 for the year. They are able to do so because they purchased their home several years ago and, thus, their mortgage

EXHIBIT 3-5 John & Kay Adams
Master Expense Budget
For the Year ____

John & Kay Adams

1. Food: Basic foods and meals budget		$2,845
2. Housing		
a. Homeowner's budget	$3,485	
b. Household furnishings and linens	1,755	5,240
3. Utilities		1,111
4. Transportation		
a. Car payments, insurance, and license	$450	
b. Gas, maintenance, parking, vacation	3,490	3,940
5. Clothing: Basic clothing expense		1,175
6. Insurance: Health and life insurance premiums		264
7. Personal Care: Personal health care and grooming		535
8. Recreation and Social		
a. Home entertainment	$245	
b. Special occasion and vacation meals	50	
c. Recreational clothing	575	
d. Recreational equipment, hobbies	305	1,175
9. Personal Improvement		655
10. Work Related		
a. Business and union dues	$285	
b. Special work clothing and care	60	
c. Meals related to career	125	470
11. Gifts, Contributions		810
12. Contingencies		600
13. Family Allowance, Allotments, Mad Money		416
14. Miscellaneous Expense Estimate		215
Total Expense Budget Estimate for Year		$19,451

EXHIBIT 3-6   John & Kay Adams
Master Budget of Income, Expenses, and Savings
For the Year _____

John & Kay Adams

Estimated Income

				Monthly Average
Gross salaries and wages		$ 28,000		
Less: Income taxes	$5,500			
Social Security	1,600	7,100		
Estimated take-home pay		$ 20,900		
Plus: Estimated other income for year		600		
Total estimated income			$21,500	$ 1,791

Estimated Expenses

Category	Fixed	Annual Variable	Total	Monthly Average
1. Food	$ 2,700	$ 145	$ 2,845	$ 237
2. Housing	3,200	2,040	5,240	437
3. Utilities	1,000	111	1,111	92
4. Transportation	2,000	1,940	3,940	328
5. Clothing	175	1,000	1,175	98
6. Health and life insurance	264	0	264	22
7. Personal care	200	335	535	44
8. Recreation and social	300	875	1,175	98
9. Personal improvement	500	155	655	54
10. Work related	300	170	470	39
11. Gifts, contributions	150	660	810	68
12. Contingencies	500	100	600	50
13. Family allowances	416	0	416	35
14. Miscellaneous (est.)	100	115	215	18
Total estimated expenses	$ 11,805	$ 7,646	19,451	1,620
Total estimated savings			$ 2,049	$ 171

TABLE 3-6 Worksheets for Expense Categories

Category	Worksheet	Exhibit
1. Food	Basic food and meals	7-1
2. Housing	Renter's	8-2
	Homeowner's	8-3
	Household furnishings and supplies	8-6
3. Utilities	Utilities expense budget	8-4
4. Transportation	Car payments, insurance, and license; gasoline, maintenance, parking; transit, vacation (partial)	9-6
5. Clothing and care	Basic clothing expense	7-7
6. Insurance	Health and life insurance	3-7
7. Personal care	Personal health care and grooming	7-10
8. Recreation and social	Home entertainment	7-3
	Recreational clothing	7-11
	Special occasion meals, parties	7-4
	Recreational equipment, hobbies	3-8
9. Personal improvement	Personal improvement and education	3-9
10. Work related	Special work clothing and care	7-8
	Meals related to career	7-2
	Business and union dues	3-10
11. Gifts and contributions	Gifts and contributions	3-11
12. Contingencies	Contingency estimate	3-12
13. Family allowance	Allowances, allotments, etc.	3-13
14. Miscellaneous	Miscellaneous expenses	3-14

payments are small. Also, their two cars are paid for and the would-be payments can be added to their savings. Therefore, their savings are substantially higher than are the savings of most families.

Kay is planning to construct a budget for the coming year. She uses canceled checks from the past couple of years and recall to determine some of the family's seasonal shopping needs as well as those commitments such as vacation and weekend activities. With pencil, paper, and pocket calculator, Kay sketches the components (the worksheets) of the various categories of expenses. The worksheet on the family's insurance needs for life, health, and income protection is shown in Exhibit 3-7.

Exhibit 3-8 relates to the family expenditures for recreational equipment, hobbies and materials and supplies, home recreational items, home entertainment equipment, and so on. Family hobbies, crafts, and recreational equipment are as varied as the expenses of a family. In fact, family members may be spending money on these items yet not really admitting that they are serious in their activities. A person may be a sort of "closet" stamp collector or an antique collector. The following is a list of hobbies and recreational activities that many people enjoy.

EXHIBIT 3-7   John & Kay Adams
Health and Life Insurance
For the Year _____

Type of Coverage	Estimate	Total
Medical & Dental Plan	*Employer paid*	$ —0—
Accidental Death Plan $150,000	$ 14 x 12 mo.	168 —
Disability Income Plan	$ 8 x 12 mo.	96 —
Life Insurance 1 yr. salary	*Employer paid*	—0—
Total Estimate for the Year		$264

EXHIBIT 3-8   John & Kay Adams
Recreational Equipment and Hobbies
For the Year _____

Types of Activities	Total
Camera film, processing, & prints	$35 —
Movies & other admission tickets	85 —
House plants, containers, plant food	30 —
Fishing and camping budget	80 —
L-P records and tapes	60 —
YWCA dues — Jill	15 —
Total Estimate of the Year	$305 —

Hobbies, Crafts, and Recreational Activities

Domestic pets: food, vet fees, shots, pedigrees
Photography: cameras, film, flash, batteries, lens
Physical fitness: Equipment, weights, benches, ropes
Model trains, planes, cars, and accessories
Stereo tapes and LP records, home videos
Movies, games, parks, museums

Collecting stamps and books

Coin collecting: Coins, holders, and security

Flower garden: Seeds, plants, containers, plant food

Fish: Tanks, foods, and other aquarium supplies

Fishing: Rods, reels, bait, license, hooks, flies, etc.

Backpacking and camping: Equipment, tents, cooking utensils

Wood crafts, rock polishing, jewelry making and materials

Painting: Oils, canvases, brushes, materials, and equipment

What the Adams expect to spend in this area for the coming year is drawn up in Exhibit 3-8.

Personal improvement and education expenditures for the Adams family relate to such things as subscriptions to a newspaper, magazines for the home, and a weekly news magazine, a few purchases of paperback books, the daugh-

The Sporting Life

"DID I MENTION MY HERBERT'S TAKEN UP MOUNTAIN CLIMBING?"

EXHIBIT 3-9 John & Kay Adams
Personal Improvement and Education
For the Year _____

Activities	Total
Daily newspapers #5 x 12 mo.	#60 –
Magazines	65 –
Paperbacks & books	30 –
Music lessons – Jill	400 –
Conferences, cultural events	100 –
Total Estimate for the Year	#655 –

ter's music lessons, estimates for some professional improvement workshops, and conferences for John and Kay on areas of supervision and management. Exhibit 3-9 shows the Adams's estimates for the coming year.

Other expenditures that could be sizable are those related to one's job. Some of these expenses do receive some income tax consideration, but the expense is likely to be incurred whether or not one files the appropriate tax return. Public employees, schoolteachers, skilled technicians and artisans, and others may belong to associations relevant to their work but whose dues and other costs are not paid for by the employer. Exhibit 3-10 illustrates examples of expenses that the Adams family will incur next year.

Gifts and contributions seem to be an integral part of one's budget. At the drop of the hat, we will organize around an issue of concern and ask for donations, contributions, and pledges to promote a cause, kill a disease, start a new religion, oust a politician, change a law, feed the hungry, and so on. Family friends and relatives are remembered by sending cards and gifts at various special occasions. Here is a good place to estimate these expenditures. Decide on

EXHIBIT 3-10 John & Kay Adams
Business and Union Dues
For the Year _____

Type of Activity	Total
Union dues	#240 –
Business & Professional Women	25 –
Laundry (John's Workclothes)	20 –
Total Estimate for the Year	#285 –

a realistic amount to give to your favorite organization, make your contribution, and stick to your limits for the year. The Adams family has for years earmarked the amounts to be spent on birthdays, anniversaries, holiday gifts, and greeting cards. Exhibit 3-11 shows their spending plans for gifts and contributions for the coming year.

Certain events may or may not happen within a specified period of time. In a modern society, most people remove the threat of a large financial loss by purchasing various forms of insurance. Even if the person has adequate insurance coverage, insurance does not and cannot protect against all kinds of losses. Most policies written today carry what are known as deductibles. A person may carry an automobile, collision, and upset policy on a car. But, to keep the cost of the premium to a reasonable level, that person may wish to assume the first $200 worth of damages out of his or her own pocket. A contingency reserve should be planned for and the money set aside in a special bank or thrift institution savings account. Consider the contingency as a monthly expense and write the check for the savings account. Once the fund has been created, it does not have to be budgeted for in the following years. The goal is to have the money when needed; it is only secondary whether or not the money is earning any interest. A major car repair, legal advice, emergency travel, or being stranded during travel fall in this category. Exhibit 3-12 shows the Adams's rough estimate of this amount to be planned for the coming year's budget.

John, Kay, and Jill have been receiving small amounts of pocket money each week purely for their own spending without any need for accountability. They may do as they wish with these small sums and not feel guilty about it. This is what one calls an allowance or mad money.

John and Kay have a mad money allowance of $3.00 a week; Jill receives $2.00 a week. This money can be counted on each week throughout the year. All three members may receive additional allowances each week, but those have to

EXHIBIT 3-11   John & Kay Adams
Gifts and Contributions
For the Year _____

Categories	Total
Christmas budget, wrapping, postage, insurance	#150 —
Church (pledge & cake sale costs)	370 —
United Way & miscellaneous contributions	150 —
Anniversaries & birthdays (family)	100 —
Greeting & other cards & postage	40 —
Total Estimate for the Year	#810 —

EXHIBIT 3-12   John & Kay Adams
Contingencies
For the Year ____

Areas of Concern	
Estimate $50 per month × 12 months *(unscheduled travel)*	$600 —
Total Estimate for the Year	$ 600 —

be accounted for. Examples are the gasoline allowance for the person who drives a car to work or the routine "bread and milk" shopping that one of the members does on his or her way home from work. A teenager might also receive a clothing allowance and one for school supplies. This is not as difficult a task to implement. Chances are that the family has had something like an allowance such as this in operation for several years, but it may not have been a specific amount and the time interval may have varied because it was developed from "left-over money" after other spending.

In brief, the allowance may be the key to having a good budgeting system; it will also save money in the long run and will help direct family efforts toward using the budget system to accomplish their important priorities. The family's allocations appear in Exhibit 3-13.

Miscellaneous expense is often misunderstood by people who are trying to make an effort at money managing. Even businesses do not know what to do with this account, and, if they are not careful, the miscellaneous expense account ends up with 10–12 percent of the firm's expenses for the year. A miscellaneous account should never amount to more than 2 percent of budget income and 1 percent or less is more realistic. For personal money management, use the miscellaneous account for those infrequent expenditures that do not fit into the

EXHIBIT 3-13   John & Kay Adams
Family Allowances and Mad Money
For the Year ____

Mad Money Allowance	Total
John $ 3 × 52 weeks	$ 156 —
Kay 3 × 52 weeks	156 —
Jill 2 × 52 weeks	104 —
Total Estimate for the Year	$ 416 —

EXHIBIT 3-14 John & Kay Adams
Miscellaneous Expense Estimate
For the Year ____

Rationale	
Estimate of 1% of $21,500 take-home pay	$215—
Total Estimate for the Year	$215—

other categories that you have established. Bank service charges is a good example of a miscellaneous expense. The cost of padlock, ball point pen refills, mending tape, a ball of twine, and so on are candidates for the miscellaneous account. A small mixed purchase from a variety store amounting to a couple of dollars or less might also be charged to this account. The miscellaneous expense account is designed to save time and get away from "nickel nursing." The technical errors that become buried in this expense account are not material and do not deserve your time. In budgeting, it's keeping an eye on the large expenditure categories that is important. Exhibit 3-14 shows the Adams's calculation.

These worksheets as well as the others (illustrated in detail in subsequent chapters) complete the planning process that should go into developing a master budget for a family. All these worksheets are summarized in the 14 categories of major expenditures. Since much of the spending is routine, the 14 categories simplify the time spent comparing the budgeted estimates with the actual expenditures. Major items such as housing, utilities, food, and transportation tend to be rather uniform throughout the year. A quick calculation of what a monthly budget estimate is for a particular item should find a close approximation with the actual expenditure. A clothing budget, on the other hand, is usually spent on two or three shopping trips during the year, it is hoped during the time of major sales. Insurance premiums, gifts, and property taxes will come in specific months rather than on a uniform monthly basis. In summary, the Adams family should have few or no surprises in their money management by making such preliminary planning so thorough.

COMPARING BUDGETED EXPENSES AND ACTUAL EXPENSES

To compare actual expenses with budgeted expenses, develop a worksheet similar to the format shown in Exhibit 3-15. Design your worksheet with the 14 categories and a total column. Be sure to include the "savings" column. Consider the savings goal as though it were just another monthly expense and write

EXHIBIT 3-15 John & Kay Adams
Comparison of Budgeted and Acutal Expenses
For the Year ___

MONTH	Total	Food	Housin-	Utility	Trans-portation	Clothing	Insurance	Personal Care	Recreation	Personal Improve-ment	Work Related	Gifts & Contri-butions	Contin-gencies	Allowances	Miscell-aneous	Savings
Total budget estimate	21,500	2,845	5,240	1,111	3,940	1,175	264	535	1,175	655	470	810	600	416	215	2,049
January actual																
Balance																
February actual																
Balance																
March actual																
Balance																
April actual																
Balance																
May actual																
Balance																
June actual																
Balance																
July actual																
Balance																
August actual																
Balance																
September actual																
Balance																
October actual																
Balance																
November actual																
Balance																
December actual																
Balance																

a check to your savings account. To be sure that your savings goal will be reached, write this check first and on the first day of the month or on payday when the money is there. Too many people try to save money at the end of the month. Chances are there will be no money left over at the end of the month. This is an example of being controlled by your expenses instead of controlling your expenses. It is this one shift in attitude, motivation, or desire that makes the difference as to who will get the most out of their money.

On the left-hand side of the worksheet, enter the months and lines for remaining subtotal balances. Summarize the information from the daily expense diary for the month, enter category totals, and bring down the new balance of the unexpended budgeted amount for each column.

SUMMARY

The first step in accomplishing one's objectives is planning, as discussed in Chapter 1. Budgeting and planning go hand in hand. The budget is an analysis of those plans expressed in dollars. A budget may be defined as a projection of income and expenditures for a specific period of time. The importance of making a budget is that it forces a person or family to think or plan ahead. Budgeting allows one to begin to control one's expenses rather than being controlled by them. On the income side of budgeting, the focus should be on disposable income. The rate of inflation during the coming budget period should also be considered because it will have an erosive effect on disposable income and reduce actual purchasing power. Good money managers should know the approximate percentage rates that they are paying on federal income taxes and Social Security. A person's income usually comes from only a few sources, and it is highly predictable. Personal living expenses are incurred in a variety of ways and may vary from only a few pennies to hundreds of dollars. Since they may not be very predictable, expenses may be viewed as either fixed or variable.

Financial emergencies (budget busters) are often expenditures that were temporarily forgotten by the individual or family or not adequately planned for. Examples of these are insurance premiums, automobile license, tire replacements, property taxes, and car trouble. Other financial emergencies may be the result of sudden illness or injury, storms, and emergency travel to relatives and friends.

The key to good budgeting is thoroughness in the development phase. Worksheets relating to major expenditure categories will help to reduce the likelihood of a major expenditure's being overlooked. Limit the number of expenditure categories to around 10 to 15 depending on your social circumstances (food, housing, transportation, etc.). Family budgeting can be a rewarding experience if family planning and participation also take place. Persons who are living on limited incomes and training grants can help their money go farther by establishing budgets.

If budgeting is still difficult, keep a daily entry of expenses in a notebook. Enter the expenses in the day incurred whether made by cash, check or credit card. At least keep this simple system going until you can regain your efforts at budgeting.

TIPS

1. If at all possible, keep a daily expense record book and note each day's expenditures. Keep sales slips in an envelope marked for the month.
2. The person who seems to be the better money manager should assume the duty of maintaining the financial record keeping and budgeting on a regular basis, but others should be able to follow the system if necessary.
3. Review spending habits from time to time to determine whether or not money is being wasted.

ADDITIONAL READINGS

Blum, J., "The Cash Clash," *Redbook*, March 1984, pp. 88—89. "Chart Your Course," *Changing Times*, January 1986, pp. 42—47.

Harris, Marlys, "Creating a Budget: A Step-by-Step Guide to Setting Saving and Spending Priorities," *Money*, October 1983, pp. 71—76.

"Kids and Money: What They Need to Know, When They Need to Know It," *Changing Times*, June 1981, pp. 17—20.

Schiller, R., "Making Ends Meet," *Reader's Digest*, February 1984, pp. 15—22.

"Where Does All The Money Go?" *Consumer Reports*, September 1986, pp. 581—92.

GLOSSARY OF USEFUL TERMS

Budget   A projection of income and expenses for a specific period of time. A budget is a plan expressed in dollars.

Cash Budget   A financial statement matching estimated cash receipts with estimated cash disbursements for a month, quarter, or year. The basic format of a cash budget is as follows:

	January	February	March
Beginning cash balance	$ 300	$400	
Plus: cash receipts	800		
Total cash available	$1,100		
Less: Cash expenditures	700		
Ending cash balance *desired*	$ 400	$420	$440

Consumer Goods   Goods purchased by the final consumer for his or her personal or household use.

Consumption   The destruction of utility. Utility is the ability to satisfy a human want.

Discretionary Income   For personal finance purposes it is the money remaining after subtracting fixed living expenses from disposable income.

Disposable Income   The amount of money one has left after subtracting income taxes and Social Security taxes.

Engel's Law   As the income of a family increases (1) a smaller percentage is expended for food; (2) the percentage of expenditures for clothing remains about the same; (3) the percentage of rent, fuel, and light remains the same whatever the income; and (4) a constantly increasing percentage is expended for education, amusements, and so on.

Fixed Living Expenses   Living expenses that cannot reasonably be changed in the near- or short-term period without major disruption of activities, for example, rent payments, mortgage payments, most utilities, property taxes, insurance premiums, basic food items, automobile license plates, and essential transportation.

Income   Money or the property received such as salary and wages, rent, interest, dividends, profits, and so on.

Income Statement   A statement summarizing total income, expenses, taxes, and savings (or loss) over a specific period of time.

Money Sense   A prudent approach to the use of money in day-to-day living. Characteristics of money sense include allocating money on the basis of essential priorities and nonessential expenditures: it is the opposite of the old expression "penny wise and pound foolish."

Murphy's Law   Everything is more difficult than it looks; if something should go wrong, it will, and it will go wrong at the worst possible time.

Purchasing Power   The amount of goods and services that money will actually buy at a given time. Also called real income.

Scale of Living   Those satisfactions that the individual or family attain through its efforts.

Utility   The ability to satisfy a human want or desire.

Variable Living Expenses   Expenses subject to control by the individual or family in the near or short term. Examples are vacation expenses, recreational and social expenses, allowances, clothing, gifts, contributions and entertainment expenses.

4

Insurance

LEARNING OBJECTIVES

Upon completion of Chapter 4, you should be able to identify and remember

- The basic purpose of any insurance.
- The basic kinds of insurance coverages for an individual or family.
- The basic kinds of insurance coverages on the things owned by people and protection against liability.
- The two basic ingredients of any life insurance coverage.
- The two basic forms of insurance companies.
- The role of the insurance agent in life and casualty insurance underwriting.
- The amount of life insurance coverage that may be obtained for a given dollar of premium paid.
- A program for insurance coverage by implementing risk reduction, risk assumption, and risk transference.
- The six steps that one can take in reviewing current insurance needs.
- The pitfalls to watch for in mail-order insurance policies.
- How to go about preparing an inventory of personal property owned and the reasons why such a list is useful in settling an insurance claim.
- The typical basic coverages that can be obtained and carried in relation to automobile ownership and driving.

2-7-77—© 1977 Newspaper Enterprise Association, Inc.

OVERVIEW

Most people who have completed a personal property inventory are often amazed at their accumulation of property as well as the value associated with it. Should all those items be destroyed by fire or some of the more valuable items stolen, a great deal of money would be necessary just to replace them. If, in attempting to reach your long-term financial goals you become ill for a long period of time or are injured permanently, you will want to be sure that some form of insurance is available to cover those months and perhaps years in which you are unable to work and earn a regular salary income. You want to be insured in the event that your car is damaged, stolen, or involved in an accident causing injury to someone and to his or her property. The purpose of this chapter is to look at what insurance is appropriate for hedging against a financial loss. It is extremely difficult to begin to cover the complex topic of insurance in just one chapter.

Because the insurance industry is changing rapidly along with the types of coverages available to the public and because of the variety of insurance advertised in all media, it is important to understand the real purpose of any insurance and then to develop a program to fit your specific needs.

INSURANCE AND ITS BASIC FUNCTION

Let us for a moment take a dispassionate view of the subject of insurance. What is the real function or purpose of insurance? The fundamental purpose of any insurance protection is to restore a financial, that is, a money, loss. For example, the major purpose of buying *life insurance* is to cover the lost salary or wages resulting from the untimely or premature death of a person usually deemed the head of a household. Since money in a family is scarce, life insurance coverage should be only on those persons in the family who provide the income or essential household services. We will treat this area more thoroughly later in the chapter.

The purpose of *property insurance* coverage is to restore the actual monetary or money loss in value of property destroyed or stolen. Here again we want to focus on the real money loss of something we own, not its sentimental value. The loss of an important family photo album, for example, may be more disheartening than the loss of a house, but it is the money loss of the house for which one buys insurance, not the photo album. Property insurance will be covered in more detail later in the chapter.

INSURANCE FOR ONE'S SELF AND ONE'S FAMILY

Proper insurance coverage is essential to sound financial money management. And, it is hoped, the reader will be sufficiently armed with information to be able to search out specific insurance coverage needs from the material in this chapter. The glossary at the end of this chapter provides essential insurance industry terms to help the reader better understand the technical portions of the material.

Employees of large corporations, governments, public schools, and many others are generally eligible for employment-based fringe benefits in the form of life and accidental death coverages and medical, hospital, and major medical insurance coverage. Dental, legal, and liability insurance coverage is also sometimes available to employees. Company group insurance programs for employees have greatly relieved employees from having to shoulder much of this task on their own.

Many employee insurance programs offer only specific coverages, so it is necessary for each individual to determine if the coverage is adequate and, if not, take the appropriate steps to fill in the gaps that may exist. Furthermore, each individual or family will have to determine the insurance coverage needed for such things as an automobile, other personal property, and maybe a house. Today, it is probably a good idea to make an effort at least once a year to review one's insurance situation and make adjustments in one's coverage according to acquisitions as well as inflation.

Your insurance coverage program should be developed by following a three-step analysis of *risk reduction, risk assumption,* and *risk transference.* Risk reduction is taking the necessary steps to remove hazardous things or situations that are in our homes and working areas. We already know many of these safety reminders: "Keep medicines and household cleaners out of reach of children." "Do not leave toys and garden tools in walk areas." "Read the label and follow instructions carefully." "Hallways and stairways should be clear and well lighted." And so on. You are always in the best position to determine your own relative safety. No one else can do this for you all the time. Moreover, do not count on the other person to always do the right thing. Following these guidelines can help to reduce the risks and hazards about you.

The second step in developing an insurance program is to determine how much of the remaining risks you are willing to assume for yourself and pay for out of your own pocket. A starting point for this is to review your balance sheet of assets and debts. Cash, car, securities, furniture and fixtures, and a house are subject to many perils. Keeping cash in insured banks or in traveler's checks is a good form of insurance protection. You may be willing to withstand the loss of small amounts of cash on your person or at home. What about your automobile? What risk do you want to assume here? You might be willing to absorb the first $100 or $200 damage to your automobile but not much more than that. How much medical expense can you absorb for a major illness or injury? What about the loss of a house due to a fire or windstorm?

To determine the amount of risk you are willing to assume, first, prepare a list of your possible risks. Next, assign a ranking to those risks. Then, make an honest review of your past experience with losses. What has been the state of your past health? What is the relative security of your apartment or house? What is your financial strength? Is your income steady or erratic? Is your job considered hazardous? These are just some of the questions that you should consider in assessing your willingness to be a self-insurer of risks.

The third step in your insurance program is to determine the insurance companies to whom the balance of the risks are to be transferred. This is a most difficult task. The only way to determine just how good your policy may be is when you try to collect. But by then, it is too late to learn how good your insurance company really is.

People who work for large corporations and various government agencies that have group health and medical and life insurance programs generally have better coverage than do those who must buy their own insurance under an individual plan. This is because of the ability of the employees' corporation or union to exert pressure on the insurance company if coverage and payment policies are not acceptable. This kind of clout seems to keep the insurance companies performing reasonably equitably. In the field of automobile insurance, however, the leverage is greatly in favor of the insurance company, because this insurance is sold largely to individuals. Instead of using the statistical data generated by police and highway patrol agencies and various transportation departments of state and local governments, auto insurers base premiums on the insured's geographical locale, type of job, age, financial status, moral repute, type of car, ability to read and write English, and so on. Entertainers and members of the military are automatically placed in a high-risk category by insurance companies. These discrimination tactics are generally known as "red lining."

Because of these peculiarities, you should consider dealing only with well-known companies that can service your claims locally. Avoid companies that function only through the mail or deal solely with the military or other special groups. Solicit the help of your credit union or bank, and do not forget to call the consumer affairs department of your state attorney general's office. The AGO may give you some insight as to companies that appear to be difficult in making settlements or that generate excessive customer dissatisfaction.

At present, auto insurance rate structures do not create incentives for safe driving. More thoughts in this area are covered in Chapter 9.

THE ROLE OF THE INSURANCE AGENT

In choosing an insurance agent, it may be advantageous to deal with someone you know and who, in turn, may know just what type of insurance you should have and what policies to avoid. If the agent is an *independent* insurance agent, he or she will select those insurance companies that have better performance records. When insuring your property, the insurance agent salesperson is the key individual as he or she holds the power to bind the insurance company to a contract. In buying life insurance, the sales representative *cannot* bind the insurance company to a contract. Only the agent's supervisory staff or persons higher up in the company can make a life insurance policy binding on the company. The words of a life insurance salesperson are not binding.

TYPES OF INSURANCE COMPANIES

Insurance companies are either *mutual* or *stock*. Mutual insurance companies are owned by the policyholders. Policyholders pay premiums based upon the experience of total member policyholders. If the group's loss experience has been low, next year's premiums may be lower or members may receive a rebate on a portion of the unused premium. If the loss experience of the member policyholders has been high, a higher premium may be levied on the group to cover losses. In stock insurance companies, stockholders own the company, with the object of earning a profit on their investment; the policyholders are just the customers. The policyholder pays a specific premium for coverage. There are no rebates to the policyholder nor are there additional assessments. Both corporate forms have advantages, but today these become more academic and will not be covered in this text. What counts is *your ability to collect from them when you have a legitimate claim*. The balance of this chapter focuses on some of the more common types of insurance available to most consumers.

TYPES OF INSURANCE COVERAGE

Life Insurance

As stated earlier, life insurance is purchased to cover the lost salary, wages, or homemaker services resulting from the untimely or premature death of a person. Almost everyone would agree that the major family income producers should carry most of the life insurance. Insurance coverage for small children is open to question. A small burial policy might be in order, but a large life insurance policy on a toddler may be unnecessary. A young, single, career-oriented man or woman with no debts and no financial responsibilities to any other person probably has little need for life insurance. If such a person wishes to take out a life insurance policy naming a charity, college, or relative as the beneficiary, that's fine, but then the life insurance becomes a sort of savings device enabling a bequest to someone at some time in the future. *Our concern for insurance coverage in this chapter is to restore a financial or money loss.*

If there is no real economic loss or hardship involved, question just what your insurance coverage goals are in the situation. Therefore, limit your life insurance coverage budget to those income earners whose deaths would cause financial hardship. With this focus, you will not be so likely to carry a policy on everyone who lives in a house or to purchase the wrong type of policy.

Life insurance is almost always needed in those households where there is a father, a mother, and young children. Some households in America have "extended families" that include retired parents, aunts, uncles, and children of deceased blood relatives. Whatever your situation, if there are several people who absolutely depend on you to provide essential household services, then the bulk of the family's insurance dollars should be on you.

How much life insurance coverage should one buy? Answering this question partly depends upon how well off the family is, the number and age of children, the surviving adults' ability to find work, whether job skills are current or dated, and the potential earnings of the surviving parent. Other important considerations are the age and health of surviving parents and children (see Table 4-1). Other questions to be asked are: "Do the children have chronic diseases or handicaps?" "Is the house paid for?" "Are there a lot of outstanding debts?" "To what extent are Social Security and or Veterans Administration benefits available to the family survivors?" "How old are the people who are to be insured?"

Because of persistent economic problems of high unemployment, high inflation rates, and the fact that family readjustment may take a longer time than anticipated, a surviving family should try to keep the total family income at about three-fourths of previous total income. There should be around six years for the family to adjust to a new life. This, for example, would allow a widow with small children to go back to school to update her education and job skills or

TABLE 4-1 Expectation of Life and Expected Deaths, by Race, Sex, and Age, 1983

AGE IN 1983 (years)	EXPECTATION OF LIFE IN YEARS					EXPECTED DEATHS PER 1,000 ALIVE AT SPECIFIED AGE				
	Total	White		Black		Total	White		Black	
		Male	Female	Male	Female		Male	Female	Male	Female
At birth	74.6	71.7	78.7	65.4	73.6	11.15	10.79	8.60	21.05	17.23
1	74.5	71.5	78.4	65.9	73.9	.75	.80	.59	1.22	.92
2	73.5	70.5	77.4	64.9	72.9	.59	.60	.47	1.00	.76
3	72.6	69.6	76.4	64.0	72.0	.47	.47	.37	.81	.62
4	71.6	68.6	75.5	63.0	71.0	.39	.39	.31	.66	.51
5	70.6	67.6	74.5	62.1	70.1	.33	.35	.26	.54	.42
6	69.7	66.6	73.5	61.1	69.1	.30	.33	.23	.45	.34
7	68.7	65.7	72.5	60.1	68.1	.26	.30	.20	.38	.29
8	67.7	64.7	71.5	59.2	67.2	.23	.27	.18	.33	.25
9	66.7	63.7	70.6	58.2	66.2	.20	.22	.16	.30	.23
10	65.7	62.7	69.6	57.2	65.2	.18	.19	.14	.30	.22
11	64.7	61.7	68.6	56.2	64.2	.18	.18	.14	.32	.23
12	63.7	60.7	67.6	55.2	63.2	.22	.25	.17	.38	.25
13	62.8	59.8	66.6	54.3	62.2	.31	.39	.21	.48	.27
14	61.8	58.8	65.6	53.3	61.2	.44	.60	.28	.61	.31
15	60.8	57.8	64.6	52.3	60.3	.59	.83	.36	.75	.36
16	59.8	56.9	63.7	51.4	59.3	.73	1.04	.43	.91	.41
17	58.9	55.9	62.7	50.4	58.3	.84	1.22	.49	1.10	.47
18	57.9	55.0	61.7	49.5	57.3	.92	1.34	.51	1.32	.54
19	57.0	54.1	60.7	48.5	56.4	.97	1.41	.51	1.55	.61
20	56.0	53.1	59.8	47.6	55.4	1.02	1.47	.50	1.81	.69
21	55.1	52.2	58.8	46.7	54.4	1.07	1.53	.50	2.06	.77
22	54.2	51.3	57.8	45.8	53.5	1.10	1.57	.50	2.27	.84
23	53.2	50.4	56.9	44.9	52.5	1.12	1.58	.51	2.42	.90
24	52.3	49.4	55.9	44.0	51.6	1.13	1.57	.52	2.53	.94
25	51.3	48.5	54.9	43.1	50.6	1.13	1.55	.53	2.62	.98
26	50.4	47.6	54.0	42.2	49.7	1.14	1.52	.54	2.74	1.04
27	49.4	46.7	53.0	41.3	48.7	1.14	1.51	.55	2.88	1.09
28	48.5	45.7	52.0	40.4	47.8	1.16	1.50	.56	3.05	1.16
29	47.6	44.8	51.0	39.6	46.8	1.18	1.51	.57	3.26	1.24
30	46.6	43.9	50.1	38.7	45.9	1.21	1.52	.59	3.49	1.33
31	45.7	42.9	49.1	37.8	45.0	1.24	1.54	.61	3.72	1.43
32	44.7	42.0	48.1	37.0	44.0	1.28	1.57	.65	3.93	1.53
33	43.8	41.1	47.2	36.1	43.1	1.33	1.61	.69	4.12	1.65
34	42.8	40.1	46.2	35.3	42.2	1.38	1.66	.74	4.30	1.77
35	41.9	39.2	45.2	34.4	41.2	1.46	1.73	.81	4.50	1.91
36	41.0	38.3	44.3	33.6	40.3	1.54	1.82	.88	4.73	2.07
37	40.0	37.3	43.3	32.7	39.4	1.64	1.92	.96	4.99	2.24
38	39.1	36.4	42.3	31.9	38.5	1.76	2.04	1.05	5.26	2.42
39	38.2	35.5	41.4	31.0	37.6	1.89	2.18	1.15	5.57	2.61
40	37.2	34.6	40.4	30.2	36.7	2.05	2.35	1.27	5.89	2.81
41	36.3	33.6	39.5	29.4	35.8	2.23	2.55	1.40	6.26	3.05
42	35.4	32.7	38.5	28.6	34.9	2.44	2.78	1.55	6.75	3.33
43	34.5	31.8	37.6	27.8	34.0	2.69	3.06	1.71	7.40	3.67
44	33.6	30.9	36.7	27.0	33.1	2.97	3.39	1.90	8.16	4.05
45	32.7	30.0	35.7	26.2	32.2	3.29	3.76	2.10	9.02	4.47
46	31.8	29.1	34.8	25.4	31.4	3.64	4.17	2.33	9.90	4.92
47	30.9	28.2	33.9	24.7	30.5	4.02	4.64	2.58	10.74	5.39
48	30.0	27.4	33.0	23.9	29.7	4.45	5.17	2.88	11.51	5.89
49	29.1	26.5	32.1	23.2	28.9	4.91	5.77	3.20	12.23	6.41
50	28.3	25.7	31.2	22.5	28.1	5.42	6.42	3.56	12.97	6.98
51	27.4	24.8	30.3	21.8	27.3	5.97	7.12	3.94	13.81	7.58
52	26.6	24.0	29.4	21.1	26.5	6.56	7.90	4.34	14.81	8.24
53	25.8	23.2	28.5	20.4	25.7	7.20	8.76	4.76	16.02	8.97
54	24.9	22.4	27.7	19.7	24.9	7.89	9.70	5.19	17.40	9.75
55	24.1	21.6	26.8	19.1	24.1	8.63	10.72	5.64	18.85	10.56
56	23.3	20.8	25.9	18.4	23.4	9.42	11.80	6.15	20.35	11.41
57	22.6	20.1	25.1	17.8	22.7	10.28	12.95	6.72	22.03	12.36
58	21.8	19.3	24.3	17.2	21.9	11.22	14.14	7.37	23.94	13.46
59	21.0	18.6	23.4	16.6	21.2	12.23	15.41	8.10	26.02	14.66
60	20.3	17.9	22.6	16.0	20.5	13.33	16.76	8.89	28.35	16.01
61	19.6	17.2	21.8	15.5	19.9	14.49	18.22	9.74	30.74	17.37
62	18.8	16.5	21.0	14.9	19.2	15.71	19.83	10.61	32.81	18.55
63	18.1	15.8	20.3	14.4	18.6	16.98	21.63	11.51	34.37	19.44
64	17.4	15.2	19.5	13.9	17.9	18.31	23.62	12.45	35.54	20.13
65	16.7	14.5	18.7	13.4	17.3	19.72	25.74	13.45	36.43	20.69
70	13.5	11.5	15.1	10.9	14.1	29.70	39.52	20.78	51.45	30.79
75	10.7	9.0	11.8	9.0	11.5	44.31	60.15	32.76	68.22	42.55
80	8.1	6.9	8.8	7.1	9.0	66.98	90.04	53.49	93.33	62.99
85 and over	6.1	5.2	6.5	6.0	7.4	1,000.00	1,000.00	1,000.00	1,000.00	1,000.00

U.S. National Center for Health Statistics, *Vital Statistics of the United States,* annual.

to learn new ones and provide for a wholesome environment for the children while they are growing up. Therefore, if the husband were earning $15,000 a year at the time of his death, the family should be carrying $67,500 worth of life insurance ($15,000 × 6 years × ¾). This $67,500 would provide $11,250 ($67,500 ÷ 6 years) each year for six years. The $67,500 can be providing additional income if the money is placed in a savings account earning, say, 6 percent interest. Using Table A 4 in Appendix A, yearly income could be increased to $13,728 ($67,500 ÷ 4.212). After you have determined the total amount of coverage, the next question is, "What is the best type of insurance to purchase to achieve this particular goal?"

All life insurance policies are basically a combination of two elements: a plan of pure insurance protection and/or a savings program. The more common types of life insurance programs will be described under the headings of term insurance, straight life or whole life, limited payment life, and endowment life insurance.

Term Insurance. Term insurance is the fastest-growing type of life insurance coverage in the United States and rightly so. It is pure protection life insurance, and one receives the most protection per dollar of premium spent. It has no savings feature or cash surrender value when the insurance term period expires. While this is probably not the only type of life insurance for a family to carry, it may be the most feasible type of life insurance to carry between the ages, say, of 20 to 55 or even 60. By the time adult members of the family reach their late fifties, their estate position of a home, savings, and investments will have grown sufficiently so that the reliance on life insurance protection will have diminished. The younger family will not have had the time or opportunity to have built an estate except through term life insurance. It seems that many life insurance representatives try to sell people types of life insurance other than term. This is mainly because the commissions earned on selling term insurance are not as large as for other life insurance policies.

Term insurance premiums become higher as you grow older for a given amount of insurance coverage. If you want the premiums to remain constant, then the amount of the *face value* of the policy must diminish as you grow older. This version of term insurance is called *decreasing term* life insurance. Term insurance gets its name from the fact that the policy must be renewed every five years. The key here is to buy *renewable* term insurance. Otherwise, the company may not want to renew your policy, particularly if you have had a sudden deterioration in health or you change to a more hazardous job. For the young and growing family, every dollar must be spent well, and term life insurance should be the major form to consider in obtaining the greatest dollar of protection for the dollar of premium.

Straight or Whole Life. The straight or whole life insurance policy, sometimes referred to as ordinary life, was the most popular form of insurance coverage before inflation began to far exceed the savings accumulation features that are part of the straight life policy. This type of policy is very profitable for the insurance company and provides good commissions to salespersons. The premiums are higher for a given amount of insurance coverage and far higher than for coverage under term insurance. The premiums remain level throughout the entire life of the policy, which terminates when the insured dies or reaches a certain age, say, 65, at which time the policy matures. Older policies often had policyholders' paying premiums until the year they died even if they lived to be 80 or 90. Since the policy has a small savings feature, it is possible to borrow money against these savings from the insurance company at a specific interest rate. At death, the growing cash value in this policy is part of the face value, *not* an additional amount over and above the face value of the policy. As long as the policyholder continues to make the premium payments, the company cannot cancel the policy regardless of how the insured's health may have deteriorated. This type of insurance had more merit when inflation rates were around 2 percent a year or less. However, in the 1970s, with inflation running at the rate of 6 percent or more (refer to Tables 1-1 and 1-2), the straight life policy has become less attractive.

Limited Payment Life. As the name suggests, this is a type of life insurance policy that requires the policyholder to make payments for a specified number of years. At the end of this period, say, 20 years, the premiums will have equaled the face amount of the policy, say, $5,000 or $10,000 or whatever the goal, although the insurance coverage remains in effect beyond that time. This type of policy as you might expect sounds more like a goal-oriented *savings* program rather than like "death insurance." The premiums each year are large and are probably too large for a young family to meet, particularly when job security is not all that well established. This type of policy even has less appeal as inflation increases or remains as it has in the past couple of years. People who are attempting to reach a specific monetary program should purchase term insurance as a hedge against premature death and invest their money in other savings media that provide a higher return than what insurance companies offer.

Endowment Insurance. An endowment policy is the most expensive in that the premiums are much larger than are those for straight life and limited payment insurance. Again, this is more of a savings program than an insurance plan. The time period may be 20 or 30 years in which to accumulate the face value of the policy of, say, $15,000. During this accumulation period, the insurance portion of the program provides insurance protection and the beneficiary named in the policy receives the $15,000 if the policyholder dies during the period. However, if at the end of the endowment period the policyholder is still alive, the policyholder receives the face amount of his or her policy. This is also the cash value of the policy. Again high levels of inflation make this type of policy unattractive.

Table 4-2 presents a hypothetical case to show the amount of the various kinds of life insurance that could be purchased by a man at age 25 per $100 of insurance premium.

TABLE 4-2 Theoretical Amounts of
Insurance Coverage per $100 Annual
Premium for an Adult Male 25
Years Old

Term	$22,000
Straight life	8,000
Limited payment (20 year)	4,500
Endowment (20 year)	2,000

While only approximations, the figures indicate that the term insurance appears to suit the needs of heads of families just starting out in life. Perhaps the major reason that savings-oriented insurance policies are still in wide use is that many people need the persuasion of an insurance policy to force them to save any money at all. This is certainly a very high price to pay for saving money. A more realistic approach to saving is building an equity in a home where the mortgage is insured in the event of death of the homeowner. While equity buildup in a home is painfully slow, inflation has worked in favor of the home-owner unlike the case of savings-oriented insurance policies for which inflation is eroding the savings by the loss of purchasing power.

Accidental Death and Dismemberment Insurance

Accidental death and dismemberment insurance (AD&D) is a form of coverage that provides benefits for certain injuries or death. The key term in this insur-ance is "accident." Accidental deaths occur less frequently than do natural deaths (perhaps as few as 1 in 12), but it is this kind of premature accident-caused death that worries many young families. Furthermore, an accident that does not result in death may leave the injured person minus an arm or leg or perhaps blind. It is here that thousands of dollars will be rapidly consumed for operations, psychological counseling, and physiotherapy. Costs of modifying a home to accommodate special recuperative equipment can be expensive. Be-cause this type of death or injury is less frequent, premiums for specific coverage are lower. For example, $100,000 of AD&D coverage for an employee might cost as little as $50 per year. The employee of a company with a group insurance program may already be covered because the employee's union may have al-ready negotiated such benefits in a contract. Employers may accept such a negotiated program because the cost is small and corporations are interested in keeping good safety records. An employee may be able to pick up additional coverage in the company plan. The employee may acquire additional increments of AD&D protection of $25,000 for around $12 per year. It is also possible for an employee to obtain very modest amounts of AD&D coverage for spouse and children.

Typical exclusions for AD&D insurance are deaths by suicide, intentionally self-inflicted injuries, deaths by self-administered poisons or chemicals; losses resulting from sickness, physical infirmity, stroke, or heart attack; and losses during the commission of a felony, violent disorder, or assaults upon others.

Long-Term Disability Insurance

Long-term disability insurance is designed to provide income protection (a portion of one's salary or wages) during one's normal working years in the event that one becomes disabled for an extended period of time. To illustrate, one evening the head of a young family is returning home from work. While driving home the person loses control of the car and plunges over an embankment; severe brain damage results. The broken bones are set and mended, all cuts and bruises heal, but the brain does not repair itself. The person lives but must be fed, washed, and looked after in the home or institution for years to come. Because the person does not die, there is no life insurance payment to help the family meet these costs. Medical and surgical insurance policies are usually worded to cover the costs of specific operations, medicines, technical assistance and equipment, and number of days' stay in a hospital. In our example, long-term disability insurance would provide a portion of the injured person's salary over these years not covered by medical and life insurance.

You may now begin to understand that the terminology in the medical health care area as well as in the field of insurance protection in general is very precise. For example, the words "one's normal working years" may mean up to the age 65. An optional plan may have to be obtained to extend beyond that age. At age 65, Social Security programs may cover one's later years. There is usually a waiting period before one receives coverage under a long-term disability insurance program. This is because employees usually have accumulated sick leave at their jobs. Limited term disability coverage of, say, 24 months may be available for disability brought about by nervous disorders or drug and alcohol addiction. Common exclusions include disabilities from war, self-inflicted injuries, common conditions arising from pregnancy, childbirth, and the postdelivery period, or time being served in jail. Today, long-term disability programs focus on rehabilitation, where possible, to retrain a person to be self-supporting. *Total disability* means the complete inability to engage in any employment or occupation for which one is qualified or to become reasonably qualified by reason of education, training, or experience. Disability is determined by a medical doctor who can decide whether or not a person can perform his or her job duties.

Remember that Social Security also has long-term disability features as do most employee retirement programs. Therefore, most long-term disability insurance programs developed by insurance companies enable employees to receive up to 60 percent of their full-time basic salaries *including* Social Security and company retirement benefits.

Medical Insurance

Having excellent medical coverage for yourself and your family is essential to accomplishing your financial goals. With the high cost of medical treatment today, this single area can bring about personal bankruptcy quicker than can a shaky business transaction or poor investments. With business transactions and investments, generally all one can lose is the money invested. However, medical expenses can add up before one is even aware of what is happening. Until the United States develops some form of comprehensive and uniform health care system (be it government or privately sponsored), your ability to meet the necessary costs of excellent medical care is either to be extremely wealthy or to spend a goodly sum of your disposable income on a preventive health and accident care program as well as on the best medical insurance you can afford.

The topic of medical care in America is a very emotional issue at present, with big money at stake. Drug manufacturers, hospital equipment manufacturers, hospital administrators, physician's unions and professional societies, medical insurance company representatives, and other lobbyist groups (labor, management, welfare agencies, etc.) are all contributing to and complicating the issue.

Because medical coverage changes rapidly, it may be necessary to review your medical insurance policy every year. Also, if you are covered by an employer's group policy, a committee of employees should continue to monitor the company program. Some corporations take pride in having the best medical programs for their employees; others try to get by with minimal programs. If you are a member of a union, be sure that the union is monitoring the company plan because your dues should be going to this kind of activity. If you work for yourself or in a small business that does not have or is too small to qualify for a group program, then you must see to it that you obtain your own quality medical insurance coverage. To keep the costs to a reasonable level, explore some of the city or county medical programs in your area.

Before going further, however, it is necessary to understand some of the key terms that relate to U.S. medical care delivery.

HMOs and PMPs   Health maintenance organizations and panel medicine plans. These medical insurance agency or group practices provide medical services; they do not make cash payments for medical services. They employ their own doctors and staffs, and they own their own hospitals and clinics. If you enroll in such a medical insurance plan you are required to use their facilities except for certain types of emergency care. Members of such programs are likely to say that they belong to a "group health," or "cooperative health," or "the Kaiser plan" when they talk to you about their medical coverage.

Blue Cross   Originally a nationwide plan designed to pay hospital expenses.

Blue Shield   Originally a plan designed to pay doctor bills. Today, Blue Cross and Blue Shield are a single nationwide coordinating agency to state programs.

FRANK & ERNEST

I'M UNDER STRICT DOCTOR'S ORDERS --- NO RICH DESSERTS, NO HEAVY DRINKING, AND A 'NO' VOTE ON NATIONAL HEALTH INSURANCE.

© 1978 by NEA, Inc., T.M. Reg. U.S. Pat. Off.   THAVES 6-30

6-30-78—© 1978 Newspaper Enterprise Association, Inc.

Commercial health insurance   A private insurance plan for the individual underwritten by many of the insurance companies that also write life insurance. These are stock or mutual companies, which also write group health insurance policies.

While you will probably subscribe to one of the HMOs, PMPs, or BLUEs, there is still a jungle of precise terms and fine print to sort out. For example, your hospital insurance policy will pay for the costs while you are in the hospital, but what about the follow-up visits that your doctor insists on at his or her office? Will your hospital insurance policy cover the office visit to take out the stitches you received during surgery? Probably not. This sort of "lack of logic" makes medical insurance coverage a jumble to the average consumer. There are no shortcuts to the effort to become aware of the kind of coverage you really need. To help you select a medical plan, the following guidelines may be useful. These are suggestions of Allen Johnson, Manager of Membership Services of the Washington Education Association.*

1. *Financial status of the company.* Does the company have sufficient assets to provide adequately for the benefits promised both now and in the future?

2. *Coverage limitation.* If there are major medical benefit limitations, they should not be less than $100,000 and preferably more. Medical expenses for a serious injury or extended medical treatment could easily exceed $100,000 in a short time.

3. *Hospital room extended benefits.* The most costly expense in medical care is hospitalization. A good medical plan will not limit the number of days of coverage since extended hospitalization could bankrupt most families.

4. *Routine medical expenses.* Although office calls and prescription drug expenses will not bankrupt most families, these represent the majority of medical

* Reprinted by permission.

expenses for the average family. First-dollar coverage is helpful, but a deductible will keep the cost of a medical plan down. A good comprehensive medical plan will provide for routine medical care with some limitations necessary to keep the cost of the plan low.

5. *Exclusions.* Exclusions cause the greatest grief when it comes to filing a claim. Exclusions to be avoided like the plague include preexisting condition, congenital birth defects, waiting periods, limitation on pregnancy coverage, athletic injuries, mental and nervous disorders, medical appliances, and the like. Every medical plan will have some exclusions and limitations, but the exclusions should be thoroughly understood before enrollment.

6. *When you leave the company.* Most medical plans are adequate while you are actively employed; however, when you are on a medical leave, when you retire, or when your employment is terminated involuntarily, your plan should provide for continued group coverage, not just individual conversion. Be particularly alert to coverage upon retirement prior to age 65. The plan should provide for this period of time when medical expenses are at their highest and when a catastrophic medical expense can least be afforded.

7. *Claim filing and appeals.* The amount of work that it takes to file a claim should be a factor in your decision. A health maintenance organization plan normally does not require claims forms. Service corporations (Blue Cross/Blue Shield) may have arrangements for health care providers to file claims directly with the service bureau. It may be helpful to talk with other plan participants to see if claim filing is a problem. You should also know who makes the final decision on a claim; the right of claim review can be crucial if there is a dispute.

8. *Geographical area covered by the plan.* Many medical plans limit themselves to a specific geographical area. Make certain that your plan will provide coverage when you travel or if you move. You also should know which hospitals may be used, which physicians and other health care providers may be utilized, and whether or not you have access to specialized medical care for unusual health conditions.

9. *Group covered by the plan.* Group insurance contracts are often based on the claim experience of the group covered. Teachers normally have a better medical claim experience than do most other groups. Larger groups (at least 1,000 or more) tend to have more stable claim experience, minimizing the risk of excessive premium rate increases.

10. *Discrimination on the basis of age or sex.* A plan may discriminate in a number of ways. For example, it may charge a different premium rate for men and for women or for those over and under age 40. It may limit benefits for certain health conditions such as pregnancy. Such practices are discriminatory in employer-provided group policies and should not be supported.

Because there is much to remember in the field of medical insurance, you might do well to have a checklist of important questions to ask an insurance representative, the people in the personnel office of your company, or your union officers. See the set of questions in Exhibit 4-1 for a guide.

Medical Insurance Exclusions

All medical insurance coverage programs have a section entitled exclusions in addition to the tightly worded sections that explain your coverages and limitations. The following list summarizes just some of the common types of exclusions. It is by no means complete.

Conditions covered by workers compensation of state and federal laws or private occupational insurance

Custodial or convalescent care

Impotency or frigidity

Routine well-baby care and circumcision

Admission or treatment primarily for rehabilitative care (including but not limited to speech and occupational therapy) except as provided by benefits

Exogenous obesity

Hospitalization primarily for diagnostic studies when hospital care would have otherwise been required

Care not medically necessary for treatment of illness or injury

Eye exams

Eyeglasses (including contact lenses)

Treatment for dyslexia, visual analysis therapy, training related to muscular imbalance of the eye and orthoptics

Hearing aids

Fitting of glasses or hearing aids

A charge in excess of usual, customary, and reasonable charges or the most prevalent semiprivate room rate

Dental care, unless part of certain surgery

Tuberculosis

Conditions resulting from major disaster, epidemic, or military action or drugs prescribed for these exclusions

Services or supplies related to sex transformations or sexual misfunctions or inadequacies

Cosmetic services

Physical examinations required for employment or licensing

Acupuncture

Reversal or voluntary infertility

EXHIBIT 4-1   Checklist of Medical Insurance Coverage

1.   Name of company or plan

2.   Are dependents covered?

3.   Any coverage limitations in terms of dollars?

4.   Any coverage limitations in terms of days of treatment?

5.   Any lifetime limitations in dollars on major medical costs?

6.   Are follow-up office calls after hospitalization covered?

7.   Are all prescription drug expenses covered? Refills?

8.   Are there any deductibles and how much?

9.   Does the deductible apply to each claim filed during a period?

10.   Are the following excluded in the policy?

Preexisting condition
Congenital birth defects
Waiting periods
Limitations on pregnancy coverage
Athletic injuries
Mental and nervous disorders
Medical appliances

11.   What are my coverage options if I leave my job or am terminated?

12.   Does my coverage change when I reach age 64 or 65 or at retirement?

13.   Upon termination from my job, can I receive group rates?

14.   How much of the paperwork do I do to file a claim?

15.   What appeal process do I have if there is a dispute?

16.   Name of the person answering your questions:

Corrective appliances and artificial aids

Organ transplants, limited to kidney transplants only

Auto accidents covered by no-fault insurance to the extent that benefits are provided by another insurer

Injuries resulting from organized sports or races

Attempted suicide and willful misconduct

Hemodialysis or other procedure for treatment of kidney failure

Cardiac bypass surgery

Conditions resulting from military service

Delay or failure to provide services in case of major disaster or epidemic, war, riot, civil insurrection, labor disputes, or similar causes

A final note. Medical insurance packages often come in two parts: "basic" and "major medical." The basic plan is designed to cover common medical expenses. Major medical refers to the method of payment of claims, not to the size of your individual medical bills. The major medical portion of your plan begins with a deductible that you pay from your own pocket.

Herman   **by Jim Unger**

"Breathe deeply and take a quick look at my bill."

Over the amount of the deductible, the major medical plan picks up all or a certain portion, say, 80 percent of all the bills in excess of the deduction.

Workers Compensation Insurance

Since the early part of this century, various state governments have enacted workers compensation laws. These state laws place the responsibility for industrial accidents on the employers. The state also holds the employer responsible for the accident even though the employee was negligent. The employer is not responsible if an employee willfully causes a self-inflicted injury while at work. Most of these insurance programs are administered by the state, with the employers' paying premiums to the state based on the various categories of skills, their relative hazards, the number of employees, and the number of hours worked in a given period of time.

These programs provide coverage for an employee and his or her family for injuries on the job for such costs as medical expenses, disability, rehabilitation, and death and survivor benefits. Today, many of these programs include coverage for diseases that sometimes result from working around certain chemicals, dust, and fumes. Since there are 50 state plans in existence, it is difficult to generalize about the coverages and benefits. You should determine whether or

Pepper . . . and Salt

THE WALL STREET JOURNAL

"You should last forever, Mr. Clemmons. The test results show you're full of preservatives."

From *The Wall Street Journal*—
Permission, Cartoon Features Syndicate.

not you are covered at your job. Your supervisor, personnel office, or union should be able to answer that question for you.

Unemployment Insurance

The Social Security Act of 1935 was designed to establish a financial base to help protect against three social economic problems: poverty, old age, and unemployment. The Federal Unemployment Tax Act (FUTA) later created the unemployment insurance program, a program in which premiums are levied against employers *only*. The employers' premiums go to fund both the federal and state unemployment programs. Unemployment insurance programs and those on unemployment often come under criticism. The interdependence that exists in a modern economy can cause even well-run businesses to lay off good employees in a recession. The following comments or observations are common in an area of high unemployment.

1. Before they find themselves on unemployment, people tend to believe that those already on unemployment are generally lazy and unmotivated.
2. Business firms are unable to do very much to solve serious unemployment problems. A business itself will survive only if cash receipts continue to exceed its cash payments during a recession.
3. Family savings are generally exhausted within six months of unemployment.
4. If people have a choice of remaining on unemployment and drawing unemployment insurance or certain welfare supplements or drawing a paycheck, most will prefer to draw a paycheck.
5. Individuals need to be better informed about the workings of the economic system in which they function.

Automobile Insurance

For those owning an automobile, it is necessary to carry appropriate and adequate automobile insurance coverage. Typical of today's automotive insurance needs are coverages for bodily injury and property damage *to others*, protection against the uninsured motorist, medical coverage *on yourself* and *your passengers*, collision and upset damage to your *own car*, comprehensive coverage *on your car*, towing coverage, and stereo and CB theft coverage. Let us take a look at the following types of coverages.

Bodily Injury and Property Damage Liability. The purpose of this coverage is to protect yourself from lawsuits brought about by the persons or their families who have been injured or killed by you while driving your car. Without this coverage, you run the risk of losing most or all of your assets to pay the legal claims. Property damage liability protection coverage is to pay for *other* people's property that you have damaged. For example, if you run into someone's automobile and damage a bumper, fender, or door or if you destroy a neighbor's hedge, your coverage will have to pay for the damage to be repaired.

The coverage limits of this portion of automobile insurance are usually expressed as 100/300/20. The 100 means $100,000 maximum limit in the form of bodily injury liability to any one person injured or killed by your automobile while you or other authorized persons were driving. The 300 stands for the total of $300,000 maximum that will be paid under the policy for all persons injured or killed in any one accident. The 20 represents $20,000, the maximum the policy will pay for property of others damaged by your car.

It is important not to be caught with skimpy liability coverage in these days. A modest increase in the premium costs could give you a sizable increase in liability coverage. Furthermore, the insurance company that represents you will probably work harder for you.

Uninsured Motorists. Basically this coverage is designed to insure you and your passengers against bodily injury expenses in the event that your car is struck by someone who does not carry any automobile insurance. Damages caused by a hit-and-run driver would be handled under this coverage assuming that a proper filing has been made to law enforcement authorities within a specified time and that the person is never apprehended. This coverage also protects you in the event that the other party's insurance company becomes insolvent within a specified time period after the accident. You are protected even if you are using another person's car or when you are walking. Most people will probably go ahead and have this insurance coverage added to their basic policy since the premium is small. People also carry this insurance because they do not always know whether or not a particular passenger has medical insurance coverage.

Medical Payments Insurance Coverage. This coverage pays for reasonable medical expenses incurred within a period of one year from the time of an accident. The coverage applies to *you*, your family, and your passengers while in your car; usually it also includes persons with permission to use your car, and it covers you while you are in someone else's car or while you are walking. Payments are made regardless of who is at fault. With some insurance carriers this coverage must be purchased as a part of the bodily injury and property damage coverage. You are covered for necessary medical, surgical, dental, ambulance, hospital care, professional nursing, drug, prosthetic device, and other charges.

There are limitations and exclusions also. Exclusions relate to using your car for commercial purposes, as a residence, or as an off-road tractor. It may be that other insurance coverage by the insured may cover the same situations. If so, the coverage in the auto policy will not be liable or will share proportionately with other coverage.

Collision and Upset Coverage. This is no-fault coverage that applies to damage sustained by your car upon hitting an object (another car, building, barrier, etc.) whether movable or fixed. This coverage is usually written with deductibles of $50, $100, $200, and $500, to keep the premium reasonable. You may decide to discontinue the coverage when the car is considered to have reached its residual value. To judge this point of discontinuance, review your past driving record, where the car is parked, how much you drive, current value of the car, status of your emergency cash reserve fund, your income, and so on. The cost might be placed in a car replacement savings fund at the bank.

Comprehensive Physical Damage. This coverage pays for any damage to your automobile except collision and upset. Protection includes payments for damage sustained resulting from storms, hail, glass breakage, theft, fire, explosion, vandalism, riot or civil unrest, animals, and so on. This policy is also sold with $25, $50, $75, or $100 deductibles. Collision and comprehensive are issued as a package to provide the car owner with 100 percent coverage.

Towing and Labor Costs. This coverage pays for the towing and labor cost of a brand-new car or a very used car that becomes disabled. The labor costs are paid for only when it is performed at the place of disablement.

MR. TWEEDY

© 1978, Los Angeles Times
Syndicate. Reprinted by
permission.

Theft. This particular coverage is in a state of transition. It appears necessary to ask the insurance agent what is covered and if there are specific dollar limits. Your $8,000 automobile may be covered, but your CB or tape recorder valued at $200 may not be. Luggage and clothing stolen from your car may be covered but only up to $300.

Fire, Lightning, and Transportation. These three categories are set out separately from the comprehensive portion of a policy. While coverage against lightning destroying your car is clear, fire and transportation losses need a word of explanation. Fire coverages include smoke and smudge damage to your car brought about by a faulty heating plant in a building where the car is garaged. Transportation refers to times when your car is being transported by truck, rail, and barge. Your insurance will cover losses sustained to your car if stranded, derailed, sunk, and so on while in transit.

In summary, when purchasing a new or used automobile, consider adequate insurance protection as an integral part of the process. Do your comparative shopping for insurance coverage *prior* to buying your car. Be adequately covered before you drive off of the car dealer's lot. A phone call to your insurance agent's office should be sufficient to obtain a "binder." Shortly after your purchase, your agent will want particulars about the car to establish the final premium cost.

If you presently own a car and are covered by insurance, the policy will usually grant automatic second car coverage for a limited number of days until you can send in details on the new purchase.

Automobile insurance premiums in the United States amount to $45 billion a year. A family or household should be very realistic and budget appropriately for this coverage. If you drive, bodily injury and property liability protection is essential. Many state laws require insurance to be secured before the automobile can be driven. Persons who do not carry insurance are required by state laws to show financial responsibility for loss if they were at fault. Exhibit 4-2 is a sample annual automobile policy premium notice.

No-Fault Automobile Insurance

The concept of no-fault automobile insurance emerged in the 1960s as an attempt to keep insurance premiums at a reasonable level. Lawsuits, attorneys' fees, and delays in settlement urged that a new approach be developed. There are currently 25 states having some form of the no-fault plan. No-fault plans are mainly applied to the bodily injuries, whereas property damages are insured under standard liability and collision coverages. There have been several attempts to have the U.S. Congress pass a no-fault automobile insurance program, but this has not been successful. Rising costs of medical services and inflation in the economy in recent years cloud the issue as to whether or not no-fault automobile insurance has lowered costs.

EXHIBIT 4-2 Sample Annual Automobile Policy Premium Notice

ALL–FARM INSURANCE COMPANY								FAP 3246548

825 Northlake Avenue
Meeker City, Washington

ANNUAL PREMIUM NOTICE

Coverages	B. I –PD (000s)	U. M. (000s)	Medical	Collision	Comprehensive	Tow	Stereo	TOTAL
Limits:	100/300/20	15/30	10,000	$100 Ded.	$25 Ded.			
1985 Ford	135.40	6.30	25.70	75.00	19.80	2.50		$264.70

POLICY NUMBER	POLICY PERIOD		
CA746251 23 1	From 04-17-X8 To 04-17-X9		

TOTAL PREMIUM DUE . . . . . | $264.70

KEEP THIS COPY FOR YOUR RECORDS

— — — — — — — — — — — — — — - detach here — — — — — — — — — — — — — —

PLEASE MAIL THIS PORTION WITH YOUR CHECK

CA746251 23 1
Charles M. Fender
1200 East Vantage Street
Bend, Washington 98204

Indicate choice
of payment plan

Quarterly	$ 68.75
Half–yearly	$134.18
Annually	$264.70

$ _____

Other Personal Property Insurance

It is difficult to go through life without accumulating things. Americans seem to accumulate more than just about anyone else in the world. In this section we concentrate on those possessions that are portable or movable other than an automobile. In essence, we need to consider insurance coverage on our furniture, clothing, kitchen and other household appliances, cameras, stereo set, record collections, TV, recreational equipment, books, typewriters, calculators, tools, linens, bedding, artwork, collectibles, hobbies, pets, and plants.

We need to know just what is normally covered in such policies, what limitations are involved, what items are normally excluded from basic coverages, and so on.

Unscheduled Personal Property. This type of coverage is what most people have in mind when they want insurance protection for the many things that they accumulate. From knowing your age, type of job, number of members in a family, type and size of dwelling, and so on, the insurance company may establish an approximate insured value of personal property owned. The policyholder will automatically be covered even if some personal property possessions are not at home—daughter's clothing, books, TV, and typewriter at a school dormitory, for example. However, policies may set limits such as 10 percent or $1,000 of policy value, whichever is greater. Note the example of requirement found in a typical property insurance policy:

> 90 Requirements in   *The insured shall give im-*
> 91 case of loss   *mediate written notice to*
> 92   *this Company of any loss,*
> 93 *protect the property from further damage, forthwith*
> 94 *separate the damaged and undamaged personal prop-*
> 95 *erty, put it in the best possible order, furnish a com-*
> 96 *plete inventory of destroyed, damaged and undam-*
> 97 *aged property showing in detailed quantities, costs,*
>   *actual cash value and amount of loss claimed . . .*

The importance of taking an inventory of personal property as well as knowing how to calculate a loss was discussed in Chapter 2. Exhibit 4-3 offers a very simple and useful worksheet for preparing a loss claim for the insurance company. Preparing such a worksheet will indicate that you have done your homework, and you will be in a better negotiating position in claim settlements.

Limitations and Exclusions. Unscheduled personal property coverage places limitations on or excludes totally certain personal property items. Excluded from coverages are animals, birds, fish, airplanes, automobiles, property of roomers and boarders, sample items held for sale, items normally rented out by the owner, and business property items. Other exclusions on personal property are wear and tear, rust, fading, evaporation, mold, cracking, and so on.

Limitations of coverage of certain personal property items are common. There may be a $100 limit on all cash, coins, bank notes, bullion, coin collection, and so on. There may be a $500 limitation on stamp collections, airplane tickets, and business documents such as notes and deeds. Jewelry and gems lost from theft as well as furs may also be limited in the aggregate to $500. Recreational equipment, boats, trailers, and outboard motors are limited to $500.

Apartment dwellers will usually purchase coverage known in the insurance field as Homeowner Contents Broad Form or Tenant Form HO-4.

Homeowner Property Insurance

Individuals and families purchasing a home or condominium will need insurance coverage for the actual dwelling and its appurtenant structures as well as personal property. The purpose of this insurance is to cover the insured against specific perils, for example, fire, windstorm, explosion, smoke damage, and vandalism.

EXHIBIT 4-3 Worksheet for Calculating Insured Loss Claims

Quantity	Description	Original Cost	Est. Life (in years)	Number of Years Used	Unused Years Lost	$\dfrac{\text{Unused years}}{\text{Est. total life}}$ $\times$	Today's est. replacement cost	Amount of Loss Claimed

Modern homeowner policy forms are written to provide coverage tailored to the insured's needs:

Basic: Homeowner 1 (HO-1) Covers 11 Perils

1. Fire or lightning
2. Property removed from premises endangered by fire or other perils
3. Windstorm or hail
4. Explosion
5. Riot or civil commotion
6. Aircraft
7. Vehicles
8. Smoke
9. Vandalism and malicious mischief
10. Theft (be aware of many exclusions)
11. Glass breakage (except in HO-3 and HO-4)

Broad: Homeowner 2 (HO-2) Covers Perils 1–11 plus

12. Falling objects
13. Weight of ice, snow, sleet
14. Collapse of building(s) or any part thereof
15. Sudden and accidental tearing asunder, cracking, burning, or bulging of heating and hot-water heating systems
16. Accidental discharge, leakage, or overflow of water or steam
17. Freezing of plumbing, heating, and air-conditioning systems and domestic appliances
18. Sudden and accidental injury from artificially generated currents to electrical appliances, fixtures, and wiring except tubes and similar electronic equipment.

Comprehensive: Homeowner 5 (HO-5) Covers

All perils except those such as war, nuclear radiation, earthquake, volcano eruption, and flood and a complete list of excluded perils in your policy.

Exclusions and Limitations. Basic exclusions in homeowner policies include loss due to enforcement of laws regulating construction, repair, or demolition of a building; any earth movement such as earthquake, volcanic eruption, landslide, mudflow, and earth sinking, rising, and shifting. Land, or the surface portion of the earth, is usually excluded from insurance coverage. The homeowner policy also excludes losses caused by flood, surface water waves, tidal waves, overflow of streams, water backed up through sewers or drains, or water seeping through leaks in sidewalks, driveways, foundations, walls, basements, floors, windows, or doors. Also excluded are losses caused by settling, cracking, bulging, shrinking, or expanding of walls, floors, ceilings, roofs, foundations, sidewalks, driveways, and patios as are losses due to rust, mildew, mold, and dry rot.

The limitations in homeowner policies include $500 maximum loss to trees and shrubs, $500 limit due to credit card theft, $1,000 limit on stolen firearms, $500 limit on loss of manuscripts, no coverage for theft in rented portion of home, and $250 maximum paid for fire department service charge.

To be assured of adequate home insurance coverage, the face value of the policy must be at least 80 percent of the *replacement cost of the house.*

Additional Living Expenses. The tenant and homeowner policy will provide reasonable living expenses because the insured's premises have been rendered untenantable by peril. Efforts must be made to repair the damages as soon as possible. There may be an upper dollar limit on this coverage.

Personal Liability. This coverage protects you against a lawsuit stemming from a visitor's injuries or damages to a neighbor's property. Backyard swimming pools, barbecue grills, lawnchairs, and uneven steps represent potential lawsuits.

Medical Payments. This coverage will pay for medical expenses resulting from a friend's or visitor's accident occurring on your property or injury caused by you, a member of your family, or a pet. This coverage makes payment regardless of who was at fault.

80% Coinsurance Clause. This is a major clause in homeowner insurance. It discourages underinsuring one's home at today's replacement costs. To assure that an insurance company will pay 100 cents on every dollar of loss up to the *policy's face value,* insurance coverage must be maintained at 80% of the structure's replacement cost.

Exhibit 4-4 shows a portion of a typical homeowner policy premium and basic coverage.

Miscellaneous Insurance Coverage

Because of the upper limitations on coverage in homeowner policies, special coverage must be sought to obtain protection against loss of high-value items. Collections of paintings, rare coins, antiques, and stamps, for example, require special separate insurance policies, and the premiums are expensive. Flood and earthquake insurance are separate and very expensive coverages.

EXHIBIT 4-4   Portion of Homeowner Insurance Premium

SECTION	REQUIRED COVERAGE	LIABILITY LIMITS	PREMIUM
I	A–Dwelling	$ 67,000	$285.00
	B–Appurtenant Structures		
	C–Unscheduled Personal Property	7,000	
	D–Additional Living Expense	1,400	
II	E–Personal Liability (each occurence)	50,000	
	F–Medical Payments (each person) (each accident)	1,000 25,000	
Form 567	Other Coverage Provisions Extended theft		Incl.
	TOTAL ANNUAL PREMIUM		$285.00

ITEMS OR EVENTS USUALLY NOT COVERED BY INSURANCE

Insurance comes into existence when there is a predictable loss, the loss can be measured, there is an economic loss but no economic gain, and the risk can be spread among several people or insurance companies or both. We have learned that pets and land are usually not covered by insurance. Insurance cannot be purchased to cover gambling losses or losses in the stock market. There is no insurance coverage for losses sustained by one while committing a crime. Failure to win elective office or failing an examination are not insurable. You must have an *insurable interest* in some item to obtain insurance coverage. You cannot insure your neighbor's automobile.

SUMMARY

The insurance industry is rapidly changing, and so are the types of coverage being offered. Life insurance is often sold on emotional appeal. Term life insurance with renewal privilege provides the most dollars of protection per dollar of premium. The purpose of any insurance is to restore a money or financial loss.

There are three steps in developing insurance coverage: risk reduction, risk assumption, and risk transference. Obtain insurance under group coverage whenever possible, as the premiums are smaller than are those of private plans. Automobile insurance companies use many subjective criteria in determining coverage and premiums. The insurance agent can bind the insuring company on a policy covering property and auto insurance. The insurance representative has no authority to bind the company in life insurance.

The two major types of insurance companies are mutual and stock. The true test of your insurance coverage is the ability to collect upon a legitimate claim. Medical insurance is the foundation of individual insurance programs. Bodily injury and property damage liability is the essential coverage in automobile insurance. Land is normally not covered by insurance. The insured must prepare a detailed inventory of goods damaged or destroyed.

It is important to understand what the exclusions and limitations are in your property or homeowner insurance. A program of insurance coverage should be at the base of a financial planning pyramid as shown in Exhibit 4-5. Note that the

EXHIBIT 4-5 Basic Financial Pyramid

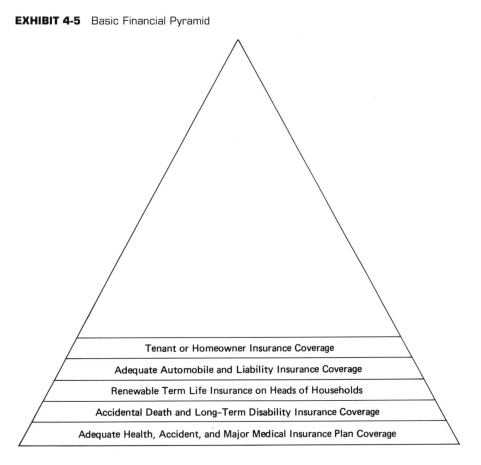

Tenant or Homeowner Insurance Coverage

Adequate Automobile and Liability Insurance Coverage

Renewable Term Life Insurance on Heads of Households

Accidental Death and Long–Term Disability Insurance Coverage

Adequate Health, Accident, and Major Medical Insurance Plan Coverage base of the pyramid begins with having adequate health, accident, and major medical insurance coverage. The other insurance needs emphasize essential basic coverages which provide the maximum protection per dollar of premium for most households.

TIPS

1. Your refrigerator may serve as vault for important documents in case of a fire.
2. Do not keep valuables concentrated in one or two rooms.
3. Reduce where possible the potential hazards around the home that could cause injury or sickness.
4. Install smoke detectors in your home or apartment if the building is not equipped with warning devices; install burglar alarms.
5. Keep insurance premiums down by buying higher deductibles; pay premiums annually; have all cars insured by the same insurance carrier.
6. Comparison shop among insurance companies.
7. If you need life insurance or additional life insurance, consider only term insurance and accidental death coverage; avoid insurance policies that are primarily savings programs.
8. Take photographs in color of personal property items.
9. Keep your coverage current.
10. Recognize the fire and health hazards of installing wood stoves, storing extra gasoline at the home, and siphoning gasoline.

ADDITIONAL READINGS

"Auto Insurance, How It Works," *Consumer Reports*, September 1984, pp. 501–13.
"Health Insurance When You're Not in a Group," *Changing Times*, March 1983, pp. 21–23.
"Keep Income Coming If You Can't Work," *Changing Times*, March 1986, pp. 53–55.
Kiester, Ed, Jr., "Health Insurance: 7 Common Gaps That Could Spell Disaster," *Better Homes and Gardens*, May 1986, pp. 107–10.
"Life Insurance: How to Protect Your Family," *Consumer Reports*, June 1986, pp. 371–402.
"What's What in Life Insurance Policies." *Better Homes and Gardens*, January 1984, p. 58.

GLOSSARY OF USEFUL TERMS

Appraisal   Survey of property that determines its value.

Assigned Risk   State-organized program whereby drivers who are unable to buy automobile insurance in the regular market are assigned to insurance companies that must sell them liability insurance. Premiums are usually higher than are those on insurance purchased through the regular market.

Assumed Liability   Liability that you assume under the terms of a contract.

Beneficiary   Person named in an insurance policy to receive the benefits in the event the insured dies.

Binder   Legal agreement issued by an agent or a company to provide temporary insurance until a policy can be written.

Bodily Injury Liability Insurance   Coverage for bodily harm, sickness, or disease, including required care, loss of services, and death resulting therefrom.

Cash Surrender Value   Value of a permanent life insurance policy if the insured terminates the policy or surrenders it to the insurance company (same as cash value).

Chartered Life Underwriter (CLU)   A designation granted by the American College of Life Underwriters, which signifies that an individual has successfully completed a series of exams in insurance, economics, life and health insurance, estate planning, and so on.

Coinsurance or Participation Clause   A provision of most major medical insurance policies stipulating that the company will pay some portion, say, 80 to 90 percent, of the amount of the covered loss in excess of the deductible.

Collision Insurance   Coverage of collision damage to the insured's car, regardless of who is at fault.

Convertible Term Insurance   Term coverage that can be exchanged for a cash value policy without evidence of insurability.

Credit Life Insurance   Insurance issued by a lender to cover payment of a loan or installment purchase if the borrower dies.

Damages   Cost of compensating those who suffer bodily injury or property damage from an accident.

Disability Insurance   Health insurance that provides income replacement if you are sick or hurt and cannot work.

Double Indemnity   A provision in some policies allowing a payment of twice the designated proceeds on a life insurance policy in case of the accidental death of the insured.

Endowment Insurance   A form of life insurance whereby premiums are paid for a specific period of time and the insured is covered during that time. If he or she is living at the end of the premium period, the face value can be collected.

Exclusions   Provisions that state what is not covered by the insurance policy.

Family Automobile Policy (FAP)   Policy that provides a package of property and liability insurances to insure against perils associated with owning an automobile.

Floater Policy   Policy that covers movable property (jewels, furs, musical instruments, etc.).

Grace Period   Period of time after the due date of premium payment during which the policy remains in force and the premium may still be paid without penalty.

Group Insurance   Insurance issued through employers, employees, or members of unions or associations covering a group of persons.

Hazard   Condition that may create or increase the probability of a loss.

Health Maintenance Organization (HMO)   An organization consisting of a group of hospitals, physicians, and other health care personnel who have joined together to provide necessary health maintenance and medical services to its members.

Hospitalization Insurance   Coverage for hospital, nursing, surgical, and miscellaneous medical expenses due to bodily injury or illness.

Inflation Endorsement   An endorsement that provides for the automatic adjustment of a building's insurance coverage to keep pace with inflation.

Liability Insurance   Any form of coverage that provides protection in case of a lawsuit brought against you.

Limited Payment Life Insurance   Whole life insurance in which the premiums are paid only for certain number of years.

Medicaid   A public assistance program under Social Security that is designed to provide medical benefits for persons who are unable to pay their health care costs.

Medicare   A health care plan administered by the federal government designed to help persons over age 65 and others who receive monthly Social Security disability benefits.

Mortality Tables   Tables that indicate expected deaths per number of population at different ages.

Mutual Company   A company that is owned by its policyholders.

No-Fault   An automobile insurance plan in which the injured party in an accident receives compensation for injuries directly from his or her insurance company regardless of who is at fault.

Peril   The cause of loss insured against (fire, windstorm, explosion, etc.).

Personal Property Insurance   Policy that covers all property, other than real property, owned by the named insured.

Policy   The printed document stating the terms of the insurance contract that is issued to the policyholder by the company.

Preexisting Condition   An illness or condition that started prior to the time an insurance policy was issued.

Premium   The payment, or one of the periodic payments, that a policyholder agrees to make for an insurance policy.

Renewable Term Insurance   Term insurance that can be renewed without evidence of insurability for a certain number of successive terms or until the insured reaches a certain age.

Riders   Special provisions not contained in the basic policy contract; also known as clauses or endorsements.

Risk   The chance of a loss now or in the future.

Straight Life Insurance   Whole life insurance on which premiums are payable for life.

Suicide Clause   Provision in some life insurance policies canceling the proceed payment if the insured commits suicide within a certain period after the policy is issued.

Term Insurance   A form of life insurance in which a person is insured for the life of the policy in exchange for premiums. If the policyholder does not die in that period, the policy ends.

Title Insurance   Special insurance that protects against loss of one's equity investment in real property if a flaw in the property's title is found.

Uninsured Motorist Insurance   Insurance that pays damages to a driver and passengers for bodily injury that occurs from an automobile accident where the liable party does not have auto insurance.

Waiver   Surrender of a right or privilege that is known to exist.

Whole Life   Insurance that covers a person for his or her entire life and pays the beneficiary no matter when the insured dies. Same as ordinary or straight life.

Workers Compensation   A form of insurance under which an employee may receive compensation for injuries sustained in the course of his or her employment.

5

Saving, Banking, and Bonds

LEARNING OBJECTIVES

Upon completion of Chapter 5, you should be able to identify and remember

- The two basic approaches to saving money and three examples of each approach.
- Ten techniques on how to save cash.
- The "Rule of 72" and how compound interest helps you to reach financial goals earlier.
- The basic services offered by a commercial bank.
- The essential elements and documents related to a personal checking account.
- Several types of bond investments providing a fixed income return.
- How to read and understand the bond market portion of the financial pages of a newspaper.
- The two well-known bond rating services.
- The meaning of the terms "yield on investment" and "yield to maturity on investment."

FRANK & ERNEST

1-28-78—© 1978 Newspaper Enterprise Association, Inc.

OVERVIEW

The preceding chapters have provided a basic framework in which to develop our comprehensive lifelong goal of successful financial management by (1) planning and goal setting, (2) organizing our records and reviewing the various property items we own (just plain taking stock of ourselves), (3) developing a budget of our estimated income and our living costs or expenses over the coming year as well as making the important determination of how much money can be realistically set aside over that period of time, and (4) taking the necessary steps to reduce potential losses by being adequately covered for those events over which we may have little control as well as those that result from carelessness.

In this chapter we look into such things as why save money, what it takes to become a millionaire, and the differences between savers and nonsavers; we then consider some techniques for saving money for different purposes. Then, we learn how to use such institutions as banks, savings and loan associations, and credit unions to protect our money, to help our money grow while it remains safeguarded, and to let these organizations provide the bulk of the bookkeeping for us. Finally, we look at alternative opportunities for investing money for long periods of time to help us reach certain specific long-term financial goals.

SAVING

The Act of Saving

Saving money is tied directly to satisfying *wants*. When one want is satisfied, another immediately takes its place. Societies learned very early that certain controls had to be exercised over these unlimited wants, beginning with Moses' tablets of "Thou shall not . . ." to modern-day superior courts' rendering "It is the law that . . .". In modern societies we have come to use money as a medium of exchange to help us satisfy our wants. The *act of saving* is a necessary ingredient to accomplish the goal of satisfying a want. The act of saving *may* take place before, during, or even after the satisfaction of a want.

Most people save money to purchase some item they have wanted or some service they need or to "buy" some peace of mind. The act of saving is taking place regardless of whether one purchases some item for cash or uses a department store credit card or an installment purchase agreement.

The person who pays cash can generally be assumed to have saved the money in some fashion. However, what about the person who acquires the item on credit? Whereas the credit buyer must also save money to make the necessary payments over the life of the credit period, this act of saving is often overlooked or lost because one's attention is often directed to other factors that may surround a credit transaction or other issues depending upon one's background in financial activities.

One person may focus his or her attention on the amount of self-discipline required to save the money for a proposed purchase. Another person may think of the convenience of having the use of an item now instead of later. Still another may point out that the credit customer sometimes has greater leverage when having an item repaired if something goes wrong with it. And another person may say that the cash buyer will pay only about 75 percent of the amount spent by the credit buyer because of the very high rates of interest associated with certain credit or financing arrangements.

Many of these issues are important and will be explored in more detail elsewhere in the text. The key point here is that the *act of saving* is taking place by payments made in cash or on credit. Since the act of saving is taking place, it is important for the consumer money manager to *take control over this function* and direct it toward accomplishing one's stated financial goals; it should not be a consequence of impulse.

Why Save Money?

Why is it necessary to save our money or at least a certain portion of it? Unless you save a portion of your money, you are forced to *earn* every penny you make throughout your entire life (excluding the *compulsory saving* of money as in Social Security when both the employee and the employer make equal cash payments to the system). Indirect saving techniques include participation in a company pension plan, the purchase of a life insurance policy, the purchase of a home. By using a combination of methods, most people can stop working eventually and enjoy some years in a form of retirement. If none of these programs existed, providing for individual security in old age would be an overriding and pervasive concern.

One could be misled into thinking that public and privately sponsored aid programs make it less necessary to provide for our own welfare during old age. While the United States has a record of helping others who are in need, most of the programs offered (including the Social Security program) at best provide only for basic needs. Most of the current government programs were developed on the grounds that the U.S. labor force would continue to expand, that the population of the nation would continue to expand, and that inflation would remain at modest levels of 1 or 2 percent. Many of the innovations of the Social Security program have been offset by dramatic changes in the composition of the work force, number of people working, number of people retiring, longer life spans of people, higher levels of permanent unemployment, lower national productivity rates, and higher than anticipated and seemingly built-in inflation rates.

It will be your own efforts at saving that will provide the bulk of your funds to cover the postworking year costs of comfortable living surroundings, travel, hobbies, entertainment, and so on.

Another incentive for saving may come from the fact that perhaps you have decided to adopt many of the concepts of budgeting discussed in Chapter 3. If members of a household decide that something does have a high priority and is very much desired, it is much easier to explain the reason why the family is not going to be spending money on certain other things. Budgeting and saving go hand in hand, and one helps to accomplish the other.

Of course, the most popular reason for saving money is to spend it on those things that make life pleasant. Other chapters will help you to get the best value for your money.

The Key to Saving: Establishing the Habit

One of the most important goals of this textbook, and perhaps the most important goal directed to the person just starting out, is that of establishing the habit of *regularly* saving some portion of one's income regardless of the source and to begin that habit *today*. Many people reading this text will say that it is absolutely impossible to save any money now because "All I have to live on is my school allowance from home," or "I only have a part-time job and money from alimony and child support," or "I have to pay off those charge account debts because the department store is charging 18 percent interest on what I still owe."

Do any of these rationales sound familiar? However, somewhere there is a place in each person's financial program where something can be saved. For example, if you were asked if you could save $5.00 out of this month's income, could you? Could you save another $5.00 in the next month and $5.00 the month after that? Chances are that almost anyone could accomplish such a goal even without really having any purposeful objective clearly in mind for saving the money.

On the other hand, some people would be quick to say, "Yes, I can save $5.00 a month; in fact, I can save $10.00 a month. But $5.00 is such a small amount to save that it just isn't worth the effort." The habit of saving starts today, right now, even when your income appears ever so small and insignificant.

Before we go deeper into the subject of saving, let us look at the true savers in the world, the people who are on their way to becoming millionaires, and get some insight into just how they reach their targets.

Millionaires—Savers or Collectors?

Some readers of this book will be seriously interested in knowing just what it takes to become a millionaire when you start from scratch. After reading the following observations, you will be in a better position to determine whether you really want the goal of becoming a millionaire during your lifetime or whether your desires are merely a case of wishful thinking.

1. Millionaires epitomize the true saver. They save money for the sake of saving. It is a goal in and of itself. They are really collectors of money. Most people save money to spend later—on vacations, a new car, new fashion clothing, or new furniture for the home. Promising young millionaires-to-be are not interested in the things that money will buy.

2. Becoming a millionaire in a span of 40 years (or the equivalent in terms of current dollars) requires overwhelming ambition. The average workweek for a potential millionaire runs 60 to 80 hours, or more. One must keep in good physical and mental condition to maintain such a schedule. Many sacrifices are faced by these people, and there are many sacrifices brought on the families of these people.

3. Starting out will require earning an income from a full-time job and a second full-time job or equivalent (such as going to college full time in the evenings) or part-time jobs with opportunities for overtime. The millionaire's goal is to save as much take-home pay as possible. Not being too much concerned with what money will buy, the potential millionaire will live a rather frugal life—a rented furnished apartment, a simple automobile if it is necessary, plain but wholesome meals (eating at home and brown bagging the others), a modest wardrobe, and so on. These people are trying to save about one-third of all their gross income and have it earning some interest and dividend income. Compare this savings rate to the average 5 percent that most American families save.

4. These people tend to keep detailed financial records, translating data into percentages, costs per day, rates of interest, the impact of compounding of interest, and rates of return on alternative investments. They develop a good understanding of the federal income tax system and seek investments where tax benefits are the greatest.

5. These people will probably go into business for themselves, as they know it is difficult to become a millionaire by moving up through the ranks in a corporation. Their motivation and egos also contribute to their being their own bosses.

6. They tend to have long lives. Downturns in the business cycle take their toll on many potential millionaires, particularly those who borrowed heavily. Loss of business revenue and cash flow problems often result in a "two steps forward and one step back" approach in reaching their goals. The compounding of interest on investments favors those who either start their savings early or those who have a long life.

7. Most of those who find their way into the ranks of millionaires are intelligent. They may or may not have high school and college diplomas, but they are well informed, have good vocabularies, and are capable of concentrating on their field. Since their goal is so clearly fixed in their minds at all times, they know where to concentrate their efforts, and they do not waste a minute of their time, at least when they are young. If something is important to remember, they will remember it, not for a while but for the rest of their lives. These people tend to think differently from anyone else in a room full of people. Their basic math skills are much better than most people's, and they work through calculations quickly.

Well, there you have some of the ingredients that go into becoming a millionaire. Their dedication to their goal may not make them the life of a party, even if you could get them to go to one. They may seem to be at a distance with most people and perhaps a little square. Their dullness may really be that they have a hard time finding something in common with other people unless those others happen to be millionaires. They were practitioners of assertiveness training long before it had a name. They are the people who understand the needs of other people (economic wants) and are willing to go about supplying those needs. They take control of their environment and do not let the environment control them.

How to Save Money

There are essentially two approaches to saving money. The first is through careful spending of your money on those basic and necessary items such as food, shelter, transportation, clothing, and so on. The second is through setting aside specific amounts of cash from your income, preferably *before* it is spent. This money should be placed regularly in checking and saving accounts with a bank, a savings and loan, or a credit union until it is needed. Our emphasis in this chapter is on this latter approach, but careful spending can help you to receive greater value for your dollar. We will discuss several techniques for saving money later on in this chapter.

Since Americans tend to spend 95 percent of their income, there are many opportunities to help get more value out of each dollar to be spent. Budgeting is one means of controlling those dollars to be spent. Let us take a closer look at the spending side of money transactions.

Saving Money Through Careful Spending. Since most of the disposable income that you earn will be spent, the following techniques may be helpful in stretching your shopping dollar. For example, before purchasing something costing, say, $50, ask yourself, "Do I honestly need this item?" "Am I really buying this item in a moment of impulse?" "Have I made a careful review of other similar items in the marketplace?" "Have I compared this product with others to determine which is the best buy for the money?" "Did I plan to buy this item when I went shopping today?" "Is this item traditionally sold at a substantial discount in certain months of the year?"

If you still have this $50 item on your mind, other useful suggestions can help you determine your spending habits and avoid impulse buying: (1) Postpone the purchase 24 or 48 hours. If you still want the item after that time, you can go ahead with the expenditure. (2) Set a family policy for group discussion on all personal expenditures that exceed a certain dollar amount. This should always be the case if the family is in the habit of using credit cards. Both adults should be aware of all the expenses being charged to a credit card. (3) Be sure to shop at a store with a good reputation and one that offers a reasonable refund policy. (4) Determine if you are buying a brand-name item or an item that the store endorses. (5) Make a careful on-the-spot inspection of any goods that you are about to purchase and be sure to read the label for special instructions on proper care and maintenance as well as any guarantees or warranties accompanying the product. (6) Ask whether the warranties are prorated or cover the total dollar cost of premature replacement. (7) Determine whether the product can be repaired locally by a certified representative or must be sent to a distant city; determine who pays the costs of mailing, packaging, and insurance. (8) Determine whether your spending is "habit spending" and question whether the habit is in your long-run interests. (9) Question whether your spending is motivated by anger, pride, or just trying to get even.

We will be taking a closer took at the various categories of spending and learning ways to get the best value for each dollar spent in the following chapters. For now, let us return to techniques of saving actual amounts of dollars.

Saving Money Before It Is Spent. Of the various ways of saving money, the best way is to set aside a specific sum before it can be spent. The amounts of money set aside from any one of the following techniques should be small so that the habit can be maintained. The 12 methods discussed will help you to accomplish a long-term, short-term, major, or minor financial goal.

1. *Automatic payroll deductions.* Have your employer transfer a few dollars from your paycheck to a savings account. The small amount withheld will not be missed, and you are not likely to take the necessary effort to withdraw the savings. You could also have your employer set aside enough to purchase a small U.S. Series EE savings bond each month. Here, too, there may be some reluctance to cash in such small investments. These small savings can be the nucleus of your emergency fund, the goal being to have money when you need it on short notice. You should not be overly concerned about amounts of interest earned or their slight erosion from inflation; rather, your concern should clearly focus on safety and the ability to obtain needed cash in a day or so.

2. *Fewer exemptions.* By claiming fewer, or zero, exemptions on your W-4 form, you could be eligible for a refund when you file your federal income tax return. This money could be used to purchase a major household appliance.

Some people will argue against this method of saving, citing the fact that the federal government is using your money and that the government, not you, is earning interest on your money. This is the kind of advice that will keep you poor or prevent you from saving. Many successful people use this simple technique to acquire household goods. Moreover, if you make this major purchase for cash, you may even get a substantial discount. In fact, the discount may exceed the interest that could have been earned in a savings account during the same period.

Consider the following purchasing alternatives. Many families will purchase items at the department store with their credit card. The interest rate on such contracts is 12 to 18 percent simple interest. Interest on a small loan from a finance company for one year often begins at 18 percent and is probably closer to 35 percent. In summary, the 5 or 6 percent lost interest because the U.S. government keeps your money is not nearly equal to the cost of buying on credit. Furthermore, your employer is doing bookkeeping for you, and this may save you time in record keeping.

3. *Automatic transfer from checking to savings accounts.* This is a simple but useful way to build a small savings fund to handle annual expenses such as license plate renewals, property tax payments, and property insurance premiums. Make these transfer payments in small amounts. In this way your checking account will not be drained, and you will not be tempted to raid this savings fund for other uses.

4. *Small Christmas savings fund.* Starting a Christmas savings fund at the beginning of the year will be helpful in two ways. First, you can *plan* what you really intend to spend for gifts on holiday activity, and second, you can set an upper limit for gift *expenditures.* You are not as likely to be taken by impulse either. Knowing the size of your fund, you have almost a year to think realistically about what presents to buy for the people on your gift list.

5. *Jar money.* A small sum can be saved by emptying your pockets or purse each day and placing the change in a small glass jar. Obviously, this is not the way to save money to buy a new sports car or take an around-the-world vacation. On the other hand, this might be just the way in which to set aside some money for that family outing, a child's birthday gift, a pizza, an extra bottle of fine table wine for that special occasion, or that small table radio for the workshop. This fund should be spent on small indulgences. The jar should be kept small so that it will be filled in a short time; it should not be a conspicuous item in the home and thus be subject to pilferage or theft.

6. *Saving a special coin.* A variation on the preceding technique is to have each member of the family save a specific coin. Young children might save pennies, older children might save nickels, and young adults and parents might save a dime or a quarter each day.

7. *Paying yourself first.* When you pay your bills, send a "bill" to yourself and place it right on top of the stack of bills that you are about to pay. Again, this bill should be for a small amount. Write the check to your savings account. This technique emphasizes the idea of saving some of your money before it is spent rather than waiting until the end of the month and saving whatever might be left over.

8. *Conducting a thrift month.* This might work for a family for a special occasion. Declare a moratorium on spending except for such essentials as food, monthly payments, and commuting to and from jobs and school. Be sure to combine commuting and shopping trips. Here, the family may eat most or all meals at home and carry a brown bag to school or work. No money should have to be spent on clothing and accessories and no furniture is to be purchased. Emphasize home entertainment or have a clean-up–fix-up month around the home. A variation on frugality is to give up a bad habit. Giving up a pack of cigarettes a day will equal saving about $400 to $450 per year.

9. *The continued payment plan.* You may be making monthly payments on the automobile or some other major household appliance. You probably have become very used to making these monthly payments. Why not capitalize on them for your own benefit. For example, say that you have just made your final payment on your automobile of $82.68. You have been making these payments for three years. Why not make a couple of more monthly payments for $82.68, except this time write the check to your savings account. Be realistic; try to make at least two or three such payments before you give in to being out of debt.

10. *The secret bank balance.* Some people have managed to "hide" a few dollars by using this simple approach. For example, you make a deposit to your bank account of $200. However, when you enter the deposit on the stub of your checkbook, enter only $180. A variation of this approach when you write a check is to enter an amount $1 higher than was actually written on the check. Use this approach only if you find that balancing your checkbook is a sort of cruel and inhumane punishment or you believe that your bank never makes a mistake.

11. *The big bill.* Some people find that they need to keep extra sums of cash around for a short time because of their particular living situation. These people will usually be reluctant to spend such cash on impulse if they keep the money in $50 or $100 bills. A variation of this is to have a few travelers checks just for special business transactions or for emergencies. If you have just returned from a vacation and still have a few travelers checks left, do not convert them into cash or spend them on routine expenses. Some people will tell you not to do this because you are not earning interest, but they are missing the point. Suppose you encounter a situation in which your personal check or credit card is not accepted; a travelers check will be taken without question.

12. *Banking your raise.* You may receive a cost-of-living adjustment increase in your salary, a merit raise, or a promotion. Try to bank this extra money for a couple of months or have it transferred automatically to your savings account from your checking account. If you feel that you cannot bank all your raise, why not split the difference and bank half?

There you have a dozen popular methods that people use to save some of their money before it is spent. You can probably think of other techniques to accomplish the same goal. At any rate putting into practice three or four of the suggestions will help you to accomplish your different saving objectives. Keep the amounts to be saved small enough so that you are not tempted to stop your program. When you are just starting out, do not be overly concerned that your savings are not adding up to large sums immediately. Be realistic; you probably cannot change your living expenses in any drastic fashion without creating anxiety for other members of the family or causing emotional stress to yourself. The only people who really must take such drastic measures are those who are on the verge of bankruptcy.

Compound Interest: "Economic Yeast"

We have all heard the saying that "A dog is man's best friend" and that "Diamonds are a girl's best friend." We should add one more: "Compound interest is the money manager's best friend." Compound interest is the "mirror" or "yardstick" that can help you measure your progress toward achieving your financial goals.

To begin, compound interest might be thought of as "interest income that in turn earns interest." The compound interest on a savings account or the "reinvestment of earnings" on other forms of investment media (stocks, real estate, a business, etc.) has a "snowballing" effect over time. If continued into the future for several years, the compounding of interest alone soon will equal and then exceed the annual amounts of "original capital inputs." These original capital inputs are the periodic amounts of money that can be set aside from your current paycheck for investment or saving purposes.

Compound interest rewards two groups of people: (1) those who begin a program of savings and investment when they are young and (2) those who will have a long life. Since it is rather difficult to determine just how long one is going to live, the emphasis should be on implementing a basic program now, regardless of how small it may appear to be at this time.

If you start a financial plan with immediate reinvestment of earnings as a young adult and carry it through for 30 or 40 years, you will be pleasantly surprised at what can be accomplished. You may not become a millionaire, but you could have accumulated $250,000 to $500,000 and will have done so almost in your spare time. The calculations in Table 5-1 are based on an 8 percent after-tax dollar return compounded annually. The illustration makes use of Table A.3 in Appendix A.

Assume that you can save $1,200 each year for 30 years without any interest being earned. It would have accumulated only $36,000 ($1,200 × 30 years). However in the illustration, $1,200 invested each year at 8 percent, *with compounding*, will amount to $135,936. Note that total interest earned is $99,936 ($135,936 − $36,000). This $99,936 (almost $100,000) would be accruing to your "accounts" day in and day out, year in and year out theoretically without your help. This is an excellent situation because, for $1 that you actually set aside and invest into a program, you will have received $3 just from the compounding of interest. Indeed, consistent investing of small money can pay off later on.

Let us now see just how long it will take you to double your money or investment (Table 5-2). For simplicity, we will ignore federal income taxes and inflation. The compounding of interest can result in slightly different answers if interest is compounded daily, monthly, quarterly, or annually. Quarterly compounding is assumed for this illustration.

You can also arrive at approximately the same answers by using a simple technique called the "Rule of 72." Simply divide the rate of interest that you want to receive on your investment into the number 72. Your answer will be the number of years required to double your money. For example, an 8 percent return on an investment compounded annually requires 9 years for it to double (72 ÷ 8% = 9 years).

TABLE 5-1 A Sketch of Compound Interest

Amount saved each month and invested at an 8% after-tax return compounded annually	Amount accumulated in 30 years	Amount accumulated in 40 years
$ 600 ($50 saved each month)	$ 67,968*	$155,436†
1,200 ($100 saved each month)	135,936	310,872
1,800 ($150 saved each month)	203,904	466,308
2,400 ($200 saved each month)	271,872	621,744

* $600 × factor 113.28 rounded = $67,968.
† $600 × factor 259.06 rounded = $155,436.

TABLE 5-2 Number of Years
Required to Double a Sum at Various
Interest Rates

Investment rate compounded quarterly	Investment will double in the following years
4%	17½
5	14
6	11¾
7	10
8	9
9	8
10	7

Let us apply this information under conditions of inflation. If inflation runs at around 6 percent per year, your salary or wages will just about have to double in 11¾ years, omitting such factors as federal income taxes. Using the "Rule of 72," the answer would be 12 years (72 ÷ 6%). The "Rule of 72" can help you to make many rough estimates quickly (Table 5-3).

By studying the dollar column in Table 5-3, you can see how each line grows at amounts greater than $80, which reflects the compounding aspect of the previous accumulation of interest left to be invested or simply "interest earning interest" on itself. If you compare the figures in the dollar column with the figures in the 8% column in Table A.1 of Appendix A, you will see a similarity. Hence, Table A.1 can be referred to as a compound interest table to determine growth of a one *lump-sum* investment.

Let us take another illustration showing how compound interest can help you reach basic financial goals (Table 5-4). Assume that you can set aside $1,000

TABLE 5-3 Application of the "Rule of 72"

Time period	Accumulated interest at 8%
Deposit on January 1, 19X1	$1,000.00
Balance on December 31, 19X1	1,080.00
" " " 19X2	1,166,40
" " " 19X3	1,259.71
" " " 19X4	1,360.40
" " " 19X5	1,469.33
" " " 19X6	1,586.87
" " " 19X7	1,713.82
" " " 19X8	1,850.93
" " " 19X9	1,999.00

TABLE 5-4 Effect of Compound Interest on a Sum

January 1	Accumulated amount at 8%
19X0	$1,000.00 (today)
19X1	2,080.00 (366 days later)
19X2	3,246.40
19X3	4,506.11
19X4	5,866.60

on January 1 each year for the next five years and that your investment earns 8 percent per year compounded annually. At the end of the period you will have not only the initial inputs of $5,000 principal but also $866.60 of accumulated interest.

The dollar column in the illustration shows the results of successive activities of periodically investing certain amounts of money and the accumulation of interest. Note that the amount of $2,080.00 on January 1, 19X1 is 366 days after the start of the program, which reflects (1) the original $1,000.00 money invested January 1, 19X0, (2) the interest earned on that money for the first year $80.00, and (3) the second deposit of money of $1,000.00 on January 1, 19X1. Use Table A.3 to save time in calculating. Note that the figures in the dollar column are similar to those listed in the 8% column of Table A.3.

Table A.3 is helpful in looking at accumulated amounts when making regular annual deposits of the same amount, year after year, for a specific number of years. The concept of fixed amounts of money being paid or received at uniform intervals of time is defined as an *annuity*. To calculate the results of the preceding illustration by using pencil and paper only may well require 15 to 20 minutes of uninterrupted work. The tables in Appendix A reduce calculation time and possibilities of error. Note that the 19X4 figure of $5,866.60 can be arrived at much more quickly by multiplying the annual deposits of $1,000 by the "factor" shown on line 5 in the 8% column of Table A.3 as follows:

$$\$1,000.00 \times \text{factor } 5.86660 = \$5,866.60$$

Today, pocket calculators sometimes have memory units to help work these kinds of problems.

Another useful technique in working with interest and compounding applies when a specific dollar goal is to be achieved. For example, you want to save exactly $3,000.00 or to have that amount available at the end of five years. Assume also that you could earn 8 percent on your investment compounded annually and that you want to make only one deposit and leave that money to draw interest. To solve such a problem, use Table A.2. Locate the factor shown on line 5 of the 8% column and multiply the goal or money to be saved ($3,000.00) by the factor:

$$\$3,000.00 \times \text{factor } .794 = \$2,382.00$$

In this case you need to deposit a lump sum of $2,382.00 today to have $3,000.00 at the end of five years.

In summary, these calculations and Tables A.1, A.2, and A.3 can be very useful when using savings institutions, credit unions, and bonds to help you accomplish certain financial goals.

Building an Emergency Fund and Liquidity

After covering some basic techniques on how to save money and how compound interest helps you to achieve certain goals sooner, we want to determine which of the many financial goals should be implemented first. Almost everyone will agree that a highly liquid, readily accessible, emergency cash fund is a good first goal. Even if we have taken all the necessary steps to reduce the risks around us and have acquired adequate insurance coverage, it is still necessary to have cash *now* to cope with the unexpected. Even when fully insured, the process of collecting on an insurance claim may take days or even weeks.

Here are some very good reasons for building a cash emergency fund: (1) Natural disasters such as blizzards, floods, tornadoes, and hurricanes cause families to seek temporary shelter and food. (2) Unexpected automobile breakdowns in a distant city may cause you to spend an extra day or so and spend money for repairs, lodging, and food. You may also have to rent a car. (3) Job loss can occur during times of recessions. (4) Family emergencies such as a sudden illness, injury, or death often require money on short notice. Sometimes it is necessary to travel great distances, live near the hospital, and help with taking care of other members of the family. (5) A true bargain on some essential and useful household appliance may present itself.

How large should this emergency cash fund be? There is no easy answer to this question. However, factors relevant to this issue are your age, job security, stability of monthly income, regularity of your paycheck, number of people dependent upon your income, state of your health, accumulated sick leave at work, state of your car, age and health of your parents or children, location of your residence in relation to emergency services, alternative job skills, other family income, and so on.

One objective might be to establish a three- to five-year program to build an emergency fund equaling three to six months' average take-home pay. Your goal could be as simple as the following: one month's take-home pay in the checking account and another two months' in a savings account, with the husband and wife each having $200 in the form of travelers checks. If your regular checking account is to be part of this emergency program, you might want to maintain a couple of hundred dollars in the account at all times. Keep in mind that the goal here is to always have money available for the unexpected. You are buying peace of mind to ease situations that might be otherwise even more unpleasant. There is nothing like money in the bank to help you cope with emergencies and to see your way through them with as little frustration as possible.

Above all, do not be overly concerned that this particular money is not earning maximum interest or that a portion of this money may be actually eroded somewhat by the effects of inflation. Your primary goal here is to have money for real emergencies when you need it. In the meantime your money is in a safe place and is insured against loss. It is good to remember that Americans in general save only around 5 percent of their income. That is, around 95 percent is spent, much of it without too much consideration for comparison shopping techniques. Therefore, an emergency cash fund developed from reduced spending should not be expected to earn a high return in the form of interest. For emergencies it is the size of the fund, its safety, and the ability to have it now that really counts here. Interest income plays a minor role in emergency funds. Your best reward, which would be greater than any amount of interest earnings, is to be able to manage your life so that emergencies requiring immediate cash are greatly reduced or at least made more tolerable.

In the following sections, we will cover some places that provide the necessary protection of emergency funds, provide most of the bookkeeping, and pay interest on your money. Saving programs for the purpose of buying major appliances, a vacation, a new car, or a home can be subject to a little greater risk and higher interest earnings. These investment media might include time deposits and bonds. Banks and credit union accounts, certificates of deposit, and most bond investments are examples of *fixed return* forms of investment.

BANKS, BANKING, AND SAVINGS INSTITUTIONS

Banking is just another service business in the United States. The banks are owned by families or by stockholders. Banks receive their charters from states or from the federal government. You can become a stockholder in many of the large banks that exist today. Their stocks are mostly traded on the *over-the-counter* market. The biggest banks may even have their stocks traded on the major stock exchange. Banks that receive their charter from the federal government are called *commercial banks* and are referred to as *national banks*. State banks may or may not be commercial banks and may function in a more limited financial area. All national banks are members of the Federal Reserve System. The reader should refer to the glossary at the end of the chapter for further information about the Federal Reserve System.

The Commercial Bank

Today's money manager probably needs at least one checking account and one savings account at a commercial bank. While not as many U.S. banks fail today as in earlier years, make a study of the banks in your area. Banks are extremely competitive today, and their services vary as do the costs of rendering those services.

Services offered by commercial banks include checking accounts, savings accounts, certificates of deposit, travelers checks, cashier checks, certified checks, safe deposit boxes, foreign exchange information and foreign currency exchange, loans, the purchase and sale of stocks and bonds for customers, financial advice, management of estates and trusts, credit card service, sale and redemption of U.S. savings bonds, 24-hour cash machines, bank-by-mail services, automatic transfers between checking and savings accounts, bank overdraft privileges, printed checks, bill-paying services, senior citizen accounts, and local economic newsletters.

By opening up a checking account with a commercial bank, you have access to vast financial skills and talent. Establishing and maintaining a good relationship with a bank over the long run will certainly pay off. The bank has an interest in you as a customer, particularly as a successful customer. Do not hesitate to have bank employees help you with reviewing your financial goals, buying a car, investing, or sending money to another city or country. Mainly, you want information. A good bank staff makes this information available and offers advice if your requests are within reason and you have done some homework. Remember, too, that a small branch may not always be able to answer your in-depth financial questions; neither should you expect a drive-in teller to sort out your banking problems. Banks are not only in heavy competition with one another, but they are under pressure to eliminate alleged red-lining practices, become equal opportunity employers, and provide upward mobility to female and minority employees. Therefore, both treatment and service costs for doing business with a bank should be better today than at any time in the past.

Commercial banks offer a variety of checking accounts designed to appeal to the needs of their customers. Some checking account services are for people who write only five or six checks a month and the service charge may simply be 10 cents or 15 cents per check; some checking accounts may have no monthly service charge as long as at least $200 or $300 is maintained in the account. While there may be ten kinds of checking services available at a modern commercial bank, your financial management goals should determine your banking needs and not the other way around.

Since a checking account should be at the center of your money management program, the checking account that requires a $200 or $300 balance with unlimited check-writing privileges appears the best type of program. Keeping $200 or $300 in the checking account at all times is only the loss of $10 or $15 a year at 5 percent interest, and the bookkeeping the bank will be performing for you is worth the cost. One of your goals is to avoid the nickel-nursing aspects of an economy checking account. You should focus upon the size of the check being written and on the merit of the thing being purchased rather than on the 10 cents that the bank will charge you for writing the check.

An important consideration when opening up a checking or savings account at a commercial bank is to determine whether or not your accounts are insured against the bank's failure. At the bank's doors, windows, and teller windows, you should see a sign that says, in effect, that the bank is a member of the Federal Deposit Insurance Corporation. All national banks are members and many state banks are members. When you see the sign "Member of FDIC" you can be assured that your checking and savings accounts are insured against bank failure up to $100,000 on *each* account maintained at the bank.

When you open a checking account, you will be asked certain basic information such as your full name, current home address, telephone number, employer's name and location of business, and so on. If your are married, the bank will want to know if you plan to have a joint bank account. If a wife uses her name on a bank account, she can build her own separate credit identity. You will be asked to sign a signature card so that the bank knows your endorsement.

Let your bank be your bookkeeper. It is a good idea to develop a basic record-keeping procedure that will provide many benefits at once. Your monthly bank statements can be a major portion of your record-keeping system and will provide nearly a complete record of your cash flow transactions. This may come in handy in the event that you are audited by the Internal Revenue Service, that you need to go to court over certain business misunderstandings, or that you just want to review some of your own past transactions.

Many business firms apply the following businesslike procedures with their bank accounts, and you can adopt them for your own use: (1) Deposit all money, regardless of sources, intact; that is, when you receive your paycheck, welfare check, pension check, GI Bill check, allotment check, or whatever, deposit it directly into your bank account. If you receive money in the form of cash, take the money directly to the bank for deposit. While it is all right to send checks and drafts through the mail for deposit by a bank-by-mail service, do not send cash. Your goal here is to avoid delays in depositing incoming checks and money before it can become lost, stolen, or spent unwisely. (2) The second procedure in a basic cash record-keeping system is to write checks for all money spent, though this may not always work for the individual consumer. Even many businesses modify this system by establishing what is known as a "petty cash fund" to cover such small expenditures for postage due, telegrams, COD charges, and reimbursement of employees for small expenditures made on behalf of the firm.

An individual or family can adopt a similar plan by writing one check each week to cover such family cash expenditures and needs as the adults' mad money allowance, adults' and children's special accountable allowances for such things as office and school lunches, school supplies, bread and milk or grocery money, or similar small amounts. This particular check should not vary in amount from one week to another. Furthermore, this check should not be sacrificed since it often is a key to getting other members of the household to go along with budgeting. On the other hand, this weekly check should not be expanded to become a sort of catchall device. For some people, even this procedure might be modified to handle certain costs for cash purchases of gasoline and parking if this is a highly routine activity.

Your checking account will generate some records for your filing system, and you will need a separate container for such items as (1) unused or blank checks, (2) used or canceled and spoiled checks, (3) check stubs or check register booklets, and (4) memoranda of deposits or deposit slips. Keep only the monthly bank statements in the file folder; the odd-sized shapes of checks, check stubs, and memoranda are difficult to "folder file."

To review the typical documents of an ordinary checking account, let us look at the following illustration of Karen S. Morgan who is opening up her first bank account. Karen has just received her first payroll check of $375.00 for two weeks of work at her new job. Assume that she has just completed the forms for opening an account at the Fourth National Bank and that the bank officer has been explaining how to make her first deposit over at the teller's window. For illustration, assume that the bank is able to print a set of checks and deposit slips with Karen's name and address, bank account number, and consecutive numbering of her first 25 checks as a special free and immediate service to new customers.

When Karen receives her paycheck at work, she should immediately protect herself financially by endorsing the back side of the check with the restrictive endorsement shown in Exhibit 5-1. This restrictive endorsement can serve as a protection in case your check or checks are stolen or disappear mysteriously. It is probably just a good habit to form when you receive any checks made out to you.

for deposit only
Karen S. Morgan

EXHIBIT 5-1 Restrictive Endorsement

EXHIBIT 5-2   Completed Checking Account Deposit Ticket

| CHECKING ACCOUNT DEPOSIT TICKET | 12–123 | | 001 |
| | 1432 | | |

Karen S. Morgan	**CASH**		
203 East Main Street	**CHECKS**		
Anytown, WA. 98321	*12 – 275*	*375*	*00*
DATE *Feb. 13* 19 *X0*			
Karen S. Morgan	**TOTAL**	*375*	*00*
Acknowledge receipt of cash	**LESS CASH W/D**	*– 25*	*00*
returned by signing the above	**NET DEPOSIT**	*350*	*00*
THE FOURTH NATIONAL BANK			
(home office branch)			
123–432–56031 721			

Karen next fills in one of her newly printed checking deposit slips and decides to deposit all the money except for a weekly cash allowance of $25.00. The bank officer says that all she had to do is enter her employer's payroll check bank number on the deposit ticket and then enter the amount in the appropriate space. The officer shows where employer bank account number is located. The number is 12-275, and it is located in the upper right-hand corner on the face of the check. When the teller takes the deposit and gives Karen the requested $25.00 in cash, the teller will ask Karen to sign the deposit slip to acknowledge the receipt of cash. The completed deposit ticket might look like the one in Exhibit 5-2.

When the teller receives Karen's deposit, Karen is given a printed deposit memo to be used for comparison purposes when she receives her monthly statement from the bank. Exhibit 5-3 illustrates this document, which briefly summarizes the total amount of the deposit to the bank account of $350.00 and the date. Other information on deposit receipts includes such items as teller's number, deposit to savings account or checkings account, bank branch number, transaction number for the day, and so on.

EXHIBIT 5-3   Sample Deposit Receipt

	DEPOSIT RECEIPT	
Check Dep .876	13FEBX0 *************************************** $350.00	
	THE FOURTH NATIONAL BANK	
	(The Home Office Br.)	

EXHIBIT 5-4 Personal Check and Account Balance Notation

No. 001	*#19.47*	Karen S. Morgan		No. 001
To: *Super Foods Inc.*		203 East Main Street		
For: *Groceries*		Anytown, WA 98321	*Feb. 18* 19 *XO*	12-123
				1432

	#	
Balance Fwd....	#	-o-
Deposits........	350	00
Total	350	00
This Check	19	47
Balance Fwd....	330	53

Pay to the Order of *Super Foods Inc.* $ *19.47*

Nineteen Dollars and 47/100 ———— Dollars

THE FOURTH NATIONAL BANK
(Home Office Branch)

Memo: *Groceries*   *Karen S. Morgan*
123 – 432 – 56031 – 721

Exhibit 5-4 illustrates Karen's first check that she writes to Super Foods, Inc., for groceries on February 18, 1988 in the amount of $19.47. Karen's home address has been printed on the face of the check. Karen's individual account number will be written in magnetic ink numbers just below the bank's name and memo line. Note that Karen writes the number 19.47 next to the dollar sign ($) so that it would be very difficult to raise the check's amount to, say, $119.47. Karen has written the check's amount in longhand and then has added a long horizontal line to eliminate any blank space remaining on the line to reduce attempts at altering the check. Another word of caution for one's protection is also in order. Since the personal checks and deposit slips carry the mark-sense numbers, it is important to protect your checkbook from theft. If you lose your checkbook, inform your bank immediately so that your account can be protected.

Exhibit 5-5 is a sample monthly bank statement. Today's monthly statements are comprehensive summaries that include not only the checking account transactions but summaries of savings accounts, loans, credit card purchases, and tax information as well. To keep the basic concepts clear, the bank statement illustrated is mailed to Karen on February 20, 1988, the end of the bank period for internal accounting purposes. The four columns, Beginning Balance, Deposits, Withdrawals, and Running Balance, have several formats; however, the concept is the same.

In this illustration, only one check has cleared the Fourth National Bank on Karen's account. Usually, the ending monthly balance on the bank statement and the depositor's balance in the check stub do not agree. In this case it is necessary to prepare what is known as a *reconciliation statement*. These informal proofs usually can be computed on the back side of the bank statement. Many banks provide a sketch of a reconciliation statement for depositors. Assuming no arithmetic errors on the part of the depositor or the bank, the differences result when some checks have not cleared the bank, a most recent deposit has not been recorded by the bank's accounting department, or such things as monthly service charges or check-printing charges have not been recorded.

EXHIBIT 5-5 Sample Monthly Bank Statement

		BANK STATEMENT	
THE FOURTH NATIONAL BANK		No. 123 – 432 – 56031 – 721	
		Period Ending: February 20, 19X0	
		Name: Karen S. Morgan 203 East Main Street Anytown, WA 98321	

Beginning Balance	Deposits	Withdrawals	Running Balance
.00	350.00	19.47	350.00 330.53
		Ending Balance	330.53

As was mentioned earlier, you may want to institute an automatic transfer of money from your checking account to a bank savings account, as when, for example, you can control your expenditures and stabilize your checking account at a minimum of $300 to $400. Then, begin a program to have $50 transferred each month to a savings account. At $50 per month, this portion of your emergency fund could reach $600 in one year. Savings accounts are sometimes called "passbook" accounts and pay interest of around 4 to 5 percent with interest compounded quarterly. An emergency fund at least equivalent to two months' take-home pay may work out very well in this type of account. The bank should be a member of the FDIC so the savings account will also be insured for up to $100,000. Usually you can draw the money out of a passbook account without a waiting period; however, you should always inquire about any types of restrictions. Finally, if you do have an automatic transfer program, remember to adjust downward your checkbook "stub" so that your checking account is kept up to date. Correcting the checkbook on the first day of each month is a good habit to establish.

Savings and Loan Associations (S&Ls)

A savings and loan association is a financial institution that provides an opportunity for people to save their money and earn interest. The money is loaned to other people mainly for the purchase of real estate such as land, houses, and home improvements. Savings and loan associations are required to offer higher rates of interest on savings accounts than commercial banks. However, savings and loan groups cannot operate as commercial banks with respect to checking accounts, though recent deregulation of certain services has made the differences in basic savings and checking more academic.

Herman

"Maybe we're over-drawn!"

Savings goals that go beyond building an emergency fund might be deposited with an S&L. Examples of these savings goals are a down payment on a home, new car savings fund, education fund for the children, money to start a future business, or vacation fund.

Savings and loan associations should be members of such insurance programs as the Federal Savings and Loan Insurance Corporation (FSLIC). When the firm displays prominently the sign "Member of FSLIC," each savings account is insured up to an amount of $100,000. Today, savings and loan associations are vigorously competing with commercial banks for your saving dollar. In times of major housing construction activity, savings institutions offer many inducements for opening an account. Radios, clocks, small TV sets, and other household appliances are given away to customers who open up savings accounts with specified minimums.

Exhibit 5-6 is a typical newspaper advertisement by a savings and loan association or a mutual savings bank. Note that the interest is higher than that offered by a commercial bank's basic savings account. The interest rates are higher, but money must be left on deposit for a much longer period of time. The savings account is often referred to as a *certificate of deposit,* but more correctly it is called a *savings certificate.* If you withdraw the money at a time prior to that specified, you may only receive interest based upon the lower "passbook" interest rate. This should emphasize the point that S&L savings accounts are not always the best place for an emergency fund. It should also be kept in mind that the chartering authorities allow local S&L officers to require advanced notice on the part of the depositor before money can be withdrawn. However, this authority is seldom exercised, and depositors can usually make immediate withdrawal of their funds.

Exhibit 5-6 also seems to indicate that two interest rates are being paid on the accounts. The *current rate of interest* is the basic annual rate of interest, much like the annual rate discussed in the section on compound interest. If the compounding is done annually, the current rate of interest will equal what is called the *effective rate of interest.* However, if compounding is done quarterly or even daily, the annual effective rate of interest return will be somewhat higher. Therefore, a 7.75 percent current rate of interest will actually turn out to be an 8.17 percent effective rate of return if the money on deposit is *compounded daily* and paid on the daily balances.

Mutual Savings Banks

Mutual savings banks are places where people may invest their money in long-term or time deposit accounts. The term "mutual" signifies that the bank is owned by its depositors and that a self-perpetuating board of trustees oversees the bank's operations. Most mutual savings banks are located on the East Coast,

EXHIBIT 5-6 Typical S&L Newspaper Ad

Current annual rate	7.75%	7.50%	6.75%	6.50%	5.25%
Annual effective rate	8.17%	7.90%	7.08%	6.81%	5.47%
Minimum deposit	$1,000	$1,000	$1,000	$1,000	$1.00
Term	6 to 10 years	4 to 6 years	2½ to 4 years	1 to 2½ years	no minimum term
Yield in dollars	$1,000 becomes $1,602.25 in 6 years $2,195.07 in 10 years	In 4 years $1,000 becomes $1,355.45	in 2½ years $1,000 becomes $1,186.58	in 1 year $1,000 becomes $1,068.11	(does not apply)
How is interest calculated	Compounded daily, paid on daily balances.				Compounded daily, paid on daily balance from day of deposit to day of withdrawal.
How is interest paid	Paid quarterly by check, or credited to certificate account or other savings account.				
Withdrawal privileges	Federal regulations on withdrawals prior to maturity require that interest be paid at passbook rate (5¼%), less 90 days on the amount withdrawn.				No restrictions, funds earn from day of deposit to day of withdrawal.
Insurance of accounts	Savings are insured up to **$100,000** by the Federal Savings & Loan Insurance Corporation, an agency of the Federal Government.				

Middle Atlantic, and West Coast. Many people will not even see much distinction between the savings and loan association and mutual savings bank. Mutual savings banks in their advertisements will state that they are members of the FDIC, and savings and loan firms will state that they are members of the FSLIC. In fact Exhibit 5-6 might also be typical of an advertisement by a mutual savings bank. States regulating state-chartered mutual savings banks may also set limits on the size of deposits and may regulate the withdrawal of funds by depositors. However, these regulations are seldom invoked.

Credit Unions (CUs)

Credit unions are cooperatives chartered by federal or state governments that handle savings and loans for their members restricted to a homogeneous industrial or employee group. Many employees of private companies as well as government agencies belong to credit unions. You can open an account for as little as $5.00 and receive a "share" of membership. There are many advantages to belonging to a credit union. They pay a higher rate of interest (referred to as dividends) on passbook savings than do banks, savings and loans, and mutual savings banks, and the member who needs to borrow money will find that the interest charges on credit loans are among the lowest if not the lowest of any type of lending firm. The amount of the personal loans is limited because of the size of the membership group. Member-savers can expect to receive 6 percent interest on their savings while a member-borrower may pay as little as 6½ percent on a secured loan. These low-cost operations often stem from the fact that employers encourage the credit union program and provide space for the CU's operations. Employees are elected to serve as the directors, on loan committees, and so on, and they often serve without pay. No advertising costs are necessary as new employees learn of the CU during the orientation period and company newsletters will carry announcements about the CU. Finally, members tend to make an extra effort to pay their loans since it was borrowed from other members in the group.

There are some drawbacks to the credit union. The amounts that can be deposited in savings or the amounts to be borrowed may be limited. Some of your associates will know more about your financial affairs if you decide to borrow money or save money. One must belong to a credit union before one can save or borrow from it. State-chartered credit unions are not always required to carry depositors' insurance.

If you have a credit union where you work or are a member of some group that has one, it is a very good place to save some of your money that is to become part of your emergency or liquidity fund. Credit unions are popular around the world and have done much to put the loan shark out of business. Information about credit unions can be obtained from The National Credit Union Administration, 2025 M Street N.W., Washington, D.C. 20456; in larger cities a state credit union agency is listed in the White Pages of the telephone directory.

NOW Accounts

The term NOW stands for negotiable order of withdrawal accounts. NOW accounts were developed by savings institutions to, in effect, turn a savings account that earns interest into a form of checking account. Commercial banks, which by law could not pay interest on checking accounts, had expressed concern over this new concept as a kind of unfair competition. However, recent federal legislation makes it possible for commercial banks to pay interest on checking accounts. The higher inflation of recent years has also caused many people to draw down their bank deposit balances and keep more in savings. The NOW account is becoming popular with credit unions and is referred to as a share draft.

Interest Earned on Checking Accounts

On November 1, 1978, the banking industry began to pay interest on checking accounts under certain conditions. While this step allows consumers to earn interest on their checking accounts, it may not always work for the average consumer. Several reasons exist for this. It may require that the customer maintain a minimum daily balance in the checking account at all times. This minimum balance may be $1,250. This is more money than many people keep in their checking accounts. If the daily balance drops below the $1,250 for any one day during the month, the bank may charge a basic monthly fee of, say, $3.50 plus 10 cents per check.

Certificates of Deposit (CDs)

A *real* certificate of deposit is a marketable security issued in the amount of $100,000 or more. These instruments pay the holder very high rates of interest, more than long-term savings accounts at banks or thrift institutions. CDs have a life of one month to one year.

Certificates of deposit issued by banks, savings and loan associations, and mutual savings banks are really "savings certificates." These minimum amounts for savings certificates are commonly $1,000.00 to $10,000.00. Savings certificates are not traded as in the case with CDs and have longer lives of six to eight years.

The term "certificate" is vague and is used for a host of financial documents.

Series H bonds were issued in denominations of $500, $1,000, $5,000, and $10,000, and the holders received checks for interest earned at 6 percent for 10 years. The new Series HH will earn a full 7½ percent if held for the full 10 years. Holders receive checks every 6 months from the federal government.

Individuals usually can hold up to $15,000 (issue price) in U.S. government savings bonds in any one year. The bonds are not transferable and cannot be used as collateral.

Series EE and HH bonds can serve as starters in reaching certain financial goals. The Series EEs are small enough to acquire under a payroll deduction plan at work. The interest may be deferred and thereby provide an income tax shelter. These bonds are exempt from state and local income taxes. No commissions are paid. They can be replaced if lost or destroyed.

Federal income taxes on matured Series E and EE can be deferred by swapping or trading them directly for Series HH bonds. The taxes will be paid when the HH bonds mature.

BONDS

U.S. Government Series E, EE, H, and HH Bonds

Over the years, two of the most popular bonds investments offered to the public have been U.S. Series E and H savings bonds. After December 1979, the federal government replaced these bonds with a new series called Series EE and Series HH bonds. Series E and H bonds that have passed their final maturity dates no longer earn additional interest. All other E and H bonds are still earning interest.

The interest rate paid on the older series was determined by shortening their maturity. In recent years the Series E bonds were issued with a five-year maturity, that is, an $18.75 bond would mature in five years to a value of $25.00. Other denominations had maturity values of $50.00, $75.00, $100.00, $200.00, $500.00, and more.

The new Series EE and HH were issued after December 1979. New Series EE are issued at amounts of one-half the maturity value. That is, a $25 bond, the smallest denomination, will have a maturity value of $50. The rate of interest is 7½ percent and the term is 10 years. All Series EE bonds purchased on or after November 1, 1982, and held 5 years, may even receive a higher rate of interest under certain conditions.

The U.S. government issues other types of bonds, notes, and bills, for example, Treasury bills, which can be purchased in amounts of $10,000. The interest paid on this type of investment is tied to the supply and demand for money in the open marketplace. Banks will help purchasers acquire these government issues and the service fees are very small, perhaps less than $20. Many banks and savings institutions developed the popular money market certificate patterned after the Treasury bills. See the glossary at the end of the chapter for more information on federal investments.

Approaching Other Bond Investments

The preceding discussions have focused on how to save money for basic emergency funds and build savings for specific financial goals. Most of these funds should be in safe and insured places to guard not only against their physical loss but also against the failure of the bank or savings institutions. These funds should be redeemable in cash with little or no waiting period and provide some income to offset some of the erosion from inflation. Another goal should be that the institution will perform much of the basic record keeping. Investments in U.S. Series E, EE, H, and HH bonds also represent virtually risk-free investments and provide income tax planning flexibility; these bonds can be purchased and redeemed with no difficulty and without commission costs.

The Basics. Investing in bonds of state and local government agencies or bonds of business corporations requires greater study and usually carries greater risks. However, learning about this field of investment can pay off in the form of higher interest rates of return without too much risk. The interest income may offset all the erosion of inflation and provide some real profit for the investor. Investment in bonds can fit those investor goals where one needs to keep money invested or saved for, say, three to five years into the future. Bonds are often suitable for the person who is retired and needs an assured income and safety of principal. Bonds serve as a basis for diversification for other investors.

A *bond* is a debt or a long-term liability of a government agency or a business corporation. Most bonds are printed in $1,000 (see Exhibits 5-7 and 5-8) denominations and pay a specified rate of interest usually every six months throughout the life of the bond. Bonds will fluctuate in price on a day-to-day basis in response to various economic events, political news, and activity of the indebted agency or firm itself. When a bond is issued for $1,000, it is said to be issued at *face value* or *par value*. If the bond is issued or traded between investors at above the face value, it is said to have been issued or traded at a *premium*. On the other hand, if the bond is issued or traded at less than its face value, it is said to be selling at a *discount*. One should view these two terms as the bond's adjustment to daily (even hourly) changes in the interest rates in the financial world. Bonds are often called by their security pledge such as a "9% first mortgage bond," "7% collateral trust bond," "8% sinking fund bond," "6% bridge bond," and so on.

Theoretically, only one interest rate is available at a given moment in time for a particular type of risk investment. However, this rate is constantly changing because of the effect of economic and political events. Bonds must be printed by a company that specializes in this work. During this process, a specific rate of interest must be printed on the documents. By the time the bonds are issued by the debtor (a government, school district, utility, manufacturing corporation, etc.), the interest rates will have probably changed by a fraction of a percentage point. To compensate for these minor changes in the interest rates, the bond is issued at a price slightly above (a premium) or slightly below (a discount) the $1,000 face value. After the bonds have been outstanding for a time, the trading value of the bonds may depart from the original issue price and/or the face value. However, as a bond moves closer to its maturity date, its value will return closer to its face value of $1,000.

Bonds may be issued in denominations other than the $1,000 illustrated, and the bonds may have a life of from 5 years to 30 or 40 years. If there is any rule of thumb for buying bonds for individuals, it might be to always buy them at a discount, perhaps three to five years before maturity.

EXHIBIT 5-7 Face of $5,000 Corporate Debenture

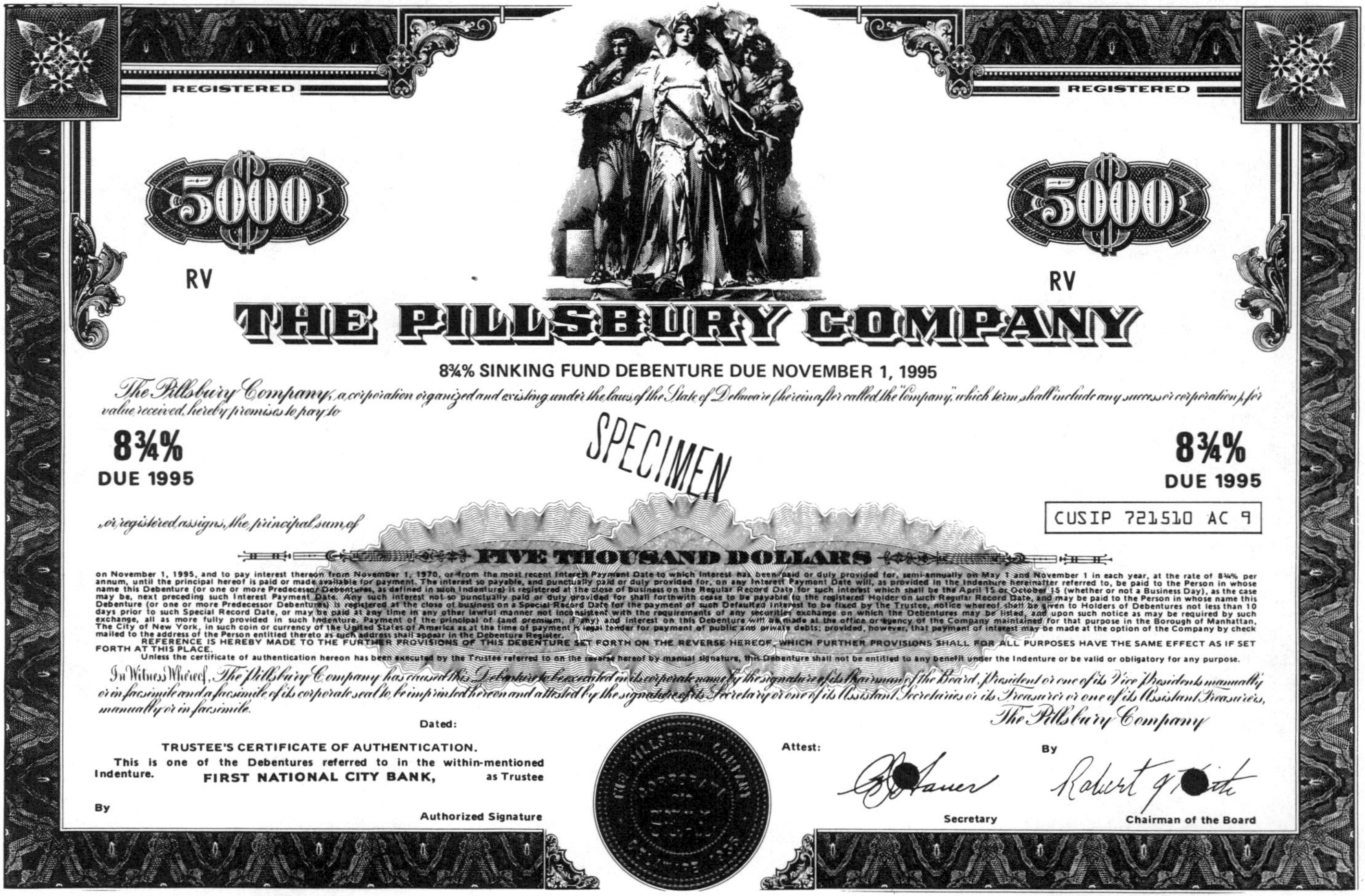

REGISTERED

5000

RV

THE PILLSBURY COMPANY

8¾% SINKING FUND DEBENTURE DUE NOVEMBER 1, 1995

The Pillsbury Company, a corporation organized and existing under the laws of the State of Delaware (hereinafter called the "Company," which term shall include any successor corporation), for value received, hereby promises to pay to

8¾% DUE 1995

SPECIMEN

CUSIP 721510 AC 9

, or registered assigns, the principal sum of

FIVE THOUSAND DOLLARS

on November 1, 1995, and to pay interest thereon from November 1, 1970, or from the most recent Interest Payment Date to which interest has been paid or duly provided for, semi-annually on May 1 and November 1 in each year, at the rate of 8¾% per annum, until the principal hereof is paid or made available for payment. The interest so payable, and punctually paid or duly provided for, on any Interest Payment Date will, as provided in the Indenture hereinafter referred to, be paid to the Person in whose name this Debenture (or one or more Predecessor Debentures, as defined in such Indenture) is registered at the close of business on the Regular Record Date for such interest which shall be the April 15 or October 15 (whether or not a Business Day), as the case may be, next preceding such Interest Payment Date. Any such interest not so punctually paid or duly provided for shall forthwith cease to be payable to the registered Holder on such Regular Record Date, and may be paid to the Person in whose name this Debenture (or one or more Predecessor Debentures) is registered at the close of business on a Special Record Date for the payment of such Defaulted Interest to be fixed by the Trustee, notice whereof shall be given to Holders of Debentures not less than 10 days prior to such Special Record Date, or may be paid at any time in any other lawful manner not inconsistent with the requirements of any securities exchange on which the Debentures may be listed, and upon such notice as may be required by such exchange, all as more fully provided in such Indenture. Payment of the principal of (and premium, if any) and interest on this Debenture will be made at the office or agency of the Company maintained for that purpose in the Borough of Manhattan, The City of New York, in such coin or currency of the United States of America as at the time of payment is legal tender for payment of public and private debts; provided, however, that payment of interest may be made at the option of the Company by check mailed to the address of the Person entitled thereto as such address shall appear in the Debenture Register.

REFERENCE IS HEREBY MADE TO THE FURTHER PROVISIONS OF THIS DEBENTURE SET FORTH ON THE REVERSE HEREOF, WHICH FURTHER PROVISIONS SHALL FOR ALL PURPOSES HAVE THE SAME EFFECT AS IF SET FORTH AT THIS PLACE.

Unless the certificate of authentication hereon has been executed by the Trustee referred to on the reverse hereof by manual signature, this Debenture shall not be entitled to any benefit under the Indenture or be valid or obligatory for any purpose.

In Witness Whereof, The Pillsbury Company has caused this Debenture to be executed in its corporate name by the signature of its Chairman of the Board, President or one of its Vice Presidents manually or in facsimile and a facsimile of its corporate seal to be imprinted hereon and attested by the signature of its Secretary or one of its Assistant Secretaries or its Treasurer or one of its Assistant Treasurers, manually or in facsimile.

Dated:

The Pillsbury Company

TRUSTEE'S CERTIFICATE OF AUTHENTICATION.

This is one of the Debentures referred to in the within-mentioned Indenture.

FIRST NATIONAL CITY BANK, as Trustee

By

Authorized Signature

Attest:

Secretary

By

Chairman of the Board

Reprinted by permission of The Pillsbury Company.

EXHIBIT 5-8 Terms of Typical Sinking Fund Debenture

THE PILLSBURY COMPANY
8¾% SINKING FUND DEBENTURE DUE NOVEMBER 1, 1995

This Debenture is one of a duly authorized issue of Debentures of the Company designated as its 8¾% Sinking Fund Debentures due November 1, 1995 (herein called the "Debentures"), limited in aggregate principal amount to \$25,000,000, issued and to be issued under an indenture (herein called the "Indenture") dated as of November 1, 1970 between the Company and First National City Bank (herein called the "Trustee", which term includes any successor trustee under the Indenture), to which Indenture and all indentures supplemental thereto reference is hereby made for a statement of the respective rights thereunder of the Company, the Trustee and the Holders of the Debentures, and the terms upon which the Debentures are, and are to be, authenticated and delivered.

The Debentures are subject to redemption upon not less than 30 nor more than 60 days' notice by mail, (1) on November 1 in each year commencing with the year 1976 through operation of the Sinking Fund at a Redemption Price equal to their principal amount, and (2) at any time, in whole or in part, at the election of the Company, at a Redemption Price equal to the percentage of the principal amount set forth below if redeemed during the twelve-month period beginning November 1 of the years indicated:

Year	Redemption Price	Year	Redemption Price
1970	108.750%	1980	104.375%
1971	108.313	1981	103.938
1972	107.875	1982	103.500
1973	107.438	1983	103.063
1974	107.000	1984	102.625
1975	106.563	1985	102.188
1976	106.125	1986	101.750
1977	105.688	1987	101.313
1978	105.250	1988	100.875
1979	104.813	1989	100.438

and thereafter at a Redemption Price equal to their principal amount, together in the case of any such redemption (whether through operation of the Sinking Fund or otherwise) with accrued interest to the Redemption Date (but interest instalments whose Stated Maturity is on the Redemption Date will be payable to the Holders of such Debentures, or one or more Predecessor Debentures, of record at the close of business on the relevant Record Date referred to on the face hereof), all as provided in the Indenture.

Notwithstanding the foregoing, the Company may not redeem any of the Debentures otherwise than through operation of the Sinking Fund prior to November 1, 1980, as a part of, or in anticipation of, any refunding operation involving the incurring of any indebtedness having an interest cost to the Company (calculated in accordance with generally accepted financial practice) of less than 8.75% per annum.

The Sinking Fund provides for the redemption of not less than \$1,250,000 principal amount nor more than \$2,500,000 principal amount of Debentures on November 1 in each year beginning with the year 1976 to and including the year 1994. Debentures acquired by the Company otherwise than by redemption may be credited against subsequent Sinking Fund requirements.

In the event of redemption of this Debenture in part only, a new Debenture or Debentures for the unredeemed portion hereof shall be

issued in the name of the Holder hereof upon the cancellation hereof.

If an Event of Default, as defined in the Indenture, shall occur and be continuing, the principal of all the Debentures may be declared due and payable in the manner and with the effect provided in the Indenture.

The Indenture permits, with certain exceptions as therein provided, the amendment thereof and the modification of the rights and obligations of the Company and the rights of the Holders of the Debentures under the Indenture at any time by the Company and the Trustee with the consent of the Holders of 66⅔% in aggregate principal amount of the Debentures at the time Outstanding, as defined in the Indenture. The Indenture also contains provisions permitting the Holders of specified percentages in aggregate principal amount of the Debentures at the time Outstanding, as defined in the Indenture, on behalf of the Holders of all the Debentures, to waive compliance by the Company with certain provisions of the Indenture and certain past defaults under the Indenture and their consequences. Any such consent or waiver by the Holder of this Debenture shall be conclusive and binding upon such Holder and upon all future Holders of this Debenture and of any Debenture issued upon the transfer hereof or in exchange herefor or in lieu hereof whether or not notation of such consent or waiver is made upon this Debenture.

No reference herein to the Indenture and no provision of this Debenture or of the Indenture shall alter or impair the obligation of the Company, which is absolute and unconditional, to pay the principal of (and premium, if any) and interest on this Debenture at the times, places, and rate, and in the coin or currency, herein prescribed.

As provided in the Indenture and subject to certain limitations therein set forth, this Debenture is transferable on the Debenture Register of the Company, upon surrender of this Debenture for registration of transfer at the office or agency of the Company in the Borough of Manhattan, The City of New York, duly endorsed by, or accompanied by a written instrument of transfer in form satisfactory to the Company and the Debenture Registrar duly executed by, the Holder hereof or his attorney duly authorized in writing, and thereupon one or more new Debentures, of authorized denominations and for the same aggregate principal amount, will be issued to the designated transferee or transferees.

The Debentures are issuable only in registered form without coupons in denominations of \$1,000 and any integral multiple thereof. As provided in the Indenture and subject to certain limitations therein set forth, Debentures are exchangeable for a like aggregate principal amount of Debentures of a different authorized denomination, as requested by the Holder surrendering the same.

No service charge shall be made for any such transfer or exchange, but the Company may require payment of a sum sufficient to cover any tax or other governmental charge payable in connection therewith.

Prior to due presentment of this Debenture for registration of transfer, the Company, the Trustee and any agent of the Company or the Trustee may treat the person in whose name this Debenture is registered as the owner hereof for all purposes, whether or not this Debenture be overdue, and neither the Company, the Trustee nor any such agent shall be affected by notice to the contrary.

ABBREVIATIONS

The following abbreviations, when used in the inscription on the face of this instrument, shall be construed as though they were written out in full according to applicable laws or regulations:

TEN COM — as tenants in common
TEN ENT — as tenants by the entireties
JT TEN — as joint tenants with right of survivorship and not as tenants in common

UNIF GIFT MIN ACT — .... Custodian ....
(Cust)   (Minor)
under Uniform Gifts to Minors
Act . . . (State) . . .

Additional abbreviations may also be used though not in the above list.

FOR VALUE RECEIVED the undersigned hereby sell(s), assign(s) and transfer(s) unto

PLEASE INSERT SOCIAL SECURITY OR OTHER
IDENTIFYING NUMBER OF ASSIGNEE

Please print or typewrite name and address including postal zip code of assignee

the within Debenture and all rights thereunder, hereby irrevocably constituting and appointing

_____ attorney
to transfer said Debenture on the books of the Company, with full power of substitution in the premises.

Dated : _____

NOTICE: The signature to this assignment must correspond with the name as written upon the face of the within instrument in every particular, without alteration or enlargement or any change whatever.

Reprinted by permission of The Pillsbury Company.

TABLE 5-5 Two Widely Used Bond Rating Systems

Moody's bond rating		Standard & Poor's bond rating	
Aaa	Highest quality	AAA	Highest quality
Aa		AA	
A		A	
Baa	Medium grade	BBB	
Ba		BB	
B	Speculative	B	Speculative
Caa		CCC	
Ca		CC	
C	Default	C	
		DDD	
		DD	Default
		D	

Bond Ratings. Before investing in these bonds, you should determine just how safe or how much risk is involved. Two well-known businesses specialize in assigning ratings to the many bond issues and periodically issue revisions. The Moody's and Standard & Poor's security analysts issue a sort of "report card" on many of the bond issues outstanding. While a student might be satisfied with receiving a "B" or a "C" for doing schoolwork, such a rating on a bond will indicate the indebted company is in serious trouble. Table 5-5 presents the ratings used by the two companies:

Reading the Bond Financial Pages. Whether you are an active investor or not, being able to read the financial pages of a newspaper can be helpful in your financial planning.

Bond quotations found in *The Wall Street Journal,* for example, provide considerable information about a bond issue. It is important to remember that bonds are expressed in terms of a percentage of face value or in terms of cents on a dollar's worth of face value. A bond quoted at 100 percent or 100 cents on the dollar would be denoting the bond's face value of $1,000.00. The number 101.5 indicates that the bond is selling at, or trading for, $1,015.00. That is, the bond is selling at 101.5 percent of the $1,000 of face value or 101.5 cents on a dollar of face value. If a bond is quoted at 98 (98 percent of face value or 98 cents on a dollar of face value), the bond can be purchased or sold for $980.00 (less commissions).

Bond interest is based on a specific percentage of the face value of the bonds. This is true even though at a given point in time the bond may be selling either above or below its face value. The *bond indenture* contract may state that it will pay 8 percent to the holder. Therefore, on a $1,000 bond, the investor can expect to receive $80 total interest each year (usually $40 every six months). The investor may receive the interest by check or through redeeming coupons attached to the bond document itself. The rate of interest on the bond document is also known as the *contract rate* or *nominal rate of interest.*

When one comes across such symbols as 8s 90, 3½ 92, or 8.7s 07 next to the corporation's name as shown in Exhibit 5-9, these can be easily interpreted as contract rates and maturity dates:

ABC Corp. 8s 96   ABC Corporation's 8% series bonds maturing in 1996
DEF Co. 3½ 92   DEF Company's 3½% bonds maturing in 1992
GHI Inc. 8.7s 07   GHI Incorporated's 8.7% series bonds maturing in 2007

The Current Yield column tells you the actual rate of interest to be earned if you were to have purchased the bond on that trading day. This also helps you to look for bonds that will give a specific rate of return without having to do your own calculating. This interest yield is determined by taking the annual dollar amount of interest to be received for a one-year period and dividing by today's bond trading price.

Another calculation usually computed by a brokerage house or a bank is the *yield to maturity.* This is the rate of return on that investment if the bond is held to its maturity. Since very few individuals intend to hold a bond until its maturity, this calculation is more academic.

The Volume column for bonds tells just how many individual bond documents changed hands on a particular trading day. The High, Low, and Close columns assist in determining the present selling (or buying) prices of the particular bond during the trading hours on a specific day. Remember that bonds are expressed in percentages of their face value. Therefore, a high of 101, a low of 99, and a close of 100 for a $1,000 bond translates into amounts of $1,010, $990, and $1,000, respectively, for that day. Note the bond listings in Exhibit 5-9.

The Net Change (Net Chg) column aids in determining a bond's price movement since the close of the preceding trading day. If a bond closed up one percentage point over the previous business day's closing price, the reader will know that a $1,000 bond closed $10 higher than the day before. On a minus one-eighth (−⅛), the bond closed $1.25 below that of the preceding trading day. These figures are found in the extreme right-hand column on a line of information. The symbol ". . ." indicates that the bond's closing price had not changed since the preceding day. Most net changes of bond prices are fractions of one percentage point. This may help to illustrate that bonds in general do have stable prices.

Among the other abbreviations to be found on the pages relating to bond quotations, one of the most common is "cv." It stands for convertible. Some bonds are issued with special provisions that allow the bondholders to exchange their bonds for so many shares of the corporation's common stock, an appealing feature to certain investors. It provides features of being a bondholder and a stockholder at the same time. At the bottom of most financial pages quoting bond information, a boxed insert explains the common symbols.

NEW YORK EXCHANGE BONDS

CORPORATION BONDS
Volume, $28,600,000

Bonds	Cur Yld	Vol	Close	Net Chg.
ANR 9⅝94	9.9	10	97⅝	+ 3⅜
ANR 11¾97	11.5	40	102	...
Advst 9s08	cv	25	84¼	...
AlaP 7⅞s02	9.3	5	84½	+ ⅜
AlaP 9½08	9.9	2	96⅜	+ ⅞
AlaP 12⅝10	12.0	17	105	...
AlskH 16¼99	14.7	45	110½	+ ½
AlskH 17¾91	14.9	5	118¾	+ ¾
AlskH 11¾92	11.4	20	103	...
Allgl 10¾99	18.6	83	57¾	− ¼
Allgl 10.4s02	18.2	98	57	− 2
Allgl 9s89	11.4	18	79	− 1¼
AlldC zr92	...	62	66	...
AlldC zr2000	...	21	31	+ ⅞
AldC dc6s90	6.4	2	93⅛	+ ⅛
AlldC zr97	...	5	42	+ ½
Alcoa 9s95	9.1	2	98⅝	+ ⅝
AForP 5s30	9.4	3	53¼	− ¾
ABrnd 8⅝90	8.7	35	99⅝	+ ⅛
AmMed 9½01	cv	48	87½	− ½
AmMed 8¼08	cv	30	75⅝	− 1⅜
AmMed 11s98	11.0	1	100	+ ½
ASmel 4⅝88	4.8	1	96 1/32	...
ATT 3⅞s90	4.2	45	93¼	...
ATT 8¾00	9.1	181	96	...
ATT 7s01	8.5	88	82¼	+ ⅛
ATT 7⅛03	8.7	172	81½	...
ATT 8.80s05	9.4	71	93½	− ⅝
ATT 8⅝s07	9.3	94	92½	+ ⅜
ATT 8⅝26	9.6	30	89⅝	...
Amoco 9.2s04	9.3	45	98¾	+ 1½
Amoco 8⅜05	9.4	10	89¼	− ¾
Amoco 7⅞07	9.3	20	85	...
Amoco 14s91	13.7	47	102½	...
Ancp 13⅞02f	cv	10	100	− 1
Apch 8.5s06	9.6	5	88¼	− 1¾
ArizP 7.45s02	9.1	9	81⅞	...
Arml 13½94	12.6	82	107½	+ 1½
Arml 9.2s00	11.0	46	84	+ 2
Arml 8½01	11.1	10	76¼	...
Asar 9¾2000	10.3	98	95	+ 1
AshO 8.8s00	9.8	10	90⅛	+ 2⅛
AshO 11.1s04	10.6	31	104¼	+ 2⅝
AsCp 11.85s89	11.4	5	104¼	+ ½
Atchsn 4s95	5.6	35	71¼	+ 1⅞
Atchn 4s95r	5.7	11	69¾	...
ARch dc7s91	7.4	50	95	+ ⅛
ARch 10⅞05	10.0	25	108½	+ ½
ARch 9¼93	9.1	100	102⅛	+ ⅛
AutDt 6½11	cv	1	120	+ ½
Avnet 8s13	cv	1	90½	+ ½
Avnet 6s12	cv	15	83	...
BRE 9½08	cv	13	99½	− ¼
Bally 6s98	cv	112	74	+ ½

Wednesday, January 20, 1988

Total Volume $28,690,000

SALES SINCE JANUARY 1

1988	1987	1986
$377,920,000	$566,321,000	$553,659,000

	Domestic Wed.	Domestic Tue.	All Issues Wed.	All Issues Tue.
Issues traded	663	701	667	703
Advances	290	355	291	356
Declines	243	212	246	213
Unchanged	130	134	130	134
New highs	11	12	11	12
New lows	12	7	12	8

Dow Jones Bond Averages

−1986− High	−1986− Low	−1987− High	−1987− Low	−1988− High	−1988− Low		---Wednesday--- −1988−		−1987−		−1986−	
93.65	83.73	95.51	81.26	88.19	86.92	20 Bonds	88.19	+0.05	95.40	+0.16	83.80	−0.04
95.79	81.85	98.23	79.51	88.75	86.65	10 Utilities	88.66	−0.09	98.20	+0.16	82.58	+0.07
91.64	84.82	93.10	83.00	87.71	86.96	10 Industrial	87.71	+0.18	92.59	+0.15	85.03	−0.14

Bonds	Cur Yld	Vol	Close	Net Chg.
CmwE 8¼07	9.9	10	83⅛	− ⅞
CmwE 9⅛08	9.9	25	91¾	+ 2¾
CmwE 13s12	11.9	10	109½	+ ¾
CmwE 10⅝95	10.1	5	105	...
Compq 5¼12	cv	959	123	− 6
ConEd 9⅜00	9.5	25	99	...
ConEd 7.9s01	8.9	6	88⅜	...
ConEd 7.9s02	9.0	20	88⅛	...
ConEd 7¾03	9.0	25	86	...
ConEd 8.4s03	9.2	11	91½	+ 3¼
ConEd 9⅛04	9.6	25	95⅛	+ ⅛
CnNG 9s95	9.1	37	98½	− 1¼
CnPw 4⅝91	5.3	5	86½	+ 2½
CnPw 5⅞96	7.8	10	75	− 1
CnPw 6⅝98	8.7	7	76	+ 1¼
CnPw 7⅝99	9.2	7	83	+ 1½
CnPw 8⅝00	9.9	1	87⅛	− 1⅞
CnPw 8⅛01	9.7	10	83¾	+ ½
CnPw 7½2020	9.6	11	77⅞	+ ¾
CnPw 11⅜94	10.9	9	104	...
CnPw 9¾06	10.4	27	94⅛	− ¾
Ctllnf 9s06	cv	7	95	− 1
CtlDat 12¾91	12.0	56	106	− 1⅝
CtlDat 8½11	cv	10	103	− 2
CoopCo 8⅝05	cv	94	60	− ½
CntryCr 7s11	cv	5	72	+ 1½
CrayRs 6⅛11	cv	42	100¼	− 1
CritAc 12s13	11.7	21	102½	+ ⅛
CritAc 13.30s14	12.8	10	104	+ ⅞

Bonds	Cur Yld	Vol	Close	Net Chg.
GTE 6⅝91	7.2	5	92⅝	...
GTE 9⅜99	9.5	19	99	− ⅞
GTCal 8⅞96	9.3	5	95⅛	− 1⅞
Gene 15¼94	14.9	10	102½	+ ⅝
Genrad 7¼11	cv	11	72	− 1
GaPw 7⅜01	9.2	25	80½	− ¾
GaPw 8⅛01	9.4	5	86⅛	− ⅜
GaPw 7⅝01	9.2	10	83	+ 1⅞
GaPw 7½02D	9.3	10	81	...
GaPw 11¾05	11.2	26	104½	− ⅜
GaPw 9⅞06	10.4	5	95	− 2
GaPw 10½09	10.5	5	99⅝	+ ⅛
GaPw 16s14	14.4	3	111⅜	+ ⅞
GaPw 10s16A	10.3	13	97	− 2
GaPw 10¾17	10.5	400	102	+ 1
GibFn 9¼08	cv	13	72¼	+ ⅞
vjGloMr 16⅛02f	...	53	22⅜	...
vjGloM dc13s03f	cv	2	21⅜	+ ¼
GdNgF 13¼95	13.0	32	101⅝	− ⅜
Gdrch 8¼94	9.0	5	91⅞	+ ¾
Gdyr 8.6s95	9.1	4	94	− 2
Grace 4¼90	cv	68	102	...
GreyF zr94	...	342	46⅜	− ⅝
GrowGp 8½06	cv	10	78½	...
Grumn 9¼09	cv	25	96¼	− 1¼
Gulfrd 6s12	cv	6	79½	− ½
GlfWn 7s03A	9.1	32	77	− ⅛
GlfWn 7s03B	9.1	2	77	− ⅛
GulfMo 5s56f	9.1	36	55	− 2

Bonds	Cur Yld	Vol	Close	Net Chg.
vjMcLn 12s03f	...	460	5	− ⅜
vjMcLn 14¼94f	...	70	5⅝	− ⅞
Mead 6s12	cv	25	87	− 1½
Melln 8.6s09	10.7	5	80⅛	− 1⅜
Melln 7¼99	9.3	25	78	...
MerLy zr06	...	53	23	...
MerLy zr91	...	27	72¼	+ 1¾
MichB 4⅜91	5.0	5	87¾	+ 1¾
MichB 9⅛18	9.6	10	95	+ 1½
MMM 8.85s	9.2	5	96¼	− ⅛
MKT 5½33f	...	3	48	...
MoAl 8.4505	9.4	5	90¼	− ⅛
Mobil 8½01	9.1	103	93	+ ¾
Mobil 14.4s04	13.3	75	108⅛	− ⅛
Mobil 13.76s04	12.7	102	108⅜	− ⅛
Mobil 8⅝94	8.7	90	98⅝	− ⅛
Mobil 8¾91	8.6	30	101⅜	+ ⅛
Monog 10s99	13.9	1	72	+ 1
Mons 8¾08	9.6	10	91⅛	+ 1¼
MntWC 7⅜88	7.4	20	99½	+ 1/32
MntWC 9s89	9.0	12	100½	...
MntWC 8⅜02	10.8	4	77⅞	+ ⅜
Moran 8¾08f	cv	4	45½	+ ½
MtSTl 9¾12	9.8	13	99⅛	− ⅞
MtSTl 8⅝18	9.5	10	91¼	+ 2¼
NAFCO 9s03	cv	35	75½	+ ½
NBI 8¼07	cv	15	52	...
Nabis 7¾s03	9.1	20	85	...
NacoFn 12s94	15.0	15	79⅞	+ 2⅞

Bonds	Cur Yld	Vol	Close	Net Chg.
PhilEl 10¼16	10.8	35	94½	+ ½
PhilM 14s91	13.7	16	102	− ¼
PhilM 15¼91	14.6	3	104⅝	+ ⅛
PhillP 12⅞92	12.3	10	105	− 1⅜
PhillP 12¼12	12.0	45	102¼	+ ¼
PhillP 11¼13	11.5	79	98⅛	− ⅜
PhilP 9¾95t	10.4	82	93¾	+ ⅛
PhillP 13⅞97	11.8	4	109¾	...
PhilP 14¾00	13.5	56	111	+ ½
Pillsb 14s91	13.8	15	101½	+ ¼
Pittstn 9.2s04	cv	37	86½	...
PopeTl 6s12	cv	70	82	− 1
PotEl 18s	cv	82	100	− ⅛
PrmCpt 5¾12	cv	24	74½	− ½
PrmeM 6⅝11	cv	7	103	− 1
Primca 6s93	7.9	5	75½	+ ⅝
ProcG 8¼05	9.0	29	91½	+ ¾
PSInd 7s02	9.1	6	77	+ ⅜
PSNH 18s89	19.2	11	93¾	+ ¼
PSNH 15¾88f	...	10	38 7/16	+ 1 3/16
PSNH 14⅜91f	...	7	34	+ ½
PSNH 15s03f	...	31	34½	+ ½
PSNH 17½04f	...	691	35	+ ⅜
PSNH 13¾96f	...	13	80¾	...
PSEG 9s95	9.1	5	99	...
PSEG 8½04	9.5	10	89¼	− 1½
PSEG 12s04	11.4	8	105	+ ½
Quak 7.7s01	8.9	1	87	+ 1
Quanx 15¼99	14.2	5	107½	+ 2
RJR 7⅜01	8.7	10	84½	+ 2⅜
RalsP 9½16	10.0	10	95	+ 2
Ramln 10s93	11.0	20	90¾	− ¼
Ramln 11⅝99	13.2	55	88	− 1
RapA72 7s94	12.9	8	54⅛	− 2⅞
RapA69 7s94	13.0	5	53¾	− 1¼
RapA 6s88	6.3	54	95 9/32	− 23/32
RapA 10¾03	16.8	30	64	− ⅝
RelGp 14s96	13.9	9	101	− ⅞
RelGp 9⅞98	12.4	5	79⅞	+ 2⅞
vjRepStl 8.9s95f	...	20	30	...
vjRepStl 12⅛03f	...	203	25	...
Revl 10⅞10	13.7	150	79½	− ⅞
Revln 11¾95	12.4	123	94⅝	+ ⅛
ReyM 6s12	cv	3	118	− 6
ReyTb 7⅞94	8.5	5	93⅛	+ ⅝
Rohr 12	...	1	77	+ 3
Rothch 7s11	cv	233	40½	− ½
Rowan 13¾96	13.4	36	102¾	...
SallM 7¾09	cv	5	193⅛	− 1⅞
Salmnln 90	...	80	97¼	− ¼
SanD 9¾08	9.8	5	99	+ ½
Savin 11⅜98f	37.6	10	30¼	− 2¾
Seagrm zr06	...	22	29	− ¼
Sears 8⅝95	8.6	25	99¾	− ¼
Sears 7⅞07	9.3	10	85	...
Sears 14⅛89	12.8	3	110	+ ⅜
Sears 12s94	10.5	26	114½	...

Tax-Exempt Bonds. Tax-exempt bonds are of interest to certain investors, as the Internal Revenue Service allows an exclusion for income tax purposes of the interest earned on certain types of public bonds. Examples of such bonds are those issued by states, counties, cities, school districts, fire and sewer districts, and so on. Perhaps the original incentive for such bonds was to have local people invest in these issues. These days investors can receive 5 or 6 percent tax-free income on such investments. That same investor might have to earn 8, 10, or 12 percent or more in taxable income just to end up with an after-tax net return of 5 or 6 percent. Another feature of the tax-exempt bond is that it allows the various governmental bodies to borrow money at lower interest rates. This helps to keep sales taxes and property taxes lower than they would otherwise be.

People who are in the higher income tax bracket find tax-exempt bonds attractive. A person earning over $200,000 and not paying any income taxes, for example, may be completely invested in these kinds of bonds. This is a legal way to avoid taxes, and you can take advantage of it. If this "loophole" is closed in the future, as some people are advocating, then the many governmental bodies will face serious problems of raising large sums of money and paying the interest.

There are drawbacks to owning state and local government issues. Many cities face serious financial problems as people have fled to the suburbs, abandoning the city to the poor and low-income people. Even shifts of the population within local areas as well as the change in the age and composition of that population can place a financial strain on school districts, parks, and basic services. Aging neighborhoods, school closings, and unused county hospitals are examples of today's problems in this area.

One must use the bond rating services of Moody's and Standard & Poor's to determine investment quality. The investor in a high-quality but small and relatively unknown sewer district bond often faces difficulty in finding a buyer when it comes time to sell the bond. Perhaps the following rule applies: Buy quality issues and ones that will mature within a few years.

Summary on Bonds. Investing in bonds other than those of the federal government requires homework in learning about bonds, a clear idea of a person's financial objectives and future income tax bracket, and an estimate of the future inflation rate. The federal bonds fulfill the need for building education funds and for retirement needs when safety and liquidity are the overriding objectives. Corporate bonds of the best quality may appeal to the person who is fully retired, that is, to someone who needs to revise his or her investments from higher risks (as with stocks and real estate) to lower risks. This shift of investments to corporate bonds is noticeable during recessionary periods, when investors are looking for a safe "parking place" for their money even though there may be some erosion resulting from inflation. Tax-exempt bonds in general appeal mostly to people in high tax brackets, people who probably have their emergency funds at satisfactory levels, and those who want a simplified invest-ment program. Tax-exempt issues appeal to large investors such as insurance companies, pension funds, and other tax-exempt foundations.

Your bank is a logical place to seek help in this area of bond investment unless you are knowledgeable on the topic and have an account with a reputable brokerage firm.

SUMMARY

Saving money is tied directly to the ability to satisfy human wants or desires. The act of saving may take place before, during, or even after the satisfaction of a want. The act of saving occurs at all times. The objective is to gain control and not let saving become the consequence of some other activity such as buying something on impulse and then saving to make the payments. Some of your savings must go toward preparing for retirement to supplement what might come from Social Security and company retirement programs. Saving and budg-eting are intermingled, and it is difficult to have one without the other. Save some of the money received regardless of how small or whatever the source. Establishing the regular habit is the key. Millionaires tend to be collectors of money rather than savers. Relatively speaking, they do not necessarily care for the things that money will buy.

The two principle ways for saving money are through careful spending and saving money (cash) before it is spent. Saving money before it is spent is usually better than trying to save money at the end of the month. Compound interest rewards two groups of people—those who start saving and investment pro-grams when they are young and those who have a long life. The time it takes to double one's income can be determined quickly by the use of the "Rule of 72."

An emergency fund should provide a minimum of three months' worth of take-home pay and up to six months' if one's job is seasonal, based upon commissions, or in the leisure recreational field. Emergency funds should be kept safe and insured in such places as commercial banks and insured savings and loan, mutual savings, and credit union institutions. U.S. Series EE and HH bonds and travelers checks may be additional means for keeping savings in a low-risk and convenient way other than in cash. High-grade corporate, state, and local government bonds may appeal to people for specific types of financial goals such as down payments on a home, children's education, or retirement. Table 5-6 summarizes financial goals and suggested low-risk media for accom-plishing it.

Exhibit 5-10 illustrates our basic financial pyramid with suggested basic insurance coverage and cash reserves. Your appropriate insurance needs can usually be implemented almost at once. Implementing plans for minimum-level checking accounts and savings programs will take time.

TABLE 5-6 Recap of Special Financial Goals and Media Strategy

Major financial goals	Beginning media strategy
Immediate cash emergency fund (1 month's take-home pay)	Bank checking and savings accounts, travelers checks
Fund to offset long-term layoff, plant shutdown, seasonal unemployment, natural disaster, strike, etc. (3 to 6 months' take-home pay)	Bank checking and savings accounts, S&L and credit union savings account
Special household appliance fund (1- or 2-year goal)	Bank, S&L, or CU savings accounts, bonuses, income tax refund, moonlighting
Vacation and long weekends' fund (specific dollar amount)	Bank, S&L, or CU savings accounts
New car replacement fund (5- to 8-year goal)	Bank, S&L, and CU savings accounts, long-term savings certificates
Car repair and maintenance fund	Separate small savings account
Home down payment fund (5-year goal)	Savings accounts, savings certificates, U.S. Series EE and HH bonds, certificates of deposit of $10,000
Corporation stock purchase plan	Savings account, deposit cash and dividends, purchase stock in $500–600 batches
Retirement fund (20- to 40-year goal)	U.S. Series EE bonds with interest deferred from taxes, other investments, stocks, real estate, CDs
Retirement income	Pension and Social Security, matured U.S. Series EE bonds that are exchanged directly for Series HH, dividend income

TIPS

1. Get on a cash-and-carry basis and avoid debt except for purchasing a modest first automobile, a home, or education.
2. If married or planning to have children, place all of one spouse's take-home pay in savings and live on one income.
3. Focus your attention on job enrichment, promotions, and moonlighting for a big chunk of income. Do not worry that savings are temporarily "parked" in insured savings account drawing 5 to 8 percent interest.
4. Open a bank account that is close to where you work or live. Avoid extra driving and time. Develop a long-term relationship with the bank for financial help.
5. When planning a vacation in a foreign country, have your bank establish an account or prepare a letter of credit with an affiliated bank in a city of that nation. This process is much cheaper and quicker than dealing through travelers check companies.

EXHIBIT 5-10   Basic Financial Pyramid

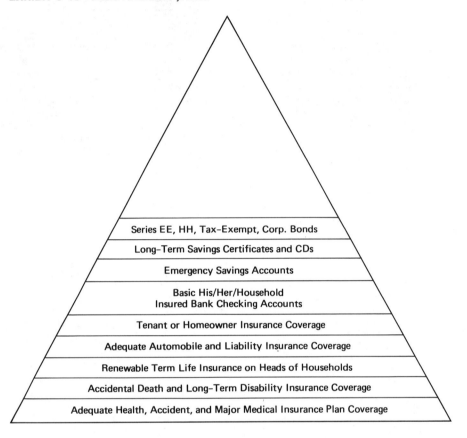

Series EE, HH, Tax-Exempt, Corp. Bonds

Long-Term Savings Certificates and CDs

Emergency Savings Accounts

Basic His/Her/Household
Insured Bank Checking Accounts

Tenant or Homeowner Insurance Coverage

Adequate Automobile and Liability Insurance Coverage

Renewable Term Life Insurance on Heads of Households

Accidental Death and Long-Term Disability Insurance Coverage

Adequate Health, Accident, and Major Medical Insurance Plan Coverage

6. The major goal of emergency money is safety, liquidity, and peace of mind, not earning the highest interest rate of return.

7. In an "equal marriage" or co-habitation arrangement, three separate bank accounts may need to be established: his, hers, and household (rent or mortgage, utilities, groceries, insurance, basic household furnishings, repairs, etc.)

8. At least one and maybe several savings accounts should be established to accomplish specific financial goals: emergency savings, vacation account, car repair and replacement, and so on.

9. Block impulse buying, take advantage of comparison shopping, and use coupons to save up to several hundred dollars a year. A $60 impulse purchase will offset the saving effort of $1,000 earning 6 percent for one whole year.

10. Avoid the banking fads, credit cards, lines of credit, overdraft privileges, and so on.

ADDITIONAL READINGS

"When Is It Your Money," *Consumer Reports,* November 1984, pp. 648–49.
"You and the Banks," *Consumer Reports,* September 1985, pp. 508–16.

GLOSSARY OF USEFUL TERMS

Annuity   Fixed amounts of money being received or paid at uniform intervals of time.

Baby Bonds   Bonds with a face value under $500.

Bank Deposit Slip   A receipt given by the bank to the depositor showing the date and the amounts deposited in the bank account.

Bank Statement   A record of account transactions in the bank account. The bank prepares a statement monthly. Included are such items as the beginning balance for the month, deposits made, checks written and other payments, and ending balance for the month.

Bearer Bonds   Bonds in which the name of the owner is not registered but is the property of whoever holds the bonds at a specific time.

Bond Discount   Bonds that are purchased for less than their face value.

Bond Premium   Bonds for which the buyer pays more than their face value.

Callable Bonds   Bonds that carry a clause stating that the indebted corporation reserves the right to retire the bonds prior to the maturity date.

Cash   Anything that a bank will accept as a deposit.

Cashier's Check   A check drawn by an authorized bank officer against the bank's own funds, more readily acceptable in commerce than a personal check.

Certificate of Accrual on Treasury Securities (CATS)   A type of zero coupon investment which are receipts representing ownership of future interest and principal payments of U.S. Treasury notes and bonds.

Certificates of Deposit (CDs)   Short-term marketable securities, paying a very high rate of interest and issued in amounts of $100,000 and above. CDs are often confused with saving certificates.

Certified Check   A check drawn by a depositor on his or her bank account stamped "certified" on the face and signed by a bank officer. At the time of certification, the amount of the check is deducted from the depositor's account.

Check   A negotiable instrument signed by a depositor directing the bank to pay a specified amount of money to a specified party.

Checking Account   Also called a demand deposit.

Collateral Trust Bonds   Bonds backed by securities of the company.

Commercial Banks   Banks that maintain checking accounts and provide a wide range of services for its customers.

Convertible Bonds   Bonds that may be exchanged by the owner for common stock of the same company under specific conditions.

Coupon Bonds   Securities having dated coupons that must be detached and presented to the bank to collect interest.

Credit Unions   Cooperatives that handle savings and loans for their members, restricted to a homogeneous industrial or employee group.

Currency   The paper money of a nation.

Debenture Bonds   Bonds backed solely by the credit of a company or governmental body.

Debit Card   Banking customer's plastic access card to automatic teller machines and electronic funds transfer.

Demand Deposit   Checking account in commercial banks. The depositor has the right to make withdrawals without advance notice.

Effective Rate of Interest   The actual rate of interest on an investment, includes interest earned on the principal, plus earnings resulting from additional compounding and payment of interest on daily, quarterly, or other balances.

Equipment Trust Bonds   Bonds used to finance the purchase of new equipment, as in the case of railroads.

Face Value   The denomination of an investment. Bonds of corporations usually have a face value of $1,000. An amount written on the document itself when printed. Face values can be at other amounts, say, $5,000 or $10,000.

FDIC (Federal Deposit Insurance Corporation)   A government insurance program providing coverage up to $100,000 on an account.

Federal Reserve System (The Fed)   A banking system consisting of a board of governors appointed by the president and Federal Reserve banks that serves as a clearinghouse for checks, is the agent for the government in distributing currency and coins, and maintains a sound credit policy for the nation by seeking to avoid sharp fluctuations in the business cycle. The United States is divided into 12 Federal Reserve districts.

FSLIC (Federal Savings and Loan Insurance Corporation)   A government insurance program providing coverage of up to $100,000 on an account.

Fully Registered Bonds   The owner's name is on the face of the bond documents; interest checks are mailed to the owner.

Indenture   The contract between the indebted corporation and the holder of a bond spelling out the rights and obligations of both parties.

Interest   Payment for the use of money that has been borrowed.

IRA (Individual Retirement Account)   A form of savings account (not a pension) designed for specific types of employees who are not covered by an employer pension plan.

M–1   The sum total of all coins, paper money, checking accounts (demand deposits), and nonbank travelers checks in the hands of the public throughout a nation. In the United States, the supply of money is announced every Thursday afternoon by the Fed.

M–2   The M–1 defined money supply plus certain checklike savings deposits.

Market Rate of Interest   The rate of interest created by the supply and demand for money.

Money   Anything generally accepted as a medium of exchange, a store of value, and a measure of value.

Municipal Bonds   A general term given to tax-exempt obligations issued by state and local governments to finance the building of roads, schools, public buildings, etc.

National Bank   Commercial banks that are chartered by the federal government and are members of the Federal Reserve System.

Negotiability   Documents such as personal checks, promissory notes, stocks, bonds, Treasury bills, etc., that can be transferred from one person to another by endorsement and delivery or by delivery without endorsement.

NOW (negotiable order of withdrawal)   A type of savings account that draws interest and on which an individual can write a check.

NSF-(not sufficient funds)   An overdraft.

Overdraft   A check drawn in an amount greater than the balance in the account at the time the check is presented to the bank for payment.

Promissory Note   A contract in which one party (the maker of the note) promises the payment of borrowed money plus interest to another party (the payee) at some specific time.

Registered Bonds   Bonds registered in the names of the owners.

Regulation Q   The provision set by the board of governors of the Federal Reserve System to establish bank interest rate ceilings on savings and time deposits.

Savings and Loan Associations   Companies that accept deposits by savers and lend funds to borrowers, usually homebuilders.

Savings Certificates   Certificates issued by banks, savings and loans, and mutual savings banks indicating that a depositor has money in the firm in special long-term deposit form.

State Bank   Commercial banks that are chartered by the individual states in which they do business.

Stop-Payment Order   A form executed by the drawer of a check ordering the drawee bank to stop payment on the instrument.

Thrift Institutions   A general term referring to credit unions, savings departments of banks, savings and loan associations, and mutual savings banks serving individual savers.

Time Deposits   Savings accounts in commercial banks or in savings and loan associations.

Travelers Check   An order, drawn on a bank's own funds, payable to the person whose name is written on the face, when countersigned by the person whose signature appears on the check.

Treasury Bill   Instruments issued by the U.S. Treasury Department in amounts of $10,000 and up for periods of three to six months. Issued (can be purchased) at a discount of, say 98 cents on the dollar and redeemed at 100 cents on the dollar at maturity. These are negotiable. Issued through Federal Reserve branches on Monday mornings. Customers of banks can usually acquire them by paying a modest commission of $15 to $20.

Usury   Illegal interest; interest in excess of the rate allowed by law.

Yield to Maturity   A term usually associated with investments purchased at less than 100 cents on the face or maturity value. The yield to maturity is higher than the current rate of interest and is as much as one would receive on the difference between the purchase price and the maturity value, hence increasing the total rate of return.

Zero Coupon Bonds   An obligation issued at a substantial discount to par ($1,000). A zero makes no periodic interest payments, but compounds semiannually at the yield-to-maturity rate. U.S. Series EE bonds are zero-type bonds. Investors might consider including zero coupon bonds in certain IRA and Keogh retirement accounts.

6

Consumer Credit, Consumer Awareness

LEARNING OBJECTIVES

Upon completion of Chapter 6, you should be able to identify and remember

- Key credit terminology such as consumer credit, credit, open account, open-end credit, acceleration clause, balloon contract, installment sales contract, and annual percentage rate.
- How a person may determine if he or she is overextended or is misusing credit.
- A three-step program to recover from a serious overextension of credit.
- The names of at least two places in your local area that assure consumers of receiving fair treatment or three groups in which to register credit complaints.
- How to calculate the true interest cost from a basic formula when information on the annual percentage rate is not shown.
- The kinds of businesses that loan money and the approximate rates of interest charged by each.
- The advantages and disadvantages of borrowing money or obtaining credit.
- The names of federal government legislation designed to protect the consumer creditor or set out rights and responsibilities.

154

OVERVIEW

Consumer credit has been a rapidly growing phenomenon in the complex maze of American economics. Some rough statistics will illustrate the growth and impact of credit.

The amount of consumer credit outstanding in the United States has jumped from a mere $6 billion in 1945 to $135 billion in 1971, $200 billion in 1976, and around $575 billion in 1987 and is still climbing. Despite its growing size, though, most families are managing this debt very well. In fact most families, 95 out of 100, tend to keep consumer credit to around 20 percent of their disposable income. This leaves only around 5 families out of 100 at any one time in serious financial trouble. Note also that not necessarily the same people are always in difficulty. Therefore, over a five-year period there could be as many as 25 families of 100 touched by a major problem.

Some 200,000 to 400,000 personal bankruptcies are filed in the United States each year. Many individuals and families are able to solve their problems before this trauma occurs. According to consumer credit counseling centers around the nation, the consumer in financial difficulty is a person 30 to 35 years of age earning $14,000 to $18,000 per year and owing $6,000 to $9,000 to 10 to 12 creditors. Estimates are that in 1987 there were more than 750 million credit cards of all versions, or just under 3 cards for every man, woman, and child. However, the 106 million Americans who have credit cards possess around 9.

It should be pointed out here that consumer credit excludes those debts related to home mortgages. When mortgage debt is added to consumer debt, then the percentage of disposable income going to debt rises to 23–25 percent. Home mortgage debt is discussed in Chapter 8.

What kinds of people have financial difficulties that cause them to seek credit counseling or bankruptcy? In general, debt is a problem for the middle-income class, but not exclusively. Low-income people usually cannot obtain credit, but the expenses that they incur from sickness, illness, or car repairs or loss of purchasing power or jobs may send them directly into bankruptcy. Credit abuse among middle- and upper-income people is similar to alcohol abuse; it cuts across the whole spectrum of white-collar and blue-collar professions. However, because of the incomes of these people, they usually can, with proper counseling, solve their problems and gain control over their finances in less than three years. Many can do so in half that time.

The recessions of 1979–1983 and the subsequent restructuring of the American economy have affected most households. Seemingly secure life-styles were suddenly in jeopardy. Economists and financial experts also found it difficult to either forecast or determine the severity of the slowdown. Other postwar recessions had been closely associated with business inventories and interest rates. The past tended to have lower inflation rates and lower interest rates. Life-styles continued to follow along more predictable and traditional patterns. As unem-

"You can't fire me! I owe money to everyone in this office!"

From *The Wall Street Journal*—
Permission, Cartoon Features
Syndicate.

ployment went up, inflation rates declined. When business inventories were once again in line with demand, the economy recovered. The following factors contributed to the inability of experts and laypersons to use past experience to guide them financially: (1) An inflation psychology influenced the purchase decisions of more people. The idea was to buy more things on credit now when the goods were affordable. (2) Housing prices had appreciated greatly, allowing many homeowners to use their houses as collateral for additional borrowing. (3) Inflation placed many Americans into higher tax brackets. While interest rates were the highest in recent history, the tax-deductible aspect softened the impact of the seemingly high cost of borrowing. (4) The impact of the energy shortage caused many people to change their life-styles and traditional spending patterns. (5) The impact of the recession was not felt uniformly across the nation. This made it difficult to develop a national policy relating to controlling interest rates, providing income tax relief, or identifying specific groups to be given relief. (6) Many U.S. commitments extended beyond its borders. The value of the dollar fluctuated, yet the nation had to sell its farm crops, arms, and machinery to pay for the crude oil necessary for automobiles, heating, and oil fuel and for other raw materials. (7) The greater emergence of the two-income household provided greater purchasing and credit power than in the past.

The U.S. economy is complex and does not always send out clear signals for the consumer to determine whether more debt or credit should be undertaken. The safest advice here is to avoid short-term consumer credit altogether. This philosophy may be easier to understand as a result of your reading the previous five chapters. However, a good money manager might well use his or her credit power to buy a long-desired piece of furniture that is advertised at a real bargain price. This is a good example of money sense. An emotional purchase made on impulse could lead to difficulties.

The balance of this chapter is designed to help you understand some of the basic terminology of credit, your rights, and your responsibilities in credit or loan transactions. You will also learn about the real cost of credit and the rates of interest charged by different lending agencies and credit grantors.

THE FIRST STEP IN CREDIT KNOWLEDGE IS . . .

The first step in credit knowledge is to know the basic credit terms:

Credit   The right granted by a creditor to a customer to defer payment of debt, incur debt and defer its payment, or purchase property or services and defer payment thereof.

Consumer Credit   Credit offered or extended to a person (not business units) in which the money, property, or service that is the subject of the transaction is primarily for personal, family, household, or agricultural purposes and for which either a finance charge is or may be imposed or which, pursuant to an agreement, is or may be payable in more than four installments.

Open Account   An account to be paid after one billing, such as a 30-day account. There is no interest or service charge.

Open-End Credit   Consumer credit extended on an open account pursuant to a plan under which (1) the creditor may permit the customer to make purchases or obtain loans from time to time, directly from the creditor or indirectly by the use of a credit card, check, or other device, as the plan may provide; (2) the customer has the privilege of paying the balance in full or in installments; and (3) a finance charge may be computed by the creditor from time to time on an outstanding unpaid balance. The term does not include negotiated advances under an open-end real estate mortgage or a letter of credit.

Revolving Account   An account with regular monthly payments based on the amount of the balance due.

Installment Sales Contract   Contracts in which a customer agrees to pay for a purchase by paying a certain amount of money each month for a specific number of months. (See sample contract, Exhibit 6-1).

With these definitions, you can determine quickly the type of credit being made available to you or sought by you when purchasing consumer goods at a department store or appliance shop or an automobile dealership.

EXHIBIT 6-1   Sample Credit Contract

Seller's Name: _____   Contract # _____

RETAIL INSTALLMENT CONTRACT AND SECURITY AGREEMENT

The undersigned (herein called Purchaser, whether one or more) purchases
from _____
(seller) and grants to _____
_____ a security interest, in,
subject to the terms and conditions hereof, the following described property.

QUANTITY DESCRIPTION AMOUNT

_____

Description or Trade in: _____

_____

Sales Tax	Sales Tax _____
	Total

Insurance Agreement

The purchase of insurance coverage is
voluntary and not required for credit.
___(Type of Ins.)___ Insurance coverage is available at a cost of $_____
for the term of credit.

☐ I desire insurance coverage

Signed_____
Date_____

☐ I do not desire insurance coverage

Signed_____
Date_____

PURCHASER'S NAME _____
PURCHASER'S ADDRESS _____
CITY _____ STATE _____ ZIP__
1. CASH PRICE $____
2. LESS: CASH DOWN
         PAYMENT $____
3.   TRADE-IN   ____
4.   TOTAL DOWN
         PAYMENT   ____ $____

5. UNPAID BALANCE OF
   CASH PRICE $ $____
6. OTHER CHARGES:
   _____ $____
   _____ $____
7. AMOUNT FINANCED $____
8. FINANCE CHARGE $____
9. TOTAL OF PAYMENTS $____
10. DEFERRED PAYMENT
    PRICE (1 + 6 + 8) $____
11. ANNUAL PERCENTAGE
    RATE   ____%

Purchaser hereby agrees to pay to ____
_____
at their offices shown above the "TO-
TAL OF PAYMENTS" shown above in
_____   monthly   installments   of
$_____   (final   payment   to   be
$_____)   the first installment being
payable _____ 19____, and all
subsequent installments on the same day
of each consecutive month until paid in
full. The finance charge applies from
_____

Signed   _____

Notice to Buyer: You are entitled to a copy of the contract you sign. You have the right to
pay in advance the unpaid balance of this contract and obtain a partial refund of the finance
charge based on the "Actuarial Method." [Any other method of computation may be so
identified, for example, "Rule of 78's," "Sum of the Digits," etc.]

WHO GETS CREDIT AND WHY

A long-standing and misunderstood feature in the money and banking world is the paradox surrounding the area of credit and loans: "Those who really want and need credit cannot usually obtain it, and those who really do not need it or want it can easily get it." When this condition is analyzed more closely, we can see why certain people can get credit. First, these individuals or families usually have a steady, full-time job and a very steady income. Steady income is the key point in the credit world. People who borrow money or who are granted credit must pay back not only the invoiced value of money, goods, or services received but also an additional amount called interest. The payments must be made regardless of any financial problems.

A second criterion that will help a person or family to acquire credit includes such things as the length of time and potential tenure with current employer, the time with past employer, the length of residence at current apartment or home, how long certain kinds of insurance have been in effect, length of customer patronage at stores where the family is known, and so on.

A third factor in the minds of credit grantors and money lenders is age. Emancipated youths still under the age of majority probably cannot obtain credit. Contracts with minors are voidable by the minor in most instances. Teenagers in a long-established family in the community may receive department store credit cards in their own names. But in such arrangement the parents may be required to make payment if the youth does not. This is tantamount to the parent's being a co-signer, a rather risky and undesirable practice. It is a better idea to allocate an accountable allowance.

A fourth factor for a good credit customer is having the right kinds of assets—another paradox. Grantors like to see cash in the bank, savings accounts, life insurance policies, shares of blue chip stocks or bonds, equity in a home, fully paid automobile, and so on.

The wrong kind of assets are those for which the resale value is low, heavy and expensive maintenance is required, insurance is expensive or very difficult to obtain, or the asset is subject to neglect, vandalism, theft, and so on. Examples are trendy clothing, expensive and difficult-to-service foreign cars, stereo equipment, TV sets, guns, and recreational equipment.

The likelihood of everyone's being an ideal credit applicant is rare. Therefore, it is possible to apply many times to various firms who give credit or make loans. If you meet the criteria and are an employee in a company that has a credit union, the credit union will probably give you the best break in interest rates. The other extreme is to use a pawnshop to obtain cash. The other sources (banks, insurance companies, finance companies, etc.) fall somewhere in between. It pays to shop around for credit. The degree of risk to be assumed by the grantor of credit or loans is noted in the annual percentage rate to be charged. Some of the rates of interest seem extremely high. However, all such firms received their guidelines from laws enacted by state legislatures.

EQUAL CREDIT OPPORTUNITY

The Federal Equal Credit Opportunity Act prohibits credit discrimination on the basis of race, color, religion, national origin, sex, marital status, or age (providing that the person has the capacity to enter into a binding contract). The act prohibits discrimination because all or a part of a person's income comes from a public assistance program. It is against federal and state laws for a creditor to place extra requirements on women. Change of name upon marriage or separation or divorce should not jeopardize one's credit history or require reapplication for credit. Creditors must consider alimony, child support, or maintenance payments as income if the credit applicant is receiving them.

ESTABLISHING CREDIT

Even when you are reasonably sure of qualifying for credit, it does not come automatically in most cases. Credit is a privilege, not a right. No corporation, utility company, department store, medical office, auto repair shop, bank, or finance company is under any obligation to extend credit to anyone.

You may be a person with seemingly the right background, and credit should be easily obtained. You have a good steady job and income, savings accounts, life insurance, some quality stocks, a home being purchased; however, you are turned down by a gasoline company or department store when you applied for a charge card. The problem here may be that you are too well organized and too financially sound for the credit world. You are on a cash-and-carry basis, almost un-American. You are a person who manages assets very well, but no one knows how you will manage credit. And, frankly, the people in the world of credit have had customers who showed good asset management abilities but had poor credit management skills.

When applying for credit with a major business firm, you are probably among hundreds, perhaps thousands, of people applying for credit. Your application is probably processed along with many others by a credit department functionary who must work within company policies and procedures. One of these procedures is called a credit history search. Companies routinely granting credit subscribe to a credit rating bureau service. If your name is not in the rating bureau's data bank, you will probably be turned down.

What can you do when you are turned down for credit, particularly if it is due to lack of credit history? First, assess the business firm with whom you are dealing. It should be a well-known company with a good reputation in the community. If you have been in the community for a long time and are well established, write a letter to the company's credit department manager stating that you were turned down and that you want to know the reasons. This letter is

Pepper . . . and Salt

THE WALL STREET JOURNAL

"If 18% credit-card interest is 'reasonable,' how come 5¼% interest on deposits is 'generous?' "

From *The Wall Street Journal*—
Permission, Cartoon Features
Syndicate.

necessary because it tells the company that you know how to use the "system," particularly if you have written a very businesslike letter, and your application is likely to be reviewed by a supervisory person in the credit department. Such a person may be able to read more from your data than the first reviewer and may grant credit to you. This person may call you and ask additional questions or ask that you come in for a second interview. This may result in your receiving the credit.

What happens if you are still turned down? You might try another firm in the community that does similar business. If a second reputable firm turns you down, then you had best reassess your situation. Are you applying for credit during the downturn of the business cycle? Are your assets the "wrong kind"? Is your job all that secure? Is the company you work for financially sound? Have you lived in the community long enough to satisfy your creditors? Are you living in a house or apartment with several other people? If someone moves out, could you stay and make the larger payments?

Lenders of money or firms extending credit are reviewing your application for a specific profile. This profile is sometimes called the "three C's of credit." The first is *character*. These are your personal characteristics for business—honesty, sense of responsibility, money sense, judgment, and so on. The second is *capacity*. This capacity relates to your ability to repay the loan or credit—your job and job security, your salary or wage, and tenure on the job. The third is *capital*. These are the "right kind" of assets—home, cars, stocks, bonds, valuables, and so on.

It may be that you will have to establish an actual credit history. This can be done by establishing a savings account at your bank or savings and loan association. Next, ask for a loan of, say, $500 for one year against your savings passbook or similar security. When you take out such a loan and repay it, this information will be on your bank records and will provide you with the credit history you need. When you apply for credit at a department store again and they ask you if you have ever had credit or borrowed money in the past, you have this history for the store's own verification.

In brief, let us assume that you have $1,000 in a savings account at the bank earning 5 percent interest. You request a loan of $500 for one year with the loan installments in the form of 12 monthly payments. The bank might charge interest of 1 percent per month on the unpaid balance for this secured loan. The real cost of borrowing the $500 is 7 percent (12 percent − 5 percent).

In many instances, people find it worth the price to pay to gain credit history, to have the convenience of credit cards versus carrying cash. Personal checks are not as acceptable as the bank cards, gasoline charge cards, and the charge cards of major national department stores. Many of these same individuals who want credit cards have no intention of "running up" large balances and using the credit. These bank and gasoline credit cards may well come in handy on trips and vacations but not in everyday situations. It is a good idea to keep some cash and travelers checks.

Before leaving this section, let us list some typical questions that are likely to be asked whether you are a new person to the world of credit or are applying for additional credit. Be sure to answer such questions in a firm and businesslike way:

1. Are you presently employed with a firm beyond the probationary period?
2. Is your current salary or wage large enough to permit making payments?
3. Do you currently owe money to department stores, banks, small loan finance companies, and so on, and, if so, how much?
4. Have you ever had your salary or wages subject to garnishments?
5. Have you ever filed for bankruptcy. When?
6. Are you now or have you been subject to legal action involving indebtedness?
7. How long have you lived in your present home?
8. What is the equity in your present home?
9. How long have you rented your apartment?
10. What credit cards do you presently have?

THE COST OF CREDIT—WHO CHARGES WHAT?

The Truth in Lending Act was passed by the U.S. Congress and went into effect July 1, 1969. The act requires that a person have sufficient information to compare the cash price of an item with the total deferred price when purchased on credit. This act is enforced under the provisions of Regulation Z of the Federal Reserve System. While this law has been on the books for many years and businesses must comply with the law, nationwide studies still indicate a high level of misunderstanding in the area of credit costs. Many schools are developing consumer survival programs to address to the lack of consumer financial skills. The following are essential terms for installment credit:

Installment or Deferred Payment Price   The total cost of the item being purchased on a credit plan or on an installment contract. It is made up of the down payment, the amount financed, and the finance charge.

Amount Financed   Amount of credit being requested or used.

Finance Charge   Cost of the credit expressed in terms of dollars.

Annual Percentage Rate   The number such as 6 percent, 12 percent, 18 percent, or 33 percent that results when the **amount financed** is compared with the **finance charge.** Rates of interest are always viewed in relation to a one-year time period, even though the contract may extend for more than one year or less than one year.

Total Number of Payments   Sum of the amount financed plus the finance charge divided by the amount of each payment.

Since 1969 anyone desiring a loan or credit must be presented with all important financial information. Suppose that you have to borrow $525.46 to have your car engine repaired. You could repay the loan back over 25 months. If you try to borrow the money from a bank or finance company, the firm would have to furnish all the information required of the Truth in Lending Act. The potential lender would probably present you with the following information before you committed yourself to such a loan: The *note is payable* in 25 equal *installments* of $29.00 each. The *amount financed* is $525.46, the *finance charge* is $199.54, and *total payments* are $725.00. The *annual percentage rate* is 31.76 percent.

The 31.76 percent annual percentage rate should cause you to shop around, even though you may well be able to handle the $29.00 monthly payments over the next two years. On the other hand, state laws allow such high interest rates. Legitimate interest rates charged by the various institutions in accordance with state laws are shown in Table 6-1. However, deregulation is changing many of these rate charges.

Whenever possible, borrowing from your own credit union is the least expensive and the pawn shop the most expensive legal place from which to obtain money.

TABLE 6-1 Sample Loan Rate Charges

Type of firms	Legal rates charged	Dollar limitations
Credit unions	6½– 12%	$ 50–3,000
Commercial bank loans	7 – 12	300–5,000
Bank credit cards	12 – 18	1–3,000
Savings and loan companies	7 – 12	Amount on deposit
Department store credit	12 – 18	1–500
Small loan finance companies	12 – 36	10–1,000
Pawn shops	36 –120	1–300
Illegal loan sharking	1,200 and up	None

DETERMINING THE ACTUAL INTEREST RATE

There may be a situation in which you are presented with an opportunity to acquire some item on a payment plan. While a business firm legally is required to present the actual interest rate to the buyer, an individual may offer some installment plan but may not understand or determine the interest rate related to the transaction.

The best way to describe the problem of determining the interest rate in a transaction is by example. Suppose that you have been looking for a good used stereo set and you see a notice on a local bulletin board: "FOR SALE! Good used stereo set—amplifier, tuner, turntable, cassette unit, and quality speakers. Cash price $275, or $25 down and $30 per month for 10 months."

How much is the interest rate on the proposed installment plan? It is necessary to use the following formula to find the approximate rate of interest charged:

$$R = \frac{2(PD)}{L(n + 1)}$$

where

R = rate of interest
P = period (when the payment periods are monthly, use the number 12; if weekly, use 52)
D = dollar costs, that is, the dollar amount of interest or finance charge
L = dollar amount of the credit extended to the buyer or money loaned to a borrower (cash price minus down payment)
n = number of payments or installment payments
2 = a constant used with this formula

To solve,

$$R = \frac{2\ (12 \times \$50)}{\$250\ (10\ +\ 1)} = \frac{\$1,200}{\$2,750} = .43636\ (43.64\%\ \text{rate of interest})$$

The $50 amount of finance charge is arrived at by two steps: (1) $25 down payment plus 10 payments at $30 equals $325, the total installment price for the stereo, and (2) the $325 installment contract price minus the cash price of the stereo of $275 ($325 − $275 = $50). The amount of the credit to be extended is $250: the $275 cash price and the cash of $25 needed for the down payment ($275 − $25 = $250).

What would you do? Would you go ahead and buy the stereo? Would you make a counteroffer with a higher down payment and smaller monthly payments? The 43.64 percent rate of interest should persuade you to reconsider your priority of a stereo set or at least do some more shopping.

A FEW MORE WORDS ABOUT INTEREST

Chapter 5 provided basic information about term interest from the investor's point of view. The other side is the debtor's responsibilities in a contractual relationship. A couple of observations are in order: (1) Charging interest has been accepted business practice since the earliest of times, and the rates of 12 to 20 percent are fairly common. (2) The act of borrowing or obtaining credit causes us to pay back more than the original or invoiced price of the goods and services, this additional amount being the interest charge. (3) The failure to make the interest payments when they become due provides the creditors with the right to institute legal action. Debtors have always been dealt with harshly. In the past, it was death or imprisonment; today, the ultimate weapon is bankruptcy, an event that stays on your credit records for 10 years.

To avoid problems relating to interest, review the following credit matters: (1) Determine if you really want this item badly enough to go into debt or borrow money. (2) Keep consumer debt below 20 percent of your disposable income. (3) Keep debt contracts below 36 months. (4) Always shop around for the best interest rate.

The term "usury" is used when there is a general belief that the interest rates charged are excessive or are being set at rates that are above legal limits. In the United States, it is the state legislatures that establish the legal interest rate ceilings for different credit- or loan-extending businesses, and it is legal for a small loan company to charge 36 percent on the first $500, 18 percent on $501–1,000, and 12 percent on $1,001–2,500.

In addition to the interest rate charged on a loan or credit request, other special fees may be added to the transaction. These become part of the basic dollar costs of borrowing or the "finance charge," for example, some form of creditor's life insurance. This is optional, but it adds another $2–3 to the con-

TABLE 6-2 Understanding the Annual
Percentage Rate

Monthly rate	Annual percentage rate
½ of 1% per month × 12 =	6%
¾ of 1% per month × 12 =	9
1% per month × 12 =	12
1½% per month × 12 =	18
2% per month × 12 =	24
3% per month × 12 =	36

tract. It is also legal to charge a fee for a credit investigation or a fee for late payment.

Many times, interest is quoted simply as 1 percent, 1½ percent, 2 percent on the unpaid balance, and so on. To understand the annual percentage rate (APR), multiply the rate times 12. Note the translations in Table 6-2.

USING CREDIT WISELY

There are only a few major areas in one's life where credit or borrowing money has merit: to buy a home, to obtain additional education or job skills, to purchase an automobile to commute to work or to buy special tools, and to meet an employer requirement. Other needs should be saved for by allocating portions of one's disposable income to special wants, travel, and contingency funds. Chapters 3 and 5 should provide sufficient information for avoiding any need for consumer credit.

There is a phase of credit that many people view as abuse of credit, as when a person purchases some toiletry items and maybe a package of candy or cigarettes and charges the items on a bank credit card. But this is probably a variation of a practice used many years ago when people normally charged purchases at the local general store day to day and then settled their account at the end of the week or month. The only problem with this practice is that a person will tend to overbuy, and the habit might get out of control. Finally, one should avoid completely any installment loan agreement where the borrower must make a very large lump-sum final payment known as a *balloon payment*.

SIGNS OF POTENTIAL DEBT TROUBLE

A major illness, the loss of a job, a lawsuit, and so on can cause debts to pile up quickly. On the other hand, many people with good, steady, well-paying jobs go to credit counselors for help in settling several thousands of dollars of high-interest installment consumer debt. These people just did not get deep into debt overnight.

A technique for spotting trouble before it becomes serious is to ask "attention-directing questions" such as, Do I pay off all my credit purchases at the end of the month? Have any outstanding balances been increasing instead of remaining stable or declining? Am I using credit cards to purchase things that I normally paid cash for a few months ago? Do I use a credit card to pay for basic groceries? Do I have to borrow money to take a vacation? Do I seem to have less cash for allowances or mad money? Have I stopped comparison shopping? Am I buying things because of emotional reasons lately? Am I using credit to impress others? Am I using credit to foster such addictive habits as tobacco, drugs, alcohol, and gambling? Have I stopped keeping track of recording and budgeting that I used to do?

Am I receiving repeated notices to pay bills? Have I been receiving calls from collection agencies to pay my bills? Have I been thinking about getting a bill consolidation or bill payer loan? Do I seem to worry about money problems most of the time? Do my consumer debts amount to more than 20 percent of my take-home pay? Do I have installment debts that run more than 36 months? Have I stopped taking the newspaper?

Have I asked for longer and longer time periods in which to pay off my debts? Do I avoid communicating with my spouse prior to buying major consumer items—TV, camera, another new car? Am I trying to borrow money from my friends and relatives to purchase consumer items? Have I bought items from high-pressure door-to-door salespeople—magazines, encyclopedias, insurance? Do I make only the minimum monthly payments?

Most people who are in control of their finances will answer "no" to these questions no matter when or how many times they are asked.

IF YOU ARE ALREADY IN DEBT . . .

One motivation for reading this type of book or enrolling in a course on personal money management is for the purpose of getting out of debt. Many students are formally counseled in these kinds of classes.

Getting out of debt is a lot like trying to lose weight. Most people are suddenly aware that their debt problems require corrective action. Like added weight, people accumulate their debt over a period of time. It is good sense to get out of debt over a specified time period. Just as a crash diet may do harm to your body, getting out of debt overnight might strain your body and psychological well-being.

The reason you can afford to get out of debt over several months, for example, is the fact that you still have income from your job. Perhaps a spouse is also working. Therefore, each month or each payday money is available for debt reduction.

The following steps are usually advocated by financial consultants and debt counselors, whether the advice is free or for a fee:

1. Destroy all your credit cards, gasoline credit cards, bank cards, and bank debit cards. Then you will have to pay for everything by cash, check, money order, or travelers check.
2. Conduct a series of frugality months by declaring a moratorium on further purchases of all clothing, major household appliances, recreational equipment, expensive outside entertainment, and so on. Limit all out-of-home meals to carried lunches.
3. Make all efforts to pay off all your creditors as soon as possible.

Most people cannot get out of debt overnight because many basic expenditures must be paid for and they are impacted by inflation, namely, food, rent or mortgage, utilities, transportation, and medical insurance. The difference between your take-home pay and these essential costs of living can be allocated for the purpose of debt repayment.

It may be a good idea to prepare a worksheet on the debts you owe. This will show you the creditor, balance owed, required monthly, or minimum monthly, payment, length of contract, and total of payments to be made for a month. The worksheet used in Exhibit 6-2 might serve as a sample.

This format will help you to design a plan to get out of debt. If you were in such a situation and incurred no additional debt, you could be completely out of debt in 25 months ($6,787.24 ÷ $277.37). If your frugality program could provide $375 per month, your total debts could be liquidated in around 18 months.

EXHIBIT 6-2 Worksheet for Determining Personal Debt

Creditor	APR	Balance Owed	Monthly Minimum Required	My Plan	
E-Z Finance (auto)	18%	$5,682.96	$210.48	Pay	$210.48
Jones Dept. Store (refrigerator)	18	478.31	31.89	Pay	31.89
Sims Dept. Store (clothing)	12	367.25	10.00	Pay	10.00
HiWay Gas Co.	12	133.72	10.00	Pay	10.00
3rd Nat'l Bank	18	75.00	10.00	Pay	10.00
Quick Loan Co.	36	50.00	5.00	Pay off	50.00
Totals		$6,787.24	$277.37		$322.37

REMEDIES

It may be that your debts cannot be paid off out of your salary. If you have lost your job or if your income has dropped sharply, you will need to contact your creditors. Explain your circumstances. The main point is not to panic. If you have let some of your bills become delinquent, you may be receiving threatening letters.

You might try to make some payment each week on your accounts. If you have explained your situation and continue to make small regular payments, your good-faith efforts may just save your credit rating and your integrity. If you have been dealing with the reputable firms in your community and if your loss of income appears temporary and your credit purchasing does not reflect gross irresponsibility, you will survive this experience. Also, credit will probably never look so appealing to you in the future. If these approaches are not successful, your next steps should be those discussed in the following sections.

Nonprofit Credit Counseling Service

There are over 200 consumer credit counseling firms operating throughout the United States. These groups receive their funding from business firms. Some charge modest fees for the services rendered beyond a credit analysis. If you sign up for a counseling program, these firms will formulate a program that will follow the steps mentioned earlier. They will also contact your creditors and negotiate longer, smaller, and more manageable payment programs. The Credit Counseling Service of (city) _____ will be found in the White Pages in the telephone directory. Department stores and Better Business Bureaus can put you in touch with these groups.

These nonprofit groups should not be confused with small loan companies that offer debt counseling through the use of high-interest "bill payer" or "debt consolidation" loans. The nonprofit groups should not be confused with the many individuals who are "financial counselors" who also charge large fees.

Chapter 13—The Wage Earner Plan

Article I, Section 8, of the U.S. Constitution offers two forms of legal relief from debts. Chapter 13 provides that individual workers can develop a three-year plan to pay off debts. There is a modest filing fee. The legal fees for going through this process can become a part of the deferred payment program. The wage earner makes payment to a federal court-appointed *trustee* who can charge a fee based on the percentage of debts plus expenses. Many creditors will go along with such a plan. While under the protection of Chapter 13, creditors cannot repossess the debtor's assets or have the wages of the debtor subject to garnishment.

Bankruptcy

Bankruptcy is the second alternative offered under the U.S. Constitution for legal relief from debts. It will cost the debtor money to file for bankruptcy. The debtor's attorney will want a cash fee paid to him or her before undertaking the case. While temporary insolvency can happen to both individuals and businesses, bankruptcy results when the total of all debts exceeds the total value of assets owned. A substantial revision in bankruptcy law was made under the Bankruptcy Reform Act of 1978.

To begin the process, proper papers must be filed. Then a court-appointed "referee" reviews the debtor's finances and claims by creditors. A trustee is appointed by the referee to carry out the process of liquidating assets and make payments to creditors according to ranking of debts. In a few months the debtor is notified that the debts have been discharged.

Bankruptcy is not a pleasant process, nor is the bankrupt party completely free from all financial responsibility. The bankrupt is allowed to keep some basic assets—limited value assets of a house and land, a modest car, clothing, tools of one's trade, and so on. However, certain financial obligations must still be paid—certain taxes and fines, education loans, willful damage to others or their property, alimony and child support, funds obtained from fraud, embezzlement, and misappropriation while in a position of trust, and so on.

At least 200,000 personal bankruptcies occur each year. That amounts to 1.0 million persons in 5 years and 2.0 million in 10 years. The numbers 7 and 10 are significant in the world of bankrupts and creditors. Bankruptcy courts will not allow you to petition for bankruptcy within 6 years of previous bankruptcy. Credit rating agencies will maintain the record of a bankruptcy for 10 years on an individual's credit records. While the process of bankruptcy is relatively brief, the effects of bankruptcy are long lasting. If you went into bankruptcy at age 25, the records of this act would be with you to around age 35. If you went bankrupt at age 32, your credit records would carry the information until you are 42. Since these years are critical to your ability to reaching financially related goals, the stigma of being a bankrupt can prevent you from taking advantage of credit at strategic points in your career or business.

Bankruptcy by an individual is a matter of public record. Furthermore, the fact that you cannot file for bankruptcy again for seven years makes you prey to all sorts of lending organizations. Don't be surprised to find your former bank or aggressive loan company wanting to offer you credit again knowing full well that you cannot become a bankrupt soon. Exhibit 6-3 presents a composite of typical ads in the classified sections of newspapers:

```
┌─────────────────────────────────────┐
│          RECENT BANKRUPT?           │
│  Want a new start? I can finance you! Let │
│  me help put you in a decent car. Don't │
│  settle for a junk heap. All you need is a │
│  good job and a reasonable down payment │
│  to drive a quality automobile.     │
│     Call Mr. Sharp     555-3660     │
└─────────────────────────────────────┘
```

EXHIBIT 6-3 Composite Loan
Company Ad

Avoid these solicitations. As a recent bankrupt, you probably still have serious shortcomings when it comes to managing money. Past mistakes and unpleasant experiences are the best (but costly) teachers in life. A cash-and-carry life-style will be a new and perhaps difficult experience, but the peace of mind from being on a cash basis should be a welcomed change from the hassle of creditors' calls and letters. Credit can be like alcohol and drugs to some people. Some people abstain from it; others deal with credit in moderation; still others will become addicted and controlled by it.

OTHER CONSUMER ASSISTANCE

This text has not emphasized the growing area of "consumerism" for a couple of reasons. First, consumerism is a rapidly expanding law-oriented field and can be the topic of a book of its own. Second, many of the consumers' rights are codified in 50 different sets of state laws, codes, and ordinances. The emphasis throughout this book is on improving your "how-to" skills and on keeping your financially oriented goals in mind. Up to now, we have been offering suggestions in planning, organizing, and budgeting, with some elements of shirt-sleeve economics being introduced. Discussion of a few areas of the field of consumerism is in order.

Consumer awareness in the marketplace has increased greatly in the 1960s and 1970s. The work of Esther Peterson, consumer advisor to presidents, and Ralph Nader, advocate of safety in transportation and products, are well known to the public. Lesser known men and women are working to improve the consumer's leverage in the marketplace.

Local newspapers, radio, and TV stations carry consumer news and tips. The consumer protection divisions of state attorney general offices have telephone hot lines, conferences, and workshops to help consumers. The position of ombudsman is becoming more common among governments, colleges, newspapers, and corporations to cut through the bureaucracy and aid the "consumer."

The final sections of this chapter will suggest ways of finding and how to get the best use of a lawyer's services. There will be a few paragraphs for the purpose of "pointing" you in the direction of groups or agencies that can help you in consumer financial matters.

Lawyer/Attorney

A *lawyer* is one whose profession it is to advise others in matters of law or to represent clients in legal matters. An *attorney* is a person legally empowered to act for another, especially a lawyer. Finding a lawyer who is well informed on the services needed at a specific time and who is sincerely interested in your legal problem is not always easy. Furthermore, knowing how to use a lawyer's services correctly and efficiently is even more difficult.

A few words are necessary to describe the role of these professional men and women in the United States. When De Tocqueville visited America in 1831, he noted the unique role of the lawyer in the nation's economic and social structure. Even today, we do not take on any major activity without involving a lawyer's advice.

Today, in the United States, there is 1 lawyer for every 390 people. In Germany, there is 1 lawyer for every 3,000 people. In Japan, there is 1 lawyer for every 14,000 people. America's multicultural heritage makes written law and lawyers' services customary for resolving disputes.

In brief, the evolution of law in the Western world has placed an emphasis on *words* to spell out the intent of a law. Two American maxims of "read the fine print" and "to the letter of the law" reflect our concern for written or statute law. This concern for fine print is again evident when American and Japanese business try to negotiate a trade contract. The Japanese might be satisfied with a 4- or 5-page letter of agreement to perform specific work. The Americans, however, will insist on a 65-page, single-space typed document with many sections, paragraphs, precise terminology, procedures, dates, time, and so on.

Therefore, Americans require their lawyers to know the English language and have the ability to read for specific purposes. All crafts, skills, and professions have special terminology and so does the profession of law. Because of the role of law in America, most basic business documents of consumers will tend to reflect this emphasis on words to spell out intent. We have all suffered to read some such document as an auto or life insurance policy, an apartment rental agreement, an installment sales contract for an automobile, or a real estate deed. Many of these documents have been made uniform, but they are still difficult for the layperson to read and understand.

All lawyers follow a basic curriculum while in law school. Those who go on to practice law will work in one of the more fundamental areas—reading contracts; advising and making recommendations; answering specific legal questions; preparing basic documents relating to land purchases or sales, contracts, simple wills, trust; representing clients in a court of law or with client's customers as an agent; and so on.

The following points develop a composite of lawyers' roles and services, not just the steps to take to find a good one.

Finding a Lawyer. Ask your friends who have had good service from a particular lawyer over a long period of time. Contact your county bar association. These people will try to determine if you have need for legal services and will refer you to a list of attorneys. If you are a college student, there may be lawyers who serve as part-time instructors in various law courses. Many lawyers are still forbidden to advertise their services, and others are reluctant to do so. Therefore, teaching, performing public service, or engaging in volunteer activities has been an acceptable and traditional custom for obtaining new clients. Approaching an attorney in these informal situations may provide an opportunity to determine a potential compatible relationship. The new legal clinics located at major shopping centers are also an attempt to have people with legal concerns begin initial contacts in a nonthreatening atmosphere.

Conflicts of Interest. A lawyer should determine very quickly and be very frank if your needs are in conflict with his or her practice. If the lawyer represents a string of apartment house owners and landlord associations, do not expect this person or firm to be an advocate if you are a tenant with landlord problems. If the legal firm derives most of its income from representing managements of business, hospitals, or schools, do not expect much help if you are an employee experiencing problems with your employer. The lawyer is supposed to be your advocate. While an attorney may be intellectually honest, just the appearance of a conflict of interest should be enough to cause you to look elsewhere.

Letters. No one ignores your attorney's letters. If you received unfair or outright dishonest treatment from a business firm, or continue receiving bills that you have already paid, or are being hassled by your present landlord or other persons, for example, a letter from your attorney will usually bring quick results. Most businesses want to resolve disputes fairly and quickly. When a business receives a letter from your attorney, it will signify two things: First, it tells the firm to look into your case immediately—you may be in the right. Second, the business is aware that you know how to work within the system.

Telephone Calls. A telephone call from your attorney to a business firm on your behalf will also bring speedy results.

Dissolution of Marriages. Some lawyers will not accept divorce cases. You should seek a lawyer who is used to this phase of legal work or specializes in this area. Moreover, your attorney should be sensitive to *your position*. Settlements might cover pension rights, job training, a decent car, child support and baby-sitting needs, cash for a working clothes wardrobe, and driving lessons.

Wills. Only you really know how you want your property distributed to your spouse, children, relatives, friends, institutions, and so on. Therefore, you must make some notes or prepare an outline of what you want done. The attorney will review your intent, offer suggestions for your review, and ask for additional specific information. Afterward, the attorney will draw up a formal will in accordance with the laws of the state and provide you with copies. Setting up a trust may also be part of the work that you want your attorney to do at the same time. Your attorney is working in the role of a technician to carry out your wishes.

Reading Installment and Real Estate Contracts. Before you sign a contract, your attorney will help you in reading these documents, calling your attention to your rights and obligations under the terms of the contract. The attorney will bring to your attention such points as creditors insurance, balloon payments, acceleration clauses, interest rates, expiration dates, penalties, and so on. This is one of the best and least costly services that your attorney can provide. However, these services diminish greatly if you have already signed such documents.

Writing Contracts to Do Business. Here, again, only you know what you want to do. For example, you are going to perform some service or build, transport, and install something. There are down payments on advance payments, hourly and daily rates for services and material and other costs. Prepare your own draft of what you plan to do. Your attorney will rewrite your draft using appropriate terms and add clauses for your protection—due dates, penalties, bonding, dispute resolutions, provisions for changes to original contract, and so on. Your attorney is your technical advisor on what you can or cannot do under local ordinances.

Taxes. Your attorney is usually well aware of or can research your specific questions relating to federal, state, county, and city taxes. The attorney can explain your rights and obligations under the law. As for preparing various tax returns, the lawyer probably has just as much trouble as you do. He or she is likely to call in a bookkeeper, tax preparer, accountant, or CPA to perform these tasks.

Courts. Except for the small claims courts, an attorney is the person to represent you in this formal arena. Most attorneys will try to keep you out of court whenever possible and determine if there is a less costly, more efficient, and equitable solution. Your attorney may suggest mediation or arbitration as alternatives to going to court.

Testimony Preparation. Contrary to TV courtroom dramas, you will need special coaching to understand your role as a defendant, plaintiff, or witness. Your attorney can help put you at ease and explain courtroom procedures, show you documents that may be used as exhibits, review possible questions that may be asked, and help you frame clear and precise answers.

Employment Discrimination. Labor law is still a relatively new and very specialized area. If you are an employee and think that you have been discriminated against, you will need a lawyer with these special skills to be your advocate. Labor unions, teachers groups, and government employees will probably know of lawyers with these skills.

Investments. Lawyers have the same problems in making sound investments as do most other people. However, in estate planning, your attorney can suggest investment media that bypass probate and how investment principal might be taxed at a lower rate or exempted completely from taxes. The attorney can set up trusts to ensure that principal and income go to a specific person in the event of your death.

Procrastination. The postponing or deferring of action or delays appears to be an integral part of technical service activity. Legal services are no different. The time required to perform professional services cannot be predicted with certainty. Frequent follow-up is helpful to keep your case from sitting on the desk. However, you can expect delays and postponements if the issues are going to a court or are matters of real estate, business located in other states, immigration, and estate settlement.

RELEVANT GOVERNMENTAL AGENCIES

Many federal, state, and city agencies provide consumer assistance programs. In fact, the function of government is to provide services to the people in return for taxes levied. However, because of the vastness of consumer-oriented agencies, only those relating to credit and borrowing or situations that generate credit instruments are emphasized here.

The Consumer Protection Division of the State Attorney General Office

This particular agency in your state should be contacted before you enter contractual relations involving large sums of money. For example, if you plan to purchase a car from a particular dealer, this agency can determine whether that

GUINDON

"Besides their other contributions to our society, lawyers could be an important source of protein."

Reprinted by special
permission of NAS, Inc.

dealer has accumulated many customer complaints in the past. If you have signed an installment contract for encyclopedias or expensive cutlery, for example, as a result of high-pressure sales tactics, check with this agency by telephone. You may have up to 72 hours after signing to change your mind. Landlord-tenant, automobile repair, product warranty service problems, and others are brought to the attention of this agency division. Look in the White Pages of your telephone directory under State of _____ for phone and hot line numbers.

Small Claims Court

You might consider this avenue for remedy of private legal disputes that amount to money damages of under $500 (or in some states $1,000). The settlement must be in terms of money. The court cannot get property back for you. There are no juries or lawyers, and the costs are usually under $10. As with anything dealing with law, there are some very precise procedures, forms, filing fees, trial dates, and times to follow. Small claims courts are part of county government.

RECENT FEDERAL CREDIT LEGISLATION

The consumer movement has produced federal legislation relating to credit transactions. Greater detail and explanation of individual rights can be obtained by writing to the Federal Trade Commission, Washington, D.C. 20580.

Truth in Lending Act of 1969

This act provides that you must be given an accurate statement of the annual percentage rate (the percentage of interest you must pay) and the finance charge (the total cost of the credit extended.)

Fair Credit Reporting Act of 1971

This act allows you to learn when an adverse credit decision is based on a credit report, to learn the nature and substance of information kept about you by a credit reporting agency, and to correct and amend erroneous information. An individual can usually find the nearest credit rating bureau listed in the Yellow Pages of the telephone directory under Credit Rating or Reporting Agencies. The local office of the Better Business Bureau and your department stores can help you contact credit rating agencies.

Equal Credit Opportunity Act of 1975

This act prohibits discrimination in the granting of credit on several bases including race, religion, national origin, sex, marital status, and age. It was the first major legislation to protect women's credit rights. It allows a wife to require creditors to show her participation in a family account and to consider her application for a separate account in her name.

Fair Credit Billing Act of 1975

This act allows credit card holders to challenge and correct billing information and prohibits creditors from sending unfavorable credit reports until the dispute rules have been followed. The act also permits merchants to set a lower price for cash-paying customers of third-party credit cards.

Fair Collection Practices Act of 1978

This act is designed to prevent abusive, deceptive, and unfair debt collection practices by debt collection agencies. It prohibits debt collectors from contracting the debtor's employer, with few exceptions. Collectors may not use threats of violence or obscene or profane language; call without identifying themselves; or repeatedly call the same person.

SUMMARY

Consumer credit has been growing rapidly in America. The great majority of Americans tend to keep consumer credit to around 20 percent of their disposable income. Personal bankruptcies in the United States run from 200,000 to 400,000 per year. Consumer credit does not include home mortgage debt. Consumer credit is offered or extended to a person primarily for personal, family, and household purposes.

Those who want credit usually cannot obtain it; those who do not need it or want it can easily get it. Grantors of credit and loans are interested in the credit applicants steady income, stability, age, and assets. The three C's of credit are character, capacity, and capital. State legislatures set the legal range of interest rates that can be charged by various credit and loan organizations. Legal annual percentage rates can range from as low as 6½ percent by credit unions up to 120 percent by pawn shops.

The first step in recovering from serious indebtedness is to destroy all credit cards. While the process of bankruptcy is relatively brief, the effects of bankruptcy are long lasting. Credit rating agencies maintain credit records relating to bankruptcy for up to 10 years. Credit transactions sometimes require the assistance and advice of a lawyer. Considerable time and money can be saved by developing an understanding of the role of lawyers in the American economy. The consumer protection division of the state attorney general office provides many areas of assistance to the consumer. Several major pieces of consumer rights legislation in the area of credit were enacted in the 1970s.

TIPS

1. The biggest drawback in borrowing is that more money has to be paid back than originally borrowed and too often it must be repaid at the most unfavorable time.
2. Wherever possible, avoid entering into consumer debt and contracts using installment sales contracts. The simple interest rate runs from 12 to 36 percent.

3. Clear all ending balances in bank and department store credit transactions at the end of each month.

4. When banks offer you a credit or debit card, you probably really have no real need for consumer-type credit. However, the card may be a real convenience while traveling, and the credit rating may carry prestige.

5. Keep the total amount of consumer credit to less than 20 percent of after-tax income, and keep the length of consumer credit contracts to less than 36 months.

6. A married woman should use her own first name in applying for credit. If you were born Nancy Jones, this is your legal name. If you marry George Smith, then you should use Nancy Jones, Nancy Smith, or Nancy Jones-Smith. It is best to be consistent.

7. When applying for credit, the creditor may ask whether you are married, unmarried, or separated but may not ask whether your are single, divorced, or widowed. Keep in mind that the terminology used in the world of credit is precise.

8. Have all terminology that you do not understand explained to you on credit contracts *before* signing.

9. In American law, your signature on a contract will bind you to that contract. Do not sign any document until you have thoroughly reviewed it.

10. Never sign a contract that contains "blanks" that could be filled in later.

11. You might use your credit when purchasing a major household appliance, particularly if you can purchase under a 90-day plan same as cash. In this way if you have warranty or service problems, you may have more leverage than if you had paid cash.

12. When having very serious debt problems, do not panic. Use the "system." That is, contact each of your creditors, explain your situation, in person if necessary. Makes some payment each week regardless of how small. This will show good faith. It may save your credit rating.

13. Persons in retirement and persons going through a divorce can often find themselves in serious debt. Stay on a cash-and-carry basis if you are in one or both of these situations.

ADDITIONAL READINGS

Consumer Information Catalog (a free federal publication listing federal consumer publications), Consumer Information Center, Pueblo, Colo.

Consumer's Resource Guide (a free publication listing places to take consumer problems and which agencies handle certain problems best), U.S. Consumer Affairs, Washington, D.C.

"How Much Debt Can You Juggle?" *Money*, March 1984, pp. 181–84.

Klein, Daniel, "Consumer Protection in the Marketplace," *Consumer's Research,* November 1984, pp. 14—17.

Quinn, Jane B, "New Handcuffs on the Cops," *Newsweek,* September 1984, p. 62.

Sylvester, David, "Going Broke on $44,500 a Year," *Pacific (Seattle Times/Seattle Post-Intelligencer),* July 12, 1987, p. 4.

"The New Rules about Bankruptcy," *Changing Times,* May 1979, pp. 31—32.

Warner, Ralph, *Everybody's Guide to Small Claims Court* (2nd ed.). Berkeley, Ca.: Nolo Press, 1985.

"What the Credit Bureau Is Saying about You," *Changing Times,* July 1983, pp. 56—59.

GLOSSARY OF USEFUL TERMS

Acceleration Clause A clause in a credit contract providing that a default on one payment makes all remaining payments due immediately.

Add-On Clause A charge account in which additional purchases are added to any remaining balance of the credit contract. All earlier purchases that are paid for under the contract are subject to repossession if there is a default.

Bait An advertised bargain that the advertiser does not intend or want to sell.

Balloon Contract A credit contract that calls for a series of relatively small payments and one large final payment.

Bankruptcy Declaring bankruptcy is a right codified by Congress from Article 1, Section 8, of the U.S. Constitution. It offers two forms of legal relief: straight bankruptcy, a legal process for discharging some of the person's debts, and the wage earner plan (Chapter 13), whereby a person can develop a three-year plan to pay off debts. Also called the Chandler Act.

Chattel Mortgage A mortgage whereby personal property is pledged as security for a debt. Buying a car on an installment loan is a common type of chattel mortgage. The lender of funds has a chattel mortgage on the vehicle.

Collateral Assets pledged as security for a loan. Collateral is used to reduce a creditor's risk.

Consumer Credit Credit offered or extended to a person in which the money, property, or service that is the subject of the transaction is primarily for personal, family, household or agricultural purposes and for which either a finance charge is or may be imposed or which, pursuant to an agreement, is or may be payable in more than four installments.

Co-signer A party who, in addition to the maker, signs a note on the face and is equally liable for payment.

Credit The right granted by a creditor to a customer to defer payment of debt, incur debt and defer its payment, or purchase property or services and defer payment thereof.

EFTS (Electronic Funds Transfer System) A computerized network of transactions processing that reduces the paperwork in doing financial business. Examples are teller machines and automated clearinghouses.

Equal Credit Opportunity Act Legislation that ensures that married women can establish credit in their names. Provisions also include women who are divorced or widowed.

Fair Credit Reporting Act   A federal law that protects consumers against the circulation of inaccurate or obsolete information by credit rating agencies.

Fair Debt Collection Practices Act   Law limiting the measures that a debt collector can employ against a consumer.

Garnishment   A process whereby wages or other property of a debtor are deducted for the purpose of payment of a debt. It requires a court order.

Installment Account   An account with a fixed number of specified payments specified as to amounts and time and including interest charges.

Installment Sales Contract   Contracts in which a customer agrees to pay for a purchase by remitting a certain amount of money each month for a specific number of months. Also called conditional sales contract.

Liabilities   Debts owed to creditors.

Lien   A claim against specified property giving the creditor the right to have the debt satisfied by selling the property if the debtor fails to pay.

Line of Credit   An amount of credit a bank determines it will lend without requiring a pledge of security.

Loan Shark   A person who makes loans and charges illegally high rates of interest.

Open Account   An account to be paid after one billing, such as 30-day account. There is no interest or service charge.

Open-End Credit   Consumer credit extended on an account pursuant to a plan under which (1) the creditor may permit the customer to make purchases or obtain loans from time to time, directly from the creditor or indirectly by use of a credit card, check, or other device, as the plan may provide; (2) the customer has the privilege of paying the balance in full or in installments; and (3) a finance charge may be computed by the creditor from time to time on an outstanding unpaid balance. The term does not include negotiated advances under an open-end real estate mortgage or a letter of credit.

Pawn   Personal property other than stocks, bonds, or negotiable paper that is pledged as security for a debt.

Regulation Z   Federal Reserve System regulation on truth in lending.

Revolving Account   An account with regular monthly payments based on the amount of the balance due.

Rule of 78's   Applies in the event of prepayment of an installment debt. If a debtor decided to pay off a one-year installment contract after one month, the creditor can assume to have earned $12/78$ of the finance charge. If the debt were to be liquidated at the end of the second month, the creditor could claim to have earned $12 + 11$ or $23/78$ of the finance charge.

Six C's of Credit   Character, capacity, capital, conditions, collateral, and common sense.

Switch   Diverting the buyer's attention to a higher-price item by disparaging, not having, or claiming not to have the "bait" item or by having advertised an item that is obviously shoddy or inferior (bait and switch).

Third-Party Cards   Credit cards such as various bank cards, American Express and Diners' Club, for example.

Truth in Lending Act   Act designed to let consumers know exactly what rate of interest they are being charged for credit.

Wage Earner Plan (Chapter 13 of the Bankruptcy Act)   *See* Bankruptcy.

7

Food, Clothing, and Personal Health Care

LEARNING OBJECTIVES

Upon completion of Chapter 7, you should be able to identify and remember

- How your food costs are associated with your quality of life.
- The estimated number of meals to be eaten over the course of a year, the number of those meals to be eaten at home by a family, food to be eaten away from home, and those meals that are associated with business, school, and social and recreational activities.
- The ratio of food to nonfood items that are routinely purchased on weekly, bi-weekly, or monthly shopping trips as well as on "bread and milk" shopping trips.
- The use of worksheets to construct an estimate of total food costs for a household unit for one year.
- Sound shopping tips intended to reduce waste and save money during supermarket shopping.
- Examples of wasteful shopping habits.
- How to draw up a basic wardrobe that would satisfactorily meet the needs for school, business and social contacts, and recreation and travel as well as necessary personal care items essential to good grooming and hygiene.
- How to develop a worksheet to determine the annual estimate of clothing and personal care needs.

- The criteria that should make for a good grocery or department store for customers.
- Five advertisements in good taste and bad taste that are currently being run in your local TV, radio, and newspaper. These may include deceptive practices.

OVERVIEW

Part IV contains three chapters relating to consumption. With the exception of insurance coverage needs, most of our disposable income will be spent on food, clothing, personal health care, housing, furnishings, utilities, and various means of transportation. While our job or career will help us to identify ourselves to the public and provide income, it is how we spend our income that establishes our self-identification, self-gratification, and social acceptance.

FOOD

Cost of Food for Household Units at Home

Spending too little for food may be harmful, and spending too much is wasteful. In Chapter 3 we were concerned with human consumption food items only, excluding from the area of food such items as soaps, kitchen cleaners, paper towels, utensils, pet food, and so on. Here we are concerned with age, life-style, amount of income, and number of people in a household and how these factors affect the amount of money to be spent on meals (again excluding nonfood purchases) for any week. Table 7-1 presents food budgets for the thrifty to the liberal and for different ages of men and women and children for food to be consumed at home. Sample figures are provided later in this section for social, work-related, vacation, and other such nonhousehold food expenditures.

Four Basic Worksheets for Food Budget

The purpose of developing four basic worksheets is to identify major areas in which food and meals are consumed: (1) basic home-prepared meals, fast foods, and school lunch meals; (2) career- or job-related meals; (3) home entertainment food and beverages; and (4) meals eaten while on vacation, long weekends, and special occasions.

Basic Foods and Meals Budget. Most people will readily identify with this budgeting activity. But a critical review of the area should be made. For example,

TABLE 7-1 Cost of Food at Home Estimated for Food Plans at Four Cost Levels, April 1985, U.S. Average*

Sex-age group	Cost for 1 week				Cost for 1 month			
	Thrifty plan	Low-cost plan	Moderate-cost plan	Liberal plan	Thrifty plan	Low-cost plan	Moderate-cost plan	Liberal plan
Families								
Family of 2†								
20–50 years	$37.40	$47.10	$57.90	$ 71.60	$161.80	$203.90	$251.10	$310.20
51 years and over	35.30	45.10	55.40	66.00	153.10	195.40	240.00	286.00
Family of 4								
Couple, 20–50 years and children								
1–2 and 3–5 years	54.40	67.60	82.50	100.80	235.40	293.10	357.60	436.90
6–8 and 9–11 years	62.40	79.60	99.20	119.20	270.40	344.90	430.30	516.60
Individuals‡								
Child								
1–2 years	9.80	11.80	13.80	16.50	42.40	51.30	59.70	71.70
3–5 years	10.60	13.00	16.10	19.20	45.90	56.40	69.60	83.20
6–8 years	13.00	17.20	21.50	25.10	56.40	74.60	93.20	108.80
9–11 years	15.40	19.60	25.10	29.00	66.90	84.90	108.80	125.80
Male								
12–14 years	16.20	22.20	27.60	32.40	70.10	96.30	119.70	140.40
15–19 years	16.80	23.10	28.50	33.00	72.80	99.90	123.30	142.90
20–50 years	17.90	22.80	28.40	34.20	77.40	98.70	123.30	148.20
51 years and over	16.20	21.60	26.50	31.60	70.30	93.60	114.70	137.10
Female								
12–19 years	16.10	19.20	23.90	28.00	69.60	83.40	100.70	121.40
20–50 years	16.10	20.00	24.20	30.90	69.70	86.70	105.00	133.80
51 years and over	15.90	19.40	23.90	28.40	68.90	84.00	103.50	122.90

United States Department of Agriculture, *Family Economics Review*, 1985, No. 3.

* Assumes that food for all meals and snacks is purchased at the store and prepared at home. Estimates for the thrifty food plan were computed from quantities of foods published in *Family Economics Review*, 1984, No. 1. Estimates for the other plans were computed from quantities of foods published in *Family Economics Review*, 1983, No. 2. The costs of the food plans are estimated by updating prices paid by households surveyed in 1977–78 in USDA's Nationwide Food Consumption Survey. USDA updates these survey prices using information from the Bureau of Labor Statistics (*CPI Detailed Report*, table 3) to estimate the costs for the food plans.

† 10 percent added for family size adjustment. See next footnote.

‡ The costs given are for individuals in four-person families. For individuals in other-size families, the following adjustments are suggested: one person—add 20 percent; two persons—add 10 percent; three persons—add 5 percent; five or six persons—subtract 5 percent; seven or more persons—subtract 10 percent.

"We usually spend $65 per week for the two of us" may be an erroneous estimate for two adults because it includes many items other than food. On the other hand, we often overlook as insignificant the "bread and milk" trips to the grocery. Also, vacations and long weekends reduce this 52-week estimate.

School lunches and meals eaten at a company cafeteria are often low cost and could well be included in this basic food budget. Coffee "kitty" dues, carried lunches, and fast-food meals should also be included. Meals at the large fast-food chains and government- and corporation-subsidized dining facilities are basically competitive with certain types of home cooking.

Reviewing the budget for John and Kay Adams family in Chapter 3, we now can see more clearly the estimate for basic foods and meals in Exhibit 7-1. Kay can prepare next year's estimate by taking this year's figures and adjusting them for regional inflation.

Career- or Job-Related Meals. To build your career and expand your business or career contacts, memberships in professional and trade organizations are ordinary and necessary investments of both time and money.

While the membership fees are modest, the speaker-dinner meeting costs run much higher than a home-cooked meal. Lunches with others at the office and retirement banquets are partly social and partly business and should be budgeted for. Conferences and workshops include no-hosted lunches. Exhibit 7-2 shows Kay Adams's estimate of these costs, which she considers necessary to John's and her life-styles.

EXHIBIT 7-1   John & Kay Adams
Basic Food and Meals Expense Budget
For the Year _____

Basic Food & Meals Expense Budget

Categories	Estimates	Total
Food: Human Consumption & Groceries	$35 for 50 weeks	$1,750 –
Bread and Milk grocery trips	$6 for 50 weeks	300 –
School Lunch Money – Jill	Est. for year	65 –
Company cafeteria meals	Est. for year	200 –
Coffee "Kitty" dues	Est. for year	20 –
Fast Food Chain meals	50 @ $10 est.	500 –
Vending machine foods	Est. for year	10 –
Total Estimate for the Year		$2,845

EXHIBIT 7-2   John & Kay Adams
Career-Related Meals Expense Budget
For the Year _____

Categories	Total
Special Office Luncheons 10 @ $7.00	$70 —
Special meetings and Meals	—0—
Retirement and Holiday Parties/Events	25—
Union and Business Association meetings	30—
Total Estimate for the Year	$125—

Home Entertainment Food and Beverage Budget. This budget includes the gourmet foods, ingredients, hors d'oeuvres, wines, and so on for special occasions. Birthday cakes, ice cream, party accessories, stock of wines, liquors, and soft drinks for parties should be a separate budget from ordinary grocery shopping. Kay Adams plans the family's budget estimate for home entertainment in Exhibit 7-3.

EXHIBIT 7-3   John & Kay Adams
Home Entertainment Food and Beverage Budget
For the Year _____

Categories	Total
Specialty and gourmet foods & beverages	$50—
Party cups, plates, napkins, candles, etc.	10—
Entertainment coffee, cakes, pies, ice cream	30—
TV snacks, nuts, popcorn, fruits	15—
Home bar and beverage stock	100—
Special soft drinks & juices	15—
Backyard cookouts, — meats, charcoal, etc.	25—
Total Estimate for the Year	$245

EXHIBIT 7-4 John & Kay Adams
Special Occasion Meals, Parties, Events Budget
For the Year _____

Categories	Total
Vacation meals (away from home) 14 @ $20	$280-
Long-weekend meals (away from home) est.	100-
Sunday brunches	-0-
Special anniversary dinners, bar, tips, sitter	100-
Birthday cakes and treats	25-
Household budget director's reward dinner	50-
T.G.I.F. & Happy hours	20-
Total Estimate for the Year	$575-

Vacations, Long Weekends, Special Occasions. This is a simple budget to prepare because of the planning that precedes vacations, weekend outings, anniversary dinners, and other events. Meals eaten during a vacation should be included in the total dollar budget for that purpose. At the budget planning stage, it is well to at least consider realistic estimates in this area. For example, planning a special birthday or wedding anniversary dinner outing should include costs for cocktails, dinner, tips, parking, baby sitting, cover charge, theater tickets, and so on. Kay Adam's estimate is illustrated in Exhibit 7-4. Readers are encouraged to modify the worksheets to fit their particular life-styles.

Meal Planning

Few people seem to have the self-discipline to sit down and write a complete menu for a whole week or month. Those who can probably will know that their food costs are well under control. For the active, perhaps single, career man or woman who is not very anxious to follow a rigid menu program after a long day at work, a fast-food restaurant with its convenience and time-saving features offset the added cost.

For those individuals and heads of households whose present income is severely restricted—for example, full-time students, welfare or Social Security recipients, and the unemployed—meal planning may either result in cash savings or in raising the quality of life on the same amount of income.

TABLE 7-2 A Week's Menus Based on the Thrifty Food Plan

	SUNDAY	MONDAY	TUESDAY	WEDNESDAY	THURSDAY	FRIDAY	SATURDAY
B R E A K F A S T	Orange juice French toast Sirup Beverage	Orange juice Ready-to-eat cereal Doughnut Beverage	Peaches, sliced Grits Cinnamon toast Beverage	Orange juice Eggs Pan-fried potatoes Toast Beverage	Peaches, sliced Ready-to-eat cereal Toast Beverage	Apple juice Farina Toast Beverage	Apples, quartered Pancakes Sirup Beverage
L U N C H	Beef pot roast Gravy Mashed potatoes Mixed vegetables Bread Ice milk Beverage	Grilled cheese sandwiches Macaroni salad Baked apples Beverage	Frankfurters Sauerkraut Bread Oatmeal cookies Beverage	Beef macaroni soup Saltine crackers Plums Beverage	Noodle soup Peanut butter and jelly sandwiches Carrot sticks Graham crackers Beverage	Frankfurter bean soup Saltine crackers Oatmeal cookies Beverage	Cheese sandwiches Gelatin (with apple juice and celery) Meringue pie Beverage
D I N N E R	Beans in tomato sauce Macaroni salad Pear halves Cornbread Gelatin Beverage	Beef stew with vegetables Cornbread Ice milk Beverage	Beef pie with vegetables Refrigerator biscuits Lettuce wedges with dressing Peanut butter cake Beverage	Fried chicken Rice Gravy Corn Bread Peanut butter cake Beverage	Beef patties Baked potatoes Stewed tomatoes Muffins Ice milk Beverage	Cheese rarebit on toast French-fried potatoes Collards Meringue pie Beverage	Spaghetti with meat sauce Tossed salad (lettuce, carrots, dressing) Bread sticks Ice milk Beverage
S N A C K	Doughnut	Bread and jelly sandwiches	Cheese and saltine crackers	Doughnut	Peanut butter cake	Graham crackers	Ready-to-eat cereal

Note: Milk for everyone at least once daily, and for children, teenagers, and pregnant and nursing women, more often.
Spreads for bread and sugar for cereal, coffee, and tea may be added, if desired.

Data are from *Family Economics Review* (Washington, D.C.: U.S. Department of Agriculture, Consumer and Food Economics Institute, Agricultural Research Service, U.S. Government Printing Office, Winter 1976), p. 24.

TABLE 7-3   Costing Out the Price of a Sample Breakfast

	Cost	Calories
1 4-oz serving orange juice (12 oz frozen @ $.80): $.80 ÷ 48 oz mixed × 4 oz =	$.067	50
1 slice toast (15-oz loaf @ $.40; 16 slices): $.40 ÷ 16 =	.025	60
1 ½-oz margarine (16 oz @ $.95 per lb): $.95 ÷ 32 pats =	.030	100
1 boiled egg (large-sized grade AA; 1 doz @ $.70): $.70 ÷ 12 =	.058	80
1 serving ready-to-eat cereal (24 oz @ $1.20): $1.20 ÷ 24 =	.050	100
1 ½-cup 2% fat-free milk (½ gal @ $.85): $.85 ÷ 64 oz × 4 oz =	.053	70
1 6-oz mug of black coffee (10 oz instant @ $4.50) estimate	.020	0
	$.303	460
Estimated cost of energy used by appliances	.030	
	$.333	

Entries are compiled from information on labels of goods purchased at a major supermarket, July 1979. Calories from labels or USDA.

Fortunately, most of our meals, particularly breakfast and lunch, are very similar during the workweek. The evening meals and weekend meals tend to have more variety. Table 7-2 provides a sample menu for a week developed by the U.S. Department of Agriculture.

One additional consideration when planning a basic food budget is the estimated cost per serving for an adult. Table 7-3 contains such a breakdown for breakfast for one adult.

Acquiring Good Shopping Habits

Acquiring good shopping habits is the key to gaining the most value for the dollar. The use of the following tips should save a couple of hundred dollars a year. You may find many that you presently practice plus a few more that you may want to include to sharpen your shopping skills.

1. Prepare a shopping list and stick to it.
2. Block all impulses to purchase items not on the list.
3. Shop on weekends as these are the days when real bargains and fresh items can be purchased.
4. Do not shop on an empty stomach. Everything looks good when you are hungry, and there is a tendency to overpurchase.
5. Shop alone or with another knowledgeable person. Accompanying spouses and children can add another $5 to $10 to your food bill.
6. Use unit pricing to find the actual cost per ounce, pound, slice, and so on.

7. Purchase the store's privately labeled brands if the quality is the same as that of major brands.

8. Purchase the cheaper lean cuts of meat and learn how to prepare them. Avoid high-fat and high-bone cuts of meat.

9. Watch the cash register when your purchases are being tallied.

10. Make use of coupons on frequently purchased items.

11. Nonfood items frequently purchased at supermarkets are often cheaper if purchased at discount stores.

12. Buy in bulk if the food items are not wasted or do not spoil.

13. Compare newspaper advertisements and shop at two stores, provided that transportation costs do not offset the savings.

14. Purchase fruits and vegetables when in season.

15. Demand "rain checks" on sale items temporarily out of stock.

These are just a few shopping strategies that informed shoppers use to get the most for their money.

A few words should be said about supermarket use of psychology. The store's floor plan is designed in the hope that you will spend more money. For example, goods with the highest markups are located near eye level; goods with small markup are located in difficult-to-reach areas. Notice that, to purchase meat, dairy products, coffee, and soft drinks, you must walk past many rows or shelves of tempting displays to reach these items.

THE WALL STREET JOURNAL

"Have I eaten enough fiber?"

From *The Wall Street Journal*—
Permission, Cartoon Features
Syndicate.

Note also that tasty goods with good profit margins are located at the end of each aisle and that many impulse goods—magazines, cigarettes, gum, candy, razor blades—are conveniently located at the checkout counter. Remember, too, that product packaging is carefully developed to capture consumers' attention.

Proper Storage of Food

Food storage is a concern for the producer as well as for the consumer. More than 90 percent of the U.S. population depends on the other 10 percent to supply foodstuffs. To prolong the shelf lives of many products the food processors use additives. Without these preservatives, varieties of foodstuffs would be vastly reduced, and shopping by the consumer would have to be done more frequently.

As consumers, we may readily understand proper storage for fresh meats, produce, dairy products, and bread. These items are purchased and consumed frequently. On the other hand, canned goods, dry cereals, flour, dried beans, instant coffee, noodles, and so on are expected to have longer shelf lives.

How much should the consumer store and for how long? There is no single answer. Refrigerator storage depends on how well the appliance is functioning and what the expected lives of your produce, meats, and so on are. Exhibit 7-5 will help you to determine the storage life of refrigerated foods.

Canned goods have codes to identify their shelf lives. Unfortunately, these codes are not uniform. The manufacturers and processors use combinations of the alphabet and numerals to indicate when the goods were packed. Some companies do write the pull-date such as May 19X8/Codes A through L or 1 through 12 signify the month; the day of packing may be signified by a number from 1–365. Day 149 would be May 28. Monday through Friday might be coded 1 through 5. To maintain a single digit for coding the months, a firm might use number 1–9 for January through September and letters A–C for the months October through December. The following examples show what a processor's code might read and the possible interpretation:

Can code	Interpretation
1498	May 28, 19X8
8149	May 28, 19X8
E288	May 28, 19X8

Raising Your Own Vegetables

Will a small garden such as the one shown in Exhibit 7-6 cut the food bill, particularly that portion presently spent on fresh and frozen vegetables? At present, the time and money needed to start a garden will not offset supermar-

EXHIBIT 7-5 Guide to proper placement of foods in the refrigerator at normal setting temperatures of 37° to 40°F (Column at right shows maximum storage periods for frozen foods stored at 0°F or lower.)

Guide to Refrigerator Storage

The chart below shows proper placement of foods in the refrigerator at normal setting, which should maintain a temperature of 37° to 40°F. Column at right shows maximum storage periods for frozen foods stored at 0°F. or lower.

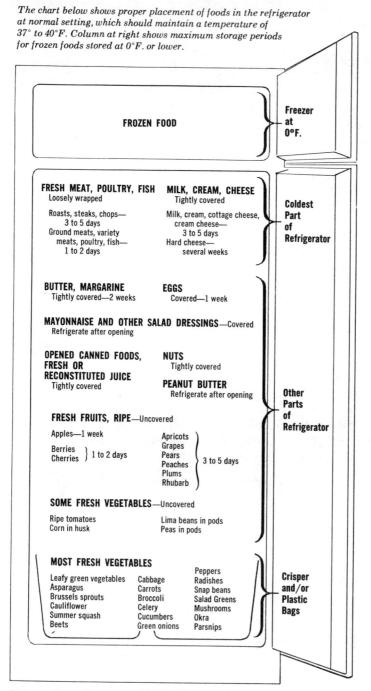

FROZEN FOOD

Freezer at 0°F.

FRESH MEAT, POULTRY, FISH
Loosely wrapped

Roasts, steaks, chops—
  3 to 5 days
Ground meats, variety
  meats, poultry, fish—
  1 to 2 days

MILK, CREAM, CHEESE
Tightly covered

Milk, cream, cottage cheese,
  cream cheese—
  3 to 5 days
Hard cheese—
  several weeks

Coldest Part of Refrigerator

BUTTER, MARGARINE
Tightly covered—2 weeks

EGGS
Covered—1 week

MAYONNAISE AND OTHER SALAD DRESSINGS—Covered
Refrigerate after opening

OPENED CANNED FOODS, FRESH OR RECONSTITUTED JUICE
Tightly covered

NUTS
Tightly covered

PEANUT BUTTER
Refrigerate after opening

Other Parts of Refrigerator

FRESH FRUITS, RIPE—Uncovered

Apples—1 week

Berries
Cherries } 1 to 2 days

Apricots
Grapes
Pears
Peaches
Plums
Rhubarb } 3 to 5 days

SOME FRESH VEGETABLES—Uncovered

Ripe tomatoes
Corn in husk

Lima beans in pods
Peas in pods

MOST FRESH VEGETABLES

Leafy green vegetables
Asparagus
Brussels sprouts
Cauliflower
Summer squash
Beets

Cabbage
Carrots
Broccoli
Celery
Cucumbers
Green onions

Peppers
Radishes
Snap beans
Salad Greens
Mushrooms
Okra
Parsnips

Crisper and/or Plastic Bags

Data are from *Consumers All: The Yearbook of Agriculture* (Washington, D.C.: U.S. Government Printing Office, 1965), p. 433.

EXHIBIT 7-6   Proposal for a Vegetable Garden

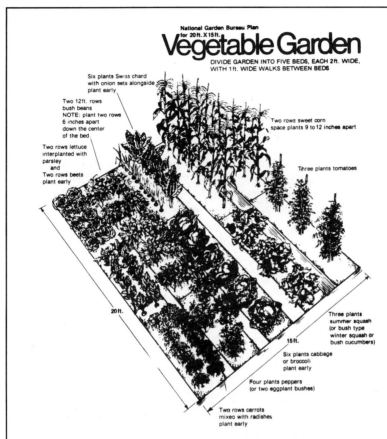

National Garden Bureau Plan for 20 ft. X 15 ft.

Vegetable Garden

DIVIDE GARDEN INTO FIVE BEDS, EACH 2 ft. WIDE,
WITH 1 ft. WIDE WALKS BETWEEN BEDS

Six plants Swiss chard
with onion sets alongside
plant early

Two 12 ft. rows
bush beans
NOTE: plant two rows
6 inches apart
down the center
of the bed.

Two rows lettuce
interplanted with
parsley
and
Two rows beets
plant early

Two rows sweet corn
space plants 9 to 12 inches apart

Three plants tomatoes

20 ft.

15 ft.

Three plants
summer squash
(or bush type
winter squash or
bush cucumbers)

Six plants cabbage
or broccoli
plant early

Four plants peppers
(or two eggplant bushes)

Two rows carrots
mixed with radishes
plant early

Here's model plan for
beginning gardeners

by ED HUME

Times garden editor

Research by the National Garden Bureau indicates that many beginning gardeners have only a hazy idea of the mature size of vegetable plants.

All it takes is one successful garden to make each succeeding one a breeze. Yet, first gardens are, more often than not, overly large, crowded and poorly arranged, with tall plants in the front and frequently harvested vegetables stuck way in the back.

Your next vegetable garden can be as pretty as a picture, sensibly arranged and of a practical size. Use this National Garden Bureau plan as a model and be sure to:

1. Plant no more than you can

care for with ease in four to six hours each week.

2. Select varieties that are adapted to your area.

3. Plant at the season recommended on seed packets.

4. Allow plenty of space for plants to grow; thin ruthlessly.

The 500 square feet of this garden is 20 x 15 feet, about the size of a one-car garage. It is designed to accommodate 13 kinds of vegetables and will supply most of the fresh vegetables needed by a family of three. It can be weeded, watered and harvested within an average of two hours time each week.

Seeds for this garden will cost about $6.50, yet from it you can harvest $100 or more of delicious

vegetables, depending on the length of the growing season in your area.

You might not care for some of the vegetables shown in the plan. Substitute others of comparable plant size. Seed packets and gardening books can advise you. Your County Cooperative Extension Service offers free bulletins on vegetable gardening and lists of locally recommended varieties.

Depending on the length of the gardening season in your area, you can plant "succession crops" as soon as you have harvested the vegetables shown in the plan. Over most of the country, leafy salad vegetables, cabbage family members and root crops can be planted as succession crops as late as August, for fall harvest.

Illustration reprinted by permission of the National Garden Bureau. Newspaper article reprinted from *Seattle Times,* 10 March 1978, by permission of Ed Hume, garden editor.

ket costs. However, starting a garden of your own could be a learning experience for yourself and children, develop a sense of accomplishment, encourage long-range and year-round planning, and serve as a way of getting some exercise and provide good therapy after a long day at work.

CLOTHING

Clothing is one of the most important investments that an individual can make and it need not be expensive: Buy sparingly, buy quality, and buy conservatively in style and color. When you are about to enter a potentially important business or career meeting or transaction, or when a positive first impression could be important to your future, take the necessary time to consider what manner of dress will be most appropriate. With the post–World War II baby-boom population entering the job market and with continuing high levels of unemployment in the United States, entering careers and advancing within them will be even more difficult to accomplish.

GUINDON

GUINDON 10 27

It has just occurred to Flo Benson that she hasn't been in street clothes for 5 years.

Reprinted by special
permission of NAS, Inc.

Clothing Purchase Guidelines

Select your clothing from the quality department stores in your community. The store should include basic tailoring or alterations in the price of the clothing. The store should have a refund policy if you should find flaws in the materials shortly after your purchase. Try to build a clothing fund so that you can purchase your clothing needs when the store has its true discount sales. Most quality department and clothing stores have one or two sales periods a year when their normal-quality stock of goods is marked down. Most other monthly sales during the year are developed through special purchases of cheaper and definitely inferior-quality merchandise.

Always try on any clothing you intend to purchase. Do not assume that the labels are correctly marked or that the clothing has been cut or sewn properly. Unless you have lots of money to waste, do not buy outer clothing for other members of the family except maybe young children. Husbands, wives, and teenagers each should have a specific upper dollar limit to be spent for clothing for the year.

Clothing Budget Worksheets

Let us return to the John and Kay Adams family as Kay considers the clothing needs of the family. In some years very little will be spent on clothing. In other years, events such as graduation, promotions, and job changes require major clothing purchases. Over the years Kay has built three distinct lists of clothing that the family tends to purchase from time to time. No doubt, if the Adams family were to meet with a severe financial hardship, almost all the budgeted amounts could be eliminated. The following three worksheets (Exhibits 7-7, 7-8, and 7-9) are Kay's estimates in the areas of regular clothing, special work clothes, and recreational attire. The last two worksheets could be combined with the first for simple budgeting.

PERSONAL HEALTH CARE AND GROOMING

A portion of our after-tax dollars must be spent on such items as medical insurance, out-of-pocket medical and medicine costs, over-the-counter remedies, food, clothing, and personal hygiene and grooming aids. Good health care practice may mean that fewer dollars will be spent on medical expenditures relating to dental work, obesity, circulatory, digestive, and respiratory ailments. Poor health care practices can bring on medical problems that even the medical profession cannot solve for us. Most people's incomes derive from their jobs, and poor health practices or habits may jeopardize career advancements and

EXHIBIT 7-7 John & Kay Adams
Basic Clothing Expense Budget
For the Year _____

Categories	Examples	Total
Men	Shirts, trousers, suits, jackets, shoes, socks, underwear, ties, hankerchiefs	$400 –
Women	Dresses, coats, pant suits, shoes, hosiery, underwear, accessories	500 –
Children	School and play clothes, shoes, socks, underwear, coats, sleepwear	175 –
Home Sewing	Patterns, yardgoods, thread, zippers, machine maintenance & access.	50 –
Special Apparel	Umbrellas, raincoats, boots, gloves, winter coats, slippers	20 –
Special Accessories	Watches, rings, pins, wallets, lighters, key case, jewelery, (if not gifts)	– 0 –
Cleaning & Repair	Laundry soap, bleaches, softeners, dry cleaning, shoe repair, polish	30 –
	Total Estimate for the Year	$1,175

promotions. We have an incentive to see that our time and money are not used in a way that is counterproductive to good health.

Personal Health Care and Career

Nothing will halt your career, advancement, or social life faster than poor health care. Be sure to budget adequately for such basic items as bath soaps, water softeners, shampoos, hair preparations, deodorants, toothpastes, and the like. These items can be expensive unless you take advantage of special sales and coupons, which can reduce your health care bill by 30, 40, or 50 percent. (These items usually follow a 60-day cycle of discounts.) Additional savings can be achieved by utilizing cents-off coupons. Also, do not forget the large discount store's private labels.

EXHIBIT 7-8 John & Kay Adams
Special Work Clothing Expense Budget
For the Year _____

Categories/Items	Est.
Safety hats, goggles, gloves, dust masks, ear plugs, safety boots & shoes, work uniforms (men & women) badges, military uniforms, ribbons, shoes, polishing materials, aprons, rain gear, hand cleaners, stain removers, lotions, special money wallets, sun glasses, hair nets, caps, business cards.	
Total Estimate for the Year	#60—

EXHIBIT 7-9 John & Kay Adams
Recreational Clothing Budget
For the Year _____

Categories/Items	Est.
Tennis, jogging, golf shoes, ski-boots, jackets, sweat bands, hats, caps, goggles, wet suits, warm-up suits, swim wear, safety helmet, elastic bandage or supporter, gym clothes and socks, scouting and drill team clothing, etc.	
Total Estimate for the Year	#50—

ZIGGY

THANK YOU FOR NOT WEARING MUSK OIL

10-14

Home Medical Needs

Today, the average home may be more hazardous than the place where we work. But, for less than $50, you can have a well-stocked medicine cabinet to handle mishaps that occur in your home. You may also want to develop a first aid emergency kit for your car or for camping.

Personal Health Care Worksheet for Budgeting

Personal health care and grooming aids are likely to be purchased more frequently than are home remedy items. However, all such items are purchased only a few times a year, as they need to be replaced. Correlate your purchases with advertised specials at major cut-rate or discount drugstores; this practice will help you to save on vitamins and first aid supplies as well.

In the long-established John and Kay Adams family, Kay prepares a rough estimate of the coming year's needs for the family. She makes some dollar estimates of the things that the family has purchased in the past. She includes the barbershop and beauty shop as well as family-planning items and small appliances. In your own budgeting, you might not need to continue the detailed listing in successive years. Remember, though, that there is tendency to underestimate in this budget section because we are not likely to view all these items in a group. Furthermore, if these items are not purchased at the discount or coupon sale times, you will be losing out on the 30–50 percent discounts that can be had. Kay estimates that $545 will be spent in the coming year as shown in Exhibit 7-10.

EXHIBIT 7-10 John & Kay Adams
Personal Health Care and Grooming Budget
For the Year _____

Categories/Items	Total
Hand, bath soaps and softners	#25 —
Shampoos, creams and rinses	30 —
Hair preparations, combs, brushes, pins, rollers	10 —
Shaving creams, blades, lotions	15 —
Dental care: pastes, powders, floss, mouthwash	20 —
Deodorants, colonges, perfumes, powders	30 —
Make-up preparations, lip sticks, eye shadow	20 —
Nail care items – clippers, emery boards, polish	10 —
Prescription & refills	20 —
Pain relievers	5 —
Cold medicines & allergy relief	5 —
Cuts & burns medicines, bandages	5 —
Feminine hygiene & family planning	50 —
Vitamin & mineral supplements	10 —
Tissues, toilet paper, cotton swabs	60 —
Infant care items	— 0 —
Appliances: dryers, blowers, mirrors, etc.	— 0 —
Suntan lotions	10 —
Barber & hairstyling, wash & set, etc.	210 —
Total Estimate for the Year	#535 —

SUMMARY

How we spend money for food, clothing, and personal health care reveals a
definite life-style to our friends and acquaintances. The money spent for food
need not be excessive, and yet it can provide a new dimension to the quality of

our life. Quality kitchen utensils and tableware may encourage you to eat more meals and do entertaining at home. Separate human consumption food from other items in developing budgets. Establish realistic amounts to be spent on food for entertainment and for other social and vacation meals.

People on a restricted budget should focus on nutrition when planning menus. Amounts spent for food can be kept to a minimum by developing good shopping and storage habits. Gardening may be a better way to get more exercise than to reduce food costs.

Clothing should be considered as an investment when it relates to career and when establishing a positive first impression is important. Purchase clothing locally and from the reputable clothing and department stores.

Good personal health care and grooming are essential for career and social success. Savings of 30 to 50 percent can be obtained by purchasing personal health care and grooming items at advertised and coupon sale times.

Each household should take measures to reduce the likelihood of injuries and illnesses at home and have on hand basic medical items for minor injuries and illnesses.

TIPS

1. Shop for groceries near the weekend when food is fresher and when there are more advertised specials. Shop on a full stomach; use a shopping list; scan newspapers for shopping sales and coupons.
2. Store food so that an easy visual inventory can be made and stored goods can be totaled.
3. Do not feel awkward or squeamish that you only purchased the advertised specials and nothing else at a store.
4. When putting together a functional wardrobe, buy quality, buy sparingly, and buy conservative styling. Consider the money spent for clothing to help you obtain a job or enhance your career as an investment.
5. Do not purchase clothing through the mail when such items can be purchased locally during a routine shopping trip.
6. Reduce health hazards around the home.
7. If you are going to conduct a "frugality month," food, clothing, and personal health care and grooming items should be purchased with care:

   Do not purchase any new clothing during the month.

   Buy only the most nutritious foods and prepare more meals at home and from scratch. Buy fresh produce in season.

   Consolidate all shopping into fewer driving trips and walk when possible to do other shopping.

   Cut back on expensive cosmetics and grooming aids.

Plan evening entertainment at home instead of outside. Visit parks, museums, and libraries in place of more expensive entertainment.

Conserve energy around the home where possible—run only full loads in dishwashers and washers. Go easy on air conditioning.

Brown bag all lunches to work and school and take a thermos of coffee, tea, soup, or milk.

Make breakfast your biggest meal of the day and cut back on the more expensive evening meal.

Consider "day-old" bakery goods and shop at those outlets if family members insist on sweets.

Go on a diet. Give up or cut back on certain impulse habits.

ADDITIONAL READINGS

Beffart, Mark, "The Visible Business Tool," *Working Woman,* November 1984, pp. 194–99.

"Clothing," *Money,* June 1985, p. 205.

Dadd, Debra Lynn, *The Nontoxic Home,* New York; St. Martin's, 1986.

Edelstein, Barbara, *The Woman Doctor's Diet for Teenage Girls.* New York: Ballantine, 1985.

Graedon, Joe, *Joe Graedon's New People's Pharmacy: Drug Breakthroughs of the 80's.* New York: Bantam, 1985.

"How to Be a Smart Shopper," *Consumers' Digest,* November 1985, pp. 122–23.

Kempton, Beverly, "The Language of Clothes," *Working Woman,* September 1984, pp. 157–59.

Kraus, Barbara. *Calorie Guide.* New York: Signet, 1986.

———, *Calories & Carbohydrates* (6th ed.). New York: Signet, 1985.

"Mail-Order Companies," *Consumer Reports,* October 1987, pp. 607–14.

Molloy, John T, *Dress for Success.* New York: Warner, 1976.

Rosenfeld, Isadore, *Modern Prevention: The New Medicine.* New York: Bantam, 1987.

Seligman, Jean, "The Shopping Addicts," *Newsweek,* March 18, 1985, pp. 81–82.

"The Good Gray Suit," *Consumer Reports,* August 1986, pp. 502–10.

"The New World of Health Care," *U.S. News & World Report,* April 14, 1986, pp. 60–66.

"Trenchcoats," *Consumer Reports,* September 1987, pp. 538–45.

"What Has All-Bran Wrought?" *Consumer Reports,* October 1986, pp. 638–39.

GLOSSARY OF USEFUL TERMS

Additive (food) A substance added in very small amounts to provide or enhance desirable properties or to suppress undesirable properties.

Biodegradable Material that decomposes naturally.

Commodity Raw materials—sugar, eggs, cotton, soy beans, tin or any standardized product—whose price is determined in a competitive market.

Consumer Goods Goods purchased by ultimate consumers for personal and household consumption. The three major areas are convenience, shopping, and specialty goods.

Convenience Goods Products sold through many retail stores, widely advertised, and purchased frequently with little or no thought given to making such purchase.

Co-op A form of business ownership rendering a service to its owner-members on a nonprofit basis.

Franchise A systemized method of conducting business. This is usually a binding arrangement between a national firm and a local businessperson to carry on a specialized activity.

Impulse Buying Buying something in a store that a person had no intention of buying when he or she came into the store.

Loss Leader An item on which little or no profit is made, offered for sale in the hope that it will attract customers who will buy other merchandise.

Merchandising Activities pertaining to buying merchandise for resale, marketing, pricing, and promoting the sale.

Nondurable Goods Tangible goods that are used up in one or a few uses.

Private Brand A brand of goods usually advertised and sold by the retailer under a house name at a cheaper price than similar goods carrying national names.

Serving Amount of each food, as established by the U.S. Department of Agriculture, needed to provide 20 grams of protein—one-third of the daily amount required by the average 20-year-old male.

Shopping Goods Products of relatively high unit value, normally purchased only after the customer has compared the price, style, and quality.

Specialty Goods Products that the consumer finds particularly attractive and will make a special purchasing effort to obtain.

Tariff A tax or duty levied on goods imported from other nations.

Unit Pricing Posted listing of prices per ounce, pound, and so on, on the shelves along with the food products.

8

Housing, Furnishings, and Real Estate

LEARNING OBJECTIVES

Upon completion of Chapter 8, you should be able to identify and remember

- The advantages of renting or buying a home.
- The advantages of owning a single-family dwelling, mobile home, co-op apartment, condominium, and motor home or recreational van.
- The portion of one's income that can be allocated to housing costs in one year.
- A budget for housing costs, including rent or mortgage payments, taxes, insurance, home and yard upkeep, tools, deposits, parking rental, appliance needs, moving costs, and so on.
- A budget for various utility service needs.
- The meaning of the basic homebuying terms such as earnest money, closing costs, title insurance, first mortgage, and so on.
- The true interest rate on a mortgage in light of inflation and federal income taxes.
- The advantages and disadvantages of investing in additional real estate.
- Resource material for investing in multiplexes, acreages, small commercial structures, and mortgages and investing in companies with large real estate holdings.

HERMAN

"Take my tip. Get yourself a couple of
nice big caves and rent them out."

OVERVIEW

The cost of housing has become the number one concern for Americans, as present housing costs may well take up from 30 to 50 percent of a household's disposable income. In almost any year in the United States, from 1.3 million to 2.0 million housing units are started. Given the 90 million or so households in existence, this means that a unit of housing must last 42 to 65 years. There are around 107 million housing units in the United States, about one-third being rental units.

Even in years when new housing starts are running at the 2 million level, there can still be a housing shortage, and those houses available may be selling at very high prices. People who rent these housing units will find their household budgets strained. Several factors have contributed to the recent rise in the price of housing: (1) The post–World War II baby boom has reached the real estate market. (2) People are remaining single longer and want their own apartments or houses. (3) The rising divorce rate has contributed additional heads of households. And (4) shifts in the nation's population from one geographical area to another, or from the city to the suburb, cause certain housing unit prices to go up dramatically.

The rising U.S. population is another important factor. Urban renewal, freeway construction, and stricter city codes for fire, health, and sanitation can temporarily reduce the number of units available in a given location. Since land remains a relatively constant factor, the demand for land and therefore its price rises. The cost of an individual dwelling may be divided equally among land, labor, and materials.

The purpose of this chapter is to help you to become aware of the options available for finding appropriate housing as well as knowing your rights and responsibilities associated with homebuying or renting. We will learn to determine just how much housing you can afford each month and how much of a mortgage you can undertake. You will also learn the basic real estate terminology. The worksheets provided in this chapter can help you to gain a perspective of the cost of housing, furnishings, maintenance, utilities, and so on. We will also spend some time on investing in real estate beyond basic housing.

HOUSING

Housing Costs

Housing costs as used in this chapter signify the expenditures related to either renting or owning a home and include (1) the rent payment for tenants or basic mortgage payment for principal and interest for buyers; (2) expected cash outlays for home furnishings such as furniture, appliances, carpeting, and draperies; (3) out-of-pocket expenditures for normal maintenance and repairs where appropriate; (4) cash expenditures for yard and garden upkeep; (5) utility costs and other related expenses; (6) cash outlays for necessary insurance coverage; and (7) cash outlays for property taxes. If you are a tenant, almost all these expenditures, except perhaps electricity, gas, garbage fee, and telephone, plus an element of profit to the owner are included in the single monthly payment.

Inflation and Housing

People who sell their home today will feel positively rich right up to the time they must purchase their next home. Today, more dollars are attached to the price of housing than in the past. A home purchased in 1970 for $25,000 may be sold for $100,000, but it is difficult to tell if the $75,000 increase in such a home is a real profit or an illusory profit until the house is sold and the money is reinvested. If the proceeds from the sale of the home are used to acquire a similar house at today's inflated value, then the increased value is more illusory than real. On the other hand, if the proceeds from the sale are applied to a home located in a place where inflation is less, or if one moves into a larger home with more amenities, then the transaction may result in a net gain in real purchasing power.

Other factors determining real or illusory profits in selling a home are the length of time the home has been owned and the tax bracket of the owner and whether the funds remain a basis for the purpose of housing only or whether some or all of the funds are invested in some income-producing investment that does not require maintenance, property tax payments, insurance outlays, and so on. A $100,000 home at today's prices may allow you to avoid paying rent. However, $100,000 of cash invested in a certificate of deposit would earn interest income in the form of cash. In other words, while housing prices have risen in recent years, with the many costs of home ownership plus the interest income lost (opportunity cost) minus the rent saved by buying, the house should be appreciating.

The house must appreciate in value if the home is viewed as an investment rather than as a place to live. If the house is viewed as an investment, then all the expenditures that exceed reasonable rent must be plowed back into the home by raising its value. Raw land probably, on the other hand, has to appreciate in value by at least 20 percent per year to have a reasonable return.

Another important related cost is transportation. Whether you commute to and from your home or drive out to see your raw land occasionally, do not forget these costs of transportation. While transportation costs will be discussed in detail in Chapter 9, it is a good idea to consider housing and transportation as one "package of costs."

Another area to be explored as it relates to housing is inflation. The recent years of inflation have impacted all costs of living, be they for food, health care, transportation, and housing. When a person retires today, payments may still be continuing, or it may be more difficult to meet these payments on a retirement income. High interest rates charged on home loans in recent years often require longer mortgage loan periods. High levels of inflation and interest rates may tend to make the concept of retirement a luxury. Keeping a job until one reaches 70 years of age may be one of the best ways of reducing all debts and maintaining purchasing power.

Housing and Life-style

Housing is often a reflection of one's chosen life-style. Whether you live in town or in the suburbs, in a house, condo, a mobile home, or in an apartment, such decision should be based on what is best for you and your family at that particular time in life and into the foreseeable future. An old rule of thumb says that total housing costs should not exceed 25 percent of a person's *disposable income.*

Another rule states that housing and transportation costs should not exceed 40 percent of your *disposable income*. However, today a two-income family may spend as much as one-third of their *gross income* on housing. In decades past, when a young couple purchased a home, it too seemed a struggle to make mortgage payments in those beginning years. And, for a time, vacations were forgone or scaled back and other personal expenditures were postponed to make house payments. All these families thought they were "house poor." However, with rising productivity, good wages, and a low inflation rate, the burden of monthly mortgage payments only lasted a few years. In addition to real wage increases, greater opportunities for advancement, and overtime in the 1950s and 1960s, these people could add many durable goods and luxuries to their life-styles. Whether this will be true with today's new homebuyers remains to be seen.

Two incomes are generally needed to even think about purchasing a traditional first home today, and this fact will be changing the pattern of the housing market. With job security less assured in recent years, the loss of one of those incomes can make it extremely difficult for a couple to keep a home. Energy and transportation fuel was kept artificially low in past decades; this is no longer the case. Energy costs in homes purchased a few years ago now equal or exceed the basic mortgage payments each month. For many, there will have to be some reordering of priorities when it comes to types of housing and affordable housing.

The American dream of owning one's home symbolized that people had "made it" in this nation. Different symbols may emerge to signal life-time fulfillment and accomplishment in the future. In other nations, corporate-subsidized housing and commuting expenditures are becoming a matter of course for regular employees.

Types of Housing Accommodations

Where one lives often depends on the life-style chosen by an individual or household. Other influences include one's career, size of family and ages, level of income, hobbies, similar interests, and avocations. In this section we discuss some of the characteristics of the more common types of housing accommodations as well as important advantages and disadvantages usually associated with the particular form. Because price ranges can be substantial in any one of the following areas, no attempt is made to establish that one type of housing is always the least expensive. Furthermore, the highly mobile American individual or family, moving once every five years, also makes it difficult to advocate consistently one type of housing.

Apartment Units. Apartments offer the widest choice of housing for those just starting out in life, for the newly marrieds, and those finding themselves single again. Apartments can be found in the heart of the city or town as well as in the suburbs. They are high rise and low rise, furnished and unfurnished. There is no large down payment associated with apartments, and the tenants can usually move in if they meet character references, have the money for deposits, and pay the first and last months' rent. Usually the tenant can vacate the apartment by giving a 20- to 30-day notice to the landlord and no penalty is incurred. The landlord also can usually give the tenant a 20- to 30-day notice to move. Apartments appeal to those people who do not want to be bothered with maintenance and repairs, mowing the lawn, and other ownership problems.

The newer larger apartments may offer security, in the form of intercom systems, and provide mail, parcel, and furniture delivery services. Security can be one of the greatest features of an apartment. You should be able to leave your unit for several weeks or months without worrying about someone breaking into your place.

Apartment living may pose problems for the tenant who is fond of pets, enjoys playing the stereo at three o'clock in the morning, or has parties with many guests until all hours of the morning. A nosy management may be concerned about guests visiting your unit. Managers may not be carrying out their tasks and if you complain, they might say that you are the only one in the building complaining about something. Some managers are not professional in their work and serve mainly as a buffer between the tenant and the absentee owner.

Perhaps the ideal manager is one who both owns the building and lives on the premises. The owner-manager tends to keep the place maintained and do a good job of screening potential new tenants.

Today, all apartment buildings should have adequate parking. Good-quality security locks and dead bolt locks should be on all unit doors. The building should meet city building and fire protection codes. A concrete building with sprinkler system and lighted interior and exterior fire escapes offers one of the best forms of protection against fire.

For a few dollars more per month, one can find an apartment equipped with a swimming pool, recreational rooms, exercise rooms, and party rooms. Some apartments capitalize on the "fun and games" side of life and may restrict their tenant applicants to those within a certain age group and single.

While monthly cash rental costs are about one-half to two-thirds of the cost of buying similar housing, at the end of 25 to 30 years, the buyers will own their homes, whereas the apartment dweller will own nothing and will have to continue meeting monthly rent payments. However, many people rent to save for a down payment on a home. The person, couple, or family who continues to rent should also be saving the same amount of money that, if not invested in a home, should be going into other real estate, stocks, bonds, or other investment media.

Renting a modestly furnished apartment near to one's work and shopping is an excellent way to save a considerable amount in a short time. If it is possible to locate near a bus line, you may save some of the cost of owning an automobile.

Single-Family Homes. The single-family home or the independent detached dwelling is still very much a part of the American dream. It symbolizes many of the basic tenets of the American economic system. The right of ownership of property, pride of ownership; the concept of "my home is my castle"; a good place to raise a family, have pets, and gain a feeling of independence; and greater freedom are given as major reasons for owning a home.

Buying a home will require more additional ready cash than is required by the apartment renter. The homebuyer must save sufficient money to make a down payment, which may be as much as 5 to 25 percent of the market price of the house. In addition, the buyer must have cash for closing costs to complete the sale. This may easily amount to $750–1,500, depending on the activities included in the closing costs. Monthly and annual payments for the homebuyer will include mortgage payments, property taxes, property insurance, and maintenance expenditures.

While houses can be found in numerous shapes, sizes, and ages, very few new houses are located close to the center of town. Your favorite home may well be located several blocks or many miles from your place of work. An automobile may be a necessity since city bus systems may not serve the area. Older houses provide more charm and square feet of floor space for the dollar spent; however, old houses may lack adequate plumbing and electrical systems for modern living. The average homeowner will spend considerable *time and money* for tools and materials to make minor repairs and maintain the property.

Mobile or Manufactured Homes. A rapidly growing segment of the housing market is the mobile home, though a better term might be "an immobile home" as these units are towed by trucks to a specific site and the mobile home is set on permanent foundation. A 12' × 60' mobile unit (720 square feet) can be purchased for, say, $14,000. Two such modules joined together can provide 1,440 square feet of living space. Efficient use of space in the design of mobile homes provides greater interior living quarters that many homes and apartments may not have. Good design, insulation, exterior and interior paneling, and uniform window designs can help reduce utility and maintenance costs.

Federal standards, after June 15, 1976, have brought construction quality to the same level as that for regular individual housing. Zoning ordinances in many cities still tend to require mobile home parks to be located at the edges of town. Various states tax the mobile home as a vehicle rather than as real estate. The consumer who plans to purchase a manufactured home should be aware of and explore the following relevant questions: Are the transporting and setup costs included in the purchase price? Should I rent, lease, or buy the lot? Do setup costs include anchoring steps, and hand rails? What are the various utility hookup costs? What deposits are involved? It is probably a good idea to talk with people who have owned and lived in several mobile homes and parks.

In the past the mobile home tended to depreciate in value as it was used. Some of the newer and better manufactured homes are holding their prices and appreciating in value, however. This industry is beginning to benefit as people find it more difficult to purchase the traditional home. Around 6 million people now live in mobile homes.

Condominiums. A condominium signifies individual ownership of a dwelling unit and an undivided interest in the common areas and facilities that serve the multiunit facility. The condo unit has the advantages of apartment living and home ownership. There is growing popularity in condominium living, and the trend to condos will likely continue in the future. This type of facility is more energy efficient, provides better use of limited land space, and reduces overall construction costs. Over 5 million people live in condominium units.

"Condomania" has drawn many real estate developers to purchase apartment buildings and then sell the individual units. In apartment conversions, evidence indicates that not many of the former tenants become buyers. Two reasons come to mind. One is that more cash flow is necessary to switch from being a renter to being an owner. The second is that tenants in the building know the problems of the heating system, plumbing, lack of soundproofing, and so on and do not want to be involved with these neglected items after the developers transfer the building to the owner's association.

If you purchase one of the better and more expensive units in a condominium, you will certainly have a major commitment to seeing that the building maintains its value. In addition to the usual "brick and mortar" problems, there is a host of people problems. Rising costs of maintenance of the "common areas" of the condominium is another aggravation.

Co-ops or Cooperative Apartments. A "co-op" is an apartment building or group of dwellings owned by the residents and operated for their benefit by their elected board of directors. The residents occupy but do not own the units. They own shares of stock in the total enterprise. Many of the advantages and disadvantages resemble those associated with condominium units.

Others. Many people add a certain uniqueness to their lives by living in recreational vans, houseboats, old train depots, train coaches, fire stations, converted fishing boats, yachts, lighthouses, old mills, converted buses, and so on. While some of these dwellings may not be desirable for the long term, they can provide an interesting life experience.

The Basic Decision—Rent or Buy

In looking at the financial aspects surrounding the decision of whether to rent or to buy your housing needs, each approach to housing has its advantages and disadvantages. The advantages of renting are often the disadvantages of buying, and vice versa.

Financial factors relating to home ownership are often expressed as follows:

You are building an equity and eventual ownership; homebuying serves as a hedge against inflation; there are charges for income tax deductions; homebuying is considered a long-term investment; there is a predictable fixed monthly mortgage payment that will continue for the next 20 to 30 years; a larger sum of money is almost always needed at the outset to make the necessary down payment and handle closing costs; there must be money available for insurance coverage, home security needs, and property taxes; and, finally, it usually takes time to sell property, so, at times of job transfers, a person or family can end up paying on two homes for a period of time.

Financial factors related to renting are as follows: It requires less money when compared with homebuying; there is no equity buildup no matter how long you live in the place; there is no guarantee that rent will remain stable as with a mortgage payment; the house or building may be sold to new owners, and you may have to terminate your stay; when your apartment building changes hands, rents are usually raised to keep the same percentage rate of return on the new owner's investment.

Importance of Knowing Your Cash Flow

Probably a good starting point is to consider an apartment building that is converted into a condominium. Assume that you are living in an apartment unit and that you are paying $200 rent per month. If the unit were made into a condominium unit, as is, you could expect your monthly cash outlays to immediately rise from the $200 per month to $375 per month. For the moment, let us not consider the money required for the down payment and closing costs. The point to be grasped here is that, for a given amount of housing space, there is a dollar difference between renting and buying. In our illustration, the monthly cash difference is $175. The original down payment and these additional increments of $175 per month will allow you to own the unit in 25 or 30 years. Many people who are renting really never consider that this increment such as the $175 could be saved and invested each month. Most likely, this money will be spent on vacations, clothing, social and entertainment activity, transportation, eating out, and so on, whereas, when a person or family buys a home, they often give up, willingly or unwillingly, those kinds of activities.

This is why many people say that the only way they could save money was to buy a home. From a money manager's point of view, this raises a couple of questions: When you are considering the topic of housing, what is your goal? Is it a place to live or is it being commingled as a place to live and as an investment? It is a good idea to consider a home as fitting in with your life-style first and an investment second. Right now, homes appear to be a good investment as their values are rising. However, sometimes a house cannot be sold for months and even years. If your work requires you to be transferred, you may find yourself making payments for housing in two places; if you lose your job, your home "investment" just may evaporate.

Old Rules of Thumb on Housing

The 1970s was characterized by soaring prices for homes and higher apartment rents. And some of the old rules of thumb to determine how much housing cost a paycheck can withstand are no longer applicable.

For example, today, the combined salaries and wages of both the husband and wife or of a household must be considered on applications for a real estate loan, whereas years ago there was only the husband's income to be considered. Another major change has been the lengthening of the mortgage contract from a traditional 20-year term to 30 to 40 years. With more people in higher income tax brackets, the real impact of high interest rates can be diminished. A family in the 28 percent income tax bracket will find that a 10 percent mortgage interest rate will have about the same impact as a 7.2 percent interest rate several years ago. There is more willingness to accept the fact that inflation is now institutionalized in the economy. Therefore, the homeowner can continue to expect to pay off the mortgage with cheaper dollars.

These rules overlook some potential problems that appear to be emerging. Job certainty is not as great as it was in the 1950s and 1960s, and there are fewer opportunities to earn extra income. Moreover, it is not certain what long-term effects on the economy will result from these extended mortgages and high interest rates.

One old rule of thumb states that you can afford a home that is priced no more than two and a half times your annual income. Suppose that a married couple, both working, has a combined income of $20,000. Then, the amount of home they can afford is $50,000 ($20,000 × 2.5 = $50,000). In today's market this family's choice of housing would be limited to a small condominium unit or to a smaller and older home. However, for a family to consider a home in the $60,000 to $70,000 range would cause the family to commit 50 percent of their take-home pay for housing. The location of a newer home in these price ranges may be in distant suburbs, which are less attractive these days with higher gasoline costs.

A second rule of thumb says that you can afford total monthly housing costs (principal, interest, utilities, insurance, taxes, etc.) up to 20 percent of your total (family) monthly income. In this case, our couple with $20,000 annual income could afford total monthly housing costs of $333.33: ($20,000 ÷ 12) × .20 = $333.33. This would mean that only $250 to $275 would actually be going toward the payment of mortgage principal and interest. For mortgage payments to fall within these amounts today, the contract would require (1) a larger down payment on the home, (2) a much longer mortgage time period, or (3) both.

A variation on the rule states that you can afford total monthly housing costs by dividing your total income by the number 60. Once again, you will arrive at $333.33 per month (20,000 ÷ 60). The couple should still only spend $250 to $275 for mortgage payments, as the balance of the funds is necessary for utilities, insurance, and taxes at the minimum. One might get by for a few years without making repairs, particularly if the housing is new. However, these expenditures cannot be postponed too long. Recent government figures indicate that people are now spending up to 30 and 40 percent of their gross incomes on housing. This must mean that the life-styles of those people have become rather austere.

A third rule, which relates to renters, says to limit monthly rental costs to no more than one week's income. In this case, the couple earning $20,000 a year should spend no more than $384.62 per month on housing costs ($20,000 ÷ 52 = $384.62). This amount would have to cover rental payment, utilities, and other costs such as a parking stall. A more realistic modification of this rule would be to use only the one week's worth of take-home pay for the purposes of rent. Our couple earning $20,000 per year would have around $14,800 after the deduction of withholding taxes and Social Security. This would mean that the amount available for monthly rent would be around $285 ($14,800 ÷ 52).

In summary, maybe old rules of thumb never die, but some should be allowed to slip away. They only work with combined incomes being taken into consideration, large down payments, and very long mortgage periods. However, they still may be useful in sorting out obviously overpriced housing. The key point in housing is not to get in over your head. Many a couple face some strained relations when they shift from the life of renters to being "tied down" financially to a home.

Initial Cash Needs: Renting Versus Buying

Both the renter and homebuyer need to have cash sufficient to meet initial transaction costs. The renter should have cash to pay for the first and last months' rent plus damage and cleaning deposits, key deposits, and various utility meter and hookup fees.

The homebuyer will usually need several thousand dollars for a down payment, settlement or closing costs, which may run $700 to $2,000, homeowners insurance, utility installation or hookup costs, and so forth.

Both the tenant and homeowner should consider and budget moving costs and temporary housing and meals. Even though a person may be reimbursed by an employer, there sometimes can be a considerable time lag. Do not overlook the possibility of some legal fees in these situations. When you move to a different city, it is a good idea to have your bank help you establish a new account and provide a letter of introduction. When you are in a new area, travelers checks and bank cards should serve as a backup. In summary it is very easy to underestimate your cash needs in moving. Therefore, plan for some contingency money at times of moving.

Calculating Your Monthly Housing Needs

While rules of thumb are useful for making crude estimates, major decisions should involve some detailed figures and substantial thinking and rethinking.

One way is by preparing a sketch of your current living costs, savings, and the amount left over that can be spent for housing. This sketch can be based upon the master budget discussed in Chapter 3. It is suggested that you determine the expenditures that provide you with the life-style that you consider important and then determine the amount of housing that you can afford. Chances are that something will have to be given up, particularly if the decision is to purchase a home instead of continuing to rent. If the decision to buy is motivated primarily by the desire for an investment rather than for a family environment, some caution should be exercised. There may be easier ways to invest money to produce good yields. A single person may find a house to be mainly an investment or a device for reducing income taxes. However, for a single person, paying modest rent and investing the difference in quality stocks might achieve similar goals with less time, effort, and cash flow worries.

Basically, our analysis begins with the take-home pay for the month. Then, outline all the categories of expenses and savings except for housing, utilities, furnishings, and repairs. The difference between take-home pay and this subtotal of expenses will be the amount available for total housing. For purposes of illustration, return to the couple who has a combined income of $20,000 a year and who expects to have $14,800 after the deduction of income taxes and Social Security. This leaves a monthly take-home pay of $1,233. After considerable revision and study, they estimated that they could allocate $425 per month to housing expenses. (Note that the format corresponds with that in Chapter 3, page 69.)

Income tax savings are ignored in these calculations because the standard deductions and personal exemptions are being raised every few years, which reduces much of the former advantages of itemizing interest expenses and property taxes for homebuyers.

Monthly take-home pay		$1,233	100%
Expenses and savings			
1. Food	$120		
4. Transportation	270		
5. Clothing	50		
6. Health and life insurance	80		
7. Personal care	30		
8. Recreation and vacation	70		
9. Personal improvement	40		
10. Work related expenses	10		
11. Gifts, contributions	20		
12. Contingencies	30		
13. Family allowances	20		
14. Miscellaneous expenses	10		
15. Savings	50		
Subtotal		800	65%
Balance for housing (2, 3)		$ 433	35%

Calculation of Monthly Mortgage Payment

Let us now assume that the couple with $20,000 of income is interested in purchasing a condominium unit for $50,000, no more than two and a half times their annual income. This condominium unit requires a 20 percent down payment and a 30-year mortgage at an interest rate of 10 percent. Other anticipated costs on such a unit are a 1 percent property tax based on the gross value of the unit, or $500 for the year, and homeowner insurance of approximately $180 annually. The couple estimates utility costs at $40 per month. Maintenance and other upkeep costs are $30 per month. They have an estimate for future household appliances and furnishings at $20 per month.

With this information and the $433 per month that can be spent on housing, we can determine the amount of money available for the mortgage payment and whether or not a mortgage of $40,000 for 30 years at 10 percent can be undertaken. The following sketch will help make the determination:

Monthly allocation for total housing		$433
Less: Property taxes (1% of $50,000 ÷ 12)	$42	
Monthly insurance ($180 ÷ 12)	15	
Estimated utility costs	40	
Maintenance and upkeep	30	
Furniture and appliance budget	20	147
Balance for monthly mortgage payment		$286

Based upon the calculations, the $433 total housing budget minus estimated expenditures will allow for a $286 monthly mortgage payment.

With the help of Table A.4 in Appendix A, the following steps will give us a very close approximation of what the monthly mortgage payment will be on a $40,000, 30-year, 10 percent mortgage. (The difference from the exact monthly amount is due to compounding, and the amount is off only by about $2.00.) Note the following three steps in finding the answer:

1. In Table A.4, find the factor in the 10 percent column and on line (year) 30. This factor is 9.42691.
2. Take the amount of the mortgage of $40,000 ($50,000 minus down payment of $10,000) and divide it by the factor

$$\$40,000 \div 9.42691 = \$4,243.17$$

3. Find one month's payment:

$$\$4,243.17 \div 12 \text{ months} = \$353.60 \text{ monthly payment}$$

Based upon these figures, the couple would be $67.60 short of their required monthly mortgage payment ($353.60 − $286). They could decide if they really wanted the condo unit badly enough to make additional cuts in their monthly living expenses. The extra money would have to come from the flexible (discretionary) portions of their budget such as recreation and vacation, clothing, and savings. Finding the extra $67.60 will increase their original total housing budget from $433 to $500. This would in turn cause their housing costs to approach 40 percent of their take-home pay.

How much mortgage could this couple assume within the $286 per month of cash available? This can be easily determined by working backward through the preceding steps. The $286 of monthly cash available could handle a $32,353.16 mortgage at 10 percent for 30 years ($286 × 12 months = $3,432 × 9.42691 = $32,353.16).

To summarize, these little sketches and the use of Table A.4 will prove most useful in reviewing various housing possibilities. These will also help a family to consider their real priorities concerning housing. The couple that can raise the large down payment, as in this illustration, appears to have made a home of their own a major goal. It might also be of interest to know how the $10,000 was accumulated. If the couple had lived in modest rental housing for several years and maintained a frugal life-style, they could probably have saved the down payment. On the other hand, if the couple has borrowed the $10,000 from relatives and has made little or no effort to save money from their combined incomes in the past, then this couple may have a very difficult time adjusting to being "tied down" and "house poor."

Total Cost of Borrowing—Principal and Interest

How much cash will our couple pay out over the 30 years on the $40,000 mortgage at a 10 percent interest rate? How much of the total payments over the years will consist of interest on the borrowing? The following calculations can be approximated using the assumed monthly mortgage payment of $353.60:

Total cash payments ($353.60 × 360 months)	$124,296
Less: Total amount of the original mortgage	40,000
Total interest paid over life of mortgage	$ 84,296

In brief, it would cost $84,296 for the use of $40,000 over 30 years.

How Much Is Your Home Costing You?

Many people who buy a home or have paid for their home often wonder just how much this asset is costing them each year. Others want to know whether they would be better off financially if they sold their homes and moved into apartments, as expenses relating to the upkeep of their homes are generally rising faster than their annual incomes.

There is no one simple answer to any of these questions. A person is moving from one kind of life-style to another. However, a couple of illustrations as well as some thoughts about long-term renting may be helpful when you are thinking of making such a change.

Let us begin by making some assumptions and calculations for the homeowner. First, assume that you are currently living in a home that has a realistic resale value of $75,000. You also have the following annual out-of-pocket costs: $1,500 for property taxes, $2,000 for heating and utilities, $800 average for maintenance and repairs to the home, and $280 for homeowner insurance premiums. Suppose that, if you had the $75,000 invested in quality corporate securities, you could be earning a 6 percent return after taxes.

The following sketch will arrive at the approximate annual cost of home ownership:

Alternate income forgone ($75,000 × .06)	$4,500
Annual property taxes paid	1,500
Total utilities and heating costs	2,000
Estimated maintenance and repairs	800
Homeowner insurance premiums	280
Annual cost of home ownership	$9,080

The calculations indicate that it is costing the homeowner $9,080 per year. This $9,080 is slightly more than 12 percent of the fair market value of the home ($9,080 ÷ $75,000). This is not unusual, and the figure might range from 10 to 15 percent, depending on components.

The $4,500 ($75,000 × .06) is the interest income lost or forsaken as the $75,000 value of the home is not invested at the moment. This $4,500 a year that is forgone or lost is what economists call *opportunity cost*. It makes no difference whether the home is completely paid for or not. This rather narrow concept is simply stating that one has a $75,000 asset and that it is not invested or earning a return. You may be thinking at this moment that, if you did not have the home, you would have to be paying rent to someone. On this point, you would be correct. The amount of rent might be subject to some variation.

To summarize, if the total cost of home ownership of $9,080 were to equal the total costs of renting a home, payment of utilities, personal property insurance, and so on, it would make no difference whether you keep your home or rent. The point is that, when the total costs of renting exceed $9,080 per year, you would be better off owning your housing. Many people feel that they can find very adequate rental units for much less than $9,080 per year.

From Homeowner to Renter: A Case Study

Let us now take the same information relating to the $75,000 fair-market-value home as well as the related annual costs of ownership and apply them to a long-term renter.

Suppose that the same home was purchased 15 years ago for $20,000 with a $1,000 down payment; the mortgage was for $19,000 with an interest rate of 6 percent for 25 years. Assume also that there is still $12,000 owed on the mortgage at the time of sale. There is a 7 percent sales commission when the home is sold. Other costs if the sale takes place would be $2,000 for fix-up expenses, legal assistance, moving costs, and a portion of the year's property taxes.

The apartment that the homeowner is thinking about renting carries a $400-per-month rent, average utility costs of $50 per month, and parking stall for one car of $20 per month; personal property insurance on belongings will be $60 per year. The following steps can be an approach for looking at the cash flows when selling a home and renting housing.

Step 1. Selling the home and collecting the proceeds

Sale for cash		$75,000
Less: Commission paid	$ 5,250	
Mortgage payoff	12,000	
Other expenditures	2,000	
Federal income taxes	0	19,250
Net cash proceeds		$55,750

The proceeds from the sale are $55,750. This is the amount of cash that can be immediately invested and earn a rate of return. Assume that any investments will yield an after-tax return of 6 percent. A recent Internal Revenue rulings change allows up to $125,000 of gain on sale of a home to be exempt from tax. This is a one-time-only opportunity.

Step 2. Determine the total cash to be available for rental costs

Income from invested proceeds ($55,750 × .06)	$3,345
Plus: Property taxes eliminated	1,500
Utilities and heating cost eliminated	2,000
Maintenance and repairs eliminated	800
Homeowner insurance canceled	280
Cash available for rent and expenses	$7,925

The $7,925 represents the cash income from investments plus the cash not spent on former necessary expenditures.

Step 3. Determine the cost of renting new apartment facilities and the amount of cash left over for future costs and rent increases

Cash available for rental costs per year		$7,925
Less: Rent on new apartment	$4,800	
($400 × 12 months)		
Utilities ($50 × 12 months)	600	
Parking ($20 × 12 months)	240	
Personal property insurance	60	
Total rental costs		5,700
Remaining cash reserve each year		$2,225

This calculation indicates that it will cost approximately $5,700 to rent the apartment and pay utilities, insurance, and parking. This still leaves $2,225 remaining of cash available to be invested or spent for other things. Perhaps most of this "left-over-cash" should be invested to hedge against utility and rent increases in the future.

This study is only concerned with establishing an approach to cash movement when one sells a house and begins renting. The many intangibles related to these two different life-styles can only be evaluated by the individual.

Factors Favoring Long-Term Renting

When exploring opportunities to buy or rent housing needs, there are some important factors about renting that are often overlooked. Many people spend much of their lives renting their housing. These people are not necessarily on low incomes. There are some real money-saving factors involved, providing that the rental building is going to be held by the owner-manager for a very long time and that the tenant can stay in the building for an equally long time. The savings to the tenant will probably cease if the building is sold to new owners at a substantially higher price.

People who own apartment buildings for a long time will want and cater to tenants who are contented with rental life-styles. Keep in mind the tenant who lives in a unit for many years saves the owner-manager expenditures on remodeling, refurbishing, advertising, and the possibility of a vacant unit for a couple of months.

Some tenants in such a building will be short-term tenants. Those new tenants moving into a building will be expected to pay the current going rate for rent. The owner-manager will be able to generate extra cash revenue from these newer tenants, and this can quickly be used for any higher costs that may be resulting from inflation. The bulk of the long-term tenants may receive only modest or no rent increases for longer periods of time. The key to low-cost renting is to remain in the same apartment for several years.

The owner-manager will not want to see a good long-term tenant leave. The reason is that the apartment unit may have to have extensive interior remodeling to make the unit competitive with others on the market. This remodeling may mean new carpets and new bathroom and kitchen fixtures—and at today's prices. In addition to this expenditure, the unit may not be ready to rent for a couple of months or longer. In brief, it may take the owner-manager three or four years to recover all those costs even with the new higher rents.

The owner-manager of an apartment building is also making payments on a mortgage, property taxes, insurance, and basic maintenance. These cash payments must be made faithfully. In normal times even the better apartments will have some vacancies. There is an incentive to see that the long-term tenant remains. This can be done simply by not raising rents or raising them very little. Owners of smaller apartment buildings and multiplexes cannot afford to have high vacancy rates as it will seriously affect their cash flow. Therefore, there is an incentive to keep happy tenants.

Owners of smaller apartments (say, less than 30 units) will probably do much of the maintenance and repair work themselves. Chances are they do this out of necessity or because they consider this work as a hobby related to their investment. As long as the land and building are appreciating in value and the cash flow remains positive, the long-term tenant of such building will usually find stable rental housing costs.

The long-term renter should take time in seeking out good apartments with these opportunities. These buildings will not be the newest, which may cater to young people who stay a few months and then leave. Newer apartment buildings are often lacking in quality building materials, have no character and charm, and are noisy. The newer units may have more modern bathroom and kitchen fixtures; however, the lack of quality will often make the newness short lived. Many new apartment buildings are made of wood materials.

Long-term tenants should look for buildings made of concrete, brick, or stone. There should be concrete interior fire escapes and metal exterior fire exit staircases. There should be sprinkler systems in the common areas of the building and garage areas. The building should have intercom systems and electronic front door locks for screening all callers. Checklists of key features of the apartment units can be helpful to see if the quality meets with your approval. The checklist in Exhibit 8-1 is designed for apartment tenants. Exhibit 8-2 is a checklist for homeowners, particularly buyers of detached houses on lots. Both checklists may be helpful for persons buying a condominium, co-op apartment, or mobile home.

In summary, because the average person is moving frequently or is set on home ownership, few people explore this side of housing. If renting meets with your life-style, the difference saved between renting and home ownership allows for larger sums to be invested each month. Investing the difference in quality stocks provides both appreciation and dividend income. Renting can provide a more worry-free life-style, and renters usually resist spending money on things a homeowner will purchase for repairs and remodeling. Apartments are usually more efficient with utilities than detached homes, and one can save considerably on these expenses. Another key factor in renting is the saving of transportation or commuting costs.

EXHIBIT 8-1 Apartment Unit Checklist

		YES OK	NOT OK	Your comment
ENTIRE APARTMENT UNIT	Thermostat working?			
	Ventilation fans working?			
	Double-lock front door, chain?			
	Furniture fit elevator/stairs?			
LIVING ROOM	Windows functioning?			
	Walls (paint/cracks)?			
	Carpet/level floor?			
	Built-in shelves			
BEDROOMS	Windows			
	Walls (paint/cracks)?			
	Carpet/level floor?			
	Built in cabinet/closet/drawers			
BATHROOMS	Tiles/walls			
	Cabinet/lights/outlets			
	Basin/stopper/water pressure			
	Faucets (backward turning)?			
	Tub (normal drainage)?			
	Shower/tile/door/pressure			
	Commode (normal flushing)?			
	Towel racks/mirror			
	Other fixtures			
KITCHEN	Refrigerator:			
	freezer section			
	lower section			
	racks/trays			
	Cabinets/shelves/hinges			
	Oven/range			
	Sink (enamel chipping)?			
	Faucet (water pressure enough)?			
	Dishwasher/washing machine			
	Garbage disposal			
	Counter top			
PUBLIC AREAS AND MANAGEMENT	Building entrance appearance			
	Hallways (vacuumed weekly)?			
	Garbage chute room			
	Elevator, clean/lighting/mirror			
	Inside staircase/			
	Outside staircase			
	Laundry room (clean)?			
	Storage room (lighting/security)?			
	Parking area (garage door)?			
	Mailbox area			
	Manager available/knowledgeable?			
MISCELLANEOUS				

EXHIBIT 8-2 Homeowner's Checklist

CATEGORY	YES OK	NOT OK	NEED AP- PRAISAL	COMMENTS
EXTERNAL:				
Roof and roofing material				
Structure sound				
Paint and weatherproofing				
Strong foundation				
Drainage				
Waterproof basement				
Adequate garage area				
Good walkways, drive, patio				
Boundary lines known				
Chimneys				
Attics and crawl space				
Street light/hydrants				
ENERGY RATING:				
Electricity 120V, 100 Amps.				
Water pressure				
Insulation R–rating				
Heating system				
Hot water system				
Storm windows/thermo panes				
MASTER BEDROOM:				
Good floor plan				
Walk–in closet space				
Sufficient room space				
Walls, paint				
Windows, locks, cranks				
Temperature controls				
BATHROOMS:				
Modern design				
Water pressure				
Sinks, faucets				
Commode (normal flushing)?				
Tub/shower/faucet				
Valves/traps/ventilation				
Tile surfaces unbroken				
Cabinets/shelves				
Mirrors/towel racks				
KITCHEN:				
Modern design				
Refrigerator				
Freezer section $0°$				
Lower section				
Racks and trays				
Door opening/venting space				
Oven/range/timers				
Adequate cabinet space				

KITCHEN (cont'd):				
Non-staining countertops				
Quality floor covering				
Quality sink/faucets				
Windows/cranks working				
Exhaust fans working				
Garbage disposal				
Quality dishwasher				
Adequate eating area				
Saves extra steps?				
DINING ROOM AREA:				
Good location/floor plan				
Adequate table and seating space				
Appropriate lighting/outlets				
Windows/walls/paint				
Quality flooring				
Stairs or steps				
LIVING ROOM:				
Room large and quiet?				
Away from kitchen noise?				
Away from foot traffic?				
Sound walls, flooring level				
Fireplace				
Stairs or steps				
UTILITY ROOM:				
Conveniently located?				
Adequate wiring				
Good water pressure?				
Adequate hot water tank?				
Washer/dryer unit				
Good lighting and outlets				
Good doors and soundproofing				
OTHER BEDROOMS:				
Good floor plan				
Walk-in closet space				
Sufficient room space				
Walls, paint				
Windows, locks, cranks				
Temperature controls				
GENERAL QUESTIONS:				
Zoning protects property value?				
Near work/shopping/bus stop?				
Convenient to school/church?				
Stable neighborhood?				
Clear driveway entry?				
New heating system?				
Security dead bolts?				
Do you fit in with neighbors?				
Is your income similar?				

An astute renter should save $100 to $300 per month more than those who "buy" their housing and commute long distances. If you can save $200 per month, that is $2,400 saved each year. Annual savings of $2,400 invested at 6 percent after taxes will amount to $31,633 in just 10 years ($2,400 × 13.18079, Table A.3 of Appendix A). Money not spent for down payments and closing costs can be retained and invested. Assume you had $7,000 available for these costs. If you do not spend this "lump-sum" fund of money, it could be earning interest or dividend income. At 6 percent after-tax return, the original $7,000 will grow to $12,536 ($7,000 × 1.79085, Table A.1 of Appendix A) in just 10 years. It is doubtful that an average home will appreciate by similar amounts at the end of 10 years when these two savings areas are combined.

Checklists for Housing

Hunting for housing is often carried out under limited time constraints. Searching for an appropriate apartment unit, condominium, or house in a couple of weeks or even months is not a welcomed task. Often, moving is associated with job changes and transfers. Because of this, it is useful to develop some checklists of key features desired in your home as well as defects and drawbacks to be avoided.

There is probably no one checklist which will be so complete or detailed as to meet individual needs. However, the examples illustrated in Exhibits 8-1 and 8-2 can be a starting place. Location will be the primary concern for a homebuyer. Long-term stability of the neighborhood will have much to do with shopping areas, schools being kept open, and property maintaining its value. Previously undesirable locations are being reviewed because of higher gasoline prices. Apartments and condominiums offer the widest location flexibility. There are other important factors to consider in housing. Older houses and apartments may have inadequate electrical amperage and low water pressure. Bathroom and kitchen facilities may be cramped and worn. Alternative transportation to and from a home during inclement weather should be considered.

Brush fires, floods, tornadoes, hurricanes, industrial pollution, and airport noise should be reviewed by homebuyers. While natural disasters are harder to prepare for, locations of creeks, rivers, airports, factories, prevailing winds, and traffic should be explored. Low-lying land may result in sewer backup and flash flooding when heavy rains occur. Secluded areas may invite vandalism and burglaries. If an apartment or condominium unit is located on the windward side of a high-rise building, higher heating costs can be expected.

Having a licensed appraiser look over your potential home purchase should be considered. This person will check out the technical areas relating to the exterior, roof, plumbing, heating system, electrical system, and attics and crawl space. He or she will also check out grading, drainage, and erosion control of the site.

Earnest Money Agreement

People who are going to purchase their housing will enter into a contract with the seller. This brief document is variously called an earnest money agreement or earnest money receipt and sales agreement. In essence, this is the *contract* between a buyer and a seller. This properly prepared document is binding and enforceable.

Many buyers do not understand this critical and vital point. Many buyers enter into this phase of homebuying thinking that this is one of several steps in the purchasing and negotiating process. Many buyers will sign this agreement and later think about trying to borrow money.

In this document, there will be statements concerning an accurate description of the property, not just its address, and the amount of the deposit money. The buyer will want to make the smallest deposit; the seller and his or her real estate agent will prefer large deposits. This money is deposited with a disinterested third party or firm in what is called an escrow trust fund. The money is not available to either party until the contract is completed, whereupon it becomes part of the down payment on the home. If the buyer cannot complete the contract or the time runs out, the money is forfeited and goes to the would-be seller.

Other information described in the earnest money agreement is the amount of down payment, size of mortgage, mortgage interest rate, term of loan, payments on taxes, agreements on any repairs to be made, and so on. Be sure to write in *escape clauses* if you are the buyer so that the contract is binding "contingent on obtaining the loan and interest rate," "contingent upon final appraisal report," "contingent upon review by attorney," and so on. As the buyer, you might include daily penalties if the seller has not moved out by a specific date. Exhibit 8-3 (p. 227) illustrates fundamental excerpts of a sample earnest money agreement. Since these basic documents must conform to state real estate laws, many real estate documents are preprinted.

Closing Costs

Closing costs, or settlement costs as they are often called, are the costs related to the purchase of a home, for example, finders fees, title insurance, fire insurance, survey fee, credit report, appraisal fee, mortgage insurance, recording of deed, recording of mortgage, property taxes, attorney's fee, tax registration, loan originating fee, and so. Until the passage of the Real Estate Settlement Procedures Act of 1974, many gimmicks were used to increase the return to the seller.

Title insurance is still a murky area, and consumers must direct their efforts to obtaining equity. Title insurance is concerned with two areas: (1) title guarantee, which provides protection for the buyer against errors in the public records, and (2) title insurance, which protects the buyer from all other defects (in other words, if you cannot teach responsibility, then offer insurance to compensate for it). Sample closing costs might be as follows, exclusive of down payments and earnest money deposit paid:

Loan application fee	$ 30
Loan origination fee	500
Mortgage insurance fee	180
Processing fee	160
Appraisal fee	60
Credit report	25
Title insurance	80
Recording fee	20
Tax registration fee	20
Total	$1,075

In addition to closing costs, down payments, and escrow deposits, other little and large batches of cash may still be required. These are prorations of real estate taxes due, fire insurance coverage, fees for drawing up legal documents, and even photographs if these are not included in the appraiser's fee. Do not forget to budget money for certain immediate repairs, modifications, painting, and so on that you plan to carry out upon moving to your new home.

A final point about closing costs should be made. Most of these costs are not deductible for income tax purposes. These various fees become part of the cost of the home. Itemizable tax deductions are limited to mortgage interest expense paid, property taxes paid, and loan fees paid. To be on the safe side, set aside cash in the amount of 5 percent of the mortgage needed to cover earnest money and closing costs.

Moving

Moving dates and moving costs should be an integrated part of decisions related to real estate activity. Renters, homebuyers, and sellers should all set dates for occupying (or vacating) their new facilities. A homebuyer may find the seller slow to move unless the earnest money agreement contains daily penalties for delay of moving.

If you engage a professional moving company, there are some basics to be aware of on charges. If you are moving within the city or town, the basic moving unit might be two movers and one truck. You will be charged by the hour, and the clock starts when the truck leaves the warehouse and stops when the truck returns to the warehouse. Total moving charges can be increased or reduced depending on how well you have prepared for the move. The number of boxes packed, access to elevators, stairways, size of truck, type of furniture, weight, number of individual pieces, and bulk will affect the total charges. The more you do yourself in preparation and packing, the more you can save on the moving bill.

EXHIBIT 8-3 Excerpts of Earnest Money Agreement (Sample)

EARNEST MONEY RECEIPT AND AGREEMENT

On this _____ day of _____ of the Year _____, in
the City of _____ in the County of _____
in the State of _____; Received from _____
_____ herein called the Purchaser the sum
of _____ Dollars ($ _____)
in the form of a check for $_____, cash for $_____,
note for $_____ due _____ paid or delivered
as earnest money as part payment of the purchase price on the following described real estate in the City of _____
in the County of _____, in the State of _____
_____.

The legal description of the property is as follows:

The total purchase price is _____
_____ ($_____), payable as follows: _____
_____
_____
_____
_____

The seller agrees to allow the purchaser

This offer is subject to the buyer securing financing needed.

_____   _____
        Buyer   Seller

Long-distance moving between state lines calls for different moving costs.
Moving van lines are regulated by the Interstate Commerce Commission when
they operate across state borders. The basic factors are weight and mileage. All
van lines charge the same rates; therefore, estimates from two or three representatives can be useful in determining the weight of your household goods. Do not
be surprised if the estimates of weight are below the actual weight of your
belongings.

   If you have several thousand pounds of furniture and household goods,
you should accompany the van to the weighing station before and after the

loading of your goods. You should observe the weighing of the vehicle and witness amounts written on documents. If you do not accompany the truck to the weigh station, extra weight could be added to your load.

Mark all boxes containing breakable items, and open these boxes while the driver is present. A record of broken items can be noted on the related moving documents before signing off the driver.

Income Taxes, Inflation, and Interest Rates

Few people will be able to purchase their homes by paying cash. Moreover, those with substantial incomes may not want to pay cash, particularly if their earnings are subject to heavy federal income taxes. Finally, inflation allows the debtor to pay off the mortgage with cheaper dollars.

Currently, in America, mortgage interest expense and real estate property taxes paid in excess of the standard deduction amount qualify as an itemizable deduction. Logic might have it that the federal income tax should be a tax based on one's income. The choice of how one selects a shelter should not be influenced by the federal income tax system. However, as taxable income rises, even though it is mainly the result of inflation, many people may feel that they are forced to become homeowners. This kind of tax policy has stimulated demand for housing. Coupled with artificially low gasoline and energy costs, U.S. housing has been very wasteful of valuable resources and contributes to urban sprawl.

The rising cost of housing may make it possible for only the well-to-do to acquire homes. The prospect of a federal tax system's continuing to provide this subsidy may end. This may be beginning to take place as the standard deduction amount is increased. Homebuyers may find that interest expense and property taxes will provide tax shelter relief for fewer years than in the past. Chapter 11 offers many comments on how the current income tax system functions.

Mortgage interest rates have doubled in the past decade to as high as 10 to 17 percent. However, demand appears just as strong as it was at 8 percent. It is useful to know the real impact of interest expense or the real interest rate on borrowing.

Assume that a person is buying a home with a mortgage. The stated interest rate on the mortgage is 11 percent, and the individual is in the 30 percent marginal income tax bracket. Furthermore, long-term inflation appears to remain at 6 percent. The following calculations will determine the real interest costs after inflation and taxes:

Stated mortgage interest rate	11.00%
Less: Long-term inflation rate	6.00
	5.00
Marginal tax rate (11% × .30)	3.30
Real cost of borrowing	2.70%

Thus, we find that the real impact of a 11 percent mortgage after inflation and income tax deductions is 2.7 percent. This helps to explain why high interest rates do not necessarily cause the demand for money to decline.

If inflation and favorable tax laws offset the impact of high interest rates, what will cause a slowdown in housing? The answer usually is that lending institutions run out of loanable funds, so that higher down payments will be required and shorter loan periods will be mandated, or both. Recession, higher unemployment, and threats to one's job security may cause certain segments of population to postpone house hunting.

Planning Worksheets for Housing

Both renters and homebuyers will need to budget adequately each year for their housing. While monthly rent and mortgage generally remain constant, other related housing expenditures may slip from memory.

The worksheet for a renter illustrated in Exhibit 8-4 is designed not only to cover basic rent but also to include the costs of other expenditures. A memoranda section is included to keep track of deposits, their refund, and their dates of return. Estimates for utilities are shown later in a separate worksheet.

EXHIBIT 8-4   Apartment/Home Renter Worksheet and Budget

Category	Monthly Expense	Multiply by	Total Amount
Apartment or house rent		x 12	
Parking stall rental		x 12	
Other fees, deposits, TV cable, hookups, etc.			
Tenant's property and liability insurance			
Security: Extra locks, keys, smoke detector, batteries			
Miscellaneous: Moving costs, fix-up, paint			
Total Estimate for the Year			

Memoranda:

Special deposits records

1. Damage $_____   Refundable?_____   When/how?_____

2. Telephone $_____   Refundable?_____   When/how?_____

3. Utility Met. $_____   Refundable?_____   When/how?_____

4. Cable TV $_____   Refundable?_____   When/how?_____

5. _____ $_____   Refundable?_____   When/how?_____

EXHIBIT 8-5   John & Kay Adams
Homeowner Budget
For the Year _____

Category	Monthly Payment	Multiply by	Total Amt.
Mortgage Payments	#180 –	12	#2,160 –
Management Fees			
Parking Stall Fees			
Fire, Property Insurance (HO-5) Type			275 –
Home insulation, wheather proofing, etc.			–
Painting – interior & exterior			50 –
Yard & Garden Care, Seeds, Plants, Chemicles			50 –
Yard & Garden tools, furniture, equip.			100 –
Do-it-yourself tools & materials			25 –
Heating System check-up fee			25 –
Property Taxes			800 –
		Total Estimate for the Year	#3,485 –

Annual homeowner costs beyond the basic mortgage payments need to be considered. The worksheet shown in Exhibit 8-4 includes the very basics of home costs and maintenance. Persons living in a condominium or co-op will need to consider the costs of the monthly management fee and parking. Basic maintenance will include expenditures for painting, yard and garden needs, and trips to the hardware store for tools and materials.

For a moment, let us return to the John and Kay Adams family and review the worksheet that Kay has put together for the year. The worksheet reflects a long-established home situation as the mortgage payments are rather modest. However, the budget for a homeowner HO-5 insurance policy reflects a home worth substantially more. Property taxes may also reflect the upward valuation of the home. Kay estimates that basic housing costs exclusive of utilities and furnishings will amount to $3,485 for the coming year as shown in Exhibit 8-5.

Planning Worksheets for Utilities

Utility costs are perhaps the fastest-rising element in housing costs today. In this section, telephone, electricity, water, gas, fuel oil, garbage, trash-hauling costs, city transit taxes, and so on are all called utilities. It is better to have a more specific view of these expenditures so that you do not overlook key costs. Using a washing machine may only show up in the water and electric bill. For a tenant, a separate entry may have to be made for use of a coin-operated washing machine and dryer.

Exhibit 8-6 reflects the estimates by Kay Adams. The estimate of $1,111 of utilities costs may appear excessive or grossly inadequate depending upon where a person lives and the type of energy used. The John and Kay Adamses invested in a solar unit a few years ago, and it has reduced the family's reliance on fuel oil. Additional insulation two years ago has brought a further substantial reduction in home energy costs. Lights are not left on when not in use, and

EXHIBIT 8-6   John & Kay Adams
Household Utilities Expense Budget
For the Year _____

Categories	Monthly Estimate	Times/Yr.	Total Amt.
Telephone – Local	#10 –	12	#120 –
– Long Distance			30 –
– Public Phones			5 –
Electricity – Lights &	40 –	12	480 –
Appliances			
Heating "Solar"			
Water	8 –	12	96 –
Gas – Natural, Propane			–
Fuel Oil – Heating – reserve			300 –
Garbage fee	5 –	12	60 –
Trash Hauling fee	2 –	5	10 –
Plastic Liner Bags			10 –
Cable T.V. Charge			–
Coin Operated Laundry			–
City Transit Tax			–
Metro Sewerage Tax			–
			–
	Total Estimate for the Year		#1,111 –

lower thermostat settings have helped to hold down the cost of energy and utilities.

Home energy and utility costs will probably continue to rise in the future. In some places these monthly expenditures now equal or exceed the basic monthly mortgage payment. Many Americans are taking measures to reduce transportation energy costs as well as home heating and electrical costs. Future developments may require people to have more technical knowledge about household appliance needs.

Appliances around the home are generally for their convenience and time-saving features. Future purchases of major appliances should require the consumer to consider annual electrical costs. Additional money spent toward a quality refrigerator, oven, or freezer may save many hundreds or even thousands of dollars in reduced electrical costs over their useful lives. The same may be true for such appliances as dishwashers, washing machines, and dryers. These last appliances may be used much more sparingly in the future than today. The key to money management with utilities will be conservation.

Home energy costs can be substantially reduced by the use of insulation. These expenditures should be considered as investments, as storm windows and insulation materials in the attic and walls will pay for themselves in just a few years. An insulation "jacket" around the hot-water heater tank unit is a similar example.

For determining the amount of insulation needed, consult a guide on R-values. (R-values refer to resistances against heat transfer or heat loss.) The higher the R, the more effective the insulation will be against heat loss in the winter and heat gain in the summer. Recommended minimum for attics is R-26 or more than 8 inches of glass fiber or rock wool. Exterior walls should have a minimum of R-11. Floor and crawl spaces under the house should also be insulated. Moreover, do not overlook the need for caulking and weather stripping around windows, sashes, and doors. Exhibit 8-7 shows recommended R-values of insulation for various temperature zones in the United States.

The type of energy—gas, electricity, oil, coal, wood—used in the home can save a couple of hundred dollars each year. The pilot light on gas stoves and furnaces can use up valuable energy in a year's time. A poorly adjusted fuel oil stove can also waste many dollars of fuel. In the future, a combination of gas, oil, and wood may be needed to provide low-cost heating to a home.

FURNISHINGS

Accumulating home furnishings should be accomplished with considerable thought, planned for with a firm budget limitation, and purchased rather sparingly. Furniture will not only last you for a lifetime if purchased with care, but quality furniture will be one of the few items that may well appreciate in *real*

EXHIBIT 8-7   Heating Zone Map

R-Values

Heating zone	Recommended for			Batts or blankets		Loose fill (poured in)		
	Ceiling	Floor		Glass fiber (in)	Rock wool (in)	Glass fiber (in)	Rock wool (in)	Cellulosic fiber (in)
0, 1	R-26	R-11	R-11	3½–4	3	5	4	3
2	R-26	R-13	R-13	4	4½	6	4½	3½
3	R-30	R-19	R-19	6–6½	5¼	8–9	6–7	5
4	R-33	R-22	R-22	6½	6	10	7–8	6
5	R-38	R-22	R-26	8	8½	12	9	7–7½
			R-30	9½–10½	9	13–14	10–11	8
			R-33	11	10	15	11–12	9
			R-38	12–13	10½	17–18	13–14	10–11

Tips for Energy Savers, Energy Conservation Now, Report no. 0-244-894, Pueblo, Colo.: GPO, 1977.

value while it is being used. The house may increase in value, but it may only be illusory because one is attempting to get back interest, taxes, maintenance costs, and imputed interest, which are part of the costs of holding a house.

In the John and Kay Adams family, Kay has been reviewing the needs for the home in the way of furniture, linens, appliances, and various household cleaners. The family has been planning to purchase some additional living room furniture. This has been a high priority for a couple of years. Kay estimates this

THE FAMILY CIRCUS

"Sometimes I wonder why we bought
a seven-room house."

Reprinted with special permission
of Cowles Syndicate.

will be around $1,500 if special sale prices are acted upon. Note the simple
planning sheet and budget in Exhibit 8-8.

INVESTING IN REAL ESTATE BEYOND HOUSING NEEDS

Home values in the 1970s rose from $21,000 to $70,000 or $90,000 for just a basic
house; in the same years, finer homes rose in value from $35,000 to $150,000 or
$200,000. People who have made a successful home purchase are encouraged to
extend their holdings.

The following features make land or real estate an attractive form of investment: (1) Land holdings have long been an accepted form of wealth by the rich
and not so rich. (2) Many people either own real estate or are members of
families that actually own property. (3) The supply of land is relatively fixed. (4)
Land does not wear out even after certain minerals are drawn out. (5) Demand
for land is related to the population. (6) Values related to real estate can fluctuate
widely when there is high mobility within the population. (7) U.S. tax laws
encourage real estate ownership, which is subsidized by generous write-offs for

EXHIBIT 8-8 John & Kay Adams
Household Furnishings and Supplies Budget
For the Year _____

Household Furnishings & Supplies Budget

Categories	Total Amt.
Bathroom linen, towels, face cloths, mats	$50—
Bedroom linen, sheets, pillows, blankets	—
Furniture (chairs, tables, lamps, sofas, beds, carpets, etc.)	1,500—
TV sets, radios, basic stereo set, batteries	5—
Kitchen appliances, utensils, & service	150—
Laundry equipment & appliances	—
Household cleaners & polish; drapery & carpet	50—
Total Estimate for the Year	$1,755—

interest expenses, property taxes, depreciation on income-producing structures, and capital gains provisions.

Certain drawbacks that can make real estate investments more expensive or less profitable include the following: (1) Certain pieces of real estate may not produce cash income (such as raw land or vacant buildings), yet cash may be necessary for mortgage payments, taxes, and maintenance. (2) In normal times, it may take months to sell a piece of real estate. (3) Real estate acquisition and ownership requires time to maintain and protect it; this labor should be considered as part of the investment cost. As a result (4) property owners must keep alert to changes of zoning ordinances, variance hearings, environmental protection regulations, and special assessments. And (5) the real estate investor should

12-5-76—© 1976 United Features Syndicate, Inc.

establish a business relationship with a knowledgeable real estate broker, banker, lawyer, and maybe an accountant.

The same basic principles for buying a house or condominium can be helpful when acquiring a duplex, triplex, fourplex, or small apartment or commercial building. Briefly, you should be able to work out the following sketches of cash needs and cash flows discussed earlier in this chapter: (1) immediate cash needs for down payment, closing costs, delinquent property taxes, insurance, and immediate repairs for governmental compliance; (2) total cash receipts estimated each month minus contingency for vacancies and emergency repairs; (3) total estimate of ordinary cash expenditures for utilities, insurance, property taxes, and maintenance and repairs relating to the real estate; (4) monthly mortgage payment; and (5) estimate of federal income tax deductions allowed for interest expense on borrowing, property taxes, depreciation expense, maintenance and repair expenditures, energy-saving expenditure, and so on.

These are key ingredients relating to the financial side of being a small-business owner. These financial principles are often tied closely with the principles of management. The basic functions of management are to plan, to organize, and to control. These are the same principles for the money managers outlined in Chapter 1.

Many people are attracted to real estate as an apparently easy way to financial success. However, as in most small-business activity, considerable time and effort must be devoted to learning about becoming a successful real estate investor.

Rental Properties

Being a landlord-owner is not a matter of appearing once a month to collect the rent. Leasing to tenants is much like hiring employees. There is need for careful soliciting, screening, and checking out prospective tenants' rental history. Once good tenants have been selected, the owner-landlord has state laws to uphold as his or her responsibility.

The key to long-term success for owner-landlords is similar to that of an employer with employees. You will want to build loyalty and reduce turnover. Success in this area is more of a human relations concern than a money problem. Good two-way communication, explicit (in writing) policies and rules, some steps for dispute resolution, and a sense of fairness will help you keep good tenants.

State laws for landlords and tenants cover in detail the following topics: landlords' responsibilities, tenants' responsibilities, discrimination, rental agreements, deposits, repairs, tenant's right to privacy, retaliation, termination of tenancy, eviction, abandonment, dispute resolution, and exemptions.

A few of the other ways to invest in real estate are discussed briefly in the following paragraphs. Keep in mind that real estate ventures over and above one's personal housing needs should be considered as medium to high risk and speculative.

Common Stock of Real Estate—Related Companies

A small investor, with only a few hundred or a few thousand dollars, might consider exploring the following areas. These real estate investments can be made by simply purchasing the common stock of specific corporations.

Shopping Centers. Local and national corporations may be open corporations in which investors may buy shares of stock. A stock brokerage firm will usually have a list of corporations with heavy investments in these centers. The investor's goal will be to receive dividends and appreciation value of the common stock held.

Manufactured Home Builders. Several corporations listed on national and regional stock exchanges build mobile homes. This will continue to be a growing market. However, finding a manufacturer that consistently turns out a quality product and guarantees it is a difficult task.

Hotel and Bank Property. Many hotel and commercial bank corporations are very active in real estate and own large office buildings on some of the most valuable land in a city or community. Banks make real estate loans and manage real estate. Hotel chains own valuable property in most of the choice vacation spots around the world.

Land, Minerals, and Timber. Many oil companies and successful railroads have vast holdings of valuable real estate, oil, coal, metals, and timber. Many of these companies hold the mineral rights and rights to lease additional land for exploration and development.

Other Options

Buying Land on Your Own. You may want to be the principal owner of raw land that might be developed into a subdivision for sale or for a commercial venture. Before committing yourself to any real estate venture, you should (1) make several actual visits to the property; (2) determine how good the drainage is for the property; (3) observe the type and amount of noise (aircraft traffic patterns, freeway roar, auto race tracks, and airports will make property unsuitable for certain ventures); (4) explore water supply and access to other basic utilities; (5) investigate other proposed building in the area (future high-rise buildings can destroy or obstruct views); (6) review the ordinances that might restrict the use of land or allow certain chemical odors; and (7) determine safety (police and fire agencies) in the area.

Developing Commercial Property. Commercial property cannot be developed in distant and sparsely populated locations. Labor supply, utilities, transportation, stores, banks, schools, hospitals, community attitude, raw materials, local taxes, recreational facilities, and customers are to be reviewed for commercial property development. The necessary study and skills required to be successful in this area are beyond the scope of this book. At the least, however, review the following points and assign to them some ranking such as low, medium, and high:

1. Profitability.
2. Cash flow generation.
3. Real appreciation in value.
4. Liquidity.
5. Ease and cost of management.
6. Tax sheltering of income.
7. Income tax credits available.
8. Depreciation write-offs.
9. Interest deduction on borrowed funds.
10. Your risk-level comfort zone.
11. Your greed factor.
12. Leveraging ability.
13. The real costs of holding on.
14. Capital gains tax treatment on the sale.
15. Diversification of your risk.
16. Concentration into one area.
17. Additional asset creation or wealth improvement from the investment.*

SUMMARY

The cost of housing is the number one concern in the 1980s. Total housing cost may well absorb from 30 to 50 percent of a family's disposable income. There are around 90 million households in the United States and around 107 million housing units of which one-third are rental units.

* Suggested by Richard H. Gradwohl of Highline Community College, successful commercial real estate developer and owner of a shopping center.

Even in years when new housing starts run at 2 million, there can still be a housing shortage in many places in the United States. The post–World War II baby boom, people remaining single longer, and a high divorce rate are three reasons for the current demand for housing. Shifts in population from one region to another and from the city to the suburb can cause housing unit prices to go up dramatically in certain areas. Urban renewal, freeway construction, stricter safety codes in apartments, and natural disasters can temporarily reduce the number of housing units available.

Housing costs include (1) basic rent or mortgage payments, (2) expected cash outlays for furnishings and appliances, (3) ordinary basic and repair expenses, (4) yard and garden upkeep, (5) utility and utility-type expenses, (6) insurance coverage, and (7) property taxes. A tenant will pay many of these expenditures in the one basic rent payment.

It is difficult to determine if a profit on the sale of a home is real or illusory until the home is actually sold and the money reinvested. Other factors determining the real profit on a home sale include the length of time for which the home was owned, the owner's income tax bracket, other investment alternatives, costs of maintenance, insurance, property taxes, and so on.

It is a good idea in personal money management to consider housing and transportation as one "package of costs." Housing is often a reflection of one's chosen life-style and should be based on what is best for the individual or family first and as an investment second. Housing costs in the past were more manageable due to low interest rates, low inflation, and rising worker productivity. Also, home energy and transportation fuel prices were artificially low.

Renting a modestly furnished apartment near one's work and shopping is an excellent way to save money in a short time.

Popular housing today includes (1) apartments, (2) single-family homes, (3) mobile or manufactured homes, (4) condominiums, and (5) co-ops (or co-operative apartments). Each of these forms of housing has its advantages and disadvantages. The basic decision is whether to rent or to buy. For a given amount of housing, there should be a measurable monthly cash difference for renting versus purchasing. This difference will allow the buyer eventually to own his or her home. For the renter, this difference should be invested in some manner.

Many popular rules of thumb are used when purchasing real estate, but recent inflation tends to make these guides less useful. Both renter and home-buyer need cash sufficient to meet initial transaction costs. The renter usually needs a much smaller amount than the buyer for a given amount of housing. Both renter and buyer can easily underestimate their real cash needs. The key point in housing is not to get in over your head.

To avoid paying too much for housing needs, an analysis can be made of take-home pay and the necessary expenditures for food, transportation, medical and other insurance, clothing, personal care, recreation, vacation, allowances, savings, and so on. The balance remaining will be available for total housing costs.

Once total housing costs in dollars is determined, this sum must be allocated among utilities and rent payments, or utilities, property insurance and taxes, maintenance, and mortgage payment.

When the size of the monthly mortgage payment affordable is known, Table A.4 in Appendix A can be used to determine the total amount of a mortgage that a homebuyer can assume.

A money manager should learn how to determine the total annual cost of owning his or her home. Annual costs may run from 10 to 15 percent of the current market value of the home. The money manager should be able to establish an approach for determining the cost of selling a home and becoming a renter.

Many factors favoring long-term renting are overlooked or not understood by many people. Place yourself in the position of being an owner-manager of an apartment building and determine the ideal tenant you would want and what steps you would take to retain that tenant.

EXHIBIT 8-9 Basic Financial Pyramid

Home Equity or Moderate Rent

Series EE, HH, Tax-Exempt, Corp. Bonds

Long-Term Savings Certificates and CDs

Emergency Savings Accounts

Basic His/Her/Household
Insured Bank Checking Accounts

Tenant or Homeowner Insurance Coverage

Adequate Automobile and Liability Insurance Coverage

Renewable Term Life Insurance on Heads of Households

Accidental Death and Long-Term Disability Insurance Coverage

Adequate Health, Accident, and Major Medical Insurance Plan Coverage

Many homebuyers are unaware that an earnest money agreement is actually a contract between the buyer and seller. This properly prepared document is binding and enforceable. Closing costs must be paid by the buyer, and these costs may run $700 to $2,000. Earnest money and closing costs may equal 5 percent of the mortgage needed.

Moving dates and moving costs should be an integral part of decisions dealing with real estate activity. Current income tax rules favor homebuying as interest expenses and property taxes paid qualify as itemizable deductions. Inflation and marginal income tax brackets tend to reduce the impact of high interest rates.

Home energy and utility costs will probably continue to rise in the future, which may require people to have a more technical knowledge about appliance energy consumption.

Accumulating household furnishings should be accomplished with considerable thought, planned for with a firm budget limitation, and purchased rather sparingly. Exhibit 8-9 illustrates how housing follows a logical level in the basic financial pyramid. The homebuyer is building an equity in the home. The tenant will have cash available for investments that will provide additional income.

TIPS

1. Consider housing and transportation costs as a package of expenditures. Money spent on long-distance commuting cannot be available for better housing.

2. When borrowing money for a mortgage, shop around for the best mortgage interest. A quarter of a percent saved on interest can result in a couple of thousand dollars of savings over the life of the mortgage.

3. Considering a home as an investment depends on long-term factors relating to job security, neighborhood trend, maintenance, marital status, inflation, and interest rates.

4. Before purchasing major appliances, consult such magazines as *Consumer Reports*. Stay with name brands, deal with reputable stores, follow instructions, and understand the key points about related warranties.

5. Home ownership will usually mean learning to do certain amounts of cleaning and maintenance yourself. Multilevel houses mean stairs, a factor that makes cleaning and vacuuming more difficult and poses extra hazards.

ADDITIONAL READINGS

"Adjustable Mortgages: Should You Gamble on One?" *Changing Times*, July 1984, pp. 30–34.

"Don't Gamble on a Teaser Mortgage," *Consumer Reports*, August 1984, pp. 431–34.

Eisenberg, Richard, "Real Estate Returns to Basic Economics," *Money*, October 1986, pp. 165–75.

Greenfield, Ellen J., *House Dangerous: Indoor Pollution in Your Home and Office—and What You Can Do About It.* New York: Vintage, 1987.

"Look Before You Lease," *Changing Times*, February 1985, pp. 59–62.

"Saving Energy at Home: There's More You Can Do," *Changing Times*, October 1983, p. 83.

Sheridan, Dan, "Strategies for Buying and Selling a Home," *Consumer Digest*, December 1985, pp. 35–37.

"Should You Take Back a Mortgage When You Sell?" *Changing Times*, April 1981, pp. 53–55.

GLOSSARY OF USEFUL TERMS

Abstract   A summary of the history of the legal title to a piece of property.

Adjustable-Rate Mortgage (ARM)   A relatively new and rapidly growing type of home mortgage where the rate of interest may vary widely during the life of the loan. The initial interest rate may start at an arbitrary 10 percent. Then, after six months, the interest rate will be adjusted to the real market rate or tied to U.S. Treasury bond rates.

Amortization   Provision for gradually paying off the principal amount of a loan, such as a mortgage loan, at the time of each payment of interest.

Appraisal   An evaluation of the property to determine its fair market value.

Appreciation   Increase in the dollar value of property over a period of time.

Certificate of Title   Document that signifies ownership of a house and usually contains a legal description of the house and its land.

Closing Cost   Cost in addition to the price of the house including mortgage service charges, title search, and insurance and transfer of ownership charges. It should be clear who pays for each of these costs.

Condominium   Individual ownership of a dwelling unit and an undivided interest in the common areas and facilities that serve the multiunit facility.

Contract   An agreement between two or more parties that they each will do certain things. The contract will be enforceable when it meets the following elements: an offer, acceptance, consideration, competent parties, and legal objective.

Conventional Loans   Mortgages offered by banks, insurance companies, mortgage companies, and savings associations. Interest rates on conventional loans are usually higher than are those on government-insured loans.

Conveyance   A written document by means of which title to real estate is transferred from one individual to another.

Cooperative Apartment   An apartment building or group of dwellings owned by residents and operated for their benefit by their elected board of directors. The residents occupy but do not own the unit; they own shares of stock in the total enterprise.

Deed   A document by which a grantor conveys an interest in real property to a grantee.

Depreciation   A decline in value of a house as a result of normal wear and tear, weather elements, and/or changing neighborhood conditions.

Durable Goods   Tangible goods that can be expected to last for a relatively long time even though used repeatedly (chairs, refrigerators, washing machines, toasters, etc.).

Earnest Money   The deposit of money given to the seller by the potential buyer to show that he or she is serious about buying the house. If the deal goes through, the earnest money is applied against the down payment. If the deal does not go through, it may be forfeited.

Easement Rights   A right of way granted to a person authorizing access over the owner's land.

Equity   The resale value of a home minus the amount owed.

Escrow   An agreement under which executed documents such as deeds are delivered into the hands of a third party to be held until specified conditions are fulfilled and then delivered over to the person so performing or, in the case of default, returned to the person executing the document.

Exclusive Right to Sell   A "sole contract" except that the real estate broker gets a commission even if the owner sells the house himself or herself.

FHA (Federal Housing Administration)   A division of HUD established for the purpose of providing mortgage and home improvement loan insurance. It does not make loans.

Lease   A contract whereby a landlord gives a tenant possession of real property for a set period of time in exchange for rent.

Lessee   One who leases property from another.

Lessor   One who leases property to another.

Mobile Home   A house on wheels that may be placed on a lot with no intention to move it later. Also called manufactured home.

Mortgage   An instrument that pledges property as security for a debt.

Mortgagee   A bank or lender who loans the money to the mortgager.

Mortgager (mortgagor)   The homeowner who is obligated to repay a mortgage loan on the property he or she has purchased.

Multiple Listing   All local real estate brokers included in a listing can handle the house, with others excluded. One generally deals with one broker, gets a free evaluation recommendation from a committee of several brokers, and has the selling efforts of all of them.

Opportunity Cost   The alternative that one gives up to do something. The withdrawal of savings from a bank to purchase a car will mean giving up the interest income that was being earned.

Points   An extra service charge initially deducted from a mortgage loan but an addition to the regular interest cost. One point is equal to initial service charge of 1 percent of the loan amount. The federal government now sets maximum interest levels on FHA and VA mortgages. Usually, two points are charged for each quarter of a 1 percent difference between the going rate available on conventional mortgages and the ceiling rate of FHA and VA mortgages.

Quit Claim Deed   A deed in which a grantor conveys to the grantee whatever rights he or she may have in the real property but without any assurance that he or she has any rights to give.

Real Property   Land or anything permanently attached thereto by people or nature.

REIT (real estate investment trust)   An investment company designed to invest in real estate, including mortgages. A REIT is to real estate what a mutual fund is to common stock.

Sole Contract   A method whereby one real estate broker has the right to work on selling a house. If the owner sells it himself or herself, however, the broker gets no commission.

Special Assessment   A tax for a specific purpose such as providing paved streets or new sewers.

Tax Shelter   A general term given to any investment that defers the payment or reduces the amount of federal income taxes for the year. Depreciation expense, property taxes paid, and interest expense paid on real estate investments generally reduce income taxes owed.

Title   The evidence of a person's legal right to possess property, normally in the form of a deed.

Title Insurance   Special insurance that usually protects lenders against loss of their interest in property due to unforeseen occurrences that might be traced to legal flaws in previous ownerships.

Title Search   A check of the title records generally at the local courthouse to make sure you are buying the house from the legal owner and that there are no liens, overdue special assessments, restrictions, and the like filed in the record.

Townhouse   A unit with a front- and backyard that shares common sidewalls.

Zoning Laws   Laws that restrict the use of real estate by specifying improvements that can be made by the owners.

9

Transportation

LEARNING OBJECTIVES

Upon completion of Chapter 9, you should be able to identify and remember

- How to determine your transportation needs and establish a budget for automobile costs.
- Two magazine resources useful in making a study of car selections.
- How to construct sketches of cash flows to stay within your car purchasing budget.
- How to determine approximate monthly car payments with information supplied.
- The expenditures and repairs normally associated with car ownership.
- The important concepts and costs related to owning a car for 100,000 miles.
- Steps for inspecting and road testing a used car.
- How to construct a budget for estimating transportation costs for the year.

OVERVIEW

If the price of gasoline goes to $1.50 a gallon, will you still drive to work or school? If the price goes to $2.50 a gallon, will there be a bus to take you there? For the American, transportation means going from one place to another by automobile. Other than buying a home, transportation costs may well be the consumer's largest expenditure. This chapter on transportation concludes Part IV, which has dealt with the major areas of consumption. The discussions concerning food, clothing, personal health care, housing, utilities, furnishings, and transportation should suggest many ways for you to save money, to get more value from each dollar spent in these areas, or both.

This chapter could be one of the most important in the text given that in many areas of the United States the automobile is your economic link with society. It is the way for you to get to and from work and shopping and to attend to other business matters. It is important to be in control over your automobile costs.

Responsible people will allocate appropriate income to keep their car(s) in good operating condition. It should be noted that even the best maintained vehicle can fail to perform when it is needed most, however. A defective battery, thermostat, or tire could leave you stranded or make you late for work or appointments. Unless alternative transportation is readily available or the destinations are very short, a well-maintained and repaired car is a must. People whose frequent car trouble causes tardiness or absence at work are simply not taken seriously by co-workers or supervisors.

This chapter offers suggestions for assessing and coordinating individual transportation needs and developing an understanding of the total costs of automobile ownership and operations; it also examines the areas of light and heavy maintenance and presents a detailed study of driving a car 100,000 miles. Budgeting for a year and tips on car buying are also presented.

ASSESSING TRANSPORTATION NEEDS

In the course of a year, most people go to and from work in an automobile or by some form of public transit. Vacation travel may use a combination of airplanes, buses, and automobiles. A few people use bicycles, mopeds, and motorcycles as a means of transportation.

The key for controlling your transportation costs is to review your daily basic work schedule. Most of us follow very routine schedules from Monday through Friday. If you are driving on the freeway every day, then you will need a car that can faithfully perform in that environment. How many people normally ride with you? If you plan to join a car pool, then you may want to consider a car that will carry four people. Other considerations in selection are things normally carried, number of miles driven each day, type of transmission, and so on.

Much of what has been just described will depend in part on the budget available for transportation and automobile expenses. A good bicycle can be obtained for less than $200, but a sound car may cost $4,000–8,000 depending upon whether it is new or used. The basic outlays for an automobile will be the vehicle's cost, options, sales taxes, registration, and insurance. The buyer should know the required down payment, amount of loan, finance charge, interest rate, length of contract, and the real cash value of the car. Exhibit 9-1 can be a starting place for determining your car and budget.

Your goals are to control your automobile needs, develop a rational approach in selection, and stay within your budget. No one should ever have to

EXHIBIT 9-1   Planning Worksheet for Automobile Needs and Budget

1. Major purpose for car? ____work ____pleasure ____a second car for the family ____other needs _____
2. Estimated miles to be driven each year _____
3. The number of people normally riding _____
4. Specific load-carrying ability, the necessity for trunk space, bicycles, trailers, luggage rack, etc. _____
5. Size and/or model of vehicle? ____full size ____intermediate ____compact ____subcompact ____2-door ____4-door ____pickup ____van ____station wagon
6. Color _____ Trim_____
7. Specific options: ____radio ____automatic transmission ____stick shift ____air conditioning ____power brakes ____power steering ____other: _____

Budget

1. Basic budget including vehicle cost, options, sales tax, license. $_____
2. Amount required for down payment. $_____
3. Amount of loan required. $_____ Interest rate _____% Total dollars of carrying interest charges. $_____ Number of months for repayment _____. (The law requires that these are explained to the buyer)
4. Emergency cash fund for unexpected repairs not covered by warranty. $_____
5. Estimated annual insurance premium for bodily injury and property liability coverage $_____; collision and upset $_____; other coverage $_____.
6. Supplemental notes and comments: _____
_____
_____

FRANK & ERNEST

1-13-78—© 1978 Newspaper Enterprise Association, Inc.

purchase a car or other vehicle on impulse, on short notice, or under pressure. Buying an automobile should involve bringing together your best efforts in making a decision. There are many makes and models to choose from, and many dealers are competing for your business. Therefore, take your time.

When planning to buy a car, build a "facts file" of automobile brochures and newspaper and magazine clippings. Talk to people who have recently purchased an automobile similar to the one you are considering. Talk to the people at service stations about what cars they think are good. Articles carried in *Consumer Reports* and *Changing Times* magazines are excellent resources. These magazines are usually available at public and college libraries. Skills developed in car buying can be carried over in other consumer transactions and may be very useful at your job.

The high cost of personal car ownership is rapidly causing people to reassess the real role of the automobile. In the past the type of car owned may have projected an economic status, a venturesome personality, or even appropriate conservatism expected of people in certain professions or callings. But greater awareness for the need to manage energy resources and protect the environment has caused people to adopt the smaller, simpler, and more fuel-efficient automobile. Still, even the small fuel-efficient car has risen dramatically in price. In 1970, you could expect to find suitable transportation for around $2,000. Today, you can expect to pay $7,000–9,000, though it is true that many of the compact cars come loaded with options.

In the future, a "package" of transportation vehicles might be used by one individual. A person might own a small car, a moped, and a bicycle. This same person may walk more often or use local transit systems to accomplish nearby errands. Consider living closer to where you work and shop.

STAYING WITHIN YOUR CAR-PURCHASING BUDGET

Suppose that you are in the market for a brand-new car and that you have set a *total budget* of $7,000 for your commitment. It is immaterial at this point whether you have the actual $7,000 cash saved or are planning to finance a portion and/or even trade in a used car with the deal.

The concern here is to stay within the $7,000. To do so, it is a good idea to prepare a sketch of how your cash may be spent during the course of the purchasing transaction. Assume, for our purposes, that license plates will cost $80 a year, desired automobile insurance coverage will be $300 per year, and state sales tax is 5 percent. Your sketch should enable you to back into the balance of your $7,000 that can actually be spend for the car you desire, the specific options needed, as well as the dealer's transportation and preparation costs.

A. Sketch of Cash Flow for Automobile

Total cash or budget target for new car	$7,000
Less: Insurance costs for one year	300
	$6,700
License costs for one year	80
Balance for automobile and sales tax	$6,620
Less: Sales tax (0.5 × $6,620)	331
Balance for the car, options, dealer's transportation, and preparation costs	$6,289

In summary, $6,289 should be the absolute top dollar that you will commit in negotiating at the car lots. If you have done the related homework of analyzing your transportation needs, you can stand firm in your determination of what you need and will be less likely to be swayed from your budget target or commitment. The person whose budget of $7,000 goes toward the automobile only will find the costs of insurance, sales tax, and license plates exceeding the original target by more than 10 percent. Such miscalculation can cause a person to have little or no discretionary income left over and, hence, be "car poor."

Let us carry the calculations a couple of steps farther. Suppose that the dealer preparation charges for cleaning and necessary detail work for showroom purposes amount to $150 and that transportation is $100. For purposes of illustration, let us assume you want a $200 AM-FM stereo-tape unit and a radial tires package costing $125 extra as options. The following sketch of cash flow will help to determine the top dollar that can actually be spent for the car itself.

B. Sketch of Cash for Automobile

Maximum price for car and options	$6,289
Less: Dealer preparation	150
	$6,139
Transportation cost	100
	$6,039
AM-FM stereo-tape unit	200
	$5,839
Radial tire option	125
Maximum price for basic car	$5,714

An amount of $5,714 is the maximum that you can pay for the "basic" car model and stay within your original $7,000 budget.

One additional and very useful calculation is to determine down payment and monthly car payments. Let us assume that you will pay the $300 auto insurance separately. You plan to make a 25 percent down payment on the car and pay the rest on installments for three years (36 months at 10 percent). The assumed maximum to be paid for a car is $6,700 as noted from the following calculation:

Total budget for automobile	$7,000
Less: Insurance to be paid	300
Balance for total car purchase	$6,700

The next step is to determine the 25 percent down payment for the $6,700 car including all other costs, options, and sales taxes. The down payment is calculated as follows:

$$\$6,700 \times .25 = \$1,675$$

The balance of $5,025 ($6,700 less $1,675 down payment) is to be paid in 36 months at 10 percent interest. We can find the approximate monthly car payment with the help of Table A.4 in Appendix A. Note the following steps in finding the answer:

1. In Table A.4, find the factor in the 10% column and on line (year) 3. The factor is 2.48685.
2. Take the amount of the balance owed on the installment contract of $5,025 ($6,700 minus down payment of $1,675) and divide it by the factor:

$$\$5,025 \div 2.48685 = \$2,020.63$$

3. Find one month's payment:

$$\$2,020.63 \div 12 \text{ months} = \$168.39$$

The estimated monthly payment on a contract of $5,025 for 36 months at 10 percent is $168.39. The total amount of *finance charges* on this contract is $1,037 for the 36 months. This is determined by the following simple calculation:

Down payment	$1,675
Plus: Monthly payment ($168.39 × 36)	6,062
Total installment contract cost	$7,737
Less: Total cash price of car	6,700
Total finance charge	$1,037

We now have an outline to follow for determining just how much car can be afforded with a given budget, the monthly car payments, and the total dollars of interest or finance charge.

OPERATING COSTS

Americans know that they can discuss the weather with a complete stranger and be on fairly safe ground. This same can be said about the miles per gallon of gas that a certain car might obtain. The latest Environmental Protection Agency ratings on new cars are common topics at lunch, during coffee breaks, and during social hours. However, gasoline costs and car mileage are the least expensive costs of owning a car, even after gasoline exceeded a dollar a gallon in 1979. It is maintenance that is difficult to both estimate and budget for properly. An arbitrary breakdown of maintenance cost is made for the purpose of discussion: light maintenance and heavy maintenance.

Light Maintenance

After purchasing a new or used car, you can anticipate ordinary and recurring expenditures as a result of driving the vehicle. When purchasing a *used* car, you should anticipate that some expenditures will be made shortly after the purchase date. And these "fixing-up" costs should be considered part of the true cost of the used car, even though they arise a few weeks or a few months after the purchase date.

Light maintenance is defined as minor maintenance and repairs that are anticipated by the owner and are performed on a regularly scheduled basis, usually in a couple of hours and at a cost of less than $75. Many will perform some of these tasks themselves. Typical groupings of light maintenance are

Oil changes and chassis lubrication, replacement of air, fuel, and oil filters, and replacement of smog-control equipment.

Windshield washer additive, radiator coolant, rust inhibitor, radiator flush, radiator cap and thermostat, water and heater hoses.

Brake fluid changes, automatic transmission fluid and power-steering fluid, air conditioning Freon.

Spark plugs, spark plug cable wires, distributor cap and rotor, ignition points and condenser, adjustment of timing.

Headlights, tail and brake lights, license plate light, turn signal flasher unit, parking lamp bulbs, and tail-light lenses.

Snow tire mounting, tire repairs, and tire rotation.

Car wash soaps, polishes, sponges, pail, vinyl top cleaners, window cleaner, chamois, WD-40, gunk, tar remover.

Heavy Maintenance

Heavy maintenance costs are defined as large, infrequent, nonrecurring expenditures necessary to replace large parts or systems in an automobile. Heavy maintenance expenditures generally occur after 20,000 miles of average driving for a new car. Factors bringing about these major expenditures are such things as heat, cold, friction, metal fatigue, corrosion, and damage. Examples are replacement of tires, batteries, exhaust pipes, mufflers, shock absorbers, brakes, engine parts, transmission, drive shaft, axles, steering system, electrical system, and so on.

Because of the role of mechanics in heavy maintenance, most of a typical bill is for labor and only a small portion is related to parts. It may be necessary for the mechanic to disassemble and reassemble parts of the car, engine, transmission, and so on. The technician may spend time testing and "trouble shooting" before he or she can determine exactly what is wrong with a vehicle.

There is persistent shortage of qualified mechanics in the United States. Studies reveal that consumers waste half their outlays for repairs because mechanics or repair shop employees lack the proper skills or business ethics. As a result of high-cost repairs and the problems associated with obtaining quality service, more and more people have found it necessary to become knowledgeable about their car operations.

It is beyond the scope of this chapter to treat the topic of heavy maintenance in great depth, but the basics are discussed in order of possible occurrence briefly in the following sections.

Tires. Whether you purchase a brand-new car or a used car, tires will probably be a major expenditure. Ordinary "original equipment" tires on a brand-new car will need to be replaced after 20,000 miles, but you may have to consider tire replacement as part of the cost of a used car.

If you are a commuter and drive on the freeway, your best insurance is to buy a top-quality tire. If your driving is off-freeway, town, and suburban, you may not need such expensive tires. Unless you have knowledge of tire quality, consult such magazines as *Consumer Reports* in selection. The Department of Transportation (DOT) has also been moving tire manufacturers toward a system of labeling and grading of tires and tire wear.

The key to long tire life is sensible driving, proper air pressure, and periodic inspection. With the popularity of self-service gasoline stations, drivers must take on the job themselves of seeing that tires are properly inflated. Investment in a good tire pressure gauge is a must these days. Irregular or uneven tire tread wear is a visual signal that the front wheels are out of alignment, tires are improperly inflated, or both. Improper suspension settings and alignment as well as worn-out shock absorbers will cause tires to wear unevenly.

Batteries. Batteries may last around two years on new cars under normal conditions. In purchasing a used car, battery replacement may be necessary in the buying process.

The best battery can become a "dead one" if headlights are inadvertently left on. One of the best presents you can give yourself is a set of jumper cables. Failure to get to work or being stranded in an out-of-the-way location because of a dead battery can cost extra time and dollars.

Brakes. Brake linings and disc pads may last from 10,000 to 40,000 miles. Stop-and-go driving will wear out the brakes sooner than long periods of highway driving. If your usual driving area is hilly, expect shorter brake life. Two important clues regarding brakes are as follows: (1) if your brake pedal must be depressed several inches (or feels "spongy") before you begin to stop, consider it a major warning and have your brake system corrected; (2) if you hear a dry grinding sound or the sound of scraping metal with a wire brush when you apply the brakes, take corrective action immediately.

Exhaust Pipes and Mufflers. The heat generated by driving your car takes its toll on exhaust pipes and mufflers. Furthermore, condensation brought on by extreme temperature inside the equipment and water splash and snow-melting chemicals to the outside will eventually wear out your exhaust system. Odorless deadly carbon monoxide is always a threat in a deteriorated exhaust system.

Your exhaust pipes and mufflers may last three to four years before they wear out under normal driving. Muffler and exhaust pipe failures are not emergencies. A money manager should plan ahead to have funds for these repairs when needed.

Shock Absorbers. Shock absorbers are vibration-damping devices used with the vehicle chassis and springs to lessen road bounce. Shock absorbers wear out so gradually that you, the driver, may not notice their deterioration.

Badly worn shock absorbers make a vehicle more difficult to control at higher speeds, reduce tire life, and place a strain on springs, drive shaft, and bearing system between the transmission and differential. While faulty shocks need not be replaced immediately, their neglect may cause major expenditure later.

Other Heavy Maintenance or Repairs. The items already mentioned are systems or parts that most people should expect to eventually wear out due to friction, vibration, tension, and corrosion. However, most people expect a long service life of other major systems such as the engine block, transmission, axles, wheels, electrical system, body, and frame. Nonetheless, a very-well-main-

THE WALL STREET JOURNAL

"There won't be any extras. $895.50 includes everything I can think of."

From *The Wall Street Journal*—
Permission, Cartoon Features
Syndicate.

tained automobile may still have rare and unpredictable breakdowns or require major repairs.

To lower some of the stress that goes along with major and expensive auto repairs, you should have (1) a cash fund to draw on and (2) the name of a reputable mechanic or repair garage. The first has been mentioned in earlier chapters. Finding a good repair shop requires some effort.

If your car is still under warranty, then the authorized auto dealership should perform the work. When the warranty period expires, you should have some idea of how well the local dealership is providing service. If you feel that its basic service is not satisfactory or is very expensive, then consider having your service station perform the light maintenance. The automobile dealer and service shop still might be the best place for major repair work when you are in a strange town, when the car is a foreign import, or when the work involves special equipment and tools.

Before building a monthly estimate for real car ownership, one more perspective is offered for review. Let us look at the costs associated with driving a car for 100,000 miles.

A 100,000-MILE CASE STUDY

Keeping a car for 100,000 miles is not rare, even for a standard, medium-priced vehicle. The key to such long automobile life is *maintenance.* The program of maintenance need not be fancy or extensive, but it should be consistent. For example, you might have the oil and filter changed every 2,000 miles and have the chassis lubricated; use quality oil; change the air filter every year; have the radiator flushed and coolant changed every other year; replace the plugs, points, and condenser every two years; when something needs to be fixed, get it fixed.

This appears to be the basic attitude of people who have owned the same car for 10 or 15 years. The external appearance of the vehicle is not a major factor to long life. Some people do keep the paint polished and the rubber insulation items cleaned. Some may even have the engine cleaned. However, these are the cosmetic aspects of the car ownership. Since the car is essential for commuting back and forth to work, which is often the major source of one's income, there is always a priority that money be available for car upkeep.

Let us review the case of a car that was driven for 100,000 miles; the car is still owned by the same person, has nearly 125,000 miles on it now, and is over 16 years old. The car in the case study is a full-size, U.S.-made vehicle, with four doors, a large V-8 engine, automatic transmission, and factory-installed air conditioning. The car was used for day-to-day commuting to work. Approximately 85 percent of the miles were driven on highways or freeways.

The first calculation is an overall summary of seven categories of costs:

1. Cost of automobile and sales taxes	$ 4,581.80
2. Total light maintenance (oil and filters, $315)	933.39
3. Heavy maintenance (tires only, $784)	3,138.52
4. Gasoline (all taxes paid at the pump)	3,676.47
5. Insurance coverage (100/300/15)	1,817.70
6. Estimated garaging, parking, and tolls	2,100.00
7. License plates for 10 years	475.00
Total costs for 100,000 miles	$16,723.08

Cost per mile = $16,723.08 ÷ 100,000 miles = $.1672

Table 9-1 illustrates the miles driven per year and cost of gasoline, light maintenance, and heavy maintenance and gives the totals in dollars. Over the whole 100,000 miles, gasoline costs averaged $31 per month, light maintenance $8, and heavy maintenance $26 per month. The total dollar costs for these three essentials averaged $65 per month. If you have never made any estimate of these cost considerations, you might consider these amounts as the *absolute minimum* in your car-operating-cost estimates.

Light maintenance of $933.39 over the 10 years and 100,000 miles is shown in Table 9-2 under nine rather arbitrarily assigned categories. Note that the crankcase oil was changed approximately every 2,400 miles and that the oil filter was changed every 3,700 miles. The owner believes that this was a key factor in being able to keep the original engine block intact. The next largest category under light maintenance was the amount spent for car cleaning and polishing materials of $94.40. A pleasant surprise in the operating cost of this car was the

TABLE 9-1 Summary of Basic Automobile Operating Cost for 100,000 Miles in 10 Years (Full-Size, 4-Door, V-8 Engine, Automatic Transmission)

| Year | Miles driven | Gasoline | Maintenance | | Total |
			Light	Heavy	
1	11,060	$ 379.29	$153.31	$ 53.25	$ 585.85
2	8,513	319.94	72.40	358.46	750.80
3	8,683	307.41	91.86	143.62	542.89
4	10,668	356.99	40.33	135.52	532.84
5	12,052	420.61	79.72	586.04	1,086.37
6	9,501	266.90	58.28	397.46	722.64
7	11,531	379.01	147.22	451.79	978.02
8	11,644	463.83	160.82	241.04	865.69
9	11,640	516.98	71.93	665.32	1,254.23
10	4,678	265.51	57.51	106.02	429.04
	100,000	$3,676.47	$933.39	$3,138.52	$7,748.38
Average per year	10,000	$368	$93	$314	$775
Average per month (rounded)	833	$31	$8	$26	$65

TABLE 9-2 Summary of Automobile Light Maintenance by Category, 100,000 Miles, 10-Year Study (Full-Size, 4-Door, V-8 Engine, Automatic Transmission)

1. Servicing by dealer and regular service stations: 41 oil changes (5-quart system, chassis lubrication, various filters, additives) averaging every 2,439 miles for a total of $205.27; oil filter changes on an average of every 3,704 miles for $110 $596.59
2. Car washing and polishing materials for exterior and interior paint, leather, chrome, touch-up paint, undercoating costs   94.40
3. Periodic replacement of coolant, pressure tests, radiator cleaner, rust inhibitor, minor soldering   80.71
4. Cost of tire repairs, mounting, and changing snow tires; one tire warranty adjustment for $21.39   60.74
5. Separate installations of spark plugs, cables, and ignition parts   60.55
6. Air-conditioning servicing and drive belts   10.21
7. Various headlight beams and bulb replacements   9.95
8. Engine carburetor and carbon cleaners   5.06
9. Miscellaneous   15.18

     Total $933.39

modest amounts spent on air conditioning ($10.21) and carburetor cleaner ($5.06). Total light maintenance for 100,000 miles and 10 years was $933.39, or $93 per year.

Most readers are concerned about possible major expenditures during the 100,000 miles of operation. In looking at Table 9-3, there are seven areas of heavy maintenance. Replacement of tires, snow tires, brakes, mufflers, and shock absorbers accounted for about half the total heavy maintenance costs. The engine, cooling system, transmission, and differential accounted for $1,452.67 over the 100,000 miles.

Perhaps all cars have a nuisance problem to contend with over the years of ownership. The automobile has a peculiarity associated with the water pump system. It seemed that every 30,000 miles, the pump failed. Fortunately, the sound of a failing water pump always allowed time to make an appointment with the repair shop. A single major expenditure resulted from gradual wearing of the gear teeth on the flywheel in back of the engine. The repair cost $323.64. An expenditure such as this one can be painful, particularly when no cash has been set aside for such contingencies.

To summarize, it is unlikely that any two automobiles will have the same profile. The important thing to remember is that car ownership costs more than most people think. Yet these periodic expenditures will be less expensive than trading in a car every two or three years. (Many people trade in their old cars for new ones because they can meet the monthly car payments but are never quite able to save additional cash for the heavy maintenance.)

TABLE 9-3 Summary of Automobile Heavy Maintenance by Category, 100,000 Miles, 10-Year Study (Full-Size, 4-Door, V-8 Engine, Automatic Transmission)

1. Engine cooling system, transmission, differential	
Engine block	0
Oil pan gaskets	59.29
Air conditioning system	0
Starter motor fly wheel (broken gear teeth)	323.64
Alternator/voltage regulator	58.90
Cooling fan clutch unit	55.28
Water pump and hose replacements	447.14
Rebuilt transmission (at 67,207 miles)	306.39
Differential—seals, pinion gears, axle	202.03
2. Tires: 3 Sets of 4 tires and 2 sets of 4 snow tires (includes 4 steel-belted radials mounted at 90,014 miles)	784.21
3. Brakes: 2 Sets of front brakes and 3 sets of rear brakes, drums turned	293.57
4. Mufflers: Various replacements on dual exhaust system	197.40
5. Shock absorbers: 2 sets of 4 shocks and labor costs	174.05
6. Front end: Ball joints and bushings, drag link	144.72
7. Batteries: 2 heavy-duty batteries replaced at months 44 and 96	91.90
Total heavy maintenance/major replacements	$3,138.52

$3,138.52 ÷ 100,000 miles = $.03139 per mile

THE REAL COST OF OWNING A CAR

Unless we are careful to consider *all* expenditures related to an automobile, we will grossly underestimate how much our car is really costing us. For example, most people focus their attention on how many miles their car will go on a gallon of gasoline. The amount spent for gasoline, even at today's prices, may not be the largest single expenditure on a month-to-month basis. The greatest single cost of an automobile is its decline in market value. Typically, a car will lose 3 percent per month on the undepreciated balance. That is, a new car will depreciate 25 percent in the first year, 15 percent in the second year, and 10 percent each year thereafter. These are the minimums, and the decline in market value can be greater if the car is not well known, a gas-guzzler, or discontinued model.

The car payments being made each month may be the largest single outlay of cash. When car payments are completed, the owner should begin to establish a fund of cash for eventual replacement of the car if replacement is contemplated. The money saved and the interest earned should reduce the need to borrow. The total finance charges for borrowing to purchase a car can easily add $500 to $1,000 to the cost. The key point in car ownership is to keep your car for a long period, say, 10, 12, or 15 years or more.

Other major costs per year are automobile insurance, parking, and license plates or tabs. We have discussed the numerous other repairs and replacements to be made for light and heavy maintenance. For analytic purposes, the sketch of cash in Table 9-4 is related to 15 categories of automobile expenditures. If you are

TABLE 9-4   Sketch of Dollar Costs per Month of an Automobile

Category	Estimated monthly cost
1. Automobile replacement fund (replacing in 10 years)	$ 60
2. License plates and inspection	7
3. Automobile insurance, ample coverage	25
4. Parking stall fee, tolls, meter money	20
5. Gasoline (monthly estimate)	40
6. Oil, lubrication, and filters (every 3,000 miles)	6
7. Radiator flush and antifreeze (every 2 years)	2
8. Battery replacement (every 3 to 5 years)	2
9. Minor tune-up, parts and labor (every 15,000–20,000 miles)	5
10. Washing, polishing, and rust prevention (as needed)	1
11. Tires, snow tires, mounting, and balancing (20,000–40,000 miles)	5
12. Brakes (every 20,000–40,000 miles)	3
13. Shock absorbers (every 30,000–40,000 miles)	3
14. Exhaust pipes and mufflers (every 3 to 4 years)	3
15. Major parts repairs fund (engine, transmission, rear end)	10
Estimated total monthly automobile costs	$192

not familiar with what some of these costs might amount to on a *monthly basis*, Table 9-4 will help you to better find the real monthly cost of your car.

Note that items in categories 1 through 4 are mostly *fixed*. That is, replacement (or car payment), license plate, automobile insurance, and parking are incurred each month whether or not the car is driven. Costs 5 through 15 tend to be associated with driving. These are called *variable* costs. Of the $192 monthly total costs, $112 appears to be fixed and the rest, $80, is variable. If a person drives 1,000 miles during the month, the variable costs per mile will equal 8 cents ($80 ÷ 1,000 miles driven = $.08). If the $192 total monthly estimate is reasonable, total annual cost for the year will be $2,304 ($192 × 12 months).

A special savings account with a monthly deposit should be considered to handle eventual repairs and replacements.

BUYING A USED CAR

While 10 million new cars are sold in the United States in a normal year, most car sales transactions are between buyers and sellers of used cars. For every new automobile sold, there can be two, three, and even four used cars sold, depending on the state of the economy.

Whether buying a new or used car, use the needs assessment, a budget, and sketches of cash flows discussed earlier in the chapter. The basic goal of car buying is to stay within your budget. The use of a realistic budget will prevent you from becoming emotional in the purchase. The budget will force you to think about day-to-day driving needs rather than about what might be nice on an infrequent vacation or outing. Remember, too, that greater skills and knowledge are needed in buying a used car. While new cars can have problems, most are minor and are covered under a warranty.

As was stated earlier, no one should have to purchase a car on short notice or under pressure. There are many makes and models, dealers, and private individuals with cars to sell. The car that you want may last you 5 or 10 years and cost you several thousands of dollars over those years. Because of this, it seems realistic to make a three- to six-month study of the kind of car you really need.

There can be some obvious advantages of buying a used car: (1) A car that is five years old can be bought for less than half its original sales price. (2) A few hundred dollars spent on a basically sound vehicle for new tires, brakes, exhaust pipes and mufflers, shock absorbers, battery, new water hoses, and a tune-up can restore the car to quality condition.

Keep in mind that the basic vehicle must be in sound condition. The basic chassis and frame must be undamaged. The body should have good paint remaining and be free of serious dents, scrapes, and rust. The interior of the car should be clean and not show excessive wear. There should be no offensive odors or evidence of leaks in the interior of the car. These are areas that you can take ample time to inspect and determine for yourself as well as assessing any trade-offs of one feature for another.

Where to Look

It is best to obtain a used car from someone you have known or have observed using the car over the years. And the patient used car buyer can seek out these kinds of good cars. There are people who are transferred overseas and must sell their car on short notice. There are elderly people who decide to give up driving and sell their cars. There are estates that must be settled and cars to be sold. Reputable auto rental agencies must turn over their stock of cars each year to keep competitive. The mileage on rental cars is often the result of highway driving by people who rent these cars for business purposes.

If you have exhausted these sources, then try the lot of a new car dealership that sells used cars. New car dealers will often take in an old car when selling a new one. Dealers will keep the best of these "trade-ins" and sell the rest at public auction.

Dealers who sell only used cars should put the buyer on notice. There may be some "new-looking" cars on these lots, but they also may be police cars, taxi cabs, and other cars that have seen many hours and miles of running time.

Employee bulletin boards and company newspapers can be a source of information about who is selling a car. Daily newspapers are a useful source for obtaining some approximate prices for certain models of cars.

In all your searching, your budget should quickly eliminate those cars that exceed it.

Inspection of a Used Car

Once you have found a prospective automobile that suits your main driving needs and budget, an extensive inspection should be made. This inspection involves two parts: (1) an on-the-lot inspection and (2) a driving test.

Your on-the-lot inspection should be coupled with your own previous research from such sources as *Consumer Reports*. This magazine gives an extensive impartial review of used car performance for most car models. The magazine will rate the items of heavy maintenance with repair histories.

If the particular automobile you are inspecting is meeting your expectations with the exception of a few minor trade-offs, it is time for a road test. This road test is essential. The seller of a car should expect a buyer to request this. If you do not receive the opportunity, then proceed no further and look elsewhere.

A quick spin around the block does not constitute a road test, however. The road test should take a half to one hour and include a skilled mechanic's check of the car.

FINANCING YOUR CAR

In Chapter 6, we covered the basics of the use of credit and installment sales contracts. Exhibit 9-2 is a Federal Trade Commission sample installment sales contract designed for an automobile transaction. While some sections are self-explanatory or were covered earlier, note the section on *insurance*. Credit life and disability insurance is not required to obtain credit. If your present life insurance is adequate and designed to cover such debts, then you should not acquire this rather expensive form of insurance.

Ideally, you should pay cash for an automobile. Consumer credit can easily run 12 to 18 percent a year. This alone should be an incentive to build a car fund of your own which earns interest as well. Only when your car is used in part for business is car leasing attractive. It is best to avoid leasing and long-term installment credit programs for personal driving needs. Leasing companies are profit-making firms, and the costs of minor infractions of the agreement, poor record keeping, and decline in the value of the vehicle below the agreed trade-in value are often absorbed by the customer (lessee). As stated earlier, no one should have to purchase a car on short notice, without reasonable planning, or under pressure.

EQUIPPING YOUR CAR FOR EMERGENCIES

Once you have acquired a car, a few dollars should be spent on some basic items to handle emergencies. These items should be acquired even though you may not know how to use them. Chances are someone else will. The following items are some of the essentials: battery jumper cables, flashlight and batteries, Phillip's screwdriver, blade screwdriver, pliers, crescent wrench (10″ size), electrical or duct tape, insulated wire, flares or reflectors, and ground cloth or jumpsuit. It is assumed that the car is properly equipped with an inflated spare tire, jack, and lug wrench.

For those living in rural and sparsely populated areas, some of the following items might be added: tire chains, small shovel, small ax-hammer, towing chains or strap, blanket or sleeping bag and gloves, a coffee can filled with dried camper's food, candy, matches, and candles, extra flashlight batteries, plastic water container, fuses, ice scraper, first aid kit, maps, and pencil and paper.

VACATION AND TRANSPORTATION

When a car is going to be used for extended travel, the engine, transmission, differential, brakes, tires, ignition system, exhaust system, battery, and cooling

SECURITY AGREEMENT AND RETAIL INSTALLMENT SALE CONTRACT (INSTALLMENT SALE OF MOTOR VEHICLE)

On this_____ day of_____ , 19_____ ,

(Name)

(Street Address)   (City)   (County)   (State)

SECURED PARTY—SELLER, hereby agrees to sell and_____

(Name)   (Street Address)

(City)   (County)   (State)_____ , DEBTOR—BUYER, hereby agrees to buy and to grant to Secured Party a

Security interest in the following described property:

New/Used	Yr. Mod.	Make	No. Cyl.	Model No.	Model Name	Body Type	Serial Number	Motor Number

☐ Radio ☐ Heater ☐ Automatic Transmission ☐ Overdrive ☐ Power Steering ☐ Power Brakes ☐ Power Windows ☐ Air Conditioning ☐ Other

This security interest is given to secure the payment and performance of the Debtor's obligations under this agreement and also to secure the payment of the Debtor's obligations on a promissory note of even date executed by Debtor and made payable to Secured Party in the principal sum of_____

_____ Dollars ($_____) payable in installments and maturing on the_____ day of_____

_____ , 19_____ .

CREDIT COST DISCLOSURE AS REQUIRED BY LAW

1. Cash Price $_____
2. vn Payment
   (2A) Cash Down Payment $_____
   (2B) Trade In (Describe) $_____

   Total Down Payment $_____
3. Unpaid Balance of Cash Price $_____
4. Other Charges (Itemize)
   (4A) Non Required Insurance
   _____ $_____
   _____ $_____
   (4B) Official Fees $_____
   (4C) _____ $_____
4D. Total Other Charges $_____

5. Unpaid Balance & Amount Financed $_____
6. FINANCE CHARGE (Composed of)
   (6A) Time Price Differential $_____
   (6B) Required Insurance (Itemize)
   _____ $_____
   _____ $_____
   (6C) _____ $_____
6. TOTAL FINANCE CHARGE $_____
7. Deferred Payment Price (1, 4D & 6) $_____
8. ANNUAL PERCENTAGE RATE _____%
9. Total of Payments (3, 4D & 6) $_____
   _____ installments of $_____ monthly beginning

LIABILITY INSURANCE COVERAGE FOR BODILY INJURY AND PROPERTY DAMAGE CAUSED TO OTHERS IS NOT INCLUDED. Number of payments, amounts thereof, due dates of each payment, and frequency thereof are disclosed in this document in the note and security agreement. The description of property to which a security interest is claimed and granted, the fact that afteracquired property is also liened and that future advances and other indebtedness to the secured party are likewise secured by the security interest in said property is disclosed within this document in the security agreement. Late charges of $5.00 or 5% of the payment, whichever is less, will be charged. Prepayment of the obligation may earn refund of the unearned FINANCE CHARGE as computed under Rule of 78s.

INSURANCE

PROPERTY INSURANCE, if written in connection with this extension of credit, may be obtained through any proper agent or company of choice by borrower, but if borrower desires such coverage to be obtained through or paid by creditor, the cost will be $_____ for the term of the credit, subject only to rate increases granted by state officials, and such charge will be added to the cost of the credit.

CREDIT LIFE AND DISABILITY INSURANCE, is not required to obtain this extension of credit. If borrower desires such coverage the costs as set out below will be added to the cost of the credit.
1. The cost for Credit Life Insurance alone will be $_____ for the term of the loan.
2. The cost for Credit Life and Disability Insurance will be $_____ for the term of the credit.

I desire Credit Life and Disability Insurance _____   I desire property insurance _____
                                           date   signed   date   signed

I desire Credit Life Insurance _____   I desire NO Insurance _____
                              date   signed   date   signed

Party(ies) stipulate and agree that all provisions on the reverse side hereof are incorporated herein by reference and constitute a part of this agreement. Notice to Buyer: Do not sign this contract before you read it or if it contains any blank spaces. You are entitled to an exact copy of the contract you sign. Under the law, you have the right to pay off in advance the full amount due and obtain a partial refund of the time price differential.

Debtor acknowledges that on the day and year first above written, this agreement was executed and that on said day a fully completed copy of this agreement executed by both Secured Party and Debtor has been delivered to him.

SECURED PARTY   DEBTOR

(Name)   (Name)

(Corporation or Partnership)   (Corporation or Partnership)

By_____   By_____

PARTIES HEREBY WARRANT AND COVENANT:

1. That Debtor will not sell, offer to sell, or otherwise transfer or encumber the collateral or any interest therein without the prior written consent of the secured Party.

2. That Secured Party will procure the insurance coverage designated above herein the proceeds therefrom to be payable to the Secured Party and Debtor as their interests appear. If insurance other than insurance on motor vehicles is designated above herein, Debtor shall be covered thereby. In the event of any default under this agreement, the Secured Party is authorized to cancel the said insurance and to receive the return premiums, if any, which shall be either credited to the unpaid balance due under this contract, or used to purchase insurance protecting the interest of the Secured Party alone, or used for both, whichever Secured Party elects.

3. That Debtor will preserve the collateral and keep it in good condition, and shall allow the Secured Party to inspect the same at any reasonable time.

4. That Debtor shall not sell or dispose of the collateral or subject it to any unpaid charge or any subsequent interest of a third person, unless the Secured Party first gives written consent to such.

5. That the Secured Party may at the Secured Party's option discharge liens, security interests, or other encumbrances on the collateral, and may pay for the repair of any damage to the collateral, the maintenance and preservation thereof and for insurance thereon, and upon so doing Debtor shall on demand reimburse the Secured Party for any payment so made. Said payments advanced shall draw interest at eight percent (8%) per annum from the date of payment until reimbursement, shall be added to the indebtedness owed by Debtor and shall be secured by this Security Agreement.

| 6. That the Debtor's residence is:
☐ At the address shown in the first paragraph herein.

☐ At _____
        (Street)   (City)   (State) | 7. That the Secured Party's place of business is:
☐ At the address shown in the first paragraph herein.

☐ At _____
        (Street)   (City)   (State) |

8. That the Debtor shall not permit the removal of the collateral from_____County, Missouri, except for its temporary removal in connection with its ordinary use, without first obtaining written consent of the Secured Party.

9. That the Debtor shall be in default under this agreement upon:

A. Default in the payment or performance of any obligation, covenant or liability contained herein;

B. Reasonable determination by Secured Party that any warranty or representation herein made was false when made;

C. Loss, theft, substantial damage, destruction, sale or encumbrance of any of the collateral, or the making of any levy, seizure or attachment there.

D. Death, dissolution, termination of existence, insolvency or business failure of Debtor, or appointment of a receiver for any part of the collateral, assignment for the benefit of creditors or the commencement of any proceeding under any bankruptcy or insolvency law by or against Debtor or any guarantor or surety for Debtor.

10. Upon such default and at any time thereafter, the Secured Party may declare all obligations secured hereby immediately due and payable and may proceed to enforce payment of the same and exercise any and all rights and remedies provided by the Uniform Commercial Code as well as all other rights and remedies possessed by the Secured Party. The Secured Party may require the Debtor to assemble the collateral and make it available to the Secured Party at a place designated by Secured Party which is reasonably convenient to both parties. Expenses for retaking, holding, preparing for sale, selling and the like shall include the Secured Party's reasonable attorney's fees and legal expenses. Any notification of sale or other disposition of the collateral required to be given by the Secured Party will be sufficient if given personally, or mailed by certified mail, not less than five (5) days prior to the day on which such sale or other disposition will be made, and such notification shall be deemed reasonable notice.

11. No waiver by the Secured Party of any default shall operate as a waiver of any other default.

12. The contents of the copy of the financing statement found immediately preceding this Security Agreement are incorporated herein by reference and made a part hereof.

13. Upon full performance of the Debtor's obligations under this agreement and full payment of the Debtor's obligations on the promissory note herein described, this agreement shall be void, otherwise to remain in full force and effect.

14. The terms of this agreement shall be binding upon the heirs, executors, administrators, successors, and assigns of the parties hereto.

ASSIGNMENT

For value received, the within agreement and all the right, title and interest of the undersigned Secured Party, to the property therein described and secured, is hereby sold, transferred, conveyed and assigned to:

_____

its successors and assigns, with full authority to do every act and thing necessary to collect and discharge the same. The undersigned expressly warrants that the within agreement arose from the bona fide time sale to the Debtor of the property described therein and secured thereby, that the title to said property at the time of said sale was vested in the undersigned free and clear of all liens and encumbrances, that the undersigned had the legal right to and did properly assign and deliver such title as well as said property to the Debtor at the time of said sale, that said property was not misrepresented to the Debtor in any way and that the statements of the Debtor and all other statements of fact in this Security Agreement are true to the best of the knowledge and belief of the undersigned, and that the down-payment indicated in said agreement was paid in full by Debtor in cash or trade-in as stated therein. The above agreement and above described note were completely executed prior to Debtor's signing the same. All warranties herein contained are made to induce the assignee to purchase this agreement and if there is any breach of any warranty, without regard to the knowledge or lack of knowledge of the undersigned, the undersigned will on demand purchase this agreement from the assignee for the balance then remaining unpaid plus any costs and expenses paid or incurred by the assignee.

SECURED PARTY

_____
(Corporation or Partnership)

_____   By_____
(Name)

Federal Trade Commission.

system should perform trouble free. These items should be inspected and tested by a reputable mechanic. Repairs can then be made ahead of time.

There are some things you can do to get the car ready for vacation even though you have a mechanic do the major repairs. The car can be cleaned, vacuumed, washed, and polished. You may want to include some of the emergency items described earlier in the car. If you feel that your particular car may be difficult to repair or parts difficult to find, a small sack of essential minor parts could be included: length of water or heater hose, clamps, points, condenser, rotor, distributor cap, thermostat, fuses, radiator cap, fan belt, tire gauge, and owner's manual.

BICYCLES AND MOPEDS

At the beginning of this chapter, we stated that a "package of transportation" may be needed in the years to come. Alternative transportation includes bicycles and mopeds.

An individual should assess his or her needs for a *bicycle* in much the same way as buying a car. There is no need to purchase an expensive bike if you plan to ride it only on weekends during the summer months. A simple sturdy bike with a single- or three-speed system may be adequate. You can purchase such a bike from a reputable and quality store, and you can probably find the bicycle you need for under $150.

Ten-speed bicycles, those priced above $150, are directed toward transportation as well as ego needs. The more expensive bike can be used for touring or daily commuting. The more expensive bicycle probably should be purchased from a store that deals principally in bicycles and has a staff that can service and repair them. Before purchasing a "quality" bicycle, start your research with a basic article from the November 1980 issue of *Consumer Reports,* "10 Speed Bikes." Another good article is in the July 9, 1979 issue of *Business Week,* "A Guide to Bicycle Shopping."

One final comment about bicycles. The Consumer Product Safety Commission ranks bicycles and bicycle equipment–related accidents first in frequency and severity from a survey of hospital emergency rooms.

A *moped* is a combination of a bicycle with pedals and a small motorcycle. Costs are $300 and up. These cycles are equipped with engines of less than 5 horsepower, and they can travel over 100 miles on a gallon of gasoline-oil mixture. Licensing requirements vary from state to state as does required safety equipment. Buy from a seller who also can service and repair the moped. Since their maximum speed is usually under 30 miles per hour, they are for city streets, not highways. Your automobile public liability insurance may not protect you, so check with your insurance company before driving a moped.

As with purchasing automobiles, be sure to understand what written warranties go along with the product. The glossary at the end of this chapter explains such terms as "full" and "limited" warranties as well as the term "as is." For further information on warranties, consult the Magnuson-Moss Warranty Act of 1975.

BUDGET AND WORKSHEET FOR TRANSPORTATION

Normal transportation needs in a household are likely to involve automobile payments and payments for licenses, gasoline, light and heavy maintenance, and parking. Other normal commuting costs include local transit and taxi fares.

Vacations and long-distance travel may require expenditures for plane, train, and bus tickets and hotels and meals.

Necessary transportation costs for a particular year are likely to be underestimated unless some thought is given to this area. By keeping records of actual expenditures, estimates can be more accurate for a future budget period.

Let us return to the John and Kay Adams family and review their budget for the coming year. The worksheet in Exhibit 9-3 that Kay has prepared is made up of three sections. Part A includes the basic *fixed* expenditures such as car payments, car insurance, and amounts for license. These cash expenditures must be made even though the cars are driven only a few miles each month. In this coming year, no automobile payments are to be made. License plates and insurance, however, are paid annually, for a total of $450.

The amount spent by a household for license plates varies widely depending on the particular state. The auto insurance premiums for the year are partly determined by driver's past record, amount of driving, urban, suburban or town size, cost of repair, type of use, and so on. If a car is old, perhaps only public liability coverage is retained. Auto insurance premiums are also reduced by having higher deductions on collision coverage.

Kay figures the cost of light and heavy maintenance on both the Adams's cars based upon probable expenditures for the coming year. Gasoline for both cars is estimated at $550, light maintenance at $140, and heavy maintenance at $120. The heavy maintenance estimate may be understated if the cars are to be driven more than originally expected for the year. However, there is a $100-per-month, or $1,200 miscellaneous, contingency and car replacement fund. Kay has made some reasonable effort to have cash available. Her estimate for part B is $2,140 for the coming year.

Part C of the worksheet is an attempt to include other probable costs related to transportation and travel. Extra gasoline and lube costs for weekend trips, plane tickets, rental car costs, lodging, and meals are written in and are estimated to amount to $1,350. Total anticipated transportation costs are $3,940 for the coming year.

SUMMARY

For the American, transportation means going from one place to another by automobile. Other than buying a home, transportation costs may well be the largest item of consumer expenditure. The automobile is your link with society. It is important to be in control over your automobile costs instead of being controlled by them.

Unless you have alternative transportation readily available, a well-maintained car is a must. The key for controlling your transportation costs is to

EXHIBIT 9-3   John & Kay Adams
Transportation Budget and Worksheet
For the Year _____

PART A	Est.	Subtotal
Auto(s) Payments for the year	#–0–	
Auto Insurance premuims	300–	
Auto Licence Plates, tabs, fees	150–	
Subtotal of Estimated Costs		#450–

PART B				Est.
Basic Cost Per Automobile	#1	#2	#3	
Gasoline – Estimate for Year	#350	#200–		#550–
Light Maintenance (oil, lub, tune)	80	60		140–
Heavy Maintenance (tires, brakes)	120			120–
Parking – work or business				–
Parking lot & meter money				70–
Tolls, camping fees, etc.				10–
Local transit fares – tokens, coupons				25–
Taxi fares & tips				25–
Cycles, maintenance, licence, etc.				–
Miscellaneous contingency, Car Replacement fund				1,200–
Subtotal of Estimated Costs				#2,140–

PART C	Est.
Vacation gasoline, oil, cleaning	#50–
Plane, train, bus, Rental Car, trailer fares	700–
Hotel, motel costs & Contingency travel cks.	600–
Subtotal of Estimated Costs	#1,350–
Total Transportation for the Year, Parts A, B, and C	#3,940–

review your daily basic work schedule. No one should ever have to purchase a car or other vehicle on impulse, on short notice, or under pressure. Skill developed in car buying can be carried over in other consumer transactions and may be very useful at your job. Living close to work and shopping should be a long-term goal.

Light maintenance is defined as minor maintenance and repairs that are anticipated by the owner and are performed on a regularly scheduled basis. Heavy maintenance is defined as large, infrequent, nonrecurring expenditures required to replace large parts or systems on an automobile. Keeping a car for 100,000 miles is not rare. The key to a long automobile life is *maintenance*. This appears to be the basic attitude or habit of people who own the same car 10 to 15 years. There is a tendency to underestimate the real cost of car ownership. The greatest single cost of new cars in the early years is their decline in market value. The total monthly cost of an automobile focuses attention on all the car's components subject to eventual replacement. Car ownership should be viewed in terms of fixed and variable costs.

More used cars than new cars are sold each year. Establishing a budget for car buying reduces emotional motives and forces one to concentrate on day-to-day driving needs. Greater skills are needed in buying a used car. Ideally, it would be best to obtain a used car from someone you have known or have observed using the car over the years. An extensive on-the-lot inspection and road test should be made before purchasing a used car.

It is best to avoid leasing and long-term installment credit programs for personal driving needs.

Vacation often means travel, and that the travel is often carried out in the family car. Extended travel may require a careful check of the car's basic overall condition and repairs made.

Bicycle and mopeds may be useful in reducing transportation costs.

TIPS

1. Remember that off-street parking is generally safer than on-street parking and it may reduce damage to your car.
2. Keep your car locked at all times when driving or not. Hide valuables in the trunk or out of sight.
3. Immobilize your car and reduce possible theft by removing the distributor rotor.
4. Equip your car for emergencies with a set of jumper cables, flashlight, a crescent wrench, a Phillip's screwdriver, a blade screwdriver, flares, a pair of pliers, roll of electrical or duct tape, some electrical wire, and a piece of ground cloth, old cloths, or jumpsuit.

5. Review your homeowner insurance or personal property insurance policy for coverage of losses of personal belongings while on vacation or business travel.

6. Learn to recognize the liquid drops or spots coming from the car.

7. While using the "self-service" pumps at the gasoline stations may save money, learn to check tires, crankcase oil level, and coolant and battery fluid levels on a regular basis. With the engine off, inspect fan belts.

8. Learn to recognize sounds that may warn you of potential car troubles if not fixed.

9. If, when traveling, you need to have your car serviced, remain with the car. Get out of the car and observe the attendant's activity when checking under the hood and checking the tires. Use the station restrooms only after the car has been completely serviced, bill is paid, and the car is parked away from the service area.

10. Permanent antifreeze is not permanent; it should be changed every two years. Automatic transmission fluid should be changed every 30,000 miles.

11. Washing your car yourself will save money, give you some exercise, and provide an opportunity to inspect the outside areas of the car.

12. Before considering the purchase of a car with a diesel engine, review your driving needs carefully. It may require keeping a car for 100,000 to 200,000 miles before there is a cost benefit for owning the diesel car. Availability of diesel fuel is a problem in many areas of the United States. Diesel engines are difficult to start in very cold weather. As the price for gasoline and diesel fuel narrows, the diesel becomes a less attractive investment.

13. Before buying a *new* car, attend a regional auto show. These are often held in November and most domestic and foreign models are on display.

14. Before you retire be sure to have a good automobile that is paid for by retirement. Retired persons can keep their cars longer than most people.

15. It is usually *not* a good idea to lease an automobile for personal use only. The cost includes the basic car maintenance and rent per month *and* the profit to the lessor.

16. Theft prevention for a bicycle can require up to $50 for a tamper-proof lock and chain.

17. A small fire extinguisher can be a useful piece of emergency equipment.

18. For determining the approximate market value of a used car desired, study the classified ads in newspapers as well as the prices found in the National Auto Dealers Association's *Official Used Car Guide*.

19. Before buying a used car, determine if the car has ever been included on any manufacturer's recall list by calling 800-424-9393. Be sure you have the year, model, and serial number of the car.

ADDITIONAL READINGS

Darack, Arthur, *Used Cars: How to Avoid Highway Robbery.* Englewood Cliffs, N.J.: Prentice-Hall, 1983.

"How to Keep Your Car Almost Forever," *Consumer Reports,* May 1984, pp. 247—59.

"Rental-Car Companies," *Consumer Reports,* July 1985, pp. 403—6.

"The Cost of Protecting Detroit," *Consumer Reports,* March 1985, pp. 149—50.

GLOSSARY OF USEFUL TERMS

As Is Term in contract indicating that there is no refund and that no warranty is provided by the seller.

Bait and Switch Advertising products that the dealer has no intention of selling. Once the customer is on the lot, the goal is to get the customer to buy higher-priced merchandise or substitute.

Blue Book Popular, monthly automotive trade booklet providing estimated selling prices and wholesale prices on various models of cars.

Cream Puff A very well-kept, clean used car. It may imply that the car has low mileage, original paint, and no dents, rust, or chrome deterioration.

Detailing Automotive trade term meaning the cleaning, polishing, adjusting, and minor repair of a car to put it in attractive condition for sale. It includes replacement of worn carpeting, arm-rests, pedal pads, steam cleaning, spray painting engine, radiator, and so on.

High Balling An inflated trade-in allowance for an old car. Also called "bushing."

Low Balling Technique used by automobile salespeople to get a customer back to the showroom after shopping. Quoting a price for a car that is much lower than other auto competitors'. Also done in the auto repair business.

Mechanic's Lien A legal claim on another's car as security against the payment for work done on the vehicle.

Puffery Exaggerated advertising or claims and the customer is deemed to recognize it.

System Sales A sales technique by auto dealers to put emotional stress on the buyer. The purportedly new car salesperson offers to sell you a car at an extremely attractive price. You are in the process of signing the papers and closing the deal when the sales manager comes in. In your presence, the sales manager threatens to fire the salesperson for selling the car at too low a price. The customer, witnessing the scene, decides to go along with the higher standard price of the car so that the salesperson will not lose his or her job.

Warranty, Full Authorization that a defective product will be fixed (or replaced) free, including removal and installation if necessary; it will be fixed within a reasonable time after you complain; you do not have to do anything unreasonable to get warranty service; the warranty is good for anyone who owns the product during the warranty period; if the product cannot be fixed after a reasonable number of tries, you get your choice of a replacement or a refund (see the Magnuson-Moss Warranty Act of 1975).

Warranty, Limited   A "limited" authorization that may cover only parts (not labor), allows only a prorata refund or credit, requires you to return a heavy product to the store, and covers only the first purchaser.

Window Sticker   Suggested retail sales price of a car. The manufacturer is required to post such document on each new car under a federal law. The sticker price is inflated. The customary haggling between dealer and buyer will usually result in a settlement price below the sticker amount.

10

Basic Investing

Upon completion of Chapter 10, you should be able to identify and remember

- How to develop a basic approach for selecting corporations as a basis for possible future investment.
- Examples of stock advisory service information about corporations.
- How to read the summaries of stock market information found in the financial pages of most daily newspapers.
- Basic financial information and ratios to assess a corporation's solvency and profitability.
- Essential terminology associated with basic stock investment.
- Other areas of basic investing for the beginner.

OVERVIEW

Part V introduces the topics of basic investing and income taxes. Chapter 10 presents a practical approach to investing with an emphasis on acquiring common stocks. Chapter 11 discusses the current Internal Revenue Code and offers approaches for completing a Form 1040; it also reviews sensible tax shelters available to the average income earner.

The first stage of money management is toward accumulating and preserving essential cash and emergency reserve funds where there is a minimum of risk. Insured bank and savings accounts, savings certificates, and government and quality corporate bonds tend to meet these objectives of low risk. Chapter 8 considered basic real estate purchases of a home as serving family needs and desires first and as a potential investment second. Additional real estate acquired for recreational or second home use was still viewed more as a family need than as an investment. These forms of real estate ownership tend not to offer excessive risk to the average person. Risk of loss on certain real estate structures is protected by the purchase of insurance.

This chapter shows you how to become a part owner in a business firm operating in a free enterprise system. Not many people have the desire, skill, or financial assets to start their very own businesses. Others do not want to belong to a partnership because it subjects the owners to unlimited liability. Also, partnerships do not always work out. However, becoming a stockholder is a way to becoming an owner (a very small one) in some of the most successful business firms in the world.

Our goal in this chapter is to remove some of the mystery surrounding investment in corporate stocks and to suggest some sound, basic investment approaches.

WHY INVEST IN STOCKS?

Investing in corporate shares allows the investor to own a part of a business for only a small amount of money. The purchase of common stocks of a corporation serves as a hedge against inflation over the long run.

Stock investment can provide a return or yield equal to those available only to larger investors of certificates of deposit and Treasury bills, where minimum investments require $1,000, $5,000, and $10,000. Investing in stocks helps the money manager to reach such long-term goals as home down payments, supplementary income, a new car, and additional retirement income. There is much information about corporate stocks in the financial pages of most newspapers. Radio and TV news programs report timely activity concerning this area of investment. Most public and college libraries subscribe to several investment resources including such standards as *Barron's, Business Week, Forbes, Moody's*

Stock Guide Handbook, Standard & Poor's Stock Guide and Investor Outlook, and *The Wall Street Journal.* There are over 45 million stockholders in America, and the securities market is subject to strong federal regulations, which accounts for this supply of information.

TAKING THE MYSTERY OUT OF STOCKS

To many, the stock market appears extremely complex and the terminology or jargon too extensive to learn. The abbreviations, letters, numbers, fractions, and so on seem to have little meaning. The stock market commentators speak a language of their own. Let us try to remove some of the mystery.

Every specialty has its own language. Just listen to any sportscaster describing the plays in a baseball or football game. Better yet, have you tried to describe your job to someone who does not know what you do? Chances are great that you routinely use special abbreviations, numbers, and vocabulary with your co-workers when describing document forms, machines, tools, tasks, departments, shops, and processes.

It is quite natural for businesses that handle stock transactions to have their own specialized jargon. The stock market in the United States goes back over 200 years. This fact alone allows for a lot of history, myth, tradition, and folklore in this business activity. Take the very term "Wall Street." It derives from a geographic location in Manhattan where the Dutch settlers erected a walled fortification in the middle of the 1500s. This walled area was located on the present site of New York City's financial district.

When you look at the stock quotations in the financial pages of a newspaper, you will notice that the names of corporations are abbreviated, that the dollar signs are eliminated (since the monetary unit used in the United States is the dollar), and that stocks are traditionally quoted only to the nearest one-eighth (⅛) of a dollar. This is because the medium of exchange in olden days was linked to the Spanish "pieces of eight" coinage. Some people still refer to the quarter as "two bits," fifty cents as "four bits," and so on. The "bit" is one-eighth of a dollar, or 12½ cents. A series of dots (· · ·) is a simple way to indicate "no change" in price.

The glossary at the end of this chapter and that in Chapter 5 should clarify most of the basic terms used in the investment world.

SHOULD YOU BE INVESTING IN STOCKS?

Before considering investing in corporate stocks, it is prudent to see whether you are ready for this area of investing. This requires a financial and personality checkup.

For example, you should have taken care of such basics as medical and major medical coverage, accidental death and disability insurance, salary insurance, and term life insurance where responsibilities require it. Other financial areas include having no consumer installment and department store credit. There should be at least 90 days of take-home pay in the checking and savings accounts.

A personality checkup includes a person's temperament, age, state of health, attitude of spouse on investing, attitude toward one's job, and job security. As we shall see, the prices of corporate stock fluctuate continuously. So, if watching your investment drop in price causes you or other members of your family to lose sleep, or become irritable, it is better to seek peace of mind and stay out of the stock market. Also, if you are thinking of getting rich quickly or you have a streak of gullibility or greed, the stock market may well be your undoing. You should put no more weight in daily stock market news than you would to a weather report or a recap of baseball scores.

Investment in stocks is supposed to reach long-term financial objectives, and the holding of good stocks for 5, 10, or 15 years should not be unusual. Long-term goals imply careful forethought, a sense of commitment, a strong dose of self-discipline, and some time for periodic review and reading. Money invested in corporate stocks should be money that you could afford to lose.

THE UPS AND DOWNS OF STOCK OWNERSHIP

In 1965 there were 25 million stockholders in the United States. By 1970, that number had risen to 30 million. By 1975, the number had dropped to 25 million. And by 1987, the number had risen to 45 million, or 19 percent of the population.

The surge of new stockholders in the late 1960s was due to individuals' enjoyment of a long and prosperous time in America. By the beginning of 1971, the nation had enjoyed well over 100 months (more than eight years) of continuous upward and prosperous times. The U.S. government was following a "guns and butter" policy for both domestic development and fighting in Vietnam. Inflation during that time had gone from less than 2 percent to over 5 percent (see Table 1-1). Unemployment was low. Conglomerates, "go-go" mutual funds, and real estate investment trusts (REITs) were buzz words of the day. Yesterday's auto mechanic was tomorrow's mutual fund sales representative.

The period from 1971 through 1975 was tough on these new stockholders. The war in Vietnam was winding down. The aerospace, housing, and farming industries began a decline. A weakened U.S. dollar in the international market brought on stringent economic policies.

There was an urgent need to control inflation, and the cost of credit went to 12 percent. The first experience of oil shortage and rising oil costs in 1973 and 1974 began to change a national economy based upon cheap fuel sources.

In the boom years of 1975–1979, many investments rose rapidly in value, including most real estate, bonds, CDs, gold, silver, collectibles, and diamonds. When the 1979–1981 recessions took place, the common stocks of many U.S. firms seemed undervalued. From August 1982, interest in the stock market has been increasing.

Which Stocks to Buy?

Many people err in investing in stocks when they rely on "hot tips," a friend's advice, a broker's recommendations, or short-term stock trader's news. Your own judgment is about as good as the next person's in the stock market when picking a stock.

Which stocks should you buy? You can make that decision on your own after you have done the following simple analysis. Compile a list of the makers of products you use or have around your home, work, or community. Take a sheet of paper and, down the left-hand side, draw up a list of the products, clothing, household appliances, car products, and stores where you like to trade. Include equipment that you use at work or school. You probably have some ideas of the products that you like or dislike or stores where you like to trade or avoid.

For example, the kitchen offers a variety of product and appliance makers. Perhaps you have come to trust certain makers of foods and appliances. "Food-stuff" might be a heading on the list. To the right of the word, write down the names of the various corporations: Heinz, Del Monte, General Mills, Pillsbury, Kelloggs, Post, Nestlé, and so on. Kitchen appliances can provide a host of corporation names such as Sunbeam, GM, Maytag, GE, Sears, Rival, Whirlpool, and so on. The bathroom and medicine chest will yield such well-known corporate names as Johnson & Johnson, Merck, Squibb, American Home Products, Procter & Gamble, and Syntex. Exhibit 10-1 is a sample listing of products, appliances, and services and some of the manufacturers.

It is a good idea to continue to add company names for several weeks, and you can probably come up with 50 to 75 different corporation names in a very short time. Shops, stores, supermarkets, and factories in your community can also be added. Do not forget the special service firms in your area such as banks, savings institutions, and the various public utilities for gas, electricity, and water.

The list that you draw up is only the starting point, but it will draw your attention to the larger, well-known, and perhaps well-established corporations. This list will probably not include the very small new corporations that are just starting out and carry a greater degree of risk. This is important because a majority of these small companies will fail in the first couple of years. Fewer than 20 percent will be around beyond a decade. Where there is both heavy competition and innovation, as in electronics, the expected life of a new electronics corporation can be very short.

EXHIBIT 10-1   List of Corporations for Review

	Makers
Foodstuffs	Del Monte, General Mills, Post, Pillsbury, Nestle, Kellogg, H. J. Heinz, Pepsi Co., Bordens, Wonder, Armour
Kitchen Appliances	G.M., G.E., Maytag, Whirlpool, Rival, Sears, J. C. Penney, Hobart
Bathroom, Drugs, Cosmetics	Johnson & Johnson, Mercle, Syntex, Avon, Squibb, Am. Home Products, Procter and Gamble, Clorox, Scott Paper, Revlon
Automotive	G.M., Ford, Chrysler, Toyota, Texaco, Shell, Mobil, Exxon, Firestone, Goodyear
Clothing	Levi Strauss, Sears, J. C. Penney, Blue Bell
Fast Food	Mc Donalds, Dennys, Pizza Hut
Chain Stores	Safeway, Sears, Woolworth, K-Mart, A & P, Marshall-Fields, Allied, Montgomery Ward
Radio TV	RCA, Sony, Zenith, Tandy, G.E., Panasonic, CBS, Magnavox
Equipment at work, tools, delivery	Clark Equipment, 3 M Co., Xerox, IBM, TRW, International Harvester, Union Pacific, du Pont, NCR, AT&T

A rather interesting feature about the list that you develop will be the names. Some of the companies on your list are no longer independently operated. Many have been purchased by or merged into much larger corporations. This can be both interesting and frustrating in your search to learn about a particular corporation. Every investor has experienced searching for a very well-known company but has failed to find the corporation's stock listed in any financial newspaper. In some instances, it may be necessary to call a public library, your bank's trust department, or a stockbroker. Even these people may not always know the answer right away.

Well known companies whose common stock is no longer available to the general public include Levi Strauss, Beatrice Foods, Safeway Stores, and Macy's. Founders and managers buy up all the stock to prevent certain "unfriendly" corporate raiders from controlling the business. Some well-known firms are simply divisions of still bigger companies. For example, Montgomery Ward is a part of Mobil Oil. Kentucky Fried Chicken, Taco Bell, and Pizza Hut are all owned by PepsiCo.* The parent company is very often traded on the largest stock exchanges around the world.

Narrowing Your List

After you have compiled a list of company names from their products, appliances, cars, tools, and so on, your next step is to find financial information about these companies. Your goal is to reduce your original list of 50 to 75 companies to 5 or 10 that fit your long-term investment goals. Many of the familiar company names may not fit with your long-term goals, and some companies are actually declining in influence (having evidence of financial difficulties, poor management, insufficient research and development, and antiquated equipment or are living on their past glory and goodwill).

Two financial services provide this information: *Moody's* and *Standard & Poor's*. The use of Standard & Poor's advisory information in this section was an arbitrary selection. Note the Standard & Poor's review of the Pillsbury Company in Exhibit 10-2.

Pillsbury is included mainly because of its familiarity. Some of its additional holdings include Burger King and Green Giant. The company was incorporated in Delaware in 1935 and is listed on the New York Stock Exchange with the symbol PSY.

No attempt was made to amend the printed information. As was mentioned, expect to find information abbreviated, dollar signs omitted, zeros dropped to save space, and simpler words such as "earnings" used instead of "net profit after taxes." You will find terms such as P-E ratio (or price-earnings ratio), dividend, yield, book value defined in the glossary.

Exhibit 10-2 provides a 10-year trend of information, so the reader can see how revenues or sales and net income have been doing over a long period. Trends are better than one- or two-year records to look at and assess. Key information is presented in percentages for easy understanding. Other useful information includes charts, number of shares of common stock in the hands of

---

* The corporations mentioned in this and other chapters are cited for the sole purpose of helping the reader to learn about corporate finances. They are not intended directly or indirectly as investment recommendations.

EXHIBIT 10-2 Standard & Poor's Corporate Information Sheets

Pillsbury Co. 1830

NYSE Symbol PSY   Options on ASE (Feb-May-Aug-Nov)   In S&P 500

Price	Range	P-E Ratio	Dividend	Yield	S&P Ranking	Beta
Apr. 15'87	1987					
38¼	46⅛-34⅛	16	1.00	2.6%	A+	0.81

Summary

This major food company operates and franchises Burger King fast-food restaurants and produces a wide range of consumer foods and industrial flour. Falling restaurant profitability has penalized earnings for fiscal 1986-7. Modest restructuring in the segment and cost cutting overall should aid a turnaround in fiscal 1987-8. PSY planned to sell a second master limited partnership for Burger King, possibly in the fiscal 1986-7 fourth quarter.

Current Outlook

Earnings for the fiscal year ending May 31, 1988 are projected to rise to $3.10 a share from fiscal 1986-7's estimated $2.30.

The quarterly dividend is likely to remain at $0.25 for the near term.

Sales for fiscal 1987-8 should continue to rise on volume improvement for food products. Although good gains are also seen for restaurants, pricing is likely to remain competitive. However, ingredient costs should remain stable at low levels, and continued recovery in commodity/marketing should help limit the pressure on margins. Productivity and other cost cutting programs would also be important to a pretax earnings uptrend, as would lower start-up costs for new concept restaurants. A lower effective tax rate should contribute a substantial amount to the expected earnings increase.

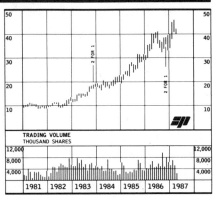

Net Sales (Million $)

Quarter:	1986-7	1985-6	1984-5	1983-4
Aug.	1,383	1,263	1,024	929
Nov.	1,688	1,583	1,256	1,125
Feb.	1,527	1,457	1,171	1,035
May	---	1,545	1,219	1,083
	---	5,848	4,671	4,172

Sales for the nine months ended February 28, 1987 rose 6.9%, year to year. Sales for the food segment were up 7.8%, and operating profits rose 22%, aided by a return to profitability in commodity marketing. Restaurant sales rose 5.7%, but operating profits declined 12% due to competitive pressures and start-up costs for new menus and restaurants. Pretax profits rose 6.8%, but after taxes at 49.7%, versus 44.2%, net income was off 3.8%, to $1.73 a share from $1.79.

Common Share Earnings ($)

Quarter:	1986-7	1985-6	1984-5	1983-4
Aug.	0.55	0.51	0.45	0.40
Nov.	0.62	0.65	0.76	0.60
Feb.	0.56	0.64	0.46	0.42
May	E0.57	0.60	0.55	0.54
	E2.30	2.39	2.21	1.96

Important Developments

Mar. '87 — PSY registered with the SEC its intent to spin off 108 to 120 Burger King restaurants to a second master limited partnership. The aftertax gain on the sale would range from $20 to $23 million. PSY sold the first Burger King limited partnership in early 1986.

Next earnings report expected in mid-June.

Per Share Data ($)

Yr. End May 31	1987	[1]1986	1985	1984	1983	1982	1981	1980	[1]1979	[1]1978
Book Value	NA	10.27	11.55	11.15	10.80	9.94	9.05	8.05	7.11	6.22
Earnings[2]	NA	2.39	2.21	1.96	1.60	1.58	1.49	[3]1.31	[3]1.16	1.02
Dividends	0.96½	0.84	0.76	0.68	0.60½	0.54½	0.48⅜	0.41⅞	0.36½	0.31⅜
Payout Ratio	NA	35%	34%	35%	38%	35%	32%	32%	34%	31%
Calendar Years	1986	1985	1984	1983	1982	1981	1980	1979	1978	1977
Prices[4]—High	41⅛	31⅞	22⅞	19½	13⅞	11½	10¾	10⅜	11⅞	11⅜
Low	29⅛	19½	16½	11¾	9⅜	8¾	6⅞	8	8½	8⅞
P/E Ratio—	NA	13-8	10-7	10-6	9-6	7-6	7-5	8-6	10-7	11-9

Data as orig. reptd. Adj. for stk. div(s). of 100% Dec. 1986, 100% Dec. 1983. 1. Reflects merger or acquisition. 2. Bef. results of disc. opers. of +0.02 in 1978. 3. Ful. dil.: 1. ⅛0 in 1980, 1.16 in 1979. 4. Cal. yr. NA-Not Available. E-Estimated.

Standard NYSE Stock Reports
Vol. 54/No. 77/Sec. 18

April 23, 1987

Standard & Poor's Corp.
25 Broadway, NY, NY 10004

Courtesy of Standard & Poor's Corporation. This report was up to date at the time of publication; subsequent changes are reflected in current Standard & Poor's reports.

EXHIBIT 10-2 *(continued)*

Income Data (Million $)

Year Ended May 31	Revs.	Oper. Inc.	% Oper. Inc. of Revs.	Cap. Exp.	Depr.	Int. Exp.	Net Bef. Taxes	Eff. Tax Rate	[1]Net Inc.	% Net Inc. of Revs.
[2]1986	5,848	670	11.5%	309	196	138	[5]377	44.8%	[4]208	3.6%
1985	4,671	536	11.5%	327	143	92	[5]340	43.6%	192	4.1%
1984	4,172	461	11.0%	282	121	86	[5]304	44.1%	170	4.1%
1983	3,686	378	10.3%	244	109	82	[5]230	39.7%	139	3.8%
1982	3,385	360	10.6%	209	93	86	[5]228	40.2%	[4]136	4.0%
[2]1981	3,302	359	10.9%	227	92	98	[5]202	40.8%	120	3.6%
1980	3,032	330	10.9%	254	80	85	192	45.4%	105	3.5%
[2]1979	2,166	244	11.2%	359	57	44	160	47.9%	84	3.9%
[2]1978	1,705	200	11.7%	134	46	31	[5]142	49.8%	71	4.2%
1977	1,461	170	11.6%	113	40	26	[5]115	49.7%	58	4.0%

Balance Sheet Data (Million $)

May 31	Cash	Current Assets	Current Liab.	Ratio	Total Assets	Ret. on Assets	Long Term Debt	Common Equity	Total Cap.	% LT Debt of Cap.	Ret. on Equity
1986	97	1,159	1,136	1.0	3,659	6.5%	973	1,314	2,490	39.1%	16.8%
1985	60	922	744	1.2	2,779	7.1%	648	1,165	2,006	32.3%	17.3%
1984	143	1,072	886	1.2	2,608	6.8%	503	1,046	1,699	29.6%	17.0%
1983	130	1,022	705	1.4	2,367	5.8%	572	956	1,637	35.0%	15.1%
1982	180	1,133	817	1.4	2,428	5.7%	597	890	1,591	37.5%	16.0%
1981	95	990	682	1.5	2,175	5.7%	631	752	1,471	42.9%	16.8%
1980	55	939	675	1.4	1,984	5.5%	552	670	1,294	42.7%	16.5%
1979	38	907	625	1.5	1,804	5.2%	509	583	1,167	43.6%	15.2%
1978	37	681	457	1.5	1,283	5.8%	298	457	818	36.4%	16.3%
1977	80	605	404	1.5	1,105	5.8%	259	388	697	37.1%	15.8%

Data as orig. reptd. **1.** Bef. results of disc. opers. in 1978. **2.** Reflects merger or acquisition. **3.** Excludes discontinued operations and reflects merger or acquisition. **4.** Reflects acctg. change. **5.** Incl. equity in earns. of nonconsol. subs.

Business Summary

Pillsbury is a major food company operating in three major segments; sales and profit contributions in fiscal 1985-6 were:

	Sales	Profits
Consumer foods	52%	41%
Restaurants	45%	59%
Commodity mktg.	3%	---

Foreign operations accounted for 8% of sales and 5% of operating income in 1985-6.

Consumer foods include a broad range of dry grocery and refrigerated fresh dough products sold primarily under the Pillsbury label, canned and frozen vegetables and frozen entrees (Green Giant), frozen pizza (Totino's, Fox Deluxe and Jeno's), and ice cream (Häagen Dazs). As a result of a realignment in fiscal 1984-5, flour milling and baking mixes operations are now included in the consumer foods segment.

Commodity marketing operations (agriproducts prior to realignment) consist of grain storage and transportation and a feed ingredient business. Consistent with its strategy of further reducing its participation in commodity-type activities, in November, 1985 PSY sold the edible dry beans / peas division.

Restaurants include the Burger King fast-food chain (4,743, mostly franchised, as of May 31, 1986) and limited-menu dinner houses under the names Steak and Ale (185) and Bennigan's (196). Operations added via the 1985 acquisition of Diversifoods Inc. include Godfather's Pizza (671).

Dividend Data

Dividends have been paid since 1927. A "poison pill" stock purchase right was adopted in 1986. A dividend reinvestment plan is available.

Amt. of Divd. $	Date Decl.	Ex-divd. Date	Stock of Record	Payment Date
0.43	Jun. 3	Jul. 28	Aug. 1	Aug. 31'86
0.50	Sep. 9	Oct. 28	Nov. 3	Nov. 30'86
2-for-1	Sep. 9	Dec. 1	Nov. 3	Nov. 28'86
0.25	Jan. 8	Jan. 27	Feb. 2	Feb. 28'87
0.25	Mar. 3	Apr. 27	May 1	May 31'87

Next dividend meeting: early Jun. '87.

Capitalization

Long Term Debt: $1,030,600,000.

Common Stock: 86,200,000 shs. (no par).
Institutions hold about 49%.
Shareholders of record: 21,300.

Office—200 South 6th St., Minneapolis, Minn. 55402. **Tel**—(612) 330-4966. **Chrmn, Pres & CEO**—J. M. Stafford. **VP-Secy**—E. C. Stringer. **VP-Treas**—J. W. Levin. **VP-Investor Contact**—J. Morris. **Dirs**—W. M. Blumenthal, D. F. Craib, Jr., A. F. Jacobson, C. E. Luhrs, K. A. Macke, J. W. McLamore, W. H. Monroe, J. H. Perkins, G. S. Pillsbury, R. A. Schoellhorn, G. J. Sella, Jr., W. H. Spoor, J. M. Stafford, P. G. Wray. **Transfer Agent & Registrar**—First National Bank, Minneapolis. **Incorporated** in Delaware in 1935.

Jane Collin

stockholders, headquarters addresses, and names of key officials. This information is summarized periodically; the date of the summary is shown at the bottom of the front side.

THE SECURITIES MARKET

The word "market" has been with us for ages—the fruit market, the meat market, the fish market. However, if we attach the word "stock" to the word market, we may feel somewhat apprehensive and uneasy. Basically, all markets tend to function in about the same way. It is a place to go to transact a specific kind of business. It is the *process* of the stock market that seems to put people off. The following illustration outlines the process of a simple buy and sell transaction.

Assume that a person living in Miami, Florida, has 100 shares of XYZ Corporation common stock to sell. Another person living in San Francisco wants to buy 100 shares of XYZ Corporation common stock. Both the buyer and seller know that the stock is worth around $25 per share. If the buyer and seller just happen to call stockbrokers in their respective cities who, in turn, just happen to be *members* of the same stock exchange or securities market, the transaction may be completed within five minutes or even less. This is true even though the securities market is located in, say, New York City.

The stock or securities exchange is an association with a specified number of memberships called *seats*. The exchange serves as a place for members to buy and sell shares of corporation stock that are listed for trading on that particular exchange. Several hundred different corporations might be listed. The exchange may have a number of trading "posts" at which specific stocks can be traded by the members.

Employees of the exchange who carry out buy and sell instructions for the stockbroker members are called *floor traders*. Where there are several buyers and several sellers for the same stock, the activity around a particular trading post will resemble an *auction*. Sellers will announce their *asking* prices while buyers will call out their *bids* for shares of stock. This is particularly so when investors instruct their broker to buy or sell a stock *at the market*, that is, at the best current price available. On the floor of the securities market, other personnel witness and confirm each transaction made on the trading floor.

House rules at the stock exchange or securities market may state that all transactions must be in amounts of 100 shares, or *a round lot*. To meet customers' needs for buying or selling fewer than 100 shares, or *odd lots*, there are exchange personnel who will handle only these transactions. Such a person is known as an *odd-lot specialist*. Many beginning investors may wish to purchase only 15 or 20 shares at a time.

Confirmations of completed floor transactions are communicated electronically to member-brokers' offices all around the country and even those in other nations. Invoices are prepared, endorsements and transfers of stock certificates are completed, and terms for settlement and brokerage commissions for services are calculated. By custom, *both* the buyer and the seller of corporate stock pay a commission in a single transaction. A stockbroker's commission might run $30 for a small transaction of $300 to $400; for a transaction amounting to $3,000, the total broker's commission may be $70.

Eventually, the old stock certificates of the seller are canceled, and substitute shares with the new owner's name are prepared and forwarded by officials of the corporation involved. There are several securities markets in the United States and other nations. The following paragraphs briefly summarize some of the major ones in America.

New York Stock Exchange (NYSE)

One of the largest and most widely known stock exchanges in the United States is the New York Stock Exchange. It is often called the "Big Board" and is located on Wall Street in the financial district of New York. There are 1,366 member seats. The price of a seat on the exchange has fluctuated over the years from just a few thousand dollars to over several hundred thousand dollars. The origins of this exchange date back to the 1790s. The shares of over 1,500 different corporations are traded on the exchange including stocks of foreign corporations. This exchange does about 80 percent of the total volume of all stock trading in the United States. The companies include the largest and most familiar in the United States including American Telephone & Telegraph, Dupont, Eastman Kodak, Exxon, General Motors, General Electric, IBM, K mart, Mobil, Sara Lee, Texaco, U.S. Steel, Xerox, and Zenith.

American Stock Exchange (AMEX)

The American Stock Exchange is also located in the financial district of New York. It is also known as the "Curb," because in its earlier days, business was actually conducted along the sidewalk and curb. Some 600 stocks are listed on the AMEX and there are 650 seats. Smaller and newer companies appear on this exchange, although well-known companies such as Hormel and Wang are traded here too.

Regional Stock Exchanges

In addition to the two major national exchanges, there are those located in other parts of the country: the Midwest Stock Exchange, Pacific Exchange, Boston

Exchange, and Philadelphia Exchange. Many of the shares listed on the large stock exchanges are also traded on these regional exchanges.

Over-the-Counter Market (OTC)

The shares of many thousands of corporations are not listed on any of the major or regional stock exchanges; in fact it is estimated that there are 40,000 *unlisted* corporation stocks compared with 3,000 or so listed companies. To be listed on major exchanges, companies must meet certain requirements as to size, number of shares, and shareholders, trading volume, annual sales, net worth, and so on. There are over 3,700 over-the-counter dealers throughout the United States and other countries. A brokerage house may be located in a community where regionally known corporations operate. The firm may be able to create a market for some of the local stocks. These brokers buy and sell securities over the telephone instead of using an auction floor.

The over-the-counter members of the National Association of Securities Dealers (NASD) maintain a computer system to accumulate the current prices of many companies traded over the counter. Some stock prices are maintained on the computer called the National Association of Securities Dealers Automated Quotations (NASDAQ). A small desk-type computer terminal at the broker's office can provide information about prices. Prices on over-the-counter stocks are quoted in *bid* and *asked* amounts and represent only approximations. Stocks traded over the counter include Apple Computer, Intel Corporation, Nordstrom, WD-40, and Yellow Freight System.

CORPORATE COMMON AND PREFERRED STOCKS

A *corporation* is a group of people (shareholders) organized to operate a business under a *charter* granted by a *state*. In a *closed* corporation, the shareholders are all members of a family or constitute a relatively small group. A *publicly owned* (open) corporation has many shareowners, and its stock is bought and sold by the general public. Our discussion will be confined to publicly owned private corporations.

A *common* stock is a certificate of ownership in a corporation. The holder usually has full voting rights to elect a board of directors and to vote on major issues that the directors bring or are required to bring before common stockholders. In addition to voting rights, there is the privilege to share in dividends, to purchase additional shares to be issued by the corporation in special offerings (preemptive rights), and to receive assets of the company (after the bondholders' distributions are made) should it be liquidated.

A *preferred* stock is a certificate of ownership in a corporation for which the holders usually receive dividend payments before holders of common stock do but have no voting rights. A preferred stock provides its holders with advantages that rank between a corporation bond and a common stock. Preferred stocks are often identified by the special privileges attached to them such as *cumulative* preferred and *participating* preferred. These features protect the investors' rights to dividends. A *convertible* preferred stock is one that may be exchanged for common stock in the same company; a noncumulative preferred stock is one in which dividends do not accrue. In this case, dividends omitted by the directors are lost.

DIVIDENDS

In general, dividends are distributions made by the corporation to stockholders. A *cash dividend* is a distribution of the profits of a corporation paid to stockholders. Cash dividends are often paid quarterly. With the exception of certain exclusions, cash dividends are subject to federal income taxes. A *stock dividend* is a distribution to stockholders in the form of shares of stock. Since it is not considered income in a real sense, it is not subject to income taxes. Nothing is changed as a result of the stock dividend. The investor receives only additional stock certificates and nothing else; the original dollar investment made to purchase the company stock remains unchanged.

For example, an individual may own 10 shares of R Corporation stock that cost a total of $500. The R Corporation board of directors, not wanting to distribute assets to stockholders, declares a 10 percent stock dividend and distributes it in the mail to investors. Now, the investor owns a total of 11 shares of stock, but the investment of $500 remains unchanged. The investor's original investment was $50 per share ($500 ÷ 10 shares). When news of a stock dividend is announced, the stock generally moves up in price for a brief time, as such dividends are interpreted as good news. (Demand for the stock may increase because of the news, and this causes the price to rise a few dollars.) As for the corporation involved, it is a case of its having its cake and eating it too.

One more activity to include with the topic of dividends is the *stock split,* a division of the outstanding shares of a corporation into a larger number of shares. The holder of 10 shares of stock before a split of, say, "2 for 1" will hold 20 shares after the split. A 100 percent stock dividend has the same net effect as a 2-for-1 split. The theoretical value of the shares of stock declines 50 percent after a 2-for-1 split.

There is some merit to issuing stock splits. A company's officials may find that the company's shares sell for a much higher price than do those of its competitors. A stock split may be a way to get the company's stock down to a more "popular" trading range. But nothing really happens as a result of a stock split. The shareholder receives no asset from the corporation. The corporation's assets, debts, and net worth are still the same.

A *reverse stock split* may occur when a corporation has experienced hard times and the price of the stock has dropped, say, from $20 a share to $2 a share. Very-low-priced stock is often equated with very speculative companies. A 1-for-10 reverse split would bring the price back up to a more "respectable" level.

It is important to remember the four important dates associated with dividend transactions: the *date of declaration*, the *ex-dividend date*, the *stockholders of record date*, and the *date of payment* or distribution. Note these important references on the Standard & Poor's sheet for Pillsbury under the heading of Dividend Data.

Cash dividends of major public corporations are paid every 90 days, or quarterly. If a corporation pays $1.00 of annual dividends on a share of common stock, then the shareholder can expect to receive $.25 per quarter on each share owned. For example, there might be a press release by a major corporation that reads as follows: "On July 27, the Board of Directors of ABC Corporation declared its regular quarterly cash dividend of $.40 to stockholders of record of August 16, to be paid on September 1."

The *ex-dividend* date is set by the securities exchange for completing stock trading transactions ahead of the stockholders' record date. The stock exchange will establish the ex-dividend date five or six days earlier than the stockholders of record date. For the ABC Corporation, the ex-dividend might be August 10. The ex-dividend date is of vital importance to investors. To receive the next upcoming cash dividend, the buyer of shares of stock should time his or her purchase before the ex-dividend date arrives. Many investors ignore this important date and often become angry when they do not receive the next dividend. As we shall see, newspapers carry the symbol "x" when a stock has gone ex-dividend.

Corporations build trust, integrity, stability, or a particular image with their dividend policies. Many large companies will take out an ad in newspapers to announce a quarterly cash dividend. This is particularly worthy to report when a company has consistently paid a quarterly dividend for 50, 75, or 100 years. Some companies can give the appearance of aggressiveness and growth by never paying cash dividends, emphasizing that the cash is being spent on research and development. Such companies hope to reward their shareholders with greater sales and profits and a higher stock valuation in the future.

Investors may view their investments in corporations partly on the basis of dividend policy. Younger people with good jobs may want to invest in companies that have good growth potential; cash dividends are not important. The elderly retired may desire good, consistent, reliable companies with stable cash dividend histories. A middle-aged investor may want both stock appreciation as a hedge against inflation as well as some cash dividends each quarter.

Herman   **by Jim Unger**

**"Remember Ralphy, the moron?
He's making $250,000 a year."**

READING THE FINANCIAL PAGES

If you have tried to read the financial pages of your newspapers but could not, you have lots of company. The goal in reporting this financial information is brevity, so the quotations eliminate dollar signs and extra zeros and express parts of a dollar values to the nearest eighth of a dollar ($\frac{1}{8}$ = $.12$\frac{1}{2}$). The breakdown of one dollar or one point, as the dollar price movements are often referred to, is

$\frac{1}{8}$ point = \$.12$\frac{1}{2}$	$\frac{5}{8}$ point = \$ .62$\frac{1}{2}$
$\frac{1}{4}$ point = \$.25	$\frac{3}{4}$ point = \$ .75
$\frac{3}{8}$ point = \$.37$\frac{1}{2}$	$\frac{7}{8}$ point = \$ .87$\frac{1}{2}$
$\frac{1}{2}$ point = \$.50	1 point = \$1.00

Included in our brief study are segments of *The Wall Street Journal* relating to the stock quotations from the New York Stock Exchange Composite, the American Stock Exchange, and the over-the-counter's NASDAQ summaries.

Exhibit 10-3 shows part of the New York Stock Exchange Composite list. In the upper left-hand side of the page is the calendar date of publication. For example, a newspaper printed on Tuesday will carry the financial information that took place on the preceding business day, or Monday, unless Monday was a holiday, in which case, the preceding business day would be Friday. The next information reported is the day's stock trading volume. It is not uncommon these days to find trading volume on the New York Stock Exchange to be 175 million shares. That is, the number of buyers of stock and the number of sellers of stock provided the opportunity for 175 million shares to change hands. Now that the U.S. stock market is part of the global economy, major news events can cause the trading to reach over 600 million shares for one day.

The stock market summary for the day will list the most actively traded stocks. While most corporation securities rest comfortably in safe deposit boxes or trust portfolios for years at a time, major events may cause some rather emotional speculative trading in the stocks of particular companies. Not all of the most actively traded issues are speculative. Some corporations have as many as 500 million shares held by a million or so shareholders, so normal or even modest buying and selling can place one of these large companies on the "most active" list. Frequently, American Telephone & Telegraph will appear on the list of most active stocks simply because it has around 3 million shareholders of common stock.

The captions at the tops of columns on the New York Stock Exchange quotations help to identify important information. The following paragraphs will help you to learn the significance of each piece of data listed on one line.

52 Weeks' High Low. The price of a share of common stock will fluctuate in dollars or points over any one-year period. For example, a high of 24¾ and a low of 18⅛ simply means that, over the past 52 weeks, the share has sold as high as $24.75 and as low as $18.125. By knowing this information, the reader can quickly determine if the current trading price (to be discussed) is near the high or low for the year. If a stock is selling near the low, this would put the reader or potential investor on notice to learn more about the possible causes.

Stocks. Under this heading are the very abbreviated names of the many corporations listed with the particular securities exchange. For example, AMF stands for American Machine and Foundry, BlackDr is Black and Decker, and G Mot is short for General Motors. There are likely to be occasions when the corporation's name is listed consecutively. The first listing refers to the company's common stock; the second and any additional listings usually refer to preferred stocks. If you see the letters "pf" to the right of the name of the company, this is the preferred stock quotation. Many public utility companies have both common and several kinds of preferred stock.

EXHIBIT 10-3 NYSE Transactions

NEW YORK STOCK EXCHANGE COMPOSITE

Wednesday, January 20, 1988

Quotations include trades on the Midwest, Pacific, Philadelphia, Boston and Cincinnati stock exchanges and reported by the National Association of Securities Dealers and Instinet

52 Weeks High	52 Weeks Low	Stock	Div.	Yld %	P-E Ratio	Sales 100s	High	Low	Close	Net Chg.
		— A–A–A —								
25 5/8	14	AAR s	.36	2.0	16	58	18 1/4	17 1/2	17 7/8	- 3/8
12	8 3/4	ACM G n	.61e	5.2	...	719	11 7/8	11 5/8	11 5/8	- 1/8
32 1/2	21	AFG s	.16	.7	8	1104	24 3/4	24	24	- 3/4
27	10 1/2	AGS s		...	13	228	15 1/2	15	15 3/8	- 1/2
9 3/8	3 1/4	AM Intl		...	38	882	5 3/8	5 1/4	5 1/4	- 1/4
33 3/4	17	AM Int pf	2.00	8.8	...	32	22 7/8	22 5/8	22 5/8	...
65 1/2	26 3/4	AMR		...	10	5827	34	32 5/8	33	- 1 1/4
27 1/4	24 7/8	ANR pf	2.67	10.6	...	2	25 1/8	25 1/8	25 1/8	...
25	19	ANR pf	2.12	10.2	...	1	20 7/8	20 7/8	20 7/8	- 1/8
12 1/4	6 3/8	ARX s		...	7	105	7 3/8	7 1/8	7 1/4	- 1/4
73 1/2	39 1/2	ASA	2.00a	4.2	...	625	49 1/8	47 7/8	47 7/8	- 1
22 3/8	9 1/2	AVX		...	18	215	14 1/8	13 3/4	13 7/8	- 1/4
67	40	AbtLab	1.00	2.1	17	3703	48 3/8	47 1/8	47 5/8	- 7/8
28	15 3/8	Abitibi g		...	...	80	20 1/8	19 3/4	20	- 1/4
16 3/4	8 1/2	AcmeC	.40	3.9	15	48	10 7/8	10 3/8	10 3/8	- 3/8
10 1/2	6 3/4	AcmeE	.32b	4.3	25	12	7 3/8	7 3/8	7 3/8	- 1/8
20	14 1/8	AdaEx	3.05e	19.5	...	138	15 7/8	15 1/2	15 5/8	- 1/8
19 1/2	6 7/8	AdamMl	.24	3.0	6	135	8 1/2	7 3/4	8	- 3/4
24 7/8	7 1/2	AMD		...	...	6540	9 3/4	8 7/8	8 7/8	- 5/8
56 3/4	29 1/4	AMD pf	3.00	9.5	...	604	31 3/4	31 1/2	31 1/2	- 3/4
11 7/8	4 5/8	Adobe		...	...	45	5 5/8	5 1/2	5 5/8	- 1/8
20 1/2	16 1/4	Adob pf	1.84	11.2	...	1	16 1/2	16 1/2	16 1/2	+ 1/4
21 7/8	17 1/2	Adob pf	2.40	11.8	...	5	20 3/8	20 3/8	20 3/8	+ 1/4
15	6 1/8	Advest	.12a	1.7	5	102	7 3/8	6 7/8	7 1/8	- 1/4
68 1/4	43 1/2	AetnLf	2.76	6.1	6	2155	46	45	45 3/8	- 7/8
83 1/2	39 1/8	AfilPub	.40	.8	8	442	53 1/2	52 1/4	53	- 3/8
26 7/8	13	Ahmans	.88	5.4	7	8420	16 7/8	16 1/8	16 1/4	- 3/8
5 3/8	1 3/4	Aileen		...	...	33	2 1/4	2	2	- 1/4
53 7/8	29	AirPrd	1.00	2.6	13	2347	38 3/4	37 1/2	37 7/8	- 5/8
36	11 1/8	AirbFrt	.60	4.3	8	110	13 7/8	13 5/8	13 7/8	...
16 1/2	6 3/4	Airgas		...	15	78	11 3/8	10 1/2	10 1/2	- 7/8
19 1/2	13 1/2	Airlease	2.16e	12.5	10	31	17 1/2	17 1/4	17 1/4	- 1/4
15/32	5/16	AlMoan		...	38	192	3/8	3/8	3/8	- 1/32
27 3/4	25 3/4	AlaP pf	1.95e	7.4	...	283	26 1/4	26 1/4	26 1/4	+ 1/8
10 3/4	7 5/8	AlaP dpf	.87	9.3	...	31	9 1/2	9 3/8	9 3/8	- 1/8
106 1/4	81 1/2	AlaP pf	9.00	9.8	...	z150	92	92	92	+ 3/8
110 1/2	103 1/2	AlaP pf	11.00	10.4	...	z1010	106 3/4	106	106	...
108	86 1/2	AlaP pf	9.44	9.6	...	z2790	99	98	98	+ 1/2
98 1/2	77	AlaP pf	8.28	10.0	...	z380	83	83	83	+ 1
27 7/8	12 1/4	AlskAir	.16	1.1	18	896	14 3/4	14	14 1/8	- 5/8
28 1/4	14 3/4	Alberto	.24	1.0	18	682	24	22 3/4	23	+ 1/4
24	12 5/8	AlbCulA	.24	1.3	14	217	19	18 1/8	18 3/8	- 1/8
34	20 1/4	Albtsn s	.48	1.9	15	844	26 1/4	25 5/8	25 3/4	- 3/4
37 7/8	18	Alcan s	.45i	1.7	13	6510	28 1/8	26 5/8	26 3/4	- 1 1/2
30	15 1/4	AlcoS s	.68	3.2	12	306	21 5/8	21 1/8	21 3/8	...
32	15 7/8	AlexAlx	1.00	5.4	13	646	18 5/8	18 3/8	18 1/2	- 1/8
59	34 3/4	Alexdr		...	123	7	41 3/4	41 5/8	41 3/4	- 1/8
92 1/2	50	AllegCp		...	6	52	69	68 1/8	69	+ 7/8
24 3/4	2 3/8	AlgInt		...	...	1721	5 1/4	4 1/2	4 3/4	- 3/4
20 1/8	5 1/4	AlgIn pr		...	...	88	10 1/8	9 1/2	9 1/2	- 5/8
88 1/2	20	Algl pfC		...	...	18	33 3/4	33 1/4	33 3/4	+ 1/4
34	15 1/8	AlgLud n	.20e	.9	...	90	23 1/2	23 1/4	23 1/2	- 1/8
49	31 3/8	AllgPw	3.00	7.7	10	584	38 7/8	38 5/8	38 7/8	+ 1/8
105 7/8	52 1/2	Allegis		...	36	2174	73 1/4	72 1/8	72 1/8	- 1
19 3/8	5 1/2	AllenG		...	...	• 370	9	8 5/8	8 7/8	+ 1/4
24 7/8	9 1/4	Allen pf	1.75	13.5	...	36	13 3/8	12 7/8	13	- 1/2
44	12 3/8	AlldPd		...	8	159	12 7/8	12 1/2	12 3/4	- 1/8
49 1/4	26	AldSgnl	1.80	6.0	9	3481	30 3/4	29 3/8	30	- 1/2
3 3/4	1	vjAllisC		...	...	90	1 1/4	1 1/8	1 1/4	...
37 1/2	4 3/4	AlisC pf		...	...	13	6 1/2	6 1/4	6 1/4	- 1/4
10 1/8	8 7/8	AlstMu n	.30e	3.0	...	651	10	9 7/8	10	...
34 1/8	23	ALLTL s	1.52	5.8	14	718	27 7/8	25 3/4	26 3/8	- 1 1/2
64 3/4	33 3/4	Alcoa	1.20	2.9	...	3362	43 1/4	41 1/8	41 3/4	- 1 1/8
32	14	AmxG n	.04e	.2	...	161	23 1/8	23	23	+ 1/4
29 1/4	12 1/2	Amax		...	6	1431	18 3/8	17 3/8	17 5/8	- 1 1/8
47 3/4	34	Amax pf	3.00	7.4	...	1	40 1/2	40 1/2	40 1/2	...
41 7/8	21 1/2	AmHes	.45e	1.8	9	2836	25 1/2	24 5/8	25 3/8	+ 5/8
30 3/8	8 7/8	ABrck s	.05e	...	...	782	20 3/8	20	20 1/8	...
60	36 1/2	AmBrnd	2.20	4.7	11	2687	47 1/2	46 1/4	46 3/8	- 1/4
34 1/2	28 5/8	ABrd pf	2.75	9.6	...	3	28 5/8	28 5/8	28 5/8	...
118 3/4	76	ABrd pf	2.67	2.9	...	10	93	93	93	- 1

52 Weeks High	52 Weeks Low	Stock	Div.	Yld %	P-E Ratio	Sales 100s	High	Low	Close	Net Chg.
16 1/4	9 1/4	Becor		...	...	9	10 7/8	10 3/4	10 7/8	...
69	42 1/4	BectDk	.86e	1.6	15	782	54 1/8	51 5/8	52 3/4	- 1 1/4
15/16	7/32	vjBeker		...	...	44	5/16	5/16	5/16	...
2 1/8	1/16	vjBekr pf		...	...	1	3/4	3/4	3/4	+ 1/16
28 3/8	18 1/4	BeldnH	.40a	1.9	10	28	21 1/4	21 1/4	21 1/4	...
75 1/4	38 1/2	BelHwl	.62	1.0	11	424	60 5/8	60 3/8	60 3/8	- 1/2
75	38 3/4	BelHw pf	.74	1.2	...	4	60 1/8	60 1/8	60 1/8	...
79 3/4	60 1/2	BellAtl	3.84	5.8	11	2200	67 1/8	64 3/4	65 7/8	- 1 1/2
23 3/8	11 1/4	BellIn s	.28	2.2	20	131	12 3/4	12 5/8	12 5/8	...
44 1/4	29 1/8	BellSo s	2.20	5.9	11	5934	38 1/2	37 1/8	37 3/8	- 1 1/8
77 1/4	42 1/4	BeloAH	.80	1.7	14	74	48 1/2	47 3/4	47 3/4	- 1
42	25 1/2	Bemis	.72	2.1	15	45	34 3/8	33 3/4	33 3/4	- 5/8
65 1/4	28 1/2	BenfCp	2.00	5.5	...	854	37 5/8	35 1/4	36 1/2	- 1 3/8
55	41	Benef pf	4.50	10.8	...	z150	43	41 1/2	41 1/2	- 1
30 3/4	23	Benef pf	2.50	10.5	...	z50	23 3/4	23 3/4	23 3/4	+ 1/2
9 7/8	2 1/2	BengtB	.05e	1.3	...	123	3 7/8	3 7/8	3 7/8	- 1/8
7 1/8	2 1/8	Berkey		...	...	86	3 1/8	2 7/8	3	- 1/8
23 1/4	5 3/4	BestBy s		...	9	145	7 1/8	6 3/4	7 1/8	...
13	6	BestPd		...	9	954	8 3/8	8	8 1/4	- 1/8
19 3/4	6 3/8	BethStl		...	7	4429	17 1/2	16 1/4	16 3/8	- 1 1/8
47 1/2	18 3/8	BethSt pf		...	...	166	44 1/4	42 3/4	43	- 1 1/4
24 1/4	9 1/4	BthS pfB		...	...	150	23 1/8	22 1/2	22 3/4	- 3/8
18 7/8	6	Bevrly	.20	3.1	...	2736	6 5/8	6	6 3/8	- 1/8
25 3/8	16 1/2	BevIP n	2.26e	12.2	12	117	18 5/8	18 3/8	18 1/2	- 1/8
28 3/8	13 1/2	Biocft		...	17	320	17 5/8	16 5/8	17	- 3/4
26 1/2	13	BlackD	.40	2.1	21	1725	19 3/4	19 1/8	19 1/2	- 3/8
25 1/4	19 1/2	BlkHC s	1.28	5.4	11	53	23 5/8	23 1/4	23 1/2	...
33 1/4	20	BlkHR s	.88	2.9	21	851	30	28 1/2	30	+ 3/8
10 1/8	4 5/8	BluChp n	.11e	2.0	...	208	5 7/8	5 5/8	5 5/8	- 1/8
54 3/4	33 5/8	Boeing	1.40	3.3	12	4101	42 7/8	41 7/8	42 1/8	- 3/4
52 1/8	28 3/4	BoiseC s		...	12	824	39 1/8	36	37 1/2	- 1 3/4
68 1/2	48	Boise pfC	3.50	6.7	...	1	52 1/2	52 1/2	52 1/2	- 1/4
29 7/8	11 3/4	BoltBr s	.06	.4	...	158	16 5/8	16 1/4	16 1/4	- 1 1/8
12 3/4	9 3/4	BordC n	e	.9	...	4072	12 5/8	12	12 1/4	- 3/8
63 7/8	31 1/4	Borden	1.28	2.6	14	903	50	48 1/2	48 3/4	- 1 1/4
24	8 1/4	Bormns	.22	2.3	...	35	9 3/8	9 3/8	9 3/8	...
15 3/4	10 3/8	BCelts	1.60e	12.7	...	82	12 7/8	12 3/8	12 5/8	- 1/8
28	16 3/4	BostEd	1.82	10.0	7	594	18 1/2	18	18 1/4	...
103	84 1/2	BosE pf	8.88	9.9	...	z340	89 3/4	89	89 3/4	- 1/4
17	13 1/2	BosE pr	1.46	9.4	...	117	15 1/2	15 1/4	15 1/2	...
44 1/2	22	Bowatr	.92	3.3	16	2180	28 3/4	27 3/4	28 1/8	- 5/8
42	20 1/4	BrigSt	1.60	6.5	15	213	25 3/8	24 1/4	24 5/8	- 1
55 3/4	28 1/4	BristM s	1.68	4.2	17	15049	41 1/2	39 7/8	40	- 1 5/8
37 1/2	22 1/8	BritAir	1.22e	4.2	6	52	29 1/4	28 3/4	29	- 1/2
32 3/4	20 1/2	BGas2 pp	1.28e	5.4	...	791	23 5/8	23 3/8	23 1/2	+ 1/2
80 3/8	44 7/8	BritPt	2.78e	5.2	11	490	54	53	53	- 3/4
21	6 1/2	BritP wt		...	...	255	7 3/4	7 5/8	7 5/8	...
18 1/8	15 1/4	BrtPt pp		...	...	1809	16 1/4	15 3/8	15 1/2	- 3/4
55 5/8	33	BritTel	1.77e	4.3	12	492	41 7/8	41 1/2	41 1/2	- 1/8
11 3/8	4 1/8	Brock n		...	16	67	5 1/8	5	5	- 1/8
1 3/4	3/8	Brock pf		...	...	3	7/16	7/16	7/16	- 1/16
60	26 1/8	Brckwy	.96	2.1	15	98	45 1/2	44 1/2	45	...
32 1/2	16 1/2	BHP n	.41e	2.1	6	487	19 5/8	19 1/2	19 1/2	- 1/4
28 1/2	18 5/8	BklyUG	1.72	7.6	9	169	23	22 1/2	22 1/2	- 3/8
24 3/8	15 1/2	BwnSh	.40	2.5	...	92	16 3/8	16 1/8	16 1/4	+ 1/8
44 1/4	26 5/8	BrwnGp	1.56	4.4	14	132	35 3/4	35 3/8	35 1/2	- 1/8
35 3/4	17 1/2	BrwnF s	.48	1.8	23	4354	26 1/2	25 1/2	26 1/8	- 3/4
30 1/4	10 3/4	Brnwk s	.36	2.3	9	3500	16 7/8	15 3/4	15 7/8	- 5/8
44 1/2	19	BrshWl	.60	2.5	19	398	24 3/4	23 7/8	24	- 3/4
26 1/4	17 3/4	Buckeye	2.20	9.9	9	179	22 5/8	22	22 1/4	- 3/8
41 5/8	19 1/2	Bundy	.92a	2.9	12	28	31 7/8	31	31 1/4	- 3/4
23 1/2	17 3/4	BunkrH	1.92a	10.1	...	20	19 1/4	19	19	- 1/4
21	12 1/4	BKInv	1.88	12.5	11	144	15	14 5/8	15	+ 1/8
34 1/2	12	BurInCt		...	9	22	15 1/8	15	15	- 1/8
84 1/4	40	BrlNth	2.20	3.5	13	1575	63	62 1/4	62 3/4	+ 1/8
20 3/8	9 3/8	Burndy		...	15	373	13 1/2	13 3/8	13 3/8	- 1/8
		— C–C–C —								
33	16	CBI In	.60	3.0	34	232	20 1/4	20	20 1/8	- 1/4
55	37 7/8	CBI pf	3.50	8.5	...	6	41	41	41	...
226 1/4	134 1/4	CBS	3.00	2.0	16	951	155 1/2	150 1/4	152	- 3
5 3/8	2 5/8	CCX		...	...	99	2 3/4	2 5/8	2 3/4	...
69 1/2	41 1/4	CIGNA	2.80	5.8	6	1928	49 3/4	48 3/8	48 3/8	- 1 3/8

Div. The next number is the annual cash dividend normally paid or paid in the most recent year. For example, 2.24 means that $2.24 was paid in cash to the holder of one share of stock in the past year. The number "1" (one) means that $1.00 has been paid last year; "3" (three) means that $3.00 was paid. Boards of directors may authorize changes in basic dividend policy. In this case, lowercase letters appear immediately to the right of the dividend amount. A key to "a," "b," "e," "g," and many others appears in Exhibit 10-4. The letter "a" means that the company pays a dividend *in addition to* the regular annual cash dividend. It may be a good idea to refer to Exhibit 10-4 and scan these many symbols before continuing.

Yld %. This term signifies the yield on an investment expressed as a percentage. For example, a company may pay an annual cash dividend of $2.00 per share on its common stock. If the current market price of the stock is $40 per share, then

EXHIBIT 10-4 Supplemental Stock Data

 a Extra or additional dividend. This is often a year-end bonus dividend of cash in addition to the regular cash dividend.
 b The annual regular cash dividend plus a stock dividend.
 c A liquidating dividend. It represents a partial return of the stockholder's original investment.
 d The stock has reached its newest low price in the past 52 weeks.
 e Amount of dividends declared or paid after a stock dividend or split up.
 j Dividends paid this year or dividend is omitted. No dividend action or a deferment taken by last board of directors meeting.
 k Dividend declared or paid this year, an issue with cumulative dividends in arrears.
 n A new issue of stock since the beginning of the year.
pf A preferred stock issue.
 r Dividend declared or paid in the preceding 12 months plus a stock dividend.
 s Stock has been split or a large (over 25 percent) stock dividend has taken place since the beginning of the year.
 t Dividend was paid in stock in the preceding 12 months.
 u Stock has reached its newest high price in the past 52 weeks.
vi Corporation is in bankruptcy or receivership or is being reorganized under the Bankruptcy Act.
 x Stock is trading ex-dividend or ex-rights. Persons owning the stock on this date will receive the dividend.
wi Price of stock at the time when it will be issued.
wt Warrant. The security traded is called a warrant. The warrant is similar to a coupon.
 y Ex-dividend and stock sales in full. A combination of symbols x and z.
 z Sales in full. This is the actual shares traded on a particular date such as 15 shares, 50 shares, 600 shares, and so on.

the yield is 5.0 percent. This $2.00 divided by $40.00 market price is .05, or 5.0 percent. This is the same as when a bank savings account earns (or yields) a 5 percent return. Having the "yield %" available saves the reader from having to calculate this number. It also permits comparison of investment return with various alternatives.

P-E Ratio. This is the market price of a share of stock divided by the net profit or earnings on one share of stock. A company's common stock may currently sell for $40 a share and the earnings for the year may be $4.00 per share. The P-E (price-earning) ratio is 10 ($40 ÷ $4). This is an important figure in that it compares the price being paid for a share of stock with its earnings. The goal is not to pay too much for a share of stock relative to its earnings. A P-E ratio of 10 also means that a person is willing to pay $10 for each $1.00 of earnings.

Stocks sell for as much as 30 to 40 times earnings and as little as 2 times earnings. Well, how high is high and how low is low? In each Monday issue of *The Wall Street Journal,* there is a brief summary of this ratio.

Sales 100s. The number of shares of a particular company traded for the day is summarized to the nearest 100 shares. That is, only "round-lot" transactions are usually recorded. If, on the line of information, the number 33 is listed under sales 100s, it means that 3,300 shares were traded for the day. It is customary in reporting to drop the two zeros. The lowercase "x" preceding this number means that the stock is trading ex-dividend. The letter "z" preceding the number means that these were the total share traded for the day. That is, the number 15 would mean 15 total shares were traded. Usually this notation is confined to rarely traded preferred stocks.

High, Low, Close. These three figures will tell the reader the price variation that occurred in a single trading day. The "High" is the highest price paid for 100 shares of the company's stock during the day. The "Low" is the lowest price at which 100 shares were traded, that is, a completed transaction by a buyer and a seller. The "Close" shows the market price of the last completed transaction of that stock for that trading day. Normally, the price fluctuation of a stock on a single day is usually minor and well within a single point. The fluctuation of $1 in market value of a stock normally selling for $10 a share is more significant than a similar variation on a stock selling for $100.

Net Chg. The "net change" is the amount of stock price movement that has taken place at the close of the trading day since the close of the preceding business day. The reader is able to determine whether the stock's price has closed either higher or lower since the close of the preceding trading date. Normally, the amount of net change is a fraction of one point (dollar). If the price of the stock at the close is the same as the preceding trading day, only a series of dots (· · ·) will appear in the "Net Chg" column. A major change appearing in

EXHIBIT 10-5 AMEX Transactions

AMERICAN STOCK EXCHANGE COMPOSITE TRANSACTIONS

Wednesday, January 20, 1988

Quotations include trades on the Midwest, Pacific, Philadelphia, Boston and Cincinnati stock exchanges and reported by the National Association of Securities Dealers and Instinet

52 Weeks High	52 Weeks Low	Stock	Div.	Yld %	P-E Ratio	Sales 100s	High	Low	Close	Net Chg.
4¼	2¼	Dsgntrn	.18t	6.3	21	26	3	2⅞	2⅞	– ⅛
9⅜	3	DesgnI	.86t	22.2	...	70	4⅛	3⅞	3⅞	– ¼
6⅜	2	DevnRs	.60	22.9	...	18	2⅝	2⅝	2⅝	+ ⅛
17	6¼	Diag A		...	11	64	8⅛	8	8	– ¼
14⅞	5⅜	Diag B		...	9	16	7	6⅞	6⅞	– ⅛
13	5⅛	DckMA g	.15e	...	...	3	6	6	6	– ⅛
13⅜	6⅜	DckMB g	.15e	...	...	3	8¾	8¾	8¾	...
57½	24	Dillard	.16	.5	12	182	29⅞	29⅜	29½	– ⅝
4⅛	1⅜	Diodes		...	...	15	1⅞	1⅞	1⅞	...
4⅜	2	DirActn		...	16	20	2¼	2¼	2¼	– ⅛
13⅞	5¾	DiviHtl	.25e	3.2	5	44	8	7¾	7⅞	...
2¼	⅛	DivHt wt		...	...	5	¼	¼	¼	+ 1/16
1⅞	½	DomeP		...	...	811	¾	11/16	¾	...
8⅞	3½	DrivHar		...	5	13	5⅝	5½	5½	– ⅛
21	6⅝	Ducom	.20	1.9	12	51	11⅛	10¾	10¾	– ⅜
23½	13¾	Duplex	.68	3.6	12	2	19⅛	19⅛	19⅛	– ¼
17¼	6½	DurTst	.40b	3.0	24	10	13⅜	13⅜	13⅜	...
		– E–E–E –								
8½	3½	EAC		...	...	10	6⅜	6⅜	6⅜	– ⅛
17⅞	5½	EECO s	.24	3.5	20	35	6⅞	6½	6⅞	– ⅛
23⅞	12¼	EAL pf	2.84	20.3	...	63	14	14	14	...
21⅝	6½	EAL pf	2.72	26.9	...	2	10⅛	10⅛	10⅛	...
21½	8⅛	EAL pf	3.24	28.8	...	30	11¼	11¼	11¼	+ ⅛
22⅝	7¼	EAL pf	3.12	29.4	...	33	10⅝	10⅝	10⅝	+ ⅛
36¾	21⅞	EstnCo	1.00a	3.4	12	9	29⅞	29½	29½	– ⅝
31¾	20	Estgp	2.90e	13.3	8	6	21⅞	21¾	21⅞	+ ⅛
30⅛	11½	EchB g s	.07	...	...	1824	21⅝	21	21¼	– ⅛
9¾	3⅝	Ecogn n		...	...	39	6⅜	6⅛	6⅛	...
29⅞	8½	EcolE n	.08e	.7	16	40	11½	11¼	11⅜	– ¼
12⅜	4⅛	EhrBbr		...	26	2	5	5	5	...
3¾	1¼	Elsinor		...	...	2470	1⅞	1⅜	1⅝	– ¼
9⅞	6	Elswth	1.00e	13.3	...	101	7⅝	7½	7½	– ⅛
4⅝	1⅛	EEdm wt		...	...	122	2⅛	2⅛	2⅛	– ⅜
7	2¼	EmpirA	.26e	7.2	...	550	3⅞	3⅝	3⅝	– ⅛
18⅝	3⅝	EmCar	.05	1.2	3	5	4¼	4¼	4¼	– ⅛
10¾	5	Endvco	1.01t	15.8	...	94	6⅝	6¼	6⅜	– ½
10⅞	6	EnDvl	1.10	14.2	3	107	7⅞	7⅜	7¾	– ⅛
7¾	1½	ENSCO		...	14	427	2¾	2½	2¾	...
14⅜	4½	Engex n		...	...	66	8¾	8⅜	8⅜	– ¼
2⅞	1⅜	Enstr pf	.18e	11.1	...	2	1⅝	1⅝	1⅝	+ ⅛
16¼	2⅝	EntMkt		...	...	811	4⅛	3⅞	4	– ¼
27¼	6	Envrpct		...	...	11	9¾	9¼	9¼	– ⅜
10⅛	7	Eqtyg	.76e	9.7	...	1	7⅞	7⅞	7⅞	...
16⅜	6½	Ero s		...	11	41	9⅛	9	9	– ¼
23½	14½	Espey	.40	2.2	16	10	18⅛	18⅛	18⅛	– ⅛
40¾	31⅜	EsqRd	.72e	2.1	13	1	34½	34½	34½	...
12¼	3¾	EtzLav		...	4	7	6½	6⅜	6⅜	– ⅛
17½	6½	EvrJ A	.20	2.6	...	10	7¾	7¾	7¾	+ ⅛
11⅞	5⅝	Excel s	.40	5.6	10	10	7¼	7⅛	7⅛	– ⅛
		– F–F–F –								
12¼	9⅜	FFP n		13.3	...	45	11¼	11⅛	11¼	...
12	5	FPA		...	...	27	7⅜	7¼	7⅜	+ ⅛
40¾	23⅜	FabInd	.60	2.2	9	444	28½	27	27	– 1¾
20¼	13½	FalCbl n	2.15	11.9	...	35	18	17⅝	18	+ ¼
7⅝	4⅛	Fidata		...	28	170	5⅝	5⅜	5⅝	+ ⅛
12¾	4⅜	FidlFn n	.06e	1.1	3	8	5⅝	5½	5½	– ⅛
15	6¾	FtAust	1.10e	14.2	...	78	7¾	7⅝	7¾	...
9⅛	6¾	FAusPr	1.13e	14.3	...	1447	8⅛	7⅞	7⅞	– ⅛
8½	4	FtCntrl		...	14	58	4¾	4⅝	4⅝	– ¼
18⅝	11¾	FtConn	1.65e	9.4	8	17	17⅝	17½	17½	+ ⅝
15¾	8¾	FstFd		...	4	128	11¾	11¼	11⅜	– ⅜
6⅜	2⅞	FFBcp n		...	...	61	4⅛	4	4	– ¼
12½	7¼	FNtCal	.05r	.5	10	1	9⅛	9⅛	9⅛	...
12½	6¼	FWymB		...	...	284	11¾	11¼	11⅜	– ¾
12½	7½	Fstcrp	.36	4.6	3	4	7⅞	7¾	7¾	– ¼
18⅜	8⅜	FischP	.81t	7.3	34	26	11½	11⅛	11⅛	– ⅛
26½	20	FitcGE	1.60	7.2	8	2	22¼	22¼	22¼	...
7¼	3⅞	Flanign		...	5	10	4½	4½	4½	...
29⅞	17⅛	FlaRck	.50	2.3	10	8	22⅜	22⅛	22⅛	– ¼
30	14	Fluke	1.26t	7.9	67	282	16	15⅝	16	– ¼
28⅜	16¾	Foodrm		...	9	4	22	21⅞	21⅞	– ¼
9⅝	5⅛	FooteM		...	...	4	9	8⅞	9	+ ¼
153½	85½	FordCn g	6.00e	...	...	z160	104	103	104	...
4½	1¾	FrdM wt		...	...	240	2⅝	2½	2½	...
40½	26¾	ForstC A	.34	1.2	63	4	29	29	29	...
40¾	27	ForstC B	.28e	1.0	63	1	28¾	28¾	28¾	...
30	13⅛	ForstL		...	22	1151	20⅜	19	19	– 1¼
15½	3⅝	Frstm n		...	11	122	4⅞	4⅝	4¾	...
14¼	7¾	Forum	1.35	13.8	...	61	10	9¾	9¾	– ¼
29½	9⅝	FreqEl		...	11	62	10⅝	10⅝	10⅝	– ¼
11⅛	7⅞	Friedm	1.00a	10.0	13	255	10⅛	9¾	10	...
5⅞	2	FriesEn		...	13	3	2⅜	2⅜	2⅜	...
45	28¾	Frischs	.24b	.6	52	33	39⅝	39	39⅝	+ ½
9¾	3⅞	FruitL n		...	...	432	5	4¾	4⅞	– ¼
12⅞	2⅞	FurVit	.20	5.7	18	226	3⅝	3½	3½	– ⅛
		– G–G–G –								

52 Weeks High	52 Weeks Low	Stock	Div.	Yld %	P-E Ratio	Sales 100s	High	Low	Close	Net Chg.
17½	10⅛	JneInt n	1.35e	9.8	...	166	13⅞	13¼	13¾	– ⅛
5⅜	1⅜	JumpJk		...	10	5	1¾	1¾	1¾	...
		– K–K–K –								
9½	2⅞	KMW		...	13	12	4¾	4½	4½	– ⅜
25	9	KV Ph s		...	127	78	14½	13⅝	14	– ⅝
7⅞	5⅜	Kappa		...	...	2	6½	6½	6½	...
14⅛	6¼	KayCp	.12	1.5	4	2	8¼	8¼	8¼	– ⅛
19½	8½	KearNt	.40	3.9	7	3	10⅜	10⅜	10⅜	– ¼
12⅝	9⅛	KlyOG n	.95e	8.0	42	6	11⅞	11⅞	11⅞	– ⅛
9¾	4⅝	KentEl	?		...	6	19	8	7⅞	8
2¼	11/16	KleerV		...	...	10	13/16	13/16	13/16	– 1/16
34½	22⅝	KogerC	2.40	9.1	120	61	26⅝	26⅛	26⅜	+ ⅛
		– L–L–L –								
25	10¼	LSB pf	2.20	18.3	...	10	12	12	12	– ¼
9	5⅝	Lajolla n	.04r	.6	16	1	7¼	7¼	7¼	...
4⅞	1⅜	LaPnt		...	...	1	2¾	2¾	2¾	+ ⅛
11⅞	4⅛	LdmkSv	.20	3.6	5	22	5½	5½	5½	...
24½	10¾	Lndmk	.40	3.0	...	12	13½	13¼	13¼	– ¼
11¼	2⅞	LdmkA s		...	3	33	3⅜	3¼	3¼	– ¼
9⅞	4⅝	Larizz n		...	11	17	7½	7¼	7⅜	– ⅛
15⅜	4¾	Laser		...	7	82	7⅛	6¾	6¾	– ½
9⅝	3¾	Lauren		...	...	20	4⅜	4⅜	4⅜	...
14¾	6¼	LawrG n	.32	3.6	10	1	9	9	9	...
14¼	7⅛	Lawsn n	.20e	2.2	...	1298	9⅜	8¾	9¼	– ⅜
2¼	⅝	LearPP		...	...	2	1	1	1	...
11½	2¾	LeePhr		...	...	87	4	3⅞	4	...
9⅜	3	LeisurT		...	3	175	4	3⅞	3⅞	– ¼
36½	16¼	LeisT pf	2.25	11.5	...	18	19¾	19½	19½	– ⅛
5¾	1⅞	Lfetime		...	30	193	3⅜	3	3	– ½
15¼	6⅛	LilVer n		...	7	18	9¾	9⅝	9⅝	– ⅛
3⅛	⅜	Lilly un		...	...	492	⅝	½	½	– ⅛
11	3	LinPro	.86e	25.5	...	2	3⅜	3⅜	3⅜	– ⅛
14	8⅝	LncNC n	1.48	14.8	7	1	10	10	10	– ⅛
1⅛	⅛	LncNC wt		...	...	1	⅜	⅜	⅜	...
9⅞	2	Lionel		...	8	1702	4¼	4	4⅛	– ⅛
1⅞	1/16	Lionl wtB		...	...	45	1/16	1/16	1/16	...
22¼	6⅝	LorTel		...	10	3346	10¼	9⅜	9½	– ⅝
28½	8	Lumex	.08	.8	10	85	10	9⅞	9⅞	– ¼
16¼	8¼	Luria		...	11	114	9⅜	9¼	9¼	– ⅛
21¾	12⅞	Lydal		...	13	5	15⅛	15	15	– ¼
24⅜	7¾	LynchC	.20	1.9	28	35	10⅝	10½	10½	– ⅛
		– M–M–M –								
17¾	7¾	MCO Hd		...	...	5	7¾	7¾	7¾	...
1⅞	¼	MCO Rs		...	...	864	⅜	5/16	⅜	...
11	7¼	MSA	1.00e	11.6	32	25	8⅝	8⅜	8⅝	+ ¼
2⅛	3/16	MSA wt		...	...	5	9/16	9/16	9/16	...
23½	12	MSI Dt		...	23	23	20¾	20¼	20⅜	– ⅜
3⅜	1¼	MSR		...	...	5	1¾	1¾	1¾	+ ⅛
15½	1⅝	MacGrg		...	...	20	2½	2⅜	2½	+ ⅛
23	11¾	MacSc s	.20	1.3	22	238	16⅛	15¼	15¼	– ⅞
11½	1	Mag Bk		...	...	11	1⅝	1⅝	1⅝	– ⅛
30⅞	23	MePS	1.80	7.3	6	3	24½	24½	24½	...
13⅛	6	Malart g	.20	...	15	11	7¾	7⅝	7¾	+ ⅛
20	9	ManfHo		...	12	194	14	13½	13¾	...
3⅜	⅞	MrthOf		...	...	14	1¼	1¼	1¼	...
5⅝	½	Marlton		...	...	5	1	1	1	+ ⅛
7½	2½	MarsG		...	9	5	3⅜	3¼	3¼	– ¼
7⅝	3¾	Matec		...	26	2	4⅞	4⅞	4⅞	...
10⅞	2¾	MatRsh		...	...	23	3¾	3⅝	3¾	...
28¾	10¾	MatSci		...	14	78	12⅞	12⅝	12⅝	– ⅜
18¾	3⅞	Matrix		...	...	34	6⅛	5⅞	6	...
12⅞	½	MattW		...	38	5	¾	¾	¾	...
7¼	⅞	Maxphrm		3.9	...	34	3½	3⅜	3⅜	– ⅛
2⅜	¼	McFad		...	...	20	7/16	7/16	7/16	– 1/16
7½	4	McRae A	.47e	8.2	7	13	5¾	5¾	5¾	...
48¼	23	Media s	.34	.9	47	221	38¼	37⅜	37⅜	– 1
11	6¼	MedPrp	1.38	17.5	...	130	7⅞	7¼	7⅞	+ ½
5⅜	2½	Mdcore		...	8	14	2⅝	2⅝	2⅝	– ⅛
1¼	¼	Mdcor wt		...	...	11	⅜	¼	⅜	...
8⅞	3¼	Mediq	.12	2.7	12	29	4½	4⅜	4⅜	– ⅛
8¾	3⅛	Mediq pf	.07	1.6	...	1250	4½	4⅜	4⅜	– ⅜
14¼	6½	MrchGp		...	5	28	8½	8⅛	8¼	– ⅛
20½	11½	MetPro	.15a	1.1	20	38	13¾	13¼	13½	...
12¾	7	Metex		...	8	12	8	8	8	– ⅛
8⅜	2⅞	MichStr		...	11	158	4⅜	4	4⅛	– ¼
8¼	3⅞	MidAm		...	22	8	4⅞	4⅞	4⅞	– ⅛
25½	14½	MidInd s	.24	1.2	7	4	20½	20½	20½	...
101½	75	MinP pf	7.36	9.4	...	z200	79	78½	78½	– 1½
13¾	6	MissnW	.32	4.5	3	16	7⅜	7⅛	7⅛	– ⅜
18¾	8¼	MtchIE	.24	2.4	49	58	10	9⅞	9⅞	...
19	8⅝	MoogB	.20	1.8	11	4	11⅜	11¼	11¼	+ ¼
19⅛	8	MoogA	.28	2.6	8	52	11¼	10⅞	10⅞	– ⅜
33¼	11½	MMed		...	11	28	16¾	16⅜	16⅝	...
3⅜	⅞	MorgnF		...	14	26	1½	1⅜	1⅜	...
23½	14¼	MtgGth	1.60	9.1	10	33	17⅝	17⅜	17⅝	+ ¼
9	6½	MtgPl n	.80e	10.5	13	45	7¾	7⅝	7⅝	– ¼

this column of two or three points in either direction should put the reader on notice that there may have been a major news event taking place affecting the company.

Now, you have a basic review of the key information found in the financial pages of the newspapers. The information found in the quotations of the American Stock Exchange is similar to that of the New York Stock Exchange. Exhibit 10-5 is an excerpt from the AMEX list. In reviewing this information, a couple of observations can readily be made. The daily volume is normally much smaller and the prices of the stocks are lower than those listed on the NYSE.

A word or two should be said about some of the summaries of stock quotations on the over-the-counter financial pages. Less data are shown on a line of information related to a specific stock (see Exhibit 10-6). Note that there is no reference to the highs or lows of the past 52 weeks, no yield calculated, and no price–earnings ratio. The day's prices for a stock are referred to as the "bid" or "asked" price. In this case, the *bid price* is the price a broker is willing to pay to buy a security from a customer. The *asked price* is the price at which a broker is willing to sell a security to a customer. The difference in the bid and asked prices is the commission to the brokerage firm.

THE DOW JONES INDUSTRIAL AVERAGE

Once you have selected a group of stocks to follow, you may want to compare them with some other index of stock activity. Many investors will compare their stock price movements with stocks that are included in the Dow Jones Industrial Average shown in Exhibit 10-7.

No radio or TV news broadcast would be complete without a fleeting reference to the venerable Dow Jones Industrial Average. The newscaster might exclaim "The Dow Jones Industrial Average closed up 2 points today on a volume of 150 million shares." Dow Jones is the publisher of *The Wall Street Journal* and has kept a running index of stocks since 1896.

Originally, there were 12 companies in the Dow Jones Industrial Average, sometimes called DJIA. Later the number of stocks were increased to 20. By 1928, the number was raised to 30 companies and has remained at this level ever since. However, companies are replaced form time to time to keep the *index* representative. For example, in June 1979, International Business Machines and Merck & Co. were added as components to the index of 30 and Chrysler Corp. and Esmark, Inc., were deleted. Theoretically, the DJIA is computed by adding the total price of the 30 companies and dividing by 30. However, when the component companies declare and issue major stock dividends and stock splits, the divisor is revised downward.

EXHIBIT 10-6 OTC Transactions

NASDAQ OVER-THE-COUNTER MARKETS

NATIONAL MARKET ISSUES

4:00 p.m. Eastern Time Prices

Wednesday, January 20, 1988

365-day High	Low	Stock	Div	Yld	P-E	Sales (hds)	High	Low	Last	Net Chg.
7¼	1⅞	Clinical Data		..	7	16	2⅜	2¼	2¼	– ⅛
5¼	1¼	Clinical Sci		..	..	21	2¾	2½	2½	– ¼
24½	4⅝	Clothestime		..	9	916	5¼	5	5	– ½
11 3-16	1¾	CMS Enhance		..	29	119	4⅜	4	4	– ½
27	19¼	CNB Bsh	.84g	3.9	10	3	21¾	21¾	21¾	...
19½	11¼	Coast Fedl SL		..	10	178	16½	15⅞	16	– ¼
12⅝	5	Coated Sales		..	16	423	8¾	8¼	8⅜	– ¼
26¾	14¾	Cobe Lab		..	14	288	19⅝	19	19	– ¾
40¼	18½	CocaBtCn	.88a	4.1	..	68	22½	21¼	21½	–1¼
8⅞	3	CoCa Mines		..	49	239	5	4⅞	4⅞	– ¼
12	5	Codenoll Tech		..	..	387	6⅜	6	6⅜	+ ⅜
2⅞	⅜	CodenollTc wt		..	..	7	⅝	⅝	⅝	– ⅛
36	14¾	Coeur d Alene		..	..	338	18¼	17¾	17¾	– ⅜
11¼	6¾	Cohasset SB		..	..	1	9	9	9	– ⅜
16¼	3⅝	Cognos Inc		..	..	1016	4⅞	4½	4½	– ⅜
16½	7⅜	Coherent Inc		..	..	197	9¾	9¾	9¾	...
9	3	Collabrt Rsch		..	..	112	4⅝	4⅛	4⅛	– ⅜
19½	4⅛	Collagen Cp		..	588	66	6	5⅞	5⅞	...
15½	7	Collectv FSB		..	4	367	10⅛	9⅞	9⅞	– ⅛
31½	19	ColnlABk	.72	3.4	13	5	21¼	21¼	21¼	+1
27¼	10½	ColBkgrpA	.60	5.2	8	639	12¼	11¼	11⅝	– ⅛
25¾	17	ColonGas	1.64	8.4	9	6	20¼	19½	19½	...
28	7½	ColonlGrA	.40	3.5	6	2239	11¾	11½	11½	– ¼
33½	19⅛	ColLifeAcc	.88	..	8	4	23¼	23	23	...
17¾	8⅞	ColoNtl Bksh		..	..	808	11⅛	10⅝	10⅞	+ ⅛
16¼	5⅞	ColumFSB	.10	.6	..	206	16¼	16	16	– ⅛
20	13	ColumbFst Fd		..	6	42	17½	17¼	17¼	...
10¼	5⅜	Comair I	.08b	1.2	34	183	6½	6⅜	6⅜	– ⅛
11	2	Comarco		..	..	4	4¼	3¾	3¾	...
27⅛	16	Comcast	.16	.7	..	3140	22½	21⅞	21⅞	– ⅝
25⅝	14	CmcastSp	.16	.8	..	527	20⅝	19½	19¾	–1
72⅝	49	Comerica	2.40	3.9	11	207	62	61¾	61¾	– ¼
3⅞	11-16	Comdial Corp		..	..	139	1	¾	⅞	– ⅛
8¼	4½	Command Air		..	7	23	7¾	7¾	7¾	+ ¼
38¾	26¾	CmrcBsh	1.12	3.8	8	18	29¾	29¼	29¾	+ ½
71	48⅜	ComrClH	1.28	2.2	20	66	59	58	58	– ½
19⅜	8⅜	CommrclFdl		..	4	267	11¾	11⅛	11⅜	– ⅝
16¾	8¾	CmrclNtl	.30	3.4	..	7	8¾	8¾	8¾	...
19⅝	10⅞	CmclShg	.56	4.0	14	41	14⅜	14⅛	14⅛	– ¼
8	(L)	Commodr Env		..	..	631	1 11-16	1½	1½	–3-16
26⅜	16½	CmwlthBc	.80	4.8	10	7	16¾	16¾	16¾	– ½
12¼	2½	Cmwlth Mtge		..	13	23	4¼	4	4¼	+ ¼
12⅝	1	Cmw Hou		..	..	61	2½	2⅛	2⅛	– ¼
3⅞	1 1-16	Com & Cable		..	..	5	3	3	3	...
12¼	6⅛	Comm Trnsm		..	..	352	6¾	6¼	6½	– ½
19½	12½	CmtyBkSy	.76	4.8	..	46	17	16	16	–1⅝
1 9-32	15-32	CmtyNB&T NY		..	..	25	⅝	⅝	⅝	...
20⅛	12	ComtySB	.24b	1.4	..	344	17½	17¼	17½	...
16½	⅝	CmtyShrs	.40	46.	..	298	1	⅞	⅞	– ⅜
9⅛	5¼	Com Syst	.20	3.4	10	246	6⅛	5⅞	5⅞	...
16	7¼	COMNET		..	9	95	10	9	10	+ ½
9½	2¾	CompuChem		..	..	117	4	4	4	...
8½	5¼	Compnt Tech		..	16	135	7⅛	6⅞	6⅞	...
15⅝	5½	ComprhCr	.40	4.5	10	1385	9	8⅞	8⅞	– ¼
8	2¼	Compresn Lab		..	..	113	3¼	3⅛	3¼	– ⅛
2	¼	Compuscn Inc		..	..	82	½	7-16	½	+1-32
17	4⅝	Computr Auto		..	28	1941	11	10	10⅜	– ¾
12¼	4⅞	C C T Corp		..	..	664	5⅝	5⅛	5¼	– ⅜
10¾	7	CmptrData	.10	1.0	10	30	10⅛	10	10⅛	+ ⅛
10⅛	4	CES		..	12	98	6	5¾	6	...
14¾	7	Comptr Horzn		..	12	35	10⅛	10	10	...
7	3½	CmptrLng	.12	2.2	..	8	5½	5½	5½	– ¼
4⅛	1¼	Computr Mem		..	..	281	1 15-16	1¾	1 13-16	+1-16
5½	1⅝	Computer Prd		..	..	1507	2 1-16	2	2	–1-16
27¾	11¾	Comshare Inc		..	60	207	15½	13¾	15½	+1¾
9¼	2⅛	Comstock Grp		..	..	1	3	3	3	+ ½
4¼	⅞	Comtrex Sys		..	..	1	1 3-16	1 3-16	1 3-16	+1-16
19⅞	6⅝	Concept Inc		..	25	356	14¼	13¾	14	– ⅛
19	8	Concord Cmpt		..	19	24	14	13¼	13¼	– ¾
23½	11	Concurrent C		..	18	36	16½	15¾	16½	...
7⅞	2¾	CONMED Cp		..	..	15	4⅝	4⅛	4⅛	– ⅜

365-day High	Low	Stock	Div	Yld	P-E	Sales (hds)	High	Low	Last	Net Chg.
11¾	6¾	DranetzTc	.24	2.6	19	3	9¼	9¼	9¼	– ½
13⅛	(L)	Dresher	.16	3.0	9	125	6	5⅜	5⅜	– ⅝
20⅜	5¾	Dress Barn		..	18	646	11¼	10¾	11	– ½
¾	9-32	Drew Ind		..	11	807	11-32	5-16	11-32	...
17¼	3¾	Drexlr Tech		..	..	93	4¼	4	4¼	...
25	11¼	Dreyers Grnd		..	38	2222	14½	13⅞	14¼	– ½
26	12¼	DS Bancr	.12d	.7	8	583	18½	18	18¼	– ½
19¼	10¼	DryClean USA		..	15	2	12¼	12¼	12¼	– ¾
10⅛	3⅞	DSC Commun		..	19	4227	5¾	5¼	5⅝	+ ⅛
26¼	7½	DST Syst	.12	1.0	11	1	11¾	11¾	11¾	– ⅝
12¼	6	Dumagmi Min		..	..	22	9	8⅞	8⅞	– ⅛
32	19½	DunkDonut	.32	1.3	13	63	24½	24¼	24¼	– ½
33¼	9	Duquesne Sys		..	25	206	19¼	18½	19	– ½
14	7½	Durakon Inds		..	10	125	9	8¾	8¾	– ⅝
24½	1¾	Duramed Ph		..	..	135	5¼	4¾	5	– ½
18⅜	11½	Duriron Co	.56	3.8	64	84	14¾	14½	14¾	...
14	7⅛	DurrFill M	.17	1.8	12	30	9⅝	9¼	9⅝	+ ¼
3 1-16	1	Dyansen Cp		..	7	82	1⅝	1⅝	1⅝	...
15¼	3¼	Dyatron Corp		..	12	51	12¾	12	12	– ½
15¾	7	Dycom Ind	5k	..	13	613	10¼	9¾	9¾	– ¾
11⅛	6⅛	Dynamic Resr		..	13	18	8	7½	7¾	...
13⅜	5⅜	Dynascan Cp		..	7	75	7	6⅞	6⅞	...
43½	14⅜	Dynatech Cp		..	10	513	19½	18¾	19	– ¼
		--E E--								
12¾	5½	E&B Marine		..	..	96	6½	6	6	...
13	8¼	Eagle Bancsh		..	..	163	10⅜	10¼	10¼	...
14½	7⅜	Eagle Fn	.10b	1.3	..	5	8½	8	8	– ⅜
3 15-16	¾	Eagle Telphnc		..	8	40	1	⅞	⅞	...
9⅜	2⅝	Earth Technol		..	..	50	4¼	4	4¼	...
13	5¾	EascoHand Tl		..	11	234	8	7½	7⅝	– ⅛
26¾	11	EastrnBc	.20b	1.2	10	77	17	16	17	– ½
11¾	3⅞	Eastex Enrgy		..	..	10	4¾	4¾	4¾	+ ½
(H)	7½	EstWeym	.20b	1.1	..	1	17¾	17¾	17¾	+ ⅛
20½	12½	Eastover	1.60	12.	13	14	13	13	13	...
13¾	5¼	Eaton Financl		..	14	37	6¼	6¼	6¼	– ¾
32¾	12⅞	EatonVan	.28	1.7	6	23	17	16¼	17	+ ½
11½	3⅞	ECAD Inc		..	..	660	6	5¾	5¾	– ¼
6	2½	ECI Telecom		..	..	7	3	3	3	...
9¼	3	EIL Instrm	5k	..	18	3	3⅝	3⅝	3⅝	...
11½	6	EIP Micro	.12	1.8	48	31	6¾	6	6¾	+ ⅛
6¼	2¾	El Chico Corp		..	..	17	3	3	3	...
23	5	Elan		..	..	1080	10⅞	9½	10¼	– ⅝
11⅝	4½	ElbitCm	.05b	1.0	5	11	4⅞	4½	4⅞	...
26¾	18	ElcoIndus	.88	3.6	11	6	24¾	24¾	24¾	...
22¾	4¼	Elco Tel Inc		..	10	314	5⅞	5⅜	5½	– ½
9	4½	Elmwood Fed		..	..	216	7½	6¾	7½	...
14	6	Eldec Corp		..	8	56	8	7½	7½	...
8½	1⅞	Electro Cathet		..	..	154	2¾	2½	2½	...
13½	5	Electro Nucln		..	..	67	7⅝	7¼	7¼	– ⅜
19¾	9	Electrmag Sci		..	13	111	11½	11¼	11½	...
12½	7¼	Eliot Savings		..	..	106	9¾	9	9	– ¾
15¼	5½	Electro Scienc		..	..	50	7	6¾	6¾	– ¼
53⅝	31⅞	Elctrlux	1.15b	3.5	..	317	33⅜	32⅝	32⅝	– ½
52¼	35	E Town	2.80	6.9	11	6	40½	40½	40½	+1
21⅝	13⅛	ElPasoEl	1.52	11.	10	250	14½	14¼	14⅜	...
6⅞	1¼	ElPollo Asado		..	..	61	1 11-16	1 9-16	1⅝	+1-16
9½	3	Elron Electrn		..	..	26	3¾	3½	3½	– ¼
1 11-16	¼	ELXSI Corp		..	..	588	⅜	11-32	11-32	–1-16
29	7¼	EMC Corp		..	12	519	14	12¼	12¾	–1½
11¾	6¾	EMC Insr	.48	6.1	6	70	7⅞	7⅝	7⅞	...
20	10¼	EMCON Assc		..	..	23	13¼	13	13¼	– ¾
4½	1¼	Empi Incorp		..	..	8	2⅛	1⅞	1⅞	– ¼
2⅞	1	Empire-Orr		..	..	13	1	1	1	...
11½	7	Empire Sv Ln		..	..	10	7½	7½	7½	– ½
3⅛	2⅛	EMS System		..	..	5	2¼	2¼	2¼	– ⅛
8½	3⅞	Emulex Corp		..	22	1725	6⅜	5⅝	5⅞	– ⅜
5	1¾	Encore Cmptr		..	..	311	2⅜	2 5-16	2⅜	+1-16
15⅝	10¾	Energas	1	7.3	10	25	13⅞	13⅝	13⅝	– ¼
37¼	7¼	Energy Convr		..	..	326	9¾	9	9½	– ¼
17¼	3¾	Energy Factr		..	..	485	6⅝	6⅜	6½	...
22	16	EnrgyNo	1.24g	7.1	10	55	17½	16¾	17½	+ ½

EXHIBIT 10-7 The Dow Jones Averages®

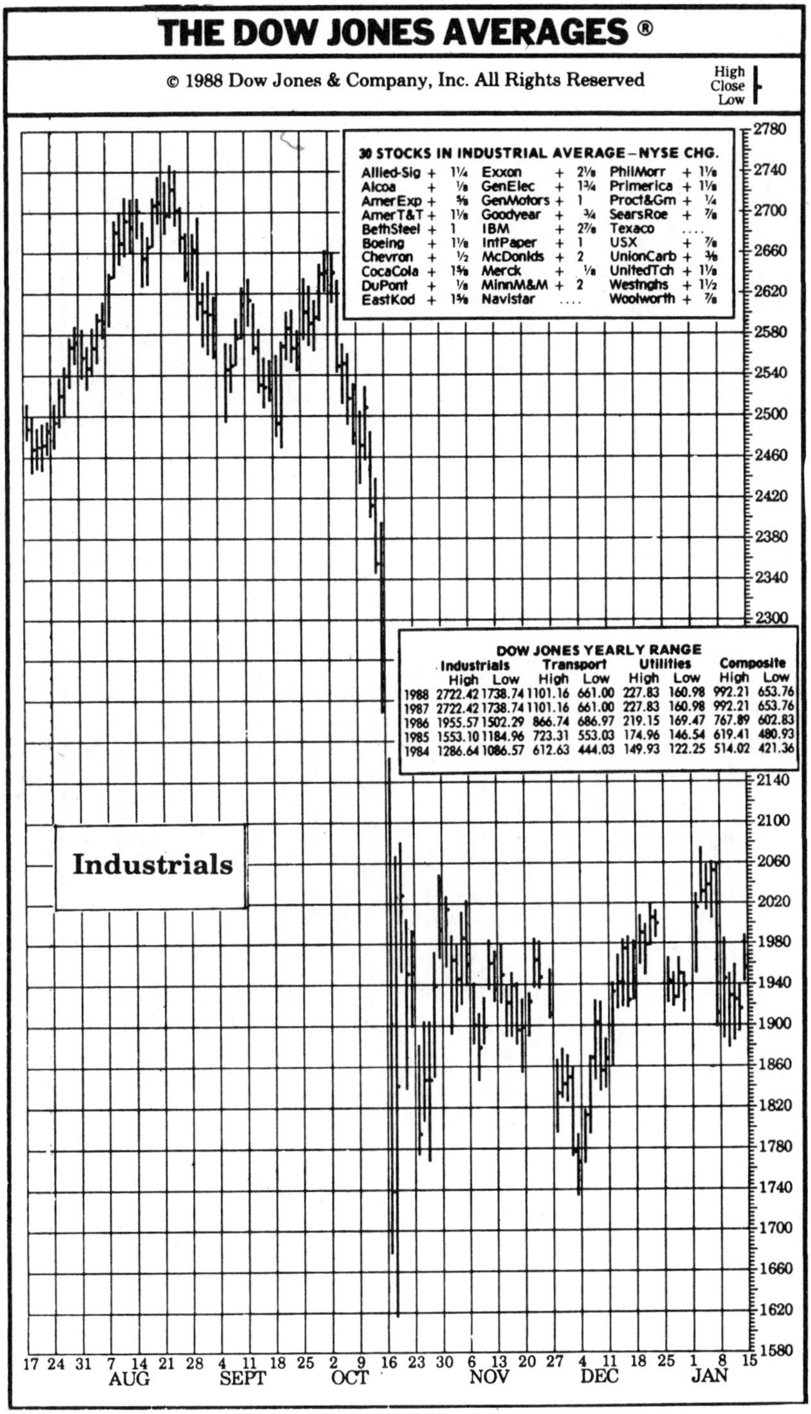
THE DOW JONES AVERAGES ®
© 1988 Dow Jones & Company, Inc. All Rights Reserved
High
Close
Low
30 STOCKS IN INDUSTRIAL AVERAGE–NYSE CHG.
Allied-Sig + 1¼ Exxon + 2⅛ PhilMorr + 1⅛
Alcoa + ⅛ GenElec + 1¾ Primerica + 1⅛
AmerExp + ⅝ GenMotors + 1 Proct&Gm + ¼
AmerT&T + 1⅛ Goodyear + ¾ SearsRoe + ⅞
BethSteel + 1 IBM + 2⅞ Texaco ....
Boeing + 1⅛ IntPaper + 1 USX + ⅞
Chevron + ½ McDonlds + 2 UnionCarb + ⅜
CocaCola + 1⅝ Merck + ⅛ UnitedTch + 1⅛
DuPont + ⅛ MinnM&M + 2 Westnghs + 1½
EastKod + 1⅝ Navistar .... Woolworth + ⅞
DOW JONES YEARLY RANGE
Industrials Transport Utilities Composite
High Low High Low High Low High Low
1988 2722.42 1738.74 1101.16 661.00 227.83 160.98 992.21 653.76
1987 2722.42 1738.74 1101.16 661.00 227.83 160.98 992.21 653.76
1986 1955.57 1502.29 866.74 686.97 219.15 169.47 767.89 602.83
1985 1553.10 1184.96 723.31 553.03 174.96 146.54 619.41 480.93
1984 1286.64 1086.57 612.63 444.03 149.93 122.25 514.02 421.36
Industrials
2780
2740
2700
2660
2620
2580
2540
2500
2460
2420
2380
2340
2300
2140
2100
2060
2020
1980
1940
1900
1860
1820
1780
1740
1700
1660
1620
1580
17 24 31 7 14 21 28 4 11 18 25 2 9 16 23 30 6 13 20 27 4 11 18 25 1 8 15
AUG SEPT OCT NOV DEC JAN

EXHIBIT 10-7 (*continued*)

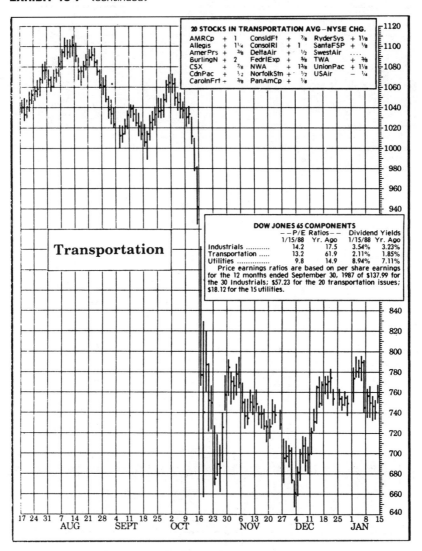

20 STOCKS IN TRANSPORTATION AVG—NYSE CHG.

AMRCp	+ 1	ConsldFt	+ 7/8	RyderSys	+ 1 1/8
Allegis	+ 1 1/4	ConsolRI	+ 1	SantaFSP	+ 1/8
AmerPrs	+ 3/8	DeltaAir	+ 1/2	SwestAir	....
BurlingN	+ 2	FedrlExp	+ 5/8	TWA	+ 3/8
CSX	+ 7/8	NWA	+ 1 3/8	UnionPac	+ 1 1/8
CdnPac	+ 1/2	NorfolkStn	+ 1/2	USAir	− 1/4
CarolnFrt	+ 3/8	PanAmCp	+ 1/8		

Transportation

DOW JONES 65 COMPONENTS

	− −P/E Ratios− −		Dividend Yields	
	1/15/88	Yr. Ago	1/15/88	Yr. Ago
Industrials	14.2	17.5	3.54%	3.23%
Transportation	13.2	61.9	2.11%	1.85%
Utilities	9.8	14.9	8.94%	7.11%

Price earnings ratios are based on per share earnings for the 12 months ended September 30, 1987 of $137.99 for the 30 Industrials; $57.23 for the 20 transportation issues; $18.12 for the 15 utilities.

EXHIBIT 10-7 (continued)

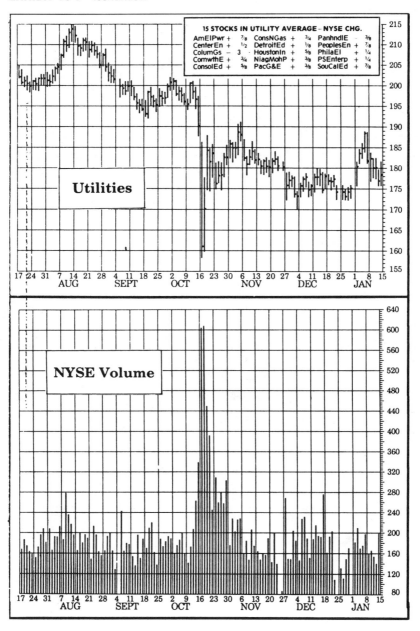

15 STOCKS IN UTILITY AVERAGE – NYSE CHG.

AmElPwr +	7/8	ConsNGas +	3/4	PanhndlE –	3/8
CenterEn +	1/2	DetroitEd +	1/8	PeoplesEn +	7/8
ColumGs –	3	HoustonIn +	5/8	PhilaEl +	1/4
ComwthE +	3/4	NiagMohP +	3/8	PSEnterp +	1/4
ConsolEd +	5/8	PacG&E +	3/8	SouCalEd +	7/8

Utilities

NYSE Volume

In addition to the 30 industrial corporation index, there is the index of 20 transportation stocks and one for 15 utility stocks. These 65 stocks are used to make still another index called the Dow Jones Composite Average. These 65 stocks were shown in Exhibit 10-7.

Another well-known and widely quoted index is the Standard & Poor's 500 stock average. It is readily found in daily newspapers and business magazines. The "S&P 500" as it is often called is a composite of 400 industrial, 20 transportation, 40 utility, and 40 financial companies' shares.

When the DJIA and S&P indicators show a long upward trend for stock prices, it is referred to as a *bull market*. When the long-term trend of indicators is downward, it is called a *bear market*. Other interesting language of Wall Street such as blue chip, growth stock, par, and proxy are found in the glossary of this chapter.

ANALYZING FINANCIAL STATEMENTS

Each year major corporations issue an *annual report*. This report includes a letter to the shareholders by the president and the chairman of the board that summarizes activities of the past year and contains brief remarks about sales, net profit, cost of doing business, new products, branches opened and closed, major staff changes, litigation, and thoughts about the future. In addition, there are pictures of products, buildings, and employees. There are financial charts, tables, and general financial statements. These financial statements include the *balance sheet, income statement,* and *statement of changes of financial position.* The two very important pieces of information accompanying these statements are the independent auditor's report and the footnotes to the statements.

FRANK & ERNEST

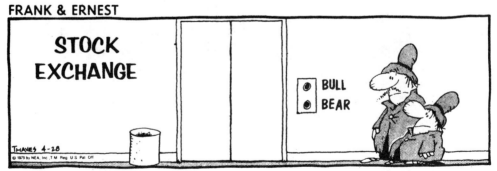

4-28-79—© 1979 Newspaper
Enterprise Association, Inc.

The following paragraphs will serve as a beginning in learning how to analyze financial statements. An in-depth study of this area is beyond the scope of this book.

Auditor's Report

Read the independent certified public accountant's (CPA) report first. You will have to hunt for this simple one- or two-paragraph statement in the annual report. You only want to deal with companies that get a "clean bill of health" from their auditors.

The key paragraph, often called the "opinion," will read something like the following:

> *In our opinion, the aforementioned financial statements present fairly the financial position of X Corporation and subsidiaries as of December 31, 19X2 and 19X1, and the results of their operations and the changes of financial position for the years then ended, in conformity with generally accepted accounting principles applied on a consistent basis.*

The auditor's signature usually follows this opinion paragraph. This opinion is a professional judgment based on the auditor's findings about the company. The auditor's opinion is not a guarantee of or warranty about the future success of the company. The auditor is stating that the amounts appearing on the various financial statements were tested and verified by various auditing techniques. Any errors and omissions found are considered so minor that collectively they will not cause any distortion of the statement. On the other hand, the reader should be more cautious about the annual report if the auditor's opinion paragraph includes additional paragraphs or contain phrases as "except for," "subject to," or "disclaims any opinion about the statement" or the statements are clearly marked with the reference "unaudited."

Footnotes

The footnotes accompanying financial statements are among the most difficult reading in the business world. The independent auditor will require the company management under audit to place important changes of accounting principles in the footnotes. The reporting requirements come to the accounting profession through the Financial Accounting Standards Board (FASB) and the Securities and Exchange Commission (SEC). The footnotes usually include information on the basis of consolidation, provisions on customer's bad debts, ending inventory determination, purchase and lease agreements, depreciation methods on plant and equipment, long-term borrowing, federal income taxes, and changes in the stockholders' investment in the corporation. Of particular

interest are changes in inventory valuation, major write-offs of inventory, abandonment of property and equipment, extensive use of debt, large repurchases of
the company's own common stock, and so on.

Financial Statements

The general-purpose financial statements that accompany the annual reports are
the (1) balance sheet, (2) earnings statement, (3) retained earnings statement,
and (4) statement of changes of financial position. Sometimes the earnings statement and retained earnings statement are combined.

The *balance sheet* is a summary of assets, liabilities or debts, and stockholders' or owners' equity in the company as of a specific date. It resembles a
"snapshot" of the corporation at an instant in time. The balance sheet speaks to
the *solvency* of the company, that is, its ability to pay debts. To exist, the company must remain solvent.

The *earnings statement* is a summary of the total revenue (fees, sales, etc.),
total cost of sales, general and administrative expenses, interest and taxes paid,
and net profit or loss for a particular period of time. The time period is usually
for one year. The income statement is similar to a motion picture about the
company. In a successful company, sales and profits increase each year.

The *retained earnings statement* is a brief summary of the profit retained in the
company. The statement will refer to the beginning balance of retained earnings,
the net profit for the year less dividends distributed or declared, and the ending
balance. A portion of net profit retained or plowed back into the company is
considered a favorable indication of management stewardship.

The *statement of changes of financial position* analyzes the corporation manager's stewardship of the company's working capital, long-term plant and
equipment, and its manner of acquiring and using working capital. The flow of
working capital in and out of the company is important. A company that continues to have net outflows of working capital will eventually go out of existence.

Financial Ratios

All the financial statements produced will not be of help unless you can interpret
them. This is done by comparing certain numbers found in the general-purpose
statements. The answers arrived at in the ratios or other calculations probably
raise more questions than they provide definite answers. Since solvency of the
business is of prime importance, some of these basic ratios or calculations for
this will be made first. The numbers in the various calculations are from the
sample financial statements of the XYZ Corp., Inc. for the years 19X1 and 19X2
shown in Exhibits 10-8a and 10-8b. The first eight ratios discussed relate to

measures of solvency. Calculations 9 through 12 are common measures of profitability. The remaining ratios or calculations measure management efficiency and decision-making ability as well as the investors' view of stock prices.

1. *Current ratio.* This ratio is the first test of a company's *solvency*. It is also known as the banker's ratio. It is computed by dividing total current assets by total current liabilities. A rule is that the company should have $2 of current

EXHIBIT 10-8a XYZ Corp., Inc.
Balance Sheet

Assets		
Current assets:	19X2	19X1
Cash and marketable securities	$ 10,000	$ 8,000
Accounts receivable, net	20,000	16,000
Inventory, December 31	30,000	26,000
Total current assets	$ 60,000	$ 50,000
Plant, property, and equipment at cost:		
Land	$ 10,000	$ 10,000
Buildings, net of accumulated depreciation	40,000	44,000
Machinery, equipment, net of accumulated depreciation	50,000	53,000
Total assets	$100,000	$107,000
	$160,000	$157,000
Liabilities		
Current liabilities:		
Accounts payable	$ 12,000	$ 10,000
Notes payable	10,000	14,000
Taxes payable	8,000	3,000
Total current liabilities	$ 30,000	$ 27,000
Long-term debt:		
Mortgage bonds payable 1990	$ 70,000	$ 75,000
Total liabilities	$100,000	$102,000
Stockholders' Equity		
Common stock 5,000 shares @ $10 par value	$ 50,000	$ 50,000
Retained earnings	10,000	5,000
Total stockholders' equity	$ 60,000	$ 55,000
Total liabilities and stockholders' equity	$160,000	$157,000

EXHIBIT 10-8b XYZ Corp., Inc.
Income Statement and Statement of Retained Earnings

Income Statement
For the year ended December 31, 19X2

	19X2	19X1
Revenue for the year	$320,000	$300,000
Less: Cost of sales	200,000	190,000
Gross profit	$120,000	$110,000
Operating expenses (general and administrative)	100,000	98,000
Net income before income taxes	$ 20,000	$ 12,000
Income taxes	8,000	4,800
Net income after taxes	$ 12,000	$ 7,200
Earnings per share	$2.40	$1.44

Statement of Retained Earnings
For the year ended December 31, 19X2

	19X2	19X1
Retained earnings, January 1	$ 5,000	$ 0
Plus: Net income	12,000	7,200
	$ 17,000	$ 7,200
Less: Dividends	7,000	2,200
Retained earnings, December 31	$ 10,000	$ 5,000

assets for $1 of current debt, or a 2:1 ratio. The notion of "current" is related to those assets that will be converted into cash within a year and debt to be liquidated within a year.

$$\frac{\text{19X2 Total current assets}}{\text{19X2 Total current liabilities}} = \frac{\$60,000}{\$30,000} = 2:1$$

2. *Acid-test ratio.* Also called the quick assets ratio, this is the second test of *solvency.* It is a critical test of a company's ability to pay all its current liabilities upon short notice. The basic rule is to have at least a 1:1 ratio. Quick assets are cash, marketable securities, and receivables.

$$\text{19X2: } \frac{\text{Cash, marketable securities, receivables}}{\text{Total current liabilities}} = \frac{\$30,000}{\$30,000} = 1:1$$

3. *Working capital.* Working capital is found by subtracting total current liabilities from total current assets. The excess is the cushion that the company has to use some current assets for purposes other than paying debts.

	19X2
Total current assets	$60,000
Less: Total current liabilities	30,000
Working capital	$30,000

This is a limited test of the company's solvency since the working capital may not be available in the form of hard cash.

4. *Accounts receivable turnover.* This is a test of the validity of the current ratio. Accounts receivable are legal claims against customers to whom the company has extended credit. Collecting from customers may be difficult at times. Here an assumption is made that all sales are made on credit. The calculation is made by dividing revenue for the year by the average accounts receivable balance.

$$19X2: \frac{\text{Revenue for the year}}{\text{Average accounts receivable}} = \frac{\$320,000}{(\$20,000 + \$16,000)/2}$$

$$= \frac{\$320,000}{\$18,000} = 17.8 \text{ times}$$

5. *Number of days to collect accounts receivable.* Most businesses establish a credit extension policy. A company may offer cash discounts as incentives for customers to pay their bills early. The policy may be to require payment within 30 days. This calculation is an easy one to work. Use 365 days in a year and divide it by the accounts receivable turnover times.

$$19X2: \frac{365 \text{ days}}{\text{Accounts receivable turnover}} = \frac{365}{17.8} = 20.5 \text{ days}$$

6. *Inventory turnover.* This is a test of the current ratio for solvency. A major item in current assets is the inventory. Critical to the solvency of a company is its ability to move the merchandise to customers by selling. Inventory that is sitting on the shelves of the business firm is not earning a penny. Unsold merchandise is as bad as keeping money hidden in a mattress. A measure of inventory movement is to divide the cost of sales by the average ending inventory balance.

$$19X2: \frac{\text{Cost of sales}}{\text{Average ending inventory}} = \frac{\$200,000}{(\$30,000 + \$26,000)/2} = 7.1 \text{ times}$$

7. *Number of days to move the inventory.* This calculation determines whether or not there is too much inventory on hand. Some companies must keep a broad selection of parts or goods on hand at all times. This could cause a very slow inventory turnover. Some businesses are expected to turn their inventory rapidly. In the case of supermarkets, the turnover of goods is 30 days; on the other hand, industrial firms and hardware stores may require 120 to 150 days to turn

their goods. The number of days to move the inventory is readily found by dividing 365 days by inventory turnovers.

$$\frac{365 \text{ days}}{\text{Inventory turnover}} = \frac{365}{7.1} = 51.4 \text{ days}$$

8. *Length of normal operating cycle.* The normal operating cycle is the time in days that it takes to move cash to inventories from inventories to accounts receivable and from the receivables back to cash. This calculation is made by adding the answers found in calculations 5 and 7. The fewer number of days in this calculation, the better.

Number of days to collect accounts receivable	20.5
Plus: Number of days to move inventory	51.4
Normal operating cycle, days	71.9

9. *Earnings per share.* This calculation is the most sought after and best understood. Earnings per share is the net income or net profit after income taxes divided by the number of shares of common stock held by the stockholders. This basic calculation is modified to adjust net income to reflect dividends owed to preferred stockholders. Corporations are required to show to stockholders any portion of the net income that resulted from extraordinary gains and losses. The shares of stock are adjusted to reflect the total potential stockholders in the event certain bondholders can exercise rights to become common stockholders.

$$19X2: \frac{\text{Net income after taxes}}{\text{Number of shares outstanding}} = \frac{\$12,000}{5,000} = \$2.40$$

10. *Rate of return on equity.* This is the best indicator of profitability when comparing dissimilar corporations and is computed by dividing net income after taxes by total stockholders' equity. The rate of return should be high enough to keep and attract investors to the company. The average return of all industries in the United States has been around 15 percent in recent years. This could be inadequate if inflation were to return to 7 or 8 percent. The large oil companies average around a 15 percent return on equity.

$$19X2: \frac{\text{Net income after taxes}}{\text{Total stockholders' equity}} = \frac{\$12,000}{60,000} = .20 \text{ (or } 20\%)$$

11. *Sales to net income.* This calculation has some limited value in determining profitability. It is determined by dividing net income after taxes by revenues for the year. It is necessary to compare the answer with the returns of other similar competing firms before any meaning can be gained. Managements of business firms often cite a low rate of return on sales as justification for raising sales prices. However, management usually will not re-cite the rate of return on equity.

$$19X2: \frac{\text{Net income after taxes}}{\text{Revenues for the year}} = \frac{\$12,000}{\$320,000} = .0375 \text{ (or 3.75\%)}$$

12. *Rate of return on total assets.* While this is a test of profitability, it is also an indicator of management's utilization of all assets. The calculation is determined by dividing net income after taxes by total assets of the firm. Some analysts modify the total assets part of the formula by using the total of plant and equipment before depreciation. Others prefer not to include any intangible assets that the company owns in their calculation. The rate of return on assets should be higher than the after-tax cost of borrowing money through mortgages and bonds. Also, it should be higher than the dividend rate paid to preferred stockholders of the company.

$$19X2: \frac{\text{Net income after taxes}}{\text{Total assets}} = \frac{\$12,000}{\$160,000} = .075 \text{ (or 7.5\%)}$$

13. *Revenue per dollar of asset.* The ratio may indicate efficient use of assets by the company's management. It is necessary to compute this ratio for several competing companies to establish a useful reference point. This ratio is found by dividing the revenues earned for the year (total sales) by the total assets of the company. The calculation for 19X2 shows $2 sales for each $1 of assets.

$$19X2: \frac{\text{Revenues for the year}}{\text{Total assets}} = \frac{\$320,000}{\$160,000} = \$2$$

14. *Debt ratio.* The debt ratio determines what percentage of the company's assets is supplied by creditors and is found by dividing total liabilities by total assets of the company. A merchandising business can afford more debt or "leverage" than can a manufacturing firm. There are limits to the amount of debt that a company may undertake. A regulated utility may borrow heavily. A retail and wholesale company may carry more debt than a manufacturing company. Maximum debt ratios might be 60 percent for retail and wholesale and 50 percent for manufacturing.

$$19X2: \frac{\text{Total liabilities}}{\text{Total assets}} = \frac{\$100,000}{\$160,000} = .625 \text{ (or 62.5\%)}$$

15. *Equity ratio.* The percentage of equity owned by the stockholders may tell whether additional debt should be undertaken. The equity ratio is found by dividing total stockholders' equity by total assets. The answer arrived at and the answer in 14 should equal 100 percent. It appears at first glance that XYZ Corp. should not undertake additional borrowing. However, assets are stated at original costs on balance sheets. Appreciation of property values and a rapid movement in the operating cycle may be creating the opportunity to use of debt.

$$19X2: \frac{\text{Total stockholders' equity}}{\text{Total assets}} = \frac{\$60,000}{\$160,000} = .375 \text{ (or 37.5\%)}$$

16. *Flow of working capital.* The movement of working capital in and out of the business is important as it can help explain here the capital is coming from and how it is being used. Most businesses rely on sales of goods and services for most of their working capital. This *basic source* of working capital is found by taking the net income for the year and adding back such bookkeeping adjustments as depreciation expense. Another *major source* of working capital is the issuance of common and preferred stock. The same is true for the issuance of long-term bonds or mortgages. Working capital can be *decreased* by the payment of cash dividends and the purchase of long-lived assets such as land, buildings, and equipment. A large net loss for the year and the retirement of part or all of a long-term debt will reduce working capital.

17. *Book value per share.* This calculation is of limited value as it only suggests what the shareholders would receive if the company stopped operation and sold all assets, paid all debts, and distributed the remaining cash to stockholders. The book value per share is found by dividing total stockholders' equity by the number of shares in the hands of investors. Investors compare the actual market price of the stock with this calculation. Most of the time, the market prices of stocks exceed their book values per share. Sometimes, however, the book value per share is higher than the actual market price. This suggests two possibilities: Investors have overlooked a bargain, or the company is heading for financial difficulty. During a recession, stock prices often fall below book values.

$$19\text{X}2: \frac{\text{Total stockholders' equity}}{\text{Number of shares of stock}} = \frac{\$60,000}{5,000 \text{ shares}} = \$12$$

To summarize briefly, these ratios are helpful when reviewing a company's annual report. Even after working up all the calculations, however, you may find that you have only raised more questions than found answers. It is better to compare at least two years of data. Trends over the past five years are even more useful. The balance sheet still has its limitations in that many important pieces of information are not shown. Such factors as employee morale, resignations of key executives, a competitor's setting up business across the street, community attitude toward the company, and rising values of land and building are not shown.

OPENING AN ACCOUNT

Opening an account to buy and sell stocks is similar to opening a bank account. There is a form to fill out that asks the usual questions of name, address, employment, bank accounts, Social Security number, age if under majority, references, full signature, special instructions on how the name or names be listed on documents, and type of account desired.

You may wish to have the stock certificates in your possession, or you may wish to leave them with the brokerage firm. If you choose the latter, there is no need for making trips to your safe deposit box to place or to withdraw securities. Your account will be similar to a checking account. You will receive a monthly statement summarizing any purchases or sales of stock, cash payments or cash receipts, dividends to your accounts, and dates of any transaction, with a line-by-line summary of the shares of stocks, bonds, and other investments held at a specific point in time. An individual account is insured up to $500,000, including some cash account balances against brokerage house failure through the Securities Investor Protection Corporation.

Once you have opened an account, you will be introduced to an account executive, a salesperson, who will buy or sell stock on *your* instructions. When you buy stocks, you must pay for them within four or five business days. It is normal to conduct all your business by telephone.

Brokerage firms may also function as *investment bankers* insofar as they help large corporations raise money by agreeing to sell shares of the corporation's preferred and common stocks for a fee. When several brokerage houses join together to help raise a large amount of capital for a corporation, it is called an *underwriting syndicate.*

The investor should be alerted to the fact that brokerage houses stay in business by buying and selling shares for which they receive commissions. Beware of the account executive who encourages you to enter into excessive buy and sell transactions without reason. This practice is known as *churning.*

Transactions and Commissions

A commission is charged each time an investor purchases or sells shares of stock through a brokerage house. The minimum commission on a buy or sell transaction for common or preferred stocks might be $30. However, as the amount of money invested increases, the impact of the commission decreases. Sample commission rates are shown in Table 10-1.

Other fees are often included. When a person purchases or sells less than 100 shares at a time, for example, the transaction is handled by an odd-lot trader. The minimum odd-lot fee is 1/8 point per share and the maximum fee is 25 cents per share if the stock sells above $55. The investor who sells shares of stock through the exchange will pay a tiny Securities and Exchange Commission fee and a fractional percentage on state transfer or excise tax.

Dollar Averaging

Dollar averaging is a simple and effective way of reaching long-term objectives when stock price fluctuations are common. For example, suppose that you are

TABLE 10-1 Selected Sample Commission Rates Common and Preferred Stocks; All Trades Subject to a $30 Minimum Commission

Share price	Number of shares					
	10	20	25	50	75	100
$ 10	$30.00	$30.00	$30.00	$30.00	$30.00	$34.25
15	30.00	30.00	30.00	30.00	36.48	43.16
20	30.00	30.00	30.00	34.25	43.16	52.06
25	30.00	30.00	30.00	38.70	49.83	60.97
30	30.00	30.00	30.00	43.16	56.51	67.13
35	30.00	30.00	32.02	47.61	62.61	73.30
40	30.00	30.69	34.25	52.06	67.13	79.46
45	30.00	32.47	36.48	56.51	71.75	85.63
50	30.00	34.25	38.75	60.25	75.70	91.25
60	30.00	37.81	43.16	67.13	85.63	93.60
70	30.00	41.37	47.61	73.30	93.60	93.60
80	30.69	44.94	52.06	79.46	93.60	93.60
100	34.25	52.06	60.97	93.60	93.60	93.60

able to set aside $75 per month to invest in corporate securities. You place the $75 temporarily in a bank savings account to earn some interest. When the savings accumulates to, say, around $600, you withdraw the money from the savings account to purchase common stock of a company that you have researched. The savings account should be one in which you earn interest from the day of deposit to the day of withdrawal.

Continue this process of setting aside cash and investing in shares in the same company in amounts of $600 until you reach a goal of, say, 25 shares. Then, select another company and begin the process until you accumulate a goal of specific shares or dollars. As interest is earned and dividends are received, these amounts should be invested as part of the next $600 of investment input.

A running tabulation of monthly cash inputs, interest income, cash dividends, and cash disbursements for stocks will help you to stay with your plan. Exhibit 10-9 is an informal worksheet of such a record.

There are several advantages to the dollar averaging approach: (1) you keep your investments in mind at all times (specific companies and stocks), (2) you continue the habit of monthly savings and earning some interest between stock purchases, (3) you avoid the pitfall of many investors of trying to outguess the stock market hoping to buy the stock at its lowest price, (4) you will have accumulated the number of shares or the dollar total of investment in due time and at an average price over the period, (5) you will have followed a very simple program consistent with long-term goal achievement, and (6) when you reach a specific dollar of investment in a company, say, $3,000 of stock, you can begin the process with the next corporation selected. The disadvantage of dollar averaging is that it is not very interesting and lacks the adventure of "wheeling and dealing."

EXHIBIT 10-9   Cash Position for Investing For the Year 19X2

Date	Transaction	Cash in	Cash out	Balance
1/1	Balance forward in Cash			#387.25
1/4	Cash in (to savings)	75.00		462.25
2/3	Cash in	75.00		537.25
2/15	Dividends from ABC. Corp.	18.00		555.25
3/2	Cash in	75.00		630.25
3/31	Interest on savings	7.23		637.48
4/5	Cash in	75.00		712.48
4/20	Purchased 15 sh ABC. Corp. @ #40 #30 com.		630.00	82.48
5/1	Cash in	75.00		157.48
5/15	Dividends from ABC. Corp. (30 sh)	36.00		193.48
6/2	Cash in	75.00		268.48
6/30	Interest on savings	2.80		271.28
7/6	Cash in	75.00		346.28
8/1	Cash in	75.00		421.28
8/15	Dividends from ABC. Corp. (30 sh)	36.00		457.28
9/2	Cash in	75.00		532.28
9/30	Interest on savings	6.58		538.86
10/2	Cash in	75.00		613.86
10/20	Purchased 20 sh BCD Co. @ 28¾ + Com.		605.00	8.86
11/2	Cash in	75.00		83.86
11/15	Dividends from ABC. Corp. (30)	36.00		119.86
12/2	Cash in	75.00		194.86
12/26	Dividends from BCD Corp. (20 sh)	10.00		204.86
12/31	Interest on savings	2.04		206.90

EXHIBIT 10-10   Dollar-Averaging Purchases of XYZ Company

Date	Shares Bought	Market Price per Share	Purchase Cost	Commission Paid	Total Cost
3/12/X1	18	$30	$540	$30	$ 570
8/05/X1	23	25	575	30	605
2/20/X2	21	27	567	30	597
7/25/X2	19	29	551	30	581
1/05/X3	18	32	576	30	606
Totals	99				$2,959

Average price for 99 shares = $29.89 ($2,959 ÷ 99)

A brief sketch of dollar averaging with the goal of investing approximately $3,000 over five purchases of XYZ Company is illustrated in Exhibit 10-10.

When computing the gain or loss on an investment, the following approach is used. The *cost* of an investment is the price of the securities *plus* the commissions paid. Net *proceeds* are found by taking the selling price of the investment and subtracting any commissions paid. The difference between the *cost* and *net proceeds* received will be the gain or loss. Income tax treatment of gains and losses is discussed in Chapter 11.

MUTUAL FUNDS

Mutual funds are corporations that sell their own stock to obtain money that is in turn invested in the securities market. The fund usually charges a commission of 5 to 9 percent of the share's value for each share or shares sold. When the mutual fund continuously issues new shares to investors, it is called an *open-end* mutual fund or a *load* fund. When new shares are being issued, a prospectus is given to the potential investor. A prospectus is a booklet containing all information about the company that would affect the value of new securities that the company wants to issue. No commission is paid when the investor sells open-end mutual fund shares.

A *closed-end investment company* is a mutual fund with a limited number of shares outstanding in the hands of investors. The closed-end fund is also called a *no-load* fund. These mutual funds employ no salespersons and charge no commissions. The shares are traded on the major stock exchanges. The investor pays only the normal brokerage fee as in any stock purchase or sale.

There are three appealing features of mutual fund investments: (1) The fund offers professionally trained investment managers. (2) The investor receives immediate diversification of his or her money over 50 or 100 corporations or more. (3) These funds are designed for meeting long-term financial objectives.

But there are also some problems encountered by the potential investor of mutual funds: (1) The fact that there are several hundred mutual funds from which to choose requires that the investor do a substantial amount of homework. (2) Managers of the many fund portfolios have not been able to demonstrate fully that they are any better at picking the "right stocks" or better at "timing" their purchases and sales than anyone else; that is, very few funds have outperformed the market over the long term. (3) The pressure for management to sell and take an early profit is always present.

In summary, you might add the favorite stocks held by mutual funds to your own list developed and discussed at the beginning of this chapter. Since it takes the same skills for finding the right mutual fund as it does to size up stocks of corporations, you are just as well off selecting the companies you want to buy. Select 8 to 10 quality firms that meet your objectives by using the *Standard & Poor's* (Exhibit 10-2) or *Moody's* services. Approach this activity with the attitude of a hobby, an avocation, or a new learning experience. If you are an employee in a company that has an employee stock purchase program and automatic dividend reinvestment privileges, consider your own company for starters.

OTHER INVESTMENT STARTERS

The basic emphasis so far has been to consider stocks as another alternative in helping you reach your investment objectives. Common and preferred stocks have deserved our attention up to this time because information about stocks is readily available, there are tax incentives for stock ownership, they may serve as a hedge against inflation, and they are a type of investment for reaching long-term financial goals. The relatively small amount of money needed to purchase stocks should hold appeal for the beginning investor of modest means.

Other investment starters could include coins, stamps, antiques, furniture, carpets, and objects of art. The following words about these investments are merely highlights, and further *reading* should be undertaken before any serious commitments are made.

Coins and Stamps

Collecting coins and stamps can be a hobby as well as a long-term investment. The avid collector will eventually run into space and security problems and, at some point, will need to consider safe deposit boxes at the bank for storage.

If you are just beginning, limit your purchase to officially minted coins by national governments; the same is true for stamps. Banks and U.S Post Offices should be your major sources. If you deal with coin and stamp shops, the dealer should have a sound reputation in the community and have been in business for several years. A coin or stamp shop that operates in a major department store might be a wise choice since the store will be concerned with its integrity. The dealer should stand behind each sale and be ready to repurchase any coin sold to you, that is, offer a money-back guarantee.

Avoid metal medallions and commemorative sets offered by private corporations. These offerings are often sold at prices well above the value of the metal, and values tend to decrease, as the opportunity for resale is negligible.

Antiques, Furniture, and Carpets

Small antiques, good-quality furniture, and carpets tend to hold or increase in value and you can enjoy their use as well. Federal law defines antiques as items made prior to the year 1830. Collectors and dealers tend to call items 100 years old or older antiques.

Quality furniture and antique reproductions can be expected to hold their value particularly in times of high rates of inflation. To assure that you are obtaining quality furniture (1) take time to determine your furniture tastes, (2) deal only with the most reputable stores in the town where the sales representatives will take the time to explain about the maker and how to recognize quality construction and finishes, and (3) look at catalogs of furniture to help make design and purchase decisions.

Develop a long-term customer relationship if you are serious in this area. In this way, store representatives will learn your tastes and can call your attention to items that might interest you. Furniture and carpets should be purchased at

THE WALL STREET JOURNAL

"My investment portfolio? You're standing on it."

From *The Wall Street Journal*—
Permission, Cartoon Features Syndicate.

local firms rather than at sales conducted at hotels and motels. You do not want to risk your money with dealers who are only in town temporarily. This is also true of art and jewelry sales. Auctions are a specialized activity. If you are not careful, you can overspend on items at an auction. Price markups in antiques of quality and in good working order can run 100 percent. You will have to hold the item several years to gain a profit.

Think ahead. Will a particular item still appeal to you 10, 20, and 30 years from now? Will the item that looks nice in your present home fit in with an apartment or condominium in the future? Furniture fads come and go, and you probably do not want items that neither reflect your taste nor will rise in value.

Objects of Art

Paintings, sculptures, prints, porcelains, pottery, custom-made jewelry, calligraphic scrolls, and so on are collectibles that often reflect individual taste and personality. Objects of art should be acquired for personal enjoyment first and as investment second. Establish a budget and purchase sparingly.

SECURITIES AND EXCHANGE COMMISSION (SEC)

After the stock market crash of 1929 and during the "Great Depression" of the 1930s, major legislation was passed by the federal government to require financial disclosure on the part of corporations to protect the investor, regulate the securities sold in interstate commerce, and prevent fraud. The Securities Exchange Act of 1934 created the Securities and Exchange Commission, a five-member agency appointed by the president of the United States and operating with the advice and consent of the U.S. Senate. It serves as a watchdog over the securities field, and its powers extend to making investigations of both civil and criminal intent of people who attempt to violate the Securities Act of 1933, the Securities Exchange Act of 1934, the Investment Advisors Act of 1940, and the Investment Company Act of 1940.

In brief, the SEC is concerned with price fixing, fraudulent financial statements, creating false appearance of active trading in stocks, excessive churning of accounts, and regulating practices surrounding mutual funds. States may also regulate corporations whose stock is not offered to buyers across state lines. State securities laws are called "blue sky" laws.

INVESTING VERSUS SPECULATING

Investing is the purchasing of stocks, bonds, land, and so on with the intention of holding such assets for long periods of time with the anticipation of appreciation in the value of the assets and income in the form of dividends, interest, rent, and so on. *Speculating* involves the taking of *considerable* risk.

A person is speculating (1) when the funds used come from savings accounts normally set aside for family emergencies or contingency funds; (2) when money is being borrowed for only a short term and the interest is high; (3) when the account customer borrows common stock from the broker and sells the stock with the hope of buying back the stock at a cheaper price, known as *selling short*; (4) when the goal is to hold common stocks, preferred stocks, or mutual funds for only a few months; (5) when purchases are made in commodities contracts of corn, pork bellies, soy beans, copper, gold, tin, and so on; (6) when the transaction involves buying shares of stock in small corporations that have one or two products that are not well known or are in an industry where larger corporations could produce similar products; (7) when the total of speculative-grade investments exceeds 5 percent of total investments; and (8) when the buy or sell decision does not have the support of the individual's own homework.

The Securities and Exchange Commission has issued a list of 10 warning signals for investors.

1. Promises of spectacular returns or profits far exceeding those normally expected.
2. Sales approaches from strangers.
3. Rumors from friends, neighbors, and acquaintances about unusual investment opportunities.
4. Telephone calls from strangers, particularly in other cities, trying to persuade you to invest.
5. Use of post office boxes in connection with communications.
6. Failure to receive full information about the people involved, the terms of the offering, the financial condition of the enterprise, and its prior business record.
7. Promise of a solution to all your financial problems.
8. Pressure to make quick investment decisions.
9. Claims of a new or exotic product or enterprise.
10. Claims that you have been selected to "get in on the ground floor."

SUMMARY

Our goal in this chapter has been to remove some of the mystery surrounding investment in corporate stocks. Investing in corporate shares allows one to own a part of a business for only a small amount of money, serves as a hedge against inflation over the long run, receives favorable treatment in federal income tax rulings, and helps to accomplish long-term financial goals. Every specialty has its own language and so does investing. Stock trading in the United States is as old as the nation, which accounts for the myth, tradition, and folklore surrounding this business. The largest stock exchange in the United States is the New York Stock Exchange. The Securities and Exchange Commission is the major regulator of securities sold in interstate commerce. It serves to protect investors and to prevent fraud.

Before investing in stocks, have a financial and personality checkup. A starting point for selecting corporations for possible investment is a review of the products found in and around the home. *Moody's* and *Standard & Poor's* are financial advisory services that are very readable and can be found in public and college libraries.

A corporation is a group of people called shareholders organized to operate a business under a charter granted by a state. A common stock is a certificate of ownership in a corporate form of business. Cash dividends are often paid quarterly by major corporations. A stock dividend is not considered income for tax purposes.

Financial pages rely on the heavy use of abbreviations, basic numbers, and letters to provide the maximum information about a company. The two most popular indicators of stock market activity are the Dow Jones Industrial Average and the Standard & Poor's 500. The most common financial statements are the balance sheet, income statements, retained earnings statement, and the statement of changes of financial position. Most financial ratios attempt to determine the solvency, profitability, and quality of management in a company.

Opening a stock investment account is similar to opening a bank account. Individual accounts are insured up to $500,000 against brokerage house failure through the Securities Investor Protection Corporation. Commissions are charged when an investor purchases or sells securities. Dollar averaging is a simple way to acquire investments when price fluctuation is common. Mutual funds are corporations that sell their own stock to obtain money that, in turn, is invested in the securities market. Other basic investments for beginners are coins, stamps, antiques, furniture, carpets, and objects of art.

Exhibit 10-11 of the Basic Financial Pyramid illustrates the sequence at which time basic long-term investments might be appropriate. Because there is greater risk associated with the purchase of stocks and certain collectibles, major commitments in these areas should be made after insurance, emergency funds, savings, and housing needs are satisfied.

TIPS

1. When you purchase corporate stock, you are really buying management talent and know-how.
2. Look for corporations whose boards of directors have long service with th company and own a substantial number of shares in the firm. These people will take a major interest in the company's future.

EXHIBIT 10-11 Basic Financial Pyramid

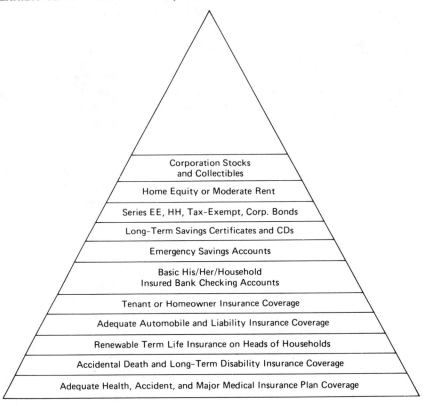

Corporation Stocks
and Collectibles

Home Equity or Moderate Rent

Series EE, HH, Tax-Exempt, Corp. Bonds

Long-Term Savings Certificates and CDs

Emergency Savings Accounts

Basic His/Her/Household
Insured Bank Checking Accounts

Tenant or Homeowner Insurance Coverage

Adequate Automobile and Liability Insurance Coverage

Renewable Term Life Insurance on Heads of Households

Accidental Death and Long-Term Disability Insurance Coverage

Adequate Health, Accident, and Major Medical Insurance Plan Coverage

3. An investment-grade company should have a well-educated management, diversity of products or product lines, adequate research and development funding for new products, and an upward trend in the past ten years in both sales and profits. The rate of earnings growth should be exceeding the inflation rate.

4. In recent years the profits of most businesses have been overstated because accounting and income tax laws do not make provisions for the higher replacement costs of future inventory needs or the higher costs of replacing worn-out or obsolete equipment.

5. As a long-term investor, keep in mind that, at any one time, some other investment will outperform yours.

6. Note particularly the 10-year trends in earnings, dividends, payout ratios, and prices of stocks. If the cost of living has doubled in the past 10 years, stock prices and dividends paid should reflect at least the same level of increase or more.

7. Businesses must remain solvent at all times to survive. Over the long run, the company must be profitable; in the short run a corporation may be in a cyclical business and experience losses in certain years.

8. The long-term investor should remember that news releases about labor strikes, new contracts or orders, federal government lawsuits, and so on generally have a short-term impact on a firm's operations.

9. Beware of percentage increases associated with business sales and profits. You may hear that X Company's profits were up 300 percent; it may mean that profits went from a penny per share to three cents a share. You must always know what the base is in any percentage-related data.

10. Remember that, for every seller of securities of a particular company, there must be a buyer for those same securities.

11. For more detailed financial information about a corporation, request the corporation's Form 10-K financial statements, which provide more information on the company's business and finances than does the annual report. Large corporations must file Form 10-K with the SEC.

12. When the national economy goes into a recession, even normally sound corporations face severe losses.

13. In interpreting earnings-per-share calculations, determine if increases resulted from profits or from a reduction of shares of stock. Take a long, hard look at a company's motives for reacquiring its common stock.

14. Factors affecting stock prices and trading volume in a free market economy include such things as bank and government holidays, religious holidays and long weekends, quarterly and yearly tax payment dates, and economic statistics such as the GNP, the CPI, unemployment, and the index of leading indicators.

15. On Thursdays and Fridays of each week, central banks around the world including the private banking systems' leaders in the Federal Reserve meet to assess a nation's money supply, prevailing interest rates, and amount of public and private debt. Any policy decisions taken or not taken are often made public after the close of the stock markets (local time). Therefore, Thursday and Friday trading can be influenced.

16. Today's long-term investor should consider a company's record in the areas of human rights, environment, criminal activity, and conduct of business in other nations.

ADDITIONAL READINGS

"A Guide to Mutual Funds," *Consumer Reports*, June 1987, pp. 352–64.

"Annual Reports: Focus on the Facts That Count," *Changing Times*, April 1985, pp. 75–81.

"Cheap Ways to Buy More Stock," *Changing Times*, January 1986, pp. 81–83.

"Financial Planners: What Are They Really Selling?" *Consumer Reports*, January 1986, pp. 37–44.

"Stock Market Basics for Beginners," *Changing Times*, June 1981, pp. 41–46.

Tobias, Andrew P., *The Only Investment Guide You'll Ever Need* (Rev. ed.). New York: Bantam, 1983.

GLOSSARY OF USEFUL TERMS

Acid-Test Ratio   Total cash, accounts receivable, and marketable securities divided by current liabilities. A key test of company solvency.

AMEX (American Stock Exchange, also called "the Curb")   Stock exchange located in New York City that lists over 600 corporations that are newer and smaller than those listed on the New York Stock Exchange.

Asking Price   Price at which a broker is willing to sell a security to a customer.

Bear   One who expects stock prices to drop.

Bear Market   A market in which stock prices are declining.

Bid Price   Price at which a broker is willing to buy a security from a customer.

Big Board   The New York Stock Exchange.

Blue Chip Stock   A term usually associated with the shares of the better known, better performing corporations of the United States.

Book Value per Share   Value of a company's assets minus liabilities divided by common stock outstanding.

Broker   A person who brings a buyer and a seller together for the purpose of handling a sale. The broker usually charges a commission for this service. The broker does not take title to the investment.

Bull   One who expects stock prices to rise.

Bull Market   A market in which stock prices are advancing.

Cash Dividend   A distribution of the profits of a corporation paid to stockholders. Cash dividends are often paid quarterly by major corporations. See *Stock dividend*.

Caveat emptor   Latin phrase meaning let the buyer beware, or buy at one's own risk.

Churning   A practice by some account executives to have the customer buy and sell stock without good reason. The practice generates extra commissions.

Closed-End Investment Company   A mutual fund with a fixed number of shares outstanding. The shares are traded on major stock exchanges. Also called a no-load mutual fund.

Common Stock   A certificate of ownership in a corporation. The holder usually has full voting rights and rights to profits after all other forms of debt and ownership have been paid.

Current Ratio   Total current assets divided by total current liabilities. Calculated from balance sheet information. A key test of company solvency.

Depreciation   Life of an asset used up over a period of time.

Disintermediation   Withdrawal of funds from savings accounts and their use to purchase U.S. Treasury bills and notes because of the latter's higher interest rates.

Dividend   *See* Cash Dividend.

Dow Jones Averages   An index of stock prices composed of four different averages of stock.

Equity Capital   Funds obtained for a business by selling ownership interests (common stock, preferred stock).

Fixed Dollar Media   Investments for which the return in interest is fixed by contract. Bank savings accounts and bonds are examples. Inflation causes these fixed media investments to erode in value.

Full-Bodied Money   Gold; money that is worth its face value as a commodity.

Growth Stocks Stocks of a company that are considered by investors to be growing at a faster rate than the economy as a whole.

Income Stocks Common stocks of company with a long, established record of regular dividends of dependable amounts for many years.

Intangible Assets Assets that have no form but do have value such as goodwill and patents.

Inventory Turnover The cost of goods sold or cost of sales for the year divided by the average inventory on hand.

Investing Purchasing stocks, bonds, land, and so on with the intention of holding them for long periods of time in anticipation of appreciation of assets and income in the form of dividends, interest, rent, and the like.

Investment Banks Financial institutions that purchase large blocks of stock from issuing companies for resale in the market.

Money Supply Total amount of currency and demand deposits in circulation in the United States; also known as M-1.

Mutual Funds Companies that sell their own stock to obtain money that, in turn, is invested in the securities market. The fund usually charges a commission for each share sold. Also called a load fund. When the mutual fund continuously issues new shares to investors, it is called an open-end mutual fund. When new shares are being issued, a prospectus is given to potential investor.

NASD (National Association of Securities Dealers) A self-regulating agency of over-the-counter dealers.

NASDAQ (National Association of Security Dealers Automated Quotations) Computerized quotation system for over-the-counter stocks.

Negotiable Instruments Stocks, bonds, promissory notes, and the like, that may have their ownership transferred from one party to another.

No-Load Fund Mutual funds that employ no salespersons and charge no commissions.

NYSE (New York Stock Exchange, also called the "Big Board") One of the largest and most important security exchanges in the world which includes the leading corporations in the United States.

Odd Lot Trading in shares of stock in lots of less than 100.

Over the Counter (OTC) Trading of unlisted securities outside the organized stock market.

Par Value An arbitrary amount assigned to a share of stock that has no relationship to either its current market value or its book value. Exists for accounting purposes.

Point On stock market price quotations, one point is equivalent to one dollar.

Portfolio Total securities held by an investor.

Preferred Stock A certificate of ownership in a corporation that usually entitles the holder to receive dividend payments before holders of common stock but has no voting rights.

Price—Earnings Ratio The market value of one share of common stock divided by its earnings.

Prospectus A booklet containing all information about a company that may affect the value of new securities that a company wants to issue.

Proxy Written authorization for another person to exercise another's vote.

Rate Earned on Owners' Equity   Profit divided by net worth or capital. Measures the amount of profit the ownership produces.

Rate of Return on Assets   Profit divided by total assets. Determines the efficient use of assets by management.

Round Lot   Trading in shares of stock in lots of 100.

Sales to Total Assets   Sales (or gross revenue) for a year divided by total assets. A test of efficient use of assets by management.

Seat   Membership on a stock exchange.

SEC (Securities and Exchange Commission)   See Securities Exchange Act of 1934.

Securities Act of 1933   Legislation designed to protect investors by regulating the sale of stock sold in interstate commerce and requiring companies to issue a prospectus when issuing new stock.

Securities Exchange Act of 1934   Legislation that established the Securities and Exchange Commission, the chief regulatory agency over corporations whose stocks are traded on major exchanges and corporations that do business inter-state.

Shares   *See* Stock Certificate.

S.I.P.C. (Securities Investor Protection Corporation)   A government organization whose purpose is to insure accounts of brokerage firms. Each account is insured up to the amount of $500,000.

Speculating   The purchase and sale of common stock, commodities, real estate, and the like with the intent of making a profit within a short period of time. Price fluctuation is emphasized over the quality of the thing purchased. High risk is involved in speculation. Compare with investing.

Standard & Poor's 500   An index of stock prices comprised of 400 industrial, 20 transportation, 40 utility, and 40 financial companies.

Stockbroker   A person who brings the buyer and seller of stocks together for a transaction. A commission is charged for this service.

Stock Certificate   A paper representing evidence of ownership in a corporation.

Stock Dividend   A payment to stockholders in the form of shares of stock instead of cash. It is not considered income in a real sense and therefore is not subject to income taxes.

Stock Exchange   A marketplace in which securities (stocks and bonds) are sold.

Stockholders   Owners of a corporation; persons who own common or preferred stock of a corporation.

Stock Split   A division of the outstanding shares of a corporation into a larger number of shares. A holder of 100 shares of stock before a split of, say, 2 for 1 would hold 200 shares after the split has taken place.

Warrant   An authorization to the owner of stock to buy that company's stock at a specified price for a specific period. Another term, *right,* is also a privilege to subscribe to new stock issues. Usually rights are contained in securities called warrants.

Working Capital   Funds used in the daily operations of the business for such purposes as payrolls, raw materials, and accounts receivable. A balance sheet calculation is made by taking total current assets and subtracting from it total current liabilities.

Yield   Income received on investments. It is usually expressed as a percentage of the market price of a security.

11

Income Taxes

LEARNING OBJECTIVES

Upon completion of Chapter 11, you should be able to identify and remember

- Concepts about the structure of the U.S. Internal Revenue Code and the purpose it serves.
- Common types of income that are considered taxable under the code as well as examples of items of income that are excluded in determining gross taxable income.
- Expenditures that qualify as being deductible from gross income, items deductible from adjusted gross income, and items not deductible under any circumstances.
- Develop a worksheet to assist in determining taxable income and income taxes.
- How to complete the simple 1040A or 1040 EZ tax return.

OVERVIEW

Earlier chapters referred to the Internal Revenue Code in terms of the federal income taxes that workers have deducted from their salaries and wages. Chapter 2 mentioned that our record-keeping system should provide for maintaining both current and past years' federal income tax records. Chapter 3 discussed the importance of one's disposable income and how it is more realistic to develop financial plans and budgets based upon income *after* the deduction of income taxes and Social Security taxes. The same chapter also described the importance of knowing your *marginal income tax bracket* so as to make a rapid calculation of just how much of each additional dollar earned can be kept for spending. Chapter 5 stated that U.S. Series EE savings bonds provide some flexibility for tax planning in that the taxes on the interest can be postponed at the election of the bondholder. The same chapter also noted that certain bonds of state and local governments are exempt from federal income taxes.

The purpose of this chapter is to draw together some thoughts about the very complex tax system and perhaps set the federal income tax laws into some workable or convenient perspective. A second goal is to help the reader to prepare his or her income tax return.

GAINING A PERSPECTIVE OF THE IRS CODE

Federal income tax legislation, as amended many times, first became law in 1913, just prior to World War I with the passage of the 16th Amendment of the U.S. Constitution wherein

> *The Congress shall have power to lay and collect taxes on incomes, from whatever source derived, without regard to any census or enumeration.*

While the Internal Revenue Code is adjusted somewhat at each session of Congress, most Americans will look to the Tax Reform Act of 1986 as a benchmark for both change and reform. For the individual, the reform has resulted in fewer and lower tax brackets. But whether the 1986 Act has brought about tax simplicity remains to be seen. One positive social objective has been to remove millions of the so-called working poor from having to file federal income tax returns. The next several paragraphs discuss some broad generalities about the American income tax system so the reader has a better understanding of the basics regardless of major reforms. The emphasis is on individuals rather than on corporations or other economic entities.

First, to be eligible to pay federal income taxes, an individual must be gainfully employed and have earned a taxable salary or wage, or have earned money through the act of saving and investing, or have obtained earnings by rendering some kind of service, or have won money or prizes as a result of a wager or contest. Retirement income from employer-sponsored pensions is also subject to federal income taxes. This is not to say that the unemployed, nongainfully employed, professional volunteer, or person relying completely on Social Security benefits do not pay taxes. They may be paying state and city sales taxes, county property taxes, state inheritance taxes, federal cigarette and gasoline taxes, federal excise taxes on tires or telephones, and so on, but they are not filing Form 1040 and paying federal income taxes.

Second, the IRS Code is complicated by the diversity of people's endeavors that go into making up the U.S. economic system. Certain parts of the code may be interpreted differently by those who read it, and this may require both the tax courts and the regular federal courts to make the final clarification. The code is simply a mirror of our complex economic society.

Third, federal income tax laws are used as a part of the government's *fiscal policy* to either stimulate or slow down the economy. By increasing or decreasing the amounts to be withheld from employee paychecks, the federal government can increase or decrease the amount of money in the hands of workers available for spending. This fiscal policy attempts to keep the nation from entering into either rapid inflationary times or times of prolonged recession or depression.

Fourth, preparation of an income tax return resembles the accounting and bookkeeping principles for compiling a profit and loss statement. Those who have prepared tax returns can readily identify with this notion. However, the IRS Code includes some rather arbitrary and sometimes rigid exceptions, provisions, credits, and allowances targeted to aid specific groups of people or businesses. These departures in the basic bookkeeping principles are due to the legitimate lobbying by special-interest groups in the House of Representatives and the Senate. Who are the lobbyists? They come from all sectors of our economy. They represent consumers, churches, businesses, education, labor, the health field, charities, state and local governments, highway interests, defense contractors, veterans, the elderly, lawyers, insurance and banking interests, and farmers. An endless stream of people is interested in seeing that "equitable taxation" takes place. If the tax break is not an equitable one, then it is likely to be viewed as a "loophole" for someone else. Raising the personal exemption to $1,950 or excluding up to $125,000 of capital gains on one's home at the time of sale are recent adjustments to the code that resulted from lobbying efforts.

Fifth, incorporated in the nation's early thinking was the philosophy that individuals tend to take better care of the nation's resources if they own those resources themselves. Another basic belief is that people should be allowed to pursue their own interests. These basic concepts probably did much to allow a *capitalistic* or *free enterprise* form of economy to grow in the United States. The IRS Code reflects these concepts by providing incentives (through allowed tax deductions or tax credits) for such things as buying a house, owning a business of your own, purchasing equipment, and investing in shares of stock in a corporation. Therefore, the tax system tends to favor those who take upon themselves greater economic or financial risks. One can readily see that the code allows ample provisions for those who buy a home rather than those who rent houses or apartments. The person who withdraws all his or her savings to start a business will receive many tax concessions. People who prefer to earn a salary as employees, save their money in an insured savings account, and retire on a company pension plan can expect to find fewer tax deductions. These tax incentives, it is hoped, will encourage people to own the resources of the nation or consider going into business for themselves, thereby creating jobs not only for themselves but for others as well. Colonel Sanders (fried chicken), Ray Kroc (McDonald's), and J. C. Penney (department stores) are people who not only created a job for themselves but also for thousands of others.

Sixth, the IRS Code tends to favor the traditional family unit over other household formations. This traditional family unit is usually one in which the husband works to earn income and the wife manages the home and cares for the children. The next most favorable tax treatment is for those who are married and only one is earning income. Third in order are those who qualify as heads of households. In general, married couples receive more tax concessions than do single individuals. This treatment raises the basic question of whether or not the IRS Code is really a "tax on income" as it claims to be. A true income tax should be based on a certain percentage of income earned without regard to whether a person plans to get married or not or to have a large family or not. Single, career-oriented people are particularly concerned with this issue as their rising incomes are subject to the progressive tax rates under the current code.

Seventh, present income tax laws assume that people will act in a prudent, rational, and responsible manner. There are few incentives for acts of carelessness, breaking the law, or not living up to contracts. The IRS does not let people deduct expenditures for traffic fines or criminal activity or other fines or penalties. The cost of a divorce (breaking a marriage contract) is not deductible. Loss of an item of value such as a diamond ring while swimming is not deductible. All income earned illegally is taxable, but the expenses associated with such income are not deductible. Child support money per se is neither income to the parent receiving it nor deductible by the parent paying it. The tax laws reflect the responsibility of both parents for the raising of children. And so on.

Eighth, consider the government's willingness to give assistance to the less fortunate, be they in this country or abroad. The code provisions reflect the desirability of giving money and certain types of property to charitable, educational, and religious organizations. Noninsured medical and dental expenses of certain amounts can also qualify as deductions for income tax determination. And the proceeds from a life insurance policy are not taxable to the person receiving it, though the premiums paid on a life insurance policy are not deductible for income tax purposes. (It should be noted, however, that life insurance proceeds might be subject to other forms of taxation such as a state inheritance tax.)

These generalities are but a sketch of the present income tax system of the federal government. If you are single, earning a good salary, living in an apartment, and enjoying good health, you will find yourself paying high federal income taxes. The same will be true for married couples both actively pursuing good jobs and having similar incomes. Conversely, if a person is sporadically employed, in marginal health, or responsible for the care of others, that person will find that most, if not all, of his or her income taxes withheld will be refunded. The person who goes into business for himself or herself will receive many tax incentives to reduce the income tax burden.

WHO MUST FILE

Whether one must file or not depends primarily on the amount of income earned. The following rules apply to U.S. citizens, resident aliens, nonresident aliens, and resident aliens who are married to citizens or residents of the United States at the end of the year. The rules will apply to persons under the age of 21. Persons will file form 1040EZ, 1040A, or 1040. Any tax owed to the Internal Revenue service is due on April 15. Newly hired employees must present proper documentation papers, show their Social Security card, and complete an Employee's Withholding Allowance Certificate, commonly called a W-4 form (Exhibit 11-1).

EXHIBIT 11-1 Employee's Withholding Allowance Certificate

Form **W-4A** Department of the Treasury Internal Revenue Service	**Employee's Withholding Allowance Certificate** ▶ **For Privacy Act and Paperwork Reduction Act Notice, see reverse.**	OMB No. 1545-0010 **1987**

1 Type or print your full name	2 Your social security number
Le Xuan Nguyen	123–45–6789

Home address (number and street or rural route)		
125 East Broad Street	3 Marital Status	[x] Single ☐ Married
City or town, state, and ZIP code		☐ Married, but withhold at higher Single rate
Anytown, CA 90083		**Note:** *If married, but legally separated, or spouse is a nonresident alien, check the Single box.*

4 Total number of allowances you are claiming (from line G above, or from the Worksheets on back if they apply) . . . | **4** | 1

5 Additional amount, if any, you want deducted from each pay . . . . | **5** $ | 0

6 I claim exemption from withholding because (check boxes below that apply):
  a [x] Last year I did not owe any Federal income tax and had a right to a full refund of **ALL** income tax withheld, **AND**
  b ☐ This year I do not expect to owe any Federal income tax and expect to have a right to a full refund of
      ALL income tax withheld. If both **a** and **b** apply, enter the year effective and "EXEMPT" here . . . ▶ | Year | 19
  c Are you a full-time student? . . . . | ☐Yes | [x] No

Under penalties of perjury, I certify that I am entitled to the number of withholding allowances claimed on this certificate or, if claiming exemption from withholding, that I am entitled to claim the exempt status.
Employee's signature ▶ *Le Xuan Nguyen*   Date ▶   March 5,   , 1987

7 Employer's name and address **(Employer: Complete 7, 8, and 9 only if sending to IRS)** | **8** Office code | **9** Employer identification number

TAXABLE INCOME

For income tax purposes, income is taxable, is excluded from taxes by statute law, or is not defined as income such as the return of borrowed money or the return of property or money that you already owned. The following is a partial alphabetical list of what the code considers *taxable income*:

Alimony received
Bonuses received as compensation
Business net profit (sales minus expenses)
Capital gains
Dividends from credit unions
Dividends in cash or check from corporations
Embezzlement proceeds
Gambling winnings
Interest on savings accounts from banks, savings and loans, mutual banks, bonds, and notes
Jury duty money or fees
Military retirement income
Partnership income or share of profits
Prizes and money received from contests
Professional fees earned
Rental income received
Retirement income, if you paid no part of its cost
Rewards
Royalties received
Salaries and wages
Tips earned
Unemployment benefits received

The following income is excluded from income for federal income tax purposes because of statute. Can you think of reasons why such items as the receipt of bequests, legacies, and gifts are not taxable? Do you see any difference in veterans' retirement income and veterans' disability compensation? Note the following exclusions:

Aid to dependent children
Bequests received
Car pool income received

Damages awarded received in personal injuries or accident insurance proceeds

Food stamps received or purchased

Gifts received

Interest on state, county, city, and school district bonds

Legacies received

Marriage settlements, lump sum received

Proceeds from an insurance policy where you were named the beneficiary

Scholarship received by student

Social Security benefits received under $25,000 on single return

The following examples are not considered income and therefore are not taxable:

The return of money loaned or borrowed

Dividends in the form of stock certificates of the same shares presently owned in that company

The return of one's original cash or capital assets on an investment

If you have difficulty in determining the status of these last items, it could be that you may have paid the taxes on them at some time in the past.

ADJUSTMENTS TO INCOME

Calculating taxable income is similar to preparing an income statement whereby revenue is first determined. Then expenses are deducted to arrive at the net profit or income for the period. Preparing a personal income tax return follows the same general outline except that the expenses allowed are established by the IRS Code. These *allowable* expenses seem to come under two broad and rather vague headings: (1) those that are business oriented or employment related or generated and (2) those that are allowed even though they are more personal or personally generated.

Deductions Allowed for Those Who Itemize

Moving expenses (for moves over 35 miles)

Unreimbursed employee business expenses

Medical and dental expenses in excess of 7.5 percent of adjusted gross income

Income taxes paid to state and local governments

Property taxes paid to state and local governments (No deductions are allowed for state and local sales taxes and gasoline taxes.)

Charitable contributions

Interest paid on mortgages of first and second homes

Forty percent of the interest incurred on allowed credit cards, auto loans, and other consumer loans (No deduction is allowed after 1988.)

Interest on loans to buy stock with some restrictions

Union dues, professional journals, job hunting costs, fees paid to tax preparers and investment counselors, and tuition expenses to the extent that they exceed 2 percent of adjusted gross income

Noninsured casualty or theft losses in excess of 10 percent of adjusted gross income

The following expenditures are *not* allowed as deductions:

Car pool expenses

Driver's license

Funeral expenses

Gambling losses in excess of gambling winnings

Hunting and fishing licenses

Losses resulting from transactions between members of a family

Losses or expenses incurred in committing a crime

Normal living expenses—food, clothing, personal care

Pet licenses and care

Vacation expenses

Standard Deductions in 1988 (Zero Bracket Amount)

It is important to remember that itemized deductions as a grand total must still exceed these standard deductions:

$5,000 on a joint return

$3,000 on those filing single returns

$4,400 for heads of households

Those who have simple life-styles and are in general good health, live in a rented house or apartment, and earn practically all their income in a salary usually find the 1040EZ short form most useful. On the other hand, if you have recently purchased a home and have a large mortgage, have a salary and income in interest or dividends, incurred major medical care costs not completely covered by insurance, or are in business for yourself, then the 1040 long form may either be required or be to your advantage. It is important for "nonitemizers" to subtract (1) their appropriate standard deduction and (2) personal exemptions from their adjusted gross income. Personal exemptions are discussed in more detail in the next section.

EXEMPTIONS

Exemptions have something to do with allowances for basic human existence. The taxpayer will always receive one exemption for himself or herself. An additional exemption can be claimed on the day a person reaches 65 years of age. The exemption for each tax filer and dependent is $1,950 in the year 1988. Nonitemizing filers get extra standard deductions of (1) for taxpayer and spouse, $600 for each condition of blindness, (2) $600 if they are more than 65 years of age when filing a joint return, or (3) $750 per condition on a single return.

If the taxpayer is married and qualifies, the taxpayer's husband or wife is also entitled to claim the over-65 and blindness exemptions. It is important to note that these extra exemptions cannot be applied to any other dependent such as a blind child or an elderly parent who is supported by the taxpayer.

Federal Income Tax Tables for 1988

One radical change in the Tax Reform Act of 1986 was the reduction of several tax brackets to just two. With the exception of very-high-tax payers the figures shown in Table 11-1 would be used:

TABLE 11-1 Federal Income Tax Brackets for 1988

Income bracket	Pay base tax of	Plus % of amount over lower bracket
1. Married Couples Filing Jointly		
$0–29,749	$ 0	15%
$29,750 and over	4,463	28
2. Single Filers		
$0–17,849	$ 0	15%
$17,850 and over	2,678	28
3. Heads of Households		
$0–23,899	$ 0	15%
$23,900 and over	3,585	28

Exemptions for Children and Other Dependents

To claim an exemption for dependent children and others, there are five tests to be met: (1) The dependent must receive less than a specified amount of income. (2) The dependent received over half his or her support from the taxpayer during the year. (3) The dependent who is married did not file a joint return with his or her spouse. (4) The dependent was a citizen or resident of the United States, a resident of Canada or Mexico, or an alien child adopted by and living with a U.S. citizen in a foreign country. (5) The dependent was (a) related to you or to your spouse if you are filing jointly (the relationship is determined by lineage, the law, and blood); (b) any other person who lived in your home as a member of your household for the *whole year*. If all five tests are met, an exemption can be claimed.

You can take an exemption for a dependent who was born or died during the tax year or even a child who was born and lived only a few minutes. A child as the term applies to income taxes includes your son, daughter, stepson, stepdaughter, or child who lived in your home as a member of your family if placed with you by an authorized placement agency for legal adoption. A foster child who lived in your home as a member of your family for the *whole year* would also qualify. Note the following paragraphs about dependents:

1. *Student dependent.* You may still claim your child as a dependent even though he or she had income if that child meets the tests in 2, 3, and 4 of the preceding list of exemptions. To qualify, the student (your child) has to have been enrolled as a full-time student at an educational organization during any five months of the tax year or has to have taken a full-time, on-farm training course during any five months of the calendar year. The educational organization must also meet certain criteria for income tax purposes.

2. *Children of divorced or separated parents.* Usually, the parent who has custody of the child for the greater part of the year can take the exemption. For 1977 and after, major changes were made in this area, and the parent may now take the exemption if the parent gave at least a specific minimum support during the year, and the decree of divorce or separate maintenance states that he or she can take the exemption, that the parent gave $1,200 or more for *each* child's support during the year, and that the parent having custody cannot prove that he or she gave more than the other parent gave. A parent who has remarried and has custody may count the support furnished by the new spouse.

3. *Dependent supported by two or more taxpayers.* When several children contribute to the care of their parents, the parent or parents being no longer able to care adequately for themselves, none of the children singularly contributes the necessary "more than half" amount that the IRS rule requires. A special rule applies when two or more taxpayers together paid more than half of another person's support. If the taxpayer paid at least 10 percent of the support and has

received a signed multiple support (Form 2120) from each of the other persons who provided more than 10 percent, the taxpayer can claim the exemption for the year.

RECORD KEEPING

As was discussed in Chapter 2, our record system should include data for federal income tax preparation. At the simplest level, there should be two file folders: one labeled "Federal Income Taxes, Current Year" and the other labeled "Federal Income Taxes, Prior Years." These two folders should be sufficient if the taxpayer files the simplified 1040 forms each year. On the other hand, it may be necessary to establish a series of folders or a separate portable file box so that one's tax records are properly maintained for the past several years. This more sophisticated record system will be needed if one acquires rental property, opens a small business, begins farming, or enters into rather complicated investment transactions.

As for the question, "How long must I keep my tax records?" there is no one answer. The IRS is required to perform a basic audit within two or three years after receiving a return. But this does not mean that you should throw away all your old tax-related records. If the IRS suspects that a taxpayer has illegally evaded paying the proper amount of taxes of several years ago, legal action can still take place. Records relating to the purchase of a home, for example, should be maintained for as long as one keeps the home; this would include expenditures for home improvements and fixing-up expenses in preparation of a sale.

Information of alleged wrongdoings by a taxpayer may come to the IRS from a former disgruntled employee or a former spouse. This may cause the IRS to make an investigation that might go back several years. The IRS may be interested in a decedent's tax history if death were from some unusual circumstance. Large sums of cash discovered in a safe deposit box of a deceased person may also cause inquiry, and the IRS may immediately claim taxes against it. If you are affluent or are holding a responsible job or public position in your community, you can anticipate investigation of your financial transactions; if you have any political aspirations, make sure that your income tax records as well as your financial activities are spotless.

WORKSHEET FOR DETERMINING INCOME TAXES

Chapter 3 provided many of the basic worksheet formats for compiling gross income and accounting for federal income taxes and Social Security taxes as well as for the many categories of personal expenses a household might encounter for a year. Exhibit 3-5 illustrated a format for a family master budget. Ideally, a person should be considering both the household budgeting and income tax planning at the same time. A taxpayer should be able to estimate total income and total taxable income for the year and also *have at all times* a close approximation of the amount of income taxes that are actually being deducted. The actual deductions should be adequate to cover your actual tax liability when it comes due in April. Since tax returns may be revised or modified each year, it is suggested that you develop a simple worksheet to prepare a sketch of your estimated income, allowed deductions, taxable income, and taxes owed. One of these worksheet estimates of total income and taxes should be developed by November of each year. This allows most taxpayers the time to legally "move" cash income or expenses into this year or postpone it to the following year.

The following case studies are designed to apply to some of the tax situations for a calendar year and are offered to show how to handle specific tax provisions being allowed at this time; the worksheet approach is also designed to call attention to several of the more common ways to shelter some of one's income from immediate tax. These four case studies progress from the simplest—that of a single taxpayer—to the most complex—that of a family that itemizes its personal deductions.

Case 1

William B. Single earned a gross salary of $10,500 for the calendar year and had $975 withheld from his salary. These data were shown on the W-2 statement he received in the following January. William is 25 years of age, not blind, and has no other dependents. Furthermore, William had no other sources of income during the year. The correct amount of Social Security taxes was taken out of his paycheck. His allowable itemized deduction amounted only to $345. William could draft the following worksheet for calculating his tax liability even without the 1040EZ form for reference (Exhibit 11-2). Since William will receive a refund, it is to his advantage to file his return as soon as possible after he receives his W-2 statement from his employer. If he were to have paid additional taxes, he would be better off filing his return around the beginning of April.

Case 2

Jane Carter is a single parent, age 35, has good vision, and provides a home and contributes the complete support for her son, Gregory, who is 6 years old. Jane's earnings for the year as a hospital employee amounted to $7,500. She earned $75

EXHIBIT 11-2 Suggested Worksheet Approach
For Filing Income Tax Forms 1040EZ and 1040A, Case I

(a) Name: *William B. Single* filing as a *single* _____.
(b) Total number of personal exemptions claimed *1* _____.

1. Estimated wages, salaries, and tips for year: $*10,500.00*
2. Estimated interest and dividends for year: $_____ *.00*
3. Add lines 1 and 2. This is your adjusted gross income: $ *10,500.00*
4. Enter appropriate standard deduction: $*3,000.00*
   $5,000 for a joint return
   $3,000 for a single return
   $4,400 for a head of household
5. Total personal exemptions __*1*__ × $1,950: $*1950.00*
6. Add line 4 and line 5 and enter the amount: $*4,950.00*
7. Subtract line 6 from line 3 above. This is your taxable income: $*5,550.00*
8. Enter estimated federal income taxes withheld: $ *975.00*
9. Calculation of tax:
   (a) If line 7 is less than $29,749 for joint return, $17,849 for single return, or $23,899 for H. of H., multiply amount on line 7 *5,550.00* × .15: $ *832.50*

   or

   (b) If line 7 is more than $29,750 for a joint return, $17,850 for single return, or $23,900 H. of H.,
      Joint: $4,464 plus .28 of excess over $29,750
      Single: $2,678 plus .28 of excess over $17,850
      H. of H.: $3,585 plus .28 of excess over $23,900
      Base $_____ plus .28 of excess: $_____
10. Compare your calculation with the amount entered on line 8 to determine whether you have a tax refund or have a remaining balance due to the IRS: *Refund* $ *142.50*

of interest from a savings account and $15 from a credit unit account at the hospital. ABC Company stock, received as a gift several years ago from her parents, paid dividends of $100. Jane has been buying small Series EE savings bonds on a payroll deduction plan at the hospital. Although the bond chart indicates that she has earned $10 of interest on the savings bonds this year, she elects to defer recognizing the interest income for tax purposes (see Exhibit 11-3). When Jane filed out her W-2 form, her employer determined that no federal income taxes should be withheld.

EXHIBIT 11-3 Suggested Worksheet Approach
For Filing Income Tax Forms 1040EZ and 1040A, Case 2

(a) Name: *Jane Carter*_____ filing as a *Head of Household*.
(b) Total number of personal exemptions claimed __2__.

1. Estimated wages, salaries, and tips for year: $ _7,500.00_
2. Estimated interest and dividends for year: $ ___190.00_
3. Add lines 1 and 2. This is your adjusted gross income: $ _7,690.00_
4. Enter appropriate standard deduction: $_4,400.00_
   $5,000 for a joint return
   $3,000 for a single return
   $4,400 for a head of household
5. Total personal exemptions __2__ × $1,950: $_3,900_
6. Add line 4 and line 5 and enter the amount: $_8,300.00_
7. Subtract line 6 from line 3 above. This is your taxable
   income: $_(610)_
8. Enter estimated federal income taxes withheld: $___0_
9. Calculation of tax:
   (a) If line 7 is less than $29,749 for joint return, $17,849
       for single return, or $23,899 for H. of H., multiply
       amount on line 7 _____ × .15: $_____
                              or
   (b) If line 7 is more than $29,750 for a joint return,
       $17,850 for single return, or $23,900 H. of H.,
       Joint: $4,464 plus .28 of excess over $29,750
       Single: $2,678 plus .28 of excess over $17,850
       H. of H.: $3,585 plus .28 of excess over $23,900
       Base $_____ plus .28 of excess: $_____
10. Compare your calculation with the amount entered on line
    8 to determine whether you have a tax refund or have a
    remaining balance due to the IRS: $___0___

Case 3

Jill Sanders is 45 years of age and has good vision. Jill is a single parent and provides a home and contributes the complete support for her daughter, Kim, who is 12 years old. Jill was divorced 5 years ago. In the settlement, she received the house and furniture but no other income or property. With the rising cost of heating and other utilities and maintenance, she was no longer able to afford the cost of her home on her salary as a secretary. She sold the house three years ago and has since moved into a more modest apartment with more security. She and her former husband purchased the home in 1968 for $25,000. When she sold the house there was still a $20,000 mortgage outstanding. She sold the house for $75,000, and, after paying off the mortgage, the sales commissions, federal income taxes, and relocating costs, she still had $50,000 remaining. She has invested the money over the past two years with $30,000 in long-term certificates of deposit, $10,000 in U.S. Series EE savings bonds, and $10,000 in U. S. Series H bonds. This is a prudent plan to follow until Jill learns more about investing. Jill will have to file her return as a head of household. Jill's salary for the year was $14,200, and her employer withheld $1,100 for the period. See Exhibit 11-4.

Case 4

Jim and Mary Johnson are married and filing a joint return. They are both under the age of 65 and have good vision. They have one child, Mark, who is 9 years old. Both Jim and Mary work, Jim as a maintenance worker and Mary as a school bus driver for nine months out of the year. Jim's salary was $18,500 for the year, and Mary's wages came to $13,000. Both had the proper amounts withheld for federal income taxes and Social Security. Jim's W-2 form shows that $2,300 was withheld on the federal income tax. Mary's withholdings were $1,400 for the year. Total bank savings interest, certificate of deposit interest, and credit union dividends (considered as interest) totaled $785 for the year. Mary has some U.S. Series EE savings bonds on which $140 of interest had been earned, but Mary elects to defer recognizing the interest on them.

The Johnsons own several shares of XYZ Corporation common stocks, on which dividends of $1,200 was earned. They sold shares in ABC Company earlier in the year. They earned a capital gain profit of $3,050 after holding this investment for several years. Jim and Mary own a modest home which they have rented out to a retired person. The net income on the rental amounted to $640 after taxes, maintenance, and depreciation. A couple of years ago Mary wrote a booklet on school bus drivers' rights and responsibilities. Her copyrighted booklet is used by many school district training programs. She earned $175 royalties for the year from her publisher. Jim did some freelance maintenance for a retirement home run by a local religious organization. He received $250 for his work. They own two bonds issued by their school district. They earned $120 tax-exempt income. While exempt for tax purposes, it must be disclosed on the tax form.

There is one downward adjustment to income: the deduction of $2,400 that Jim must pay each year in alimony to his former wife per a court settlement. As for other deductions, most medical expenses and medicines were covered by insurance. The out-of-pocket costs are way below the 7.5 percent of adjusted gross income requirement. The allowable state and local property and income taxes amounted to $1,212: charitable contributions were $500; interest paid on their home mortgage was $3,650; and miscellaneous expenses for Jim and

EXHIBIT 11-4 Suggested Worksheet Approach
For Filing Income Tax Forms 1040EZ and 1040A, Case 3

(a) Name: *Jill Sanders*   filing as a *head of household*
(b) Total number of personal exemptions claimed **2**

---

1. Estimated wages, salaries and tips for year: **$14,200.00**
2. Estimated interest and dividends for year: **$ 2,500.00**
3. Add lines 1 and 2. This is your adjusted
   gross income: **$16,700.00**
4. Enter appropriate standard deduction: **$4,400.00**
      $5,000 for a joint return
      $3,000 for a single return
      $4,400 for a head of household
5. Total personal exemptions **2** × $1,950: **$3,900.00**
6. Add line 4 and line 5 and enter the amount: **$ 8,300.00**
7. Subtract line 6 from line 3 above. This is your taxable
   income: **$ 8,400.00**
8. Enter estimated federal income tax withheld: **$ 1,100.00**
9. Calculation of tax:
      (a) If line 7 is less than $29,749 for joint return,
          $17,849 for single return, or $23,899 for
          H. of H., multiply amount on line 7 $**8400** × .15:   **$ 1,260.00**

                            or

      (b) If line 7 is more than $29,750 for a joint return,
          $17,850 for single return, or $23,900 for
          H. of H.,
             Joint: $4,464 plus .28 of excess over
                $29,750
             Single: $2,678 plus .28 of excess over
                $17,850
             H. of H.: $3,585 plus .28 of excess over
                $23,900
             Base $_____ plus .28 of excess: $
10. Compare your calculation with the amount entered on   *Balance due.*
    line 8 above to determine whether you have a tax
    refund or have a remaining balance due to the IRS: **$ 160**

Mary's union dues, trade journals, safe deposit rental for investment papers totaled $864. The deductible portion with the amount remaining in excess of 2 percent of adjusted gross income. The Johnsons suffered a casualty loss of trees and shrubs due to a prolonged and unusually severe dry season. The uninsured portion still did not meet the required excess of 10 percent of adjusted gross income. They claim three exemptions. The following worksheet (Exhibit 11-5) shows their tax liability.

EXHIBIT 11-5　Suggested Worksheet Approach
For Filing Income Tax Form 1040, Case 4

(a)　Name _Jim and Mary Johnson_ filing as a _joint return_.
(b)　Total number of personal exemptions claimed:　_3_.

INCOME

1.　Estimated wages, salaries, tips for the year (from W-2s)	$31,500
2.　(a)　Estimated taxable interest for the year	785
(b)　Show amount of tax-exempt interest in box　$\boxed{\$120}$	
3.　Estimated dividend income from stocks	1,200
4.　Capital gains and (losses)	3,050
5.　Net income or loss from rental property	640
6.　Net income or (loss) from a business	
7.　Royalty income	175
8.　Other income	250
9.　Total Income	$37,600

ADJUSTMENTS

10.　Keogh payments and alimony paid	$2,400
11.　IRA account deposits (omit if covered by pension plans)	
12.　Allowed moving expenses	
13.　Other adjustments	
14.　Total of adjustments	$2,400
15.　Adjusted Gross Income (AGI)	$35,200

DEDUCTIONS

16.　Medical and dental expenses in excess of 7.5% of AGI	$
17.　Allowable state and local taxes	1,212
18.　Charitable contributions	500
19.　Interest paid on first and second homes	3,650.

EXHIBIT 11-5 (*continued*)

20. Allowed credit card, auto loan interest (40% of the total is allowed for 1988; no deduction is allowed after 1988) $ _____

21. Allowed interest on investments   _____

22. Miscellaneous expenses exceeding 2% of AGI   *160*

23. Other expenses and casualty losses   _____

24. Total Deductions $ *5,522*

25. Enter appropriate Standard Deduction $ *5,000*
       $5,000 JR, $3,000 SR, $4,400 H of H

26. Enter here the larger number of line 24 or line 25   *5,522*

27. Subtract line 26 from line 15 above (AGI) $ *29,678*

28. **EXEMPTIONS:** *3* × $1950   *5,850*

29. **TAXABLE INCOME:** Subtract line 28 from line 27 $ *23,828*

30. Tax from table $ *3,574*

31. Taxes withheld during the year (and allowed credits)   *3,700*

32. Determine your amount of refund or additional taxes due $ *126 Refund*

	Income bracket	Pay base tax of	Plus % of amount over lower bracket
1.	Married Couples Filing Jointly		
	$0–29,749	$ 0	15%
	$29,750 and over	4,463	28
2.	Single Filers		
	$0–17,849	$ 0	15%
	$17,850 and over	2,678	28
3.	Heads of Households		
	$0–23,899	$ 0	15%
	$23,900 and over	3,585	28

MISCELLANEOUS

It may be too early to say, but the Tax Reform Act of 1986 is just one more piece of evidence that America is changing. The U.S. economy has done relatively poorly in the emerging global economy, and the U.S. federal income tax system must begin to influence decisions of individuals and businesses in an effective, efficient, and productive way. Individuals must be encouraged to save more and spend less. Investors and businesses must look to the increased productivity and profitability of a venture rather than sheltering of income from federal taxes.

The tax system may still not have addressed concerns of the eroding middle-class population in America. The new code seems to have businesses and the wealthy shouldering more of the tax burden and taking some of the sting of the ever-growing ranks of the full-time and part-time working poor.

The 1986 Reform Act has created a popular but questionable concept of the "home equity loan." Since interest paid on car loans is no longer deductible, lending institutions have now made it possible to use your home mortgage and your home equity to cover the car loan. During the auto loan payoff period the interest incurred just becomes part of your interest expense on the home mortgage, which is still tax deductible. This highly advertised financial device could be very risky to the consumer. Chances are the new lower tax brackets, the higher standard deduction, and higher dependency exemption really make the home equity loan program of marginal value.

SUMMARY

The federal income tax system reflects concepts regarded as important by the people of the nation. Remember, too, that the tax laws are actively used either to stimulate or to slow down the economy. Who must file an income tax return depends primarily on the amount of income earned and one's filing status. Not all income received by a taxpayer is taxable, and some income is excluded by statutes. Expenses allowable for income tax purposes tend to be those related to business and those primarily personal but allowed. Dependents are usually persons for whom the taxpayer provides a home and contributes more than half their support. If the dependent meets five specific tests, the taxpayer may claim the person as an exemption, which will lower the taxpayer's tax liability. The IRS requires the taxpayer to keep records to support such deductions.

Developing worksheets can help the taxpayer to maintain a uniform method for estimating income tax liability when tax forms are not available for reference. The taxpayer of average income has several alternatives to shield income from being taxed immediately or completely through homebuying, acquiring U.S. savings bonds, and buying tax-exempt municipal bonds. Long-range financial planning requires that the taxpayer know his or her marginal tax bracket. Investment decisions directed at lowering one's federal income taxes should be based on whether or not the decision will affect one's cash flow adversely and are compatible with one's life-style.

TIPS

1. Save newspaper articles that relate to changes in tax laws and include tax-saving tips of interest to individual taxpayers.

2. Prepare a worksheet of your estimated taxable income and tax deductible related expenditures in November. This will allow you time to shift expenses into this taxable year or postpone them to the next taxable year.

3. File early after the end of the tax year if you expect a refund.

4. Claiming fewer exemptions and even having additional specific amounts withheld from your wages can help to match more closely the actual tax liability to avoid having to write a large check or having to borrow money to pay your income taxes.

5. Claiming fewer exemptions and having additional dollar amounts withheld can be a way of saving money for specific financial goals, particularly if you find saving money very difficult. Do not worry that the money will not earn any interest. Consider the interest not earned as a tuition fee for learning how to save.

6. Remember the rule of thumb that, if the income is not taxed or it is specifically exempted from taxes, then the expenses related to that income are usually not deductible (as in life insurance proceeds, car pool income, income from municipal bonds, Social Security income, etc.).

7. While tax literature often concentrates on the deductibility and limitations of specific rules, do not overlook the fact that one should concentrate on earning a higher income and remaining solvent.

8. If you have capital losses, you can deduct up to $3,000 to offset your taxable income.

9. If you moved during the year and the distance was over 35 miles, you may deduct premove house-hunting and temporary living expenses.

10. You may exclude the gain on the sale of a home from taxes for an amount up to $125,000 on a one-time basis, providing you meet all qualifications.

ADDITIONAL READINGS

"Don't Let the IRS Scare You," *Changing Times*, March 1980, pp. 29–32.
"Income-Tax Guides," *Consumer Reports*, March 1985, pp. 129–32.
Karmin, Monroe W., "The Bad News for the Middle Class," *U.S. News & World Report*, June 30, 1986, pp. 43–45.

GLOSSARY OF USEFUL TERMS

Accounting Period   A 12-month period used as the basis for a taxpayer's records.

Adjusted Gross Income   The gross income of the taxpayer minus the deductions from gross income that are allowed by the tax laws.

Aliens   Persons living in the United States who are not citizens of the United States.

Alimony   Payments made by one party to another under divorce decree or separate maintenance agreement, with no restrictions on the use of the money by the recipient.

Arm's-Length Transaction   A concept frequently used by the IRS and the law that considers circumstances surrounding a transaction between a buyer and a seller. Often gains and losses resulting from transactions among members of a family are disallowed or omitted from income tax determination.

Capital Assets   For the IRS it means any property other than that used in a trade or business; capital assets include stocks, bonds, residences, personal automobiles, household furnishings, and jewelry.

Capital Gain   A gain realized upon the disposition of a capital asset.

Contributions   Monetary and nonmonetary gifts made to qualified charities but not to private individuals.

Earned Income   Includes wages, salaries, tips, or other employee compensation, but not Social Security benefits, interest, dividends, capital gains, rents, royalties, pensions, or annuity payments.

Exclusions   Certain revenues and gains that can be excluded in the computations of taxable income.

Filing Status   The taxpayer's marital status, age, amount of earned income, other income, and other relevant data.

Form 1040   The basic form used to file the individual and joint federal income tax return. The short forms are called Form 1040A and 1040EZ.

Gross Income   All income not excluded by law.

Itemized Deductions   Allowed individual expenditures composed of interest expenses, state and local taxes, charitable contributions, medical and dental expenses, casualty losses, and so on with certain limitations.

Progressive Tax   A tax that collects an increasingly larger percentage from the taxpayer at rising income levels.

Qualified Dependent   A person meeting the five dependency tests of the taxpayer (age, support, relation to taxpayer, marital status, citizenship, or residency).

Salaries   Compensation paid to employees by employer usually on a weekly, biweekly, monthly, or yearly basis.

Spouse   Husband or wife of taxpayer.

Tax Avoidance   The legitimate reduction of tax liability by taking advantage of laws and regulations that reduce taxes due.

Tax Evasion   The underpayment of taxes due by illegal means.

Total Income   All income from whatever source derived.

W-2 Form   Form showing the amount of gross salaries and wages earned for the past 12 months and the amounts of income and Social Security taxes (FICA) withheld.

W-4 Form   Form filed by employee authorizing employer to withhold income taxes based on the number of deductions shown and sworn to on the W-4.

Wages   Compensation paid to employee by employer usually on a per hour basis.

12

Retirement

Upon completion of Chapter 12, you should be able to identify and remember

- The number of years ahead before your retirement, the year in which you plan to retire, and an estimate of the number of years that you might spend in retirement.
- Factors to consider in developing a retirement program.
- Expected total annual retirement income needs for maintaining a comfortable standard of living during a period of inflation.
- The four basic financial planning tables for income-planning purposes.
- A list of specific activities, major financial purchases, and personal decisions to be contemplated in those years just prior to retirement.

OVERVIEW

As we noted in Chapter 1, of 100 persons reaching the age of 65, some 84 will probably have no savings accumulated to provide an income. That is, there will be no cash income available in the future. For these people their only cash income will be from employment, Social Security benefits, cash, and commodities and services received from social welfare agencies, charitable organizations, family, friends, and so on. Many of these same people reaching retirement may have a house, furniture, a car, and other items of value. However, these assets will not by themselves produce weekly or monthly amounts of cash income. Cash will be forthcoming only when these assets are sold or rented.

Why are there so many people in this precarious position? The reason is that many of the people are women who have spent their years as wives and home-makers raising and caring for a family. And many working men and women were never able to save for any investments of the kind that would provide them with cash income in the form of dividends, interest, profits, or rent. Other groups of this large category of people without savings are the disabled, those incapacitated by physical or mental stress, victims of alcohol and drug abuse, and those who will spend long years in various institutions. The other 16 people in the sample of 100 reaching 65 will have been more or less successful in accumulating assets that provide them with periodic receipts of cash beyond income from subsistence programs.

In our overview, let us explore the topic of retirement a little further. How do men and women view retirement? A career man or woman employed 20, 30, or 40 years at jobs will retire from the job market to some other activity. That is, these people will leave their working routines, co-workers, commuting, vacations, and so on. They may retire with a company or independent retirement program and also receive Social Security or similar benefits. Be they single, married, or widowed, their environment will remain relatively unchanged.

For someone whose career has centered on the home (as a wife, mother, and homemaker), retirement needs are more difficult to determine. And, should a person become widowed or divorced in the middle years, his or her environment will change drastically and most likely for the worse—no salable or current job skills, no job, and maybe no adequate income but perhaps too well-off to qualify for welfare. With no salable or dated skills, these divorced or widowed individuals constitute a growing segment of the adult population in the United States.

What does retirement mean to you? Will retirement mean moving to a new community, establishing new roots, and making new friends? Do you really have the personality and temperament to make such a move? If you are married, will retirement mean doing those things that you *both* enjoy?

Do the numbers "2010" bring to mind a movie title rather than a retirement date? Have you thought much about the year in which you might retire? Suppose that you are 42 years old in the year 1990 and that you plan to retire at the age of 65. You have approximately 23 years still ahead of you before you retire. Your year of retirement at 65 would be 2013. If you are 22 years of age in 1990 and plan to retire at age 65, your retirement year will be 2033. If you retire at age 70, your retirement year will be 2038. If you are presently earning $10,000 per year and the annual rate of inflation remains at 6 percent, your *annual* salary in the last working year (2038) will have to be around $180,000 just to stay even. It is no wonder that inflation is the overriding concern for anyone contemplating retirement. Can a person of average means afford to retire if the inflation rate remains at 6 percent or higher? Yes, but only if you make retirement a long-term goal and you plan for it.

CHANGES IN THE TRADITIONAL RETIREMENT AGE

Until recently, age 65 was the magic year for retirement. German Chancellor Otto von Bismark arbitrarily selected 65 as old age when he established the world's first state-supported old age pension system in 1889. Age 65 was also a benchmark in the U.S. Social Security programs implemented in the 1930s. Many corporations adopted mandatory retirement at the age of 65 for both executives and other employees. Insurance companies have structured many of their policies and benefits around the age 65. In the United States, some 5,000 people per day reached their 65th birthday. In 1900, only 1 person in 25 was 65 or older; today it is 1 in 10. In 2025, it may be 1 in 6.

Recent changes in Social Security survivor benefits reflect awareness of changing life-styles such as the following who can get survivor benefits: "Divorced widow or widower after 10 years of marriage—full benefits at 65 or any age if caring for an entitled child (under 16 or disabled) of the deceased worker. Reduced payments at 60 (or 50 if disabled). Remarriage after 60 (50 if disabled) will not prevent the payment of benefits . . .". Many state and local governments as well as some businesses have raised the retirement age or abandoned mandatory retirement.

There are certain factors contributing to the changes in traditional retirement ages. First, the U.S. Social Security funding programs have recently reviewed by a presidential commission. The program has been adjusted to accommodate the retiring baby-boom generation starting in the years 2015. But many people are apprehensive beyond that era. Social Security taxes have been among the fastest-rising taxes in the United States in the decade, with the tax in 1970 being $374.40 and in 1980 $1,587.67. No doubt, the Social Security program as we know it today will go through many changes in the next 40 years. Unfortunately, far too many people still consider their Social Security benefits as a retirement program. Social Security cannot provide you with anything like a "carefree" retirement. It is at best a "supplement" or a basic subsistence program. A *separate retirement program is a necessity.*

A second factor causing changes in the 65 retirement age concept is the presence of inflation, which is making it more difficult for people to retire on reduced income programs. People who retired only 15 years ago on relatively fixed incomes are finding that their money is no longer covering the rising property taxes, utilities, food, gasoline, home repairs, and medical expenses. These rising costs have brought an incentive for many people to continue working full-time several years past the age of 65. Continued employment may be the best way for many people to cope with inflation.

A third reason for the change in retirement age is that Americans are living much longer than they did 40 or 50 years ago. There should be no reason to retire if you enjoy your work and are able to carry on with your duties. When Social Security first began, the longer life span was not considered a major factor in the program.

A fourth reason for the change in attitude toward retirement is the fact that there is a tremendous amount of experience and accumulated technology held

Herman

"Here's your watch, Johnson. You're retiring early."

by the older population in the nation and it should not become a wasted asset, particularly in a time of global competition. The United States has neglected the older population who have experience and wisdom. Other nations tend to find useful and meaningful opportunities for their older citizens.

RETIREMENT AND INFLATION

If people could relate to their years in retirement and the problem of inflation, many of today's decisions might be undertaken differently. Greater prudence would be exercised by the government, businesses, and consumers if they understood the full impact of their decisions on the role of inflation. Developing the stability of the U.S. dollar should be the basis of decisions in the marketplace. Questionable governmental expenditures, uncontrolled urban and suburban real estate growth, and lack of concern over energy consumption by businesses, government units, and individuals have contributed to the wide swings in the strength of the dollar.

The United States has not committed itself to a concept of long-term planning, whether by business, government, or the people. Elected officials often are not versed in economic laws, too many business firms seek short-term profits, and many individuals are motivated by immediate gratification and instant success.

Once inflation exceeds some high percentage rate per year, meaningful retirement as many envision it will be an illusion.

THE GRAYING OF AMERICA

The median age of the American population is moving upward each year. Around 1965, the median age had reached one of its lowest points, that being around 25 years. There are several reasons for the rising age level in the United States. Americans enjoy a longer life span today. The people of the post–World War II baby boom (some 43 million born between 1947 and 1957) are now entering their forties. They represent about 20 percent of today's population. The postponement of marriage by more men and women and the decision to have fewer children in a marriage are also reasons for an aging population.

As the average age of U.S. citizens rises, it will bring about substantial government, economic, and social change. Some of these changes have already begun. The older American is becoming an effective lobbying voice in government (laws on age discrimination, low-income housing, property tax relief, senior transit passes, etc.). Businesses are beginning to respond to the older citizen (in food preparation, packaging, clothing design, senior citizen menus in restaurants, etc.). There will be more services tailored to the needs of an older population (health and medical care, social and recreational facilities). Florida already faces these demographic problems.

Financial Planning for Retirement

When we retire from our chosen careers, we should be retiring to activities that have been long desired and are eagerly waiting for us. In this section, we want to develop a concept of financial needs during retirement to assure this flexibility.

Let us assume that you are single and plan to retire this year after 40 years of work. For the last 25 years you worked for the same company. Your annual salary is $20,000 in this final working year. You are 65 years of age and have paid into Social Security the maximum amounts each year. Your company has a retirement pension program that, when combined or integrated with Social Security benefits, will be equal to 50 percent of your full salary in your *last* working year.

Let us note that retirement on 50 percent of your full salary is not unusual. Many retired people could retire this way, particularly when the inflation rate was only 1 or 2 percent because (1) people really do not live on their full salaries (consider the federal income tax and Social Security contributions deductions), and (2) work-related expenses are eliminated. That is, upon retiring, people are no longer commuting regularly to and from work, clothing and lunch budgets are curtailed, and dues to unions and business and trade associations are no longer necessary. Moreover, one's home may be paid for and the children are grown and on their own.

Inflation in the 1970s was worldwide, and it is expected to continue for several years. It may have become institutionalized as reflected in high interest rates on long-term business and individual borrowing, and automatic cost-of-living adjustments in wage and salary agreements, Social Security, and government salaries. Reliance on higher-cost energy is pervasive and affects the cost of almost any item we purchase in the marketplace. The lack of real productivity by our business sector will mean higher prices. The 1980s and 1990s may well cause most Americans to have a lower standard of living in general. People on fixed incomes have already seen their purchasing power decline rapidly. Let us sketch some hypothetical cash flow needs at retirement. Table 12-1 shows the most recent 12 months at full salary and the next 12 months on retirement. Again, we are assuming that the individual is 64 years old and single and is retiring at age 65. Retirement income includes Social Security benefits plus a company retirement income sufficient to equal 50 percent of gross salary. The sketch assumes $4,500 of federal income taxes and around $1,500 of Social Security taxes paid on a $20,000 salary. This leaves $14,000 as take-home pay for the last working year.

TABLE 12-1 Sketch of Cash Flows

Single individual		Last working year age 64	First retirement year age 65
Gross salary		$20,000	—
Deduct: Income taxes	$4,500		—
Social Security	1,500	6,000	—
Take-home pay		$14,000	—
Social Security benefits			$ 5,400
Company retirement plan			4,600
Retirement income: 50% of gross salary			$10,000

At retirement, Social Security benefits would approximate $450 per month, or $5,400 over the next 12 months. Next, the company retirement plan provides the balance of dollars so that retirement income will equal one half of full salary *at date of retirement*, or $4,600 for a year.

Two more factors should be added to this illustration. Assume in the future that Social Security benefits will be adjusted for periodic cost-of-living increases. However, also assume that the company pension remains fixed at $4,600, a very common practice.

Table 12-2 is a simple review of total cash income over the next 20 years of retirement (ages 65 through 84) assuming an inflation rate of 6 percent. As can be seen, Social Security benefits would rise from $5,400 in the first year to $16,338 in year 20 of retirement. The $4,600 annual company pension may seem adequate for now. However, the $4,600 will have lost two-thirds to three-fourths of its purchasing power in year 20 of retirement. In summary, the $20,938 retirement income to be received at age 84 will not buy as much as the $10,000 income received at age 65.

Suppose your target is to retire at the amount of $14,000 per year, the take-home pay of your last working year. You would then be short $4,000 per year. You could find a job and earn the amount, but you could also have saved money and invested it so that it would be earning $4,000 per year and increasing thereafter to keep up with inflation. We will explore techniques to provide exactly $4,000 per year later in this chapter.

Inflation causes loss of purchasing power on fixed income receipts. If inflation continues at 6 percent per year, for each $1,000 needed this year, you would need around $1,800 in 10 years and $3,200 in 20 years. This means that you would have to have investments in common stocks, income-producing real estate, or other assets that act as a hedge against inflation. Again, the "Rule of 72" can be helpful in determining how often you must double your income. At 6

TABLE 12-2 Retirement Income Program for 20 Years, Ages 65–84
(Assuming a 6% Inflation Rate)

Age	Social Security benefits	Company pension plan (fixed)	Total income
65	$ 5,400*	$4,600†	$10,000
66	5,724	4,600	10,324
67	6,067	4,600	10,667
68	6,431	4,600	11,031
69	6,817	4,600	11,417
70	7,226	4,600	11,826
71	7,660	4,600	12,260
72	8,120	4,600	12,720
73	8,607	4,600	13,207
74	9,123	4,600	13,723
75	9,671	4,600	14,271
76	10,251	4,600	14,851
77	10,866	4,600	15,466
78	11,518	4,600	16,118
79	12,209	4,600	16,809
80	12,941	4,600	17,541
81	13,718	4,600	18,318
82	14,541	4,600	19,141
83	15,413	4,600	20,031
84	16,338	4,600	20,938

* Single individual receiving benefits adjusted for inflation at an average annual rate of 6%.
† Fixed company pension program with no adjustments for inflation.

percent inflation, the $1,000 received annually must double to $2,000 annually in 12 years (72 ÷ 6%).

Assuring ample additional income for retirement can be accomplished by planning and investing early in life. These investments should be ones that traditionally serve as a hedge against inflation. Investments in quality corporate common stocks help in two ways. The periodic cash dividend payments tend to rise over the years. For example, a person might buy a common stock today with a cash dividend payout that equals a 5 percent yield. However, if the stock is held 9 or 10 years, the periodic increases in dividend payments when divided by the original price may yield a 9, 12, or 15 percent annual return when compared with the original cost of the stock. Most people overlook this vital point when considering the investment in common stocks. The value of common stock tends to go up during inflationary times. Income-producing real estate investments tend to provide protection from inflation. Selling a hobby of coins, stamps, or quality collectibles held for several years will produce cash income when needed.

Worksheet Approach for Determining Retirement Income

How much income will be needed in retirement? Will a company retirement plan and Social Security benefits be sufficient? What about the impact of inflation during retirement years? If you retire at age 65 or 70, how much income will you need when you are 80 or 85? What will you need to do if it looks as if you will outlive your savings and investments? In this section, we will learn how to map out a strategy to gain the income needed during those future years in retirement.

A simple but useful technique is to target your future retirement income at 100 percent of the basic take-home pay or some other percentage of that figure. You can determine whether your scale of living has been reasonable at your take-home-pay level while working. If it has not been so, then project your income needs above your take-home-pay level. For example, you might project 10 percent above take-home pay.

Exhibit 12-1 uses the earlier information about a person who will retire soon at age 65; it strives for retirement income at the take-home-pay level adjusted for continued inflation at 6 percent. The worksheet can be extended to project more than the five retirement years illustrated.

A person who is 45 years of age now should project his or her take-home pay and some estimate of inflation over the next 20 years to determine an approximate take-home pay at age 65. Then, the person could construct the following worksheet. Do not be surprised if projected annual retirement income needs run as high as $90,000 per year.

The worksheet sets out four areas of concern in determining retirement income needs: (1) the last working year to determine the net take-home pay, (2) estimated formal retirement income from a sanctioned pension plan and Social Security benefits, (3) the income from personal efforts as a result of working, saving, and investing; and (4) the excess saved or the shortfall against some target such as your former take-home pay or percentage thereof. This target should be adjusted for some rate of inflation.

The worksheet can be modified and extended to cover several years into retirement. However, the key point is to focus on the bottom line of the worksheet. Note that in only three years after retirement, the retired person would begin experiencing a shortfall of income. The principal reasons here are the decision to not carry on part-time work and the erosion impact that inflation has on fixed return investment income.

The retired person in this situation should consider continuing full-time work for a few more years if he or she is able to. The goal would be to either save as much income as possible or make sure that major purchases and repairs of household items have been completed. Here is a person retiring with $6,000 anticipated income over and above money from a pension and Social Security. Some may say that was good planning. However, when extending this work-

EXHIBIT 12-1 Worksheet for Planning Retirement Income Pegged to Former Take-Home Pay

Work/Retirement	Last Working Year	Retirement Years				
Age (in years)	64	65	66	67	68	69
Retirement years		(1)	(2)	(3)	(4)	(5)
1. Last working year						
Estimated gross salary	$20,000	(Assumes a 6% annual inflation rate for a theoretical take-home-pay equivalent: $14,000 × 1.06 = $14,840 × 1.06 = $15,730, etc.)				
Less:						
Income taxes	$4,500					
Social Security	1,500					
Total Deductions	6,000					
Net take-home pay	$14,000	$14,840	$15,730	$16,674	$17,675	$18,735
2. Estimated formal retirement income						
From company pension		$ 4,600	$ 4,600	$ 4,600	$ 4,600	$ 4,600
From Social Security		5,400	5,724	6,067	6,431	6,817
Total basic retirement income		$10,000	$10,324	$10,667	$11,031	$11,417
Balance needed to equal "take-home pay"		$ 4,840	$ 5,406	$ 6,007	$ 6,644	$ 7,318
3. Personal efforts and investments						
From part-time work		$ 2,000	$ 1,500	$ 1,000	$ 800	$ 0
Dividend income		1,200	1,400	1,650	1,850	2,000
Interest income		2,000	2,000	2,000	2,000	2,000
Keogh plan from part-time job		800	800	800	800	800
Total other income		$ 6,000	$ 5,700	$ 5,450	$ 5,450	$ 4,800
4. Excess saved or (shortfall)		$ 1,160	$ 294	($ 557)	($ 1,194)	($ 2,518)

sheet another 15 years, when the retired person is approaching 80 years of age, the retirement income will be grossly inadequate.

Elderly retired people who are outliving their savings or have inadequate income have to make very important decisions sometimes. They may have to sell their homes and move into modest apartments. They may have to convert other investments into lifetime annuities so as not to outlive their dwindling savings. Many elderly persons today find it difficult to accept government and charitable assistance.

To summarize, planning retirement income needs is essential. What appears at first glance to be adequate usually turns out to be too little and too late.

Key Financial Planning Tables for Projecting Retirement Income

In Chapter 5 we discussed compound interest and illustrated how interest income accumulates on investments. Appendix A presents the four tables for financial planning. (Tables A.1 through A.4 consider the interest rate is compounded annually.) Most financial planning consultants and insurance companies use these basic tables. A few illustrations on how to use these tables for retirement planning are discussed here. In this way, you can calculate both present and future desired cash needs.

Using Table A.1. Table A.1 can help you determine how much money you will need at some point in the future when inflation is maintaining some common rate over the long run. Note the following examples.

Example A. You are 64 years of age and you plan to retire at age 65. In your last year of employment, you determine that your take-home pay will be $14,000. How much income will you need at age 84 (20 years later) if inflation stays at a rate of 6 percent per year? Calculation: Use Table A.1, 6% column, 20 years.

$$\$14,000 \times 3.20714 = \$44,899.96$$

Example B. You are 25 years of age today and your take-home pay is $8,750 per year. Assuming inflation will average 5 percent per year over the next 40 years (age 65), what would be your required income 40 years from now just to maintain your present financial situation? Calculation: Use Table A.1, 5% column, 40 years.

$$\$8,750 \times 7.03999 = \$61,599.91$$

Example C. You are 30 years old and have just received an inheritance of $5,000. You decide to make this the cornerstone for retirement 40 years from now at age 70. You purchase some high-quality stock in a corporation with automatic reinvestment of dividends. This plan will give you an after-tax rate of income of 7 percent compounded annually. To what amount will the $5,000 lump-sum investment grow over the next 40 years? Calculation: Use Table A.1, 7% column, 40 years.

$$\$5,000 \times 14.97446 = \$74,872.30$$

Using Table A.2. Table A.2 is most helpful in determining what amounts of investment must be made today to reach a specific dollar goal 5, 10, or 20 years from now.

Example A. You are 50 years of age and you want to invest a specific amount of money so that at age 70 you will have $70,000. Assume that you can earn an after-tax income of 6 percent. What lump-sum investment must be made today? Calculation: Use Table A.2, 6% column, 20 years.

$$\$70,000 \times .31180 = \$21,826$$

Example B. You want to accumulate $100,000 at retirement in just 15 years. You plan to buy a piece of property that will appreciate at an after-tax rate of 10 percent. How much cash will you have to pay for the piece of property to achieve this goal? Calculation: Use Table A.2, 10% column, 15 years.

$$\$100,000 \times .23939 = \$23,939$$

Example C. You are 64 years old and will be retiring at age 65. While your retirement income will be reasonably adequate, additional supplemental income will be necessary during the 10 years age 70 through 79. If you do not provide for this supplemental income, you may have to sell your home earlier than you anticipated. Table 12-3 is a sketch of cash needs for those years, including adjustments for inflation averaged at 5 percent per year.

TABLE 12-3 Cash Needs to Supplement Basic Retirement Program

Age	Supplemental cash needs
70	$ 3,200
71	3,500
72	4,000
73	3,000
74	3,500
75	3,800
76	4,000
77	4,000
78	4,500
79	5,000
	$38,500

Assume further that you want the $38,500 fund completely established at age 64 even though you will not need the fund for five years. The money is to be saved in the form of a certificate of deposit for five years earning an interest rate of 8 percent per year. During the withdrawal years, the money will be in a savings account earning 5 percent interest, the same as inflation. The following steps will help you determine the exact amount to be deposited in one lump sum at age 64 to provide for your supplemental income when needed.

Step 1. Develop a sketch of the cash needs adjusted back to a lump sum at age 69. Calculation: Use Table A.2, 5% column, years 1–10. Refer to Table 12-4 for a sample format.

Step 2. Determine the lump sum needed for the certificate of deposit that will earn 8 percent per year for five years. Remember, the fund is to be established at age 64. Calculation: Use Table A.2, 8% column, 5 years.

$$\$29,245 \times .68058 = \$19,903$$

The $19,903, or nearly $20,000, is the amount needed to be invested at age 64 to provide for those 10 years of special need.

Using Table A.3. Table A.3 as well as Table A.4 are the most useful in contemplating retirement income goals and needs. Table A.3 takes into consideration the setting aside and investing of *equal amounts* (an annuity) of money each year to achieve a specific money goal. Table A.3 projects the notion that, during the year in which one is "saving" for the annual investment deposit, no interest has been earned. However, once deposited or invested, it earns interest compounded annually. This is a conservative approach, but that is realistic to take such a position for retirement purposes. The following examples will help you understand how to use this table.

TABLE 12-4 Calculating the Present Value of Future Supplemental Cash Needs

Age	Supplemental cash needs	×	Table A.2, 5%	=	Present value at age 69
70	$3,200	×	.95238	=	$ 3,048
71	3,500	×	.90703	=	3,175
72	4,000	×	.86384	=	3,455
73	3,000	×	.82270	=	2,468
74	3,500	×	.78353	=	2,742
75	3,800	×	.74622	=	2,836
76	4,000	×	.71068	=	2,843
77	4,000	×	.67684	=	2,707
78	4,500	×	.64461	=	2,901
79	5,000	×	.61391	=	3,070
Lump sum needed at age 69					$29,245

Example A. You plan to save $1,200 *each year* for the next 30 years at an after-tax income rate of 6 percent per year. How much will you have at the end of 30 years? Calculation: Use Table A.3, 6% column, 30 years.

$$\$1,200 \times 79.05819 = \$94,869.83$$

Example B. Suppose that you need a fund of $75,000 at age 65 to help you with supplemental retirement income. You are 45 years old and you want to accumulate the $75,000 in 20 years. You consider that you can earn a 7 percent after-tax return on your investment compounded annually. How much will you have to set aside *each year* to reach the $75,000 goal? Calculation: Use Table A.3, 7% column, 20 years.

$$\$75,000 \div 40.99549 = \$1,829.47$$

Example C. Before you retire in eight years, you need to replace the roof on your home. You estimate by then the cost will be $9,000. How much money do you have to save *each year* at 5 percent compounded annually? Calculation: Use Table A.3, 5% column, 8 years.

$$\$9,000 \div 9.54911 = \$942.50$$

Using Table A.4. This table is very useful when you need to determine your level of spending or to set an upper limit on spending from a special money fund. Since you will not use up all the fund in one year, the amount of the fund remaining can still be earning interest. The following examples will help you gain efficiency with this interesting table.

Example A. You have been saving and investing for more than 20 years, and when you reach 65 years of age, the value of this investment is now $75,000. You want this fund to supplement your Social Security and company pension. What amount can you withdraw *each year* over the next 20 years so that at the end of year 20 the $75,000 will be exhausted? Assume that the unused portion can earn interest at 6 percent. Calculation: Use Table A.4, 6% column, 20 years.

$$\$75,000 \div 11.46992 = \$6,538.84$$

Example B. You are retired and your current retirement income is no longer sufficient to maintain your retirement expenses. You have 10 acres of land that you have owned and lived on for the past 15 years since you retired. You decide to sell 5 acres to a real estate developer at $8,000 per acre for $40,000. After taxes and fees and other costs, you have $36,000 remaining. How much money can you withdraw *each year* for the next 8 years that will exhaust the fund? Assume that you can earn a 7 percent return compounded annually on the remaining funds. Calculation: Use Table A.4, 7% column, 8 years.

$$\$36,000 \div 5.97130 = \$6,028.84$$

Comprehensive Problem. Let us go through a complete planning program which should help you learn the basics of long-range planning for your retirement income needs. You may want to refine the process by using variations in potential income, inflation rates, retirement dates, marital status, and financial setbacks.

Step 1. Assume that you are 25 years of age and earn $11,000 a year; with federal income tax withholdings and Social Security contributions, your annual take-home pay is $8,900 this year.

You expect to retire 40 years from now, at age 65. You anticipate that, with promotions and merit and cost-of-living adjustments, your take-home pay will increase at an 8 percent rate per year over the next 40 years.

Calculation (Table A.1): $8,900 take-home pay at age 25 × 21.72452 the factor in 8% column, line 40 = $193,348 take-home pay for the year at age 65.

Step 2. After you have calculated your take-home pay at age 65 at $193,348, it is necessary to estimate what your retirement and Social Security benefits might be after retirement. Let us assume that retirement income is 75 percent of take-home pay, or $145,501 ($193,348 × .75).

Step 3. You expect to live 20 years after retirement. You expect some inflation to continue after retirement. You estimate a 5 percent rate of inflation. During your 20 years of retirement, you will have to increase your income if cost-of-living adjustments do not take place. What will be your retirement at year 20?

Calculation (Table A.1): $145,501 retirement income at age 65 × 2.65330 factor in 5% column, line 20 = $386,058 annual income needed at age 84.

Step 4. Assume that you need to have a contingency of $1,500,000 established on your own to be available at age 65 in the event you cannot work. Furthermore you estimate a 7 percent after-tax return compounded annually over the next 40 years. How much will have to be set aside *each year* to accomplish the $1,500,000 fund?

Calculation (Table A.3): $1,500,000 contingency fund ÷ 199.6351 factor in 7% column, line 40 = $7,513.71 invested each year (or $626.14 per month).

Step 5. You want the $1,500,000 contingency reserve to last the 20 years of retirement. How much can be withdrawn each year so that the fund is exhausted at year 20? Assume that you can earn the same 7 percent interest compounded annually.

Calculation (Table A.4): $1,500,000 contingency fund ÷ 10.59401 factor in 7% column, line 20 = $141,589 can be withdrawn each year.

In summary, the four tables provide quick answers to a variety of questions relating to retirement income. A common question is, "How does one know which table should be used to compute a particular situation?" Unless one earns a living working with these tables, it is not worthwhile attempting to memorize their particular usages. It is suggested that the models be adopted to specific needs or goals. They will make good tools.

PROGRAMS OR TOOLS OF RETIRMENT PLANNING—THE BASICS

This section covers some of the basics that relate to retirement planning. Almost anyone who enters the world of work and spends his or her career as an employee should review the following six programs or tools: (1) the balance sheet or net worth statement, (2) personal and family facts and factors, (3) personal savings and investment programs, (4) employer pension coverage programs, (5) the Social Security program, and (6) Medicare. Each of the basic six programs or tools is discussed to call out important points or questions as it might fit into a person's retirement goals.

The Balance Sheet or Net Worth Statement

The first step in a financial plan is to take stock of where you are at a point in life. Financial progress is determined by comparing the net worth of the current year with that of earlier years. Ideally, the annual increase in net worth should be pegged to a specific rate of growth each year. A goal might state that there should be an annual rate of increase of 15 percent. Balance sheets of business firms list their assets at original cost. However, for individuals and households, the listing of assets at their approximate fair market value is more realistic. Exhibit 12-2 lists the assets, debts, and net worth of a middle-aged family on December 31, 19X1.

The assets and debts reflect a long-established family. How well are they doing financially? At first glance it looks very good. A comparison of the past five years of balance sheets would be more useful to determine real progress. Presently the Wong family has a net worth of $142,480. Ralph Wong is 45 years old and no doubt will consider retirement in 20 to 25 years when he is 65 or 70. How much net worth should he and his wife Sharon have when he reaches age 65? Just to stay even with inflation at 6 percent over the next 20 years, they would need $456,953 as their net worth ($142,480 × 3.20714, Table A.1, 6% column, 20 years). A 12 percent annual increase over the next 20 years of their net worth would amount to $1,374,440.

Personal and Family Facts and Factors

The ability to reach specific financial goals as well as enjoy a financially independent retirement depends on many individual and household concerns. Inflation,

EXHIBIT 12-2 Sample Balance Sheet

Ralph (45) and Sharon (42) Wong and Family
Balance Sheet
December 31, 19X1

Assets

Cash in bank	$ 2,700
Cash in savings account	5,000
Certificate of deposit 8%	10,000
Cash surrender value of life insurance	1,200
Vested portion of retirement plan	14,000
Keogh plan, part-time freelancing	2,750
100 shares IBM common (cost $6,845)	7,600
200 shares General Motors (cost $14,000)	13,500
House and land (cost $32,500)	84,000
Furnishings and household items	12,000
Automobiles (cost $11,700)	7,300
Collectibles and hobbies (cost $2,500)	4,800
Stereos, cameras, tools	4,100
Objects of art	1,850
Total assets	$170,800

Debts

Department store charge account	320
Income taxes balance due (est.)	1,700
Property taxes owed (3 months)	400
Mortgage on home, balance	16,700
Tuition payments owed (children)	2,400
Automobile payments owed	6,800
Total debts	$ 28,320

Net worth	$142,480

changes to alternative energy sources, and international economics may change the whole social fabric of the nation and disrupt the financial goals of the best money managers. Other factors influencing your retirement decisions include the state of your health as well as your spouse's, the type of job or career, whether both husband and wife work, the number of dependents, education level, savings and investments accumulated to date, the amount of debt outstanding, income tax bracket, the opportunity to continue working beyond traditional retirement years, and so on. Good, continuous, long-range planning can help achieve financial goals to compensate for what may appear to be, for the near term, factors preventing you from reaching your objective.

Personal Saving and Investment Programs

With the interest earned by saving and investing, one can develop additional income for a better life-style and more financial independence during retirement. Personal investment programs should be in areas that provide a hedge against inflation as would be the case of high-yield U.S. Treasury bill, common stocks of corporations, and real estate. Personal investment activity requires a certain amount of homework to learn about the fundamentals and having the temperament to deal with risk.

Employer Pension Coverage Programs

Most employees will qualify for the company pension or retirement program after completing a probation period, working full time, and reaching a certain minimum age of 25 or similar criteria. Companies with retirement plans periodically provide employee handbooks to answer common inquiries.

The following questions are important in determining the usefulness of the company's plan for your retirement years. How long must you be in the plan to become vested? Is the plan portable? What is the normal retirement age? Does the plan contain a cost-of-living adjustment clause? What happens if you retire early? Are the benefits reduced for early retirement? What provisions are made for widows(ers) if the employee dies?

What percentage of your final working year salary will you receive? Are there survivor benefits for other members of the family? Can you lose your retirement income related to the amount to be received from Social Security? Most large companies try to keep employees informed of changes in the plan. The personnel office can answer most questions.

With the passage of the 1974 Employee Retirement Income Security Act (ERISA), all pension plans must offer workers the following options relating to widows' (and widowers') benefits: (1) When a worker becomes eligible for early retirement, the employee can sign up for spouse benefits in the event that the employee dies before retirement so that the spouse will have a pension for life. (2) When the employee reaches retirement age, the individual can choose a pension that will provide for the spouse for the rest of his or her life.

The Social Security Program

Persons covered by Social Security should periodically check their account to be sure that there are no errors. This may be done by obtaining a "Request Statement of Earnings" form from the post office or by writing directly to the Social Security Administration, P.O. Box 57, Baltimore, Maryland 21203.

A second important point to remember is the amount of credit needed to be considered *fully insured*. No one can be fully insured with credit for less than 1½ years of work; a person who has credit for 10 years of work can be sure that he or she will be fully insured for life. Tables 12-5 and 12-6 show how much credit for work under Social Security one needs to be fully insured. It should be noted that, while one may be fully insured to receive certain kinds of benefits, it does not determine the *amount*. The amount will usually depend on the worker's average earnings covered by Social Security.

Contact the near-by Social Security office approximately three months before you actually retire. In this way the necessary paperwork will have been processed and your first check should arrive in the first month of your retirement.

Social Security gives you the option of retiring at age 62 or at age 65. Part of this decision will be related to current income, the state of one's health, other pension programs, and current job satisfaction. If you retire at age 62, you

TABLE 12-5 Years of Work Credit For Retirement Benefits (fully insured)

If you reach age 62 in	Years you need
1984	8¼
1985	8½
1986	8¾
1987	9
1988	9¼
1989	9½
1990	9¾
1991 or later	10

Data are from U.S. Department of Health and Human Services, Social Security Administration, SSA Publication No. 05-10035, January 1987, p. 18.

TABLE 12-6 Work Credit for Survivors and Disability Benefits

Born after 1929, die or become disabled at	Born before 1930, die or become disabled before 62 in	Years you need
28 or younger		1½
30		2
32		2½
34		3
36		3½
38		4
40		4½
42		5
44		5½
46		6
48		6½
50		7
52		7½
54		8
56	1985	8½
58	1987	9
60	1989	9½
62 or older	1991 or later	10

Data are from U.S. Department of Health and Human Services, Social Security Administration, SSA Publication No. 0510035, January 1987, p. 20.

receive 80 percent of the benefits at age 65. If you wait to age 65, you will have lost some benefits. It will take 12 years to regain the advantage if you retire at 65 versus 62.

A career homemaker whose husband had made contributions to Social Security during his working years can begin receiving "widow's benefits" at age 60. The benefits are at a reduced percentage as shown in Table 12-7. It should be noted that a recent U.S. Supreme Court decision permits widowers the same benefits. Remarriage after age 60 no longer affects the receipt of benefits as it did earlier.

The Social Security Administration has set requirements on the amount of *earned income* received in a year while drawing benefits. The upper limits of the amounts one can earn in the form of *salary* and *wages* vary due to fluctuations in the amount of the inflation rate. During 1987, if you are between the ages of 65 and 69, you could earn up to $8,160 and continue to receive full benefits. However, if you earned above that amount, you would lose benefits at the rate of $1

TABLE 12-7
Calculation of Widows'
Benefits

Age	Percentage
60	71.5%
61	77.2
62	82.9
63	88.6
64	94.3
65	100.0

for every $2 of earned income. On the other hand, if you are 70 years of age and older, you can earn all the income you want and not lose Social Security benefits.

Finally, for retirement income planning, one should know the meaning of *exempt income* under Social Security. The following types of income can be received without reducing benefits: income from pensions, dividend income, veterans' benefits, annuities, rental income, savings account interest, bond interest, gifts, inheritances, gain on the sale of property or other capital assets, or royalties from patents and copyrights. Both the income tax laws and Social Security provide incentives to make investments in these areas.

Medicare

Medicare is discussed separately from Social Security benefits to call attention to medical insurance. Most medical insurance programs written to cover employees under various group plans terminate at age 65, the traditional retirement date. Thus, when employees retire, they lost their medical benefits at the time when they are most needed. To carry equivalent coverage privately would be prohibitive for most people.

Medicare takes over after retirement to provide basic and essential medical coverage. Medicare should not be confused with national health care insurance such as that found in Canada. Planning for retirement should include preparing a cash reserve or specific insurance coverage to fill in the gaps not covered by Medicare.

Almost anyone who is 65 or older or eligible for hospital insurance can enroll for Medicare medical insurance. You do not need any Social Security or government work credits to get medical insurance. Aliens 65 or older who are not eligible for hospital insurance must be permanent residents and must reside in the United States for five years before they can enroll in medical insurance. If you want medical insurance protection, you pay a monthly premium for it. The basic premium at this writing is approximately $25.00 per month. If you are receiving Social Security benefits or retirement benefits under the railroad retirement system, you will be automatically enrolled for medical insurance—unless you refuse it—at the same time you become entitled to hospital insurance.

Medicare hospital insurance can help pay for inpatient hospital care, inpatient care in a skilled nursing facility, home health care, and hospice care.

Inpatient Hospital Care. If you need inpatient care, hospital insurance helps pay for up to 90 days in any participating hospital in each benefit period. In 1987, hospital insurance paid for all covered services for the first 60 days, *except* for the first $540. For the 61st through 90th day, hospital insurance pays for all covered services *except* for $130 a day. If you ever need more than 90 days of hospital care in any benefit period, you can use some or all of your 60 nonrenewable "reserve days." For each reserve day you use, hospital insurance pays for all covered services *except* for $260 a day. Covered services include semiprivate room, all meals, regular nursing services, operating and recovery room, anesthesia services, intensive care and coronary care, drugs, lab tests, X rays, medical supplies and appliances, rehabilitation services, and preparatory services related to kidney transplant surgery.

Skilled Nursing Facility Care. If you need daily skilled nursing or rehabilitation services after a hospital stay and meet certain other conditions, hospital insurance can help pay for inpatient care in a participating skilled nursing facility. A skilled nursing facility is a specially qualified facility that mainly provides nursing and rehabilitation services. Most nursing homes are *not* skilled nursing facilities and are *not* certified by Medicare. Hospital insurance can help pay for up to 100 days in a skilled nursing facility in each benefit period *if* you need skilled nursing or rehabilitation services that long. In 1987, hospital insurance pays for all covered services for the first 20 days and all but $65 a day for up to 80 more days. Covered services include semiprivate room, all meals, regular nursing services, rehabilitation services, drugs, medical supplies, and appliances.

Home Health Care. If you are confined to your home and meet certain other conditions, hospital insurance can pay the full approved cost of home health visits from a participating home health agency. There is no limit to the number of covered visits you can have. Covered services include part-time skilled nursing care, physical therapy, and speech therapy. If you need one or more of those services, hospital insurance also covers part-time services of home health aides, occupational therapy, medical social services, and medical supplies and equipment.

Hospice Care. Under certain conditions, hospital insurance can help pay for hospice care for terminally ill beneficiaries if the care is provided by a Medicare-certified hospice. Special benefit periods apply to hospice care. Hospital insurance can pay for a maximum of two 90-day periods and one 30-day period. Covered services include doctors' services, nursing services, medical appliances, and supplies, including outpatient drugs for pain relief, home health aide and homemaker services, therapies, medical social services, short-term inpatient care including respite care, and counseling. Hospital insurance pays part of the cost of outpatient drugs and inpatient respite care. For all other covered services, hospital insurance pays the full cost.

Medical Insurance Benefits. Medicare medical insurance helps pay for your doctor's services and a variety of other medical services and supplies that are *not* covered by hospital insurance. Most of the services needed by people with permanent kidney failure are covered only by medical insurance. Each year, as soon as you meet the annual medical insurance deductible, medical insurance generally will pay 80 percent of the approved charges for covered services you receive during the rest of the year. In 1987, the annual deductible was $75. Medical insurance covers doctors' services no matter where you receive them in the United States. Covered doctors' services include surgical services, diagnostic tests, and X rays that are part of your treatment, medical supplies furnished in a doctor's office, services of the office nurse, and drugs which are administered as part of your treatment and cannot be self-administered.

Medical insurance covers the services you receive in an emergency room or outpatient clinic of a hospital. It can cover an unlimited number of home health visits if all required conditions are met.

What Medicare Does Not Cover. Medicare provides basic protection against the high cost of illness, but it will not pay all your health care expenses. Services and supplies that Medicare does not pay for include custodial care, such as help with bathing, eating, and taking medicine; dentures and routine dental care; eyeglasses, hearing aids, and examinations to prescribe or fit them; personal comfort items such as a phone or TV in your hospital room; prescription drugs and patent medicines; most nursing home care; and routine physical checkups and related tests.

It is suggested that Blue Cross or Blue Shield supplemental plans be purchased to fill in the gaps of Medicare. Avoid the heavily advertised commercial plans.

In summary the six programs are fundamental to any basic retirement plan. The first three—periodic balance sheets, facts and factors about you or your family, and personal savings and investment—tend to rely heavily on your own efforts. The last three—employee pension coverage, Social Security, and Medicare—usually accrue to you by spending your career years being gainfully employed.

THE INDIVIDUAL RETIREMENT ACCOUNT

Individual retirement accounts (IRAs) were created January 1, 1975 as a result of the 1974 Employee Retirement Income Security Act (ERISA). An IRA account is a *tax-sheltered* "pension" plan for workers not covered by employee plans, that is, businesses or not-for-profit associations that have no formal retirement program. The eligible employee can set aside up to a maximum of $2,000 each year ($2,250 for a married person with a spouse who has no earned income) and deduct the amount to reduce one's taxable income.

The money must be deposited in qualified plans. The individual selects his or her investments. Banks, savings institutions, mutual funds, and insurance companies offer a variety of plans that qualify. These plans offer fixed and variable returns. The bank or other qualified institution reports on the account periodically to both the federal government and to you.

An employee is fully "vested" immediately in an IRA as opposed to many company pension plans that often require 10 years of continuous and uninterrupted service before qualifying for benefits. Earnings on IRA investments are tax deferred. The compounding of these tax-deferred dollars can be continued until the investor reaches 70½ years of age. The earliest retirement for an individual without incurring a substantial penalty is 59½ years of age. Withdrawals from the IRA accounts must start no later than age 70½, or a substantial penalty tax will be levied on the account.

In summary, IRA accounts should be viewed more as a savings account than as a pension. Pension income continues until your death and your surviving spouse's death. IRA income stops when the account is exhausted. IRA income is taxable when you receive it. The contributions to an IRA are frozen and unavailable to you until age 59½ under normal circumstances. The program is also limited to single filers earning less than $25,000 or $40,000 on a joint return. To remain competitive in the global economy, more companies are eliminating pension programs.

SELF-EMPLOYED RETIREMENT PLAN

Persons who are self-employed should consider establishing retirement programs. The type of savings and investment program will be determined in part by the success of their business, type of business service, and income tax bracket. These retirement plans are sometimes referred to as Keogh or HR-10 plans.

Persons who start their own business will find this just one more income tax area to investigate. It is best to go to the local Internal Revenue Service office for assistance. If you are planning to use a plan administered by a bank, then use IRS Form 3672 as part of your paperwork.

The net income or net profit of the business is considered as earned income. It is the result of subtracting business expenses from the gross sales or fees. Nontaxable income earned overseas or income received by an inactive partner does not qualify for a Keogh plan. The rules are very strict to prevent diversion of funds and allow for undue enrichment to certain persons or owners of several businesses.

Rules for Keogh plans for the self-employed require that employees who meet certain requirements *must* be included in the retirement plan. If this is not the intention of the owner of a business, then the owner should consider the IRA account.

Under a Keogh plan, the self-employed person may set aside up to 25 percent or $30,000 of specifically defined net profit each year, whichever is less. Here, net profit is defined as profit *after* the retirement contribution. That is, you can make a 20 percent contribution but only deduct 13 percent. People engaged in self-employment "moonlighting" or part-time jobs may also set aside the net profit. If part-time earnings are very small, an individual may put every dollar of net profit into a Keogh plan. Under normal conditions, the minimum retirement age is 59½ unless disabled. Distributions must be made no later than age 70.

TAX-SHELTERED ANNUITIES

This form of annuity is available to employees of tax-exempt religious, charitable, education, and not-for-profit governmental organizations. Employees may set aside as much as 20 percent of their gross income in a tax-sheltered annuity. This allowable deduction will reduce the employee's taxable income for the year. The money is available to you in cash or monthly income when you retire, or before. The money is subject to taxes as normal income in the years it is withdrawn. The Tax Reform Act of 1986 fixed $9,500 as the total contribution that can be set aside in any one year by the employee.

INCREASING INCOME DURING RETIREMENT

For persons who have been retired for several years and are finding that their retirement income is inadequate, the following topics may be explored in an attempt to increase monthly income and ensure not outliving certain savings and investment funds.

Higher Yield on Invested Income

Investment portfolios should be reviewed to increase dividend and interest income. Growth stocks that have appreciated over the years but do not pay much in the way of dividends should be sold and the funds invested in high-grade preferred stocks and common stocks of sound basic utility corporations. This approach will improve income and serve as some hedge against inflation. Present investments in corporate stocks should be sold and high-grade invest-ment bonds acquired. Bond interest in recent years has risen to 8, 9, and 10 percent per annum. Short-term certificates of deposit tied to the interest rate of U.S. Treasury bills also provide high-yield, low-risk investments. If much of the owner's investments have been sold off to provide income, then these recom-mendations will probably not be useful regardless of how much higher yield is forthcoming.

Annuities

When one's savings accounts and investments in stocks, bonds, real estate, and so on no longer provide adequate income, one may be forced to sell such assets and invest the proceeds in an annuity. An annuity is usually sold by insurance companies. Basically one purchases an annuity by paying a single lump-sum cash premium. In return, the insurance company makes specific monthly payments to the purchaser or *annuitant* for a specified or indefinite period of time.

The *straight-life annuity* pays the highest monthly income during one per-son's lifetime. The fixed dollar amount to be received depends on how much is available for the principal, the annuitant's age, and the total lump sum invested. Upon death of the annuitant, the annuity contract is complete, and there are no funds remaining to revert to one's estate. Depending on the insurance company, it might require roughly $10,000 lump-sum investment to be able to receive $100 a month for life if a person is 70 years of age. By careful shopping among insurance companies, one might gain a few dollars a month more than the $100. The greatest disadvantage of the straight life fixed annuity is in-flation.

The *joint and survivor annuity* pays monthly cash income benefits over the lifetimes of the participants. Again, there is no residual after the death of the second annuitant. It tends to have the same advantages and disadvantages as the straight life annuity.

There are other types of annuities such as a life annuity with time certain, variable annuities, and refund annuities, but none of these is likely to provide the higher income needed by the elderly retired. They may be more useful for meeting other financial-planning goals.

Reverse Mortgage

The reverse mortgage, which is fairly new, might provide a way for the elderly retired to increase their income if they own a home. The homeowner makes a contract with a bank using a paid-for home as collateral in return for a $150-a-month loan. The interest rate would be the same as that for a regular mortgage.

SUMMARY

Planning for retirement should begin early in life. Lack of purchasing power due to inflation is the chief problem of those on retirement. Retirement is directed more to the career worker rather than to the career homemaker. Most people give little thought to the year in which they may retire. Recent court rulings have made Social Security more equitable between men and women. The Social Security program in the United States faces serious funding problems over the next 30–40 years. Social Security is not a retirement program. Each person must take steps to be covered by a bona fide retirement program. Business, government, and others have yet to develop a long-range goal to address the problem of inflation. The World War II baby boom of 43 million constitutes 20 percent of the U.S. population. These people are now in the work force. They will be retiring in the years 2020–2030.

People today will spend 25 percent of their life in retirement. A person's retirement goals will be influenced by career, marriage, number of children, retirement planning, and state of health. Inflation rates of 6 percent and above raise serious doubts about one's ability to retire.

The worksheet approach to retirement income planning focuses on the adequacy or shortfall of planned retirement incomes. Continuing full-time work beyond 65 may be the best retirement plan during periods of high inflation. Knowledge of the four financial planning tables is essential to developing various career-retirement models.

The six basic planning tools and programs for retirement planning are (1) the balance sheet or net worth statement, (2) knowledge of the facts and factors of the individual or family, (3) personal savings and investment programs, (4) employer-sponsored pension programs, (5) Social Security programs, and (6) Medicare.

The Individual Retirement Account is basically a tax-deferred savings program rather than a pension. IRAs are for employees not covered by company pension plans or for whom no pension plan exists. The Keogh plan is basically a retirement program for the self-employed. Tax-sheltered annuities are available to employees of not-for-profit charitable, educational, and religious organizations. Annuities may provide additional income to the retired.

EXHIBIT 12-3 Basic Financial Pyramid

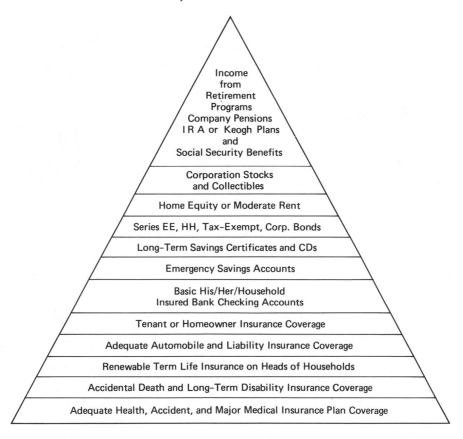

Income
from
Retirement
Programs
Company Pensions
I R A or Keogh Plans
and
Social Security Benefits

Corporation Stocks
and Collectibles

Home Equity or Moderate Rent

Series EE, HH, Tax–Exempt, Corp. Bonds

Long–Term Savings Certificates and CDs

Emergency Savings Accounts

Basic His/Her/Household
Insured Bank Checking Accounts

Tenant or Homeowner Insurance Coverage

Adequate Automobile and Liability Insurance Coverage

Renewable Term Life Insurance on Heads of Households

Accidental Death and Long–Term Disability Insurance Coverage

Adequate Health, Accident, and Major Medical Insurance Plan Coverage

Exhibit 12-3 of the Basic Financial Pyramid is completed with long-term retirement financial programs reviewed. Social Security benefits will serve as the cornerstone. Financial independence in retirement will require additional company-sponsored and individual retirement programs.

TIPS

1. If inflation continues at the 6 percent plus level of recent years and you are in good health, exercise all your rights to remain employed. Working may be the best hedge against inflation.

2. Initiate your own separate long-term savings and investment program to supplement your company pension program and Social Security benefits. Lack of money is still the retired person's greatest worry.

3. Take advantage of any legal income tax opportunities to postpone the payment of taxes on both earned income and exempt earnings.

4. Be aware that, as long as inflation-adjusted Social Security benefits are integrated with the company's pension program payment schedule, retiring employees at the median and lower wage levels will tend to receive a declining proportion of the benefits in the company pension fund.

5. Read, clip, and save tax and pension information appearing in company newspaper as well as other newspaper and magazine articles.

6. Enroll in a course or seminar designed for preretirement employees and family members.

7. Prior to retirement years, periodically request a statement of Social Security accumulations.

8. Before leaving your full-time job and salary for retirement, be sure your home is in new or nearly new condition. Weigh the possibility of moving to a home more suitable to your retirement needs. Assess the future trend of the neighborhood in which you will be retiring.

9. If married, prepare your retirement program to allow the surviving spouse the broadest flexibility for continued financial security. If there are children, avoid promising them assets that might reduce financial security to the surviving spouse.

10. Be very realistic about job opportunities after you retire. The continued high level of unemployment and underemployment in the United States will most likely continue in the 1990s.

11. Consider continued high-cost housing, transportation, and energy as being interrelated in the decision for retirement living as well as the places in which you will live (home, condo, apartment, retirement home, etc.).

12. Consider income taxes and retirement and estate planning as being interrelated topics for study and review.

13. If married, prepare your spouse to be able to take on financial matters in case he or she outlives you.

ADDITIONAL READINGS

"Know Your Medicare Rights," *Consumer's Digest*, February 1986, p. 74.
"Retirement: Problem or Paradise," *Consumer's Digest*, May/June 1984, pp. 74–79.
"Saving Through an Annuity," *Consumer Reports*, January 1988, pp. 35–45.
"Will You Ever Collect a Pension?" *Consumer Reports*, March 1982, pp. 124–30.

GLOSSARY OF USEFUL TERMS

Compound Interest   Interest earned on interest already paid on the invested principal when it is left to accumulate with the principal.

Defined Benefit Plan   A retirement plan that provides for specific benefits on retirement and requires contributions to be based on actuarial data to provide the fixed benefit.

ERISA (Employee Retirement Income Security Act of 1974)   Legislation that deals with eligibility, benefit formulas, early retirement, disability retirement, preretirement death benefits, and vesting.

Imputed Interest   The interest that could be but is not earned on a sum of money that is put to some alternative use. The money invested in a fully paid home could have been earning interest, dividends, or rent if invested elsewhere.

Individual Retirement Account (IRA)   For a person with no employer-sponsored pension, a plan whereby up to each year a maximum of $2,000 may be invested in an approved savings medium or mutual fund. This contribution and earnings on it are tax free until retirement after age 59½. (See Chapters 5 and 11.)

Insurance Annuity   A contract usually made with an insurance company that provides an annual payment to a person until the person dies.

Keogh Plan   Legislation allowing self-employed people to set up their own retirement program with certain tax savings.

Life Annuity with Time Certain   Guarantee of a minimum number of income payments regardless of the life span of the annuitant. If the person dies before the term (10 years, for example), the annuity continues to pay the same monthly amount to a designated beneficiary.

OASDHI (Old Age, Survivor's, Disability, and Hospital Insurance)   The technical name for Social Security under the Federal Insurance Contribution Act (FICA).

Portable Pension   Benefits that can be transferred by a worker to a new place of employment.

Self-Directed IRA   An individual retirement account in which, instead of saving cash in an account and earning interest, the deposit might be in the form of diamonds, gold coins, stamps, limited partnerships, and so on.

Social Security Act   Federal statute that provides for old age and survivor insurance, unemployment insurance, and old age assistance.

Straight Life Annuity   Annuity that pays the highest monthly income during one person's lifetime. The fixed dollar amount depends on (1) how much principal is available, (2) the lump-sum total, and (3) the annuitant's age. Upon the death of the annuitant, the annuity contract is complete and no funds remain for one's estate.

Supplemental Security Income   Federally financed payments made to the elderly and disabled who are poor and whose Social Security benefits payments are deemed inadequate.

Tax-Sheltered Annuity   A type of annuity under which that portion of a taxpayer's income paid into the program is not subject to federal income tax while the fund accumulates.

Variable Annuity   A type of annuity in which the earnings from investment in variable investment media (as in common stocks) determine the amount of the annual payment to the person or persons named in the annuity.

Vesting   The retention by a person of part or all of his or her pension rights accumulated under one employer after he or she has left the employer.

13

Estate Planning

LEARNING OBJECTIVES

Upon completion of Chapter 13, you should be able to identify and remember

- A list of essential tools or documents for estate planning.
- The essential elements of a simple will.
- The basic purpose of a living will.
- How to prepare a simple letter of last instructions regarding one's own funeral, memorial, burial, service, and so on.
- The basic purpose of a trust.

OVERVIEW

Estate planning is a complex and technical subject for the following reasons: (1) Each state has its own laws governing the disposition of property, wills, probate, and so on. (2) Federal and state tax rulings influence the direction of estate settlement. (3) The individual should do the necessary homework to minimize both the costs and the time relating to the settling of his or her estate. Doing the "homework" is the most difficult. It is unpleasant to think about. Only you best understand what you want done with the material items after you are gone. It may seem expensive to have the proper documents drawn. We may tend to feel that there is plenty of time in which to do this work. We gain little experience in learning how to settle affairs since a death in immediate families occurs only once in every 15 to 20 years.

ESTATES AND ESTATE PLANNING

The idea of estate planning may conjure up visions of multimillionaires and their attorneys and accountants plotting to ensure that their asset holdings will pass on to their heirs and that not a farthing will go to the tax collectors. Let us look more realistically at the topic of estate planning as it might pertain to a small business owner, office worker, welder, or career homemaker. Once, again, we need to focus our attention on a key term, "estate."

Estate, according to the dictionary, is a condition or stage of life; one's property or possessions; an individually owned piece of land containing a residence. A legal definition of estate is "property which is governed by a will and passes to other people through it." For estate and gift tax purposes, an estate is all property that is governed by a will plus all joint tenancy bank accounts, insurance proceeds, and community property that passes outside a will.

Using the broader definition, your estate consists of *all the assets* that you own at the current time or owned at the time of death. Any time that you purchase a car, sell a stereo set, buy a home, own a business, sell shares of stock, and so on, you are working within the framework of estate planning.

Estate planning may not be significant to you if you are under the age of majority. It will not be important if you have used up, consumed, or sold all your assets in the process of living to a very old age and are now being cared for by the state. Those between these two groups, however, will need to consider the several features of estate planning, settlement, and possible taxes.

The real possibility of premature or untimely death as an adult provides two general reasons to do some estate planning now. First, you may have certain wishes that, in the event of your death, specific assets go directly to designated individuals. Second, all state laws prescribe for the distribution of your assets unless you have written a will.

An unplanned estate often adds to the complications surrounding the death of an individual. In addition to the emotional strain relating to a death, there will be a laborious task of searching, inventorying, accounting, and settling the estate in accordance with state laws. It is such times as these that family members argue over the way in which matters were handled. The arguing does not stop after the funeral but can go on and on over years and generations.

In summary, there are three overriding goals in estate planning: (1) to provide protection for those who need it the most, for example, if you are married, you will want your spouse and children to be cared for properly; (2) to avoid legally the payment of taxes wherever possible; and (3) to reduce the time and costs and even avoid the probate courts. To gain a better understanding of estate planning, a quick review of the "basic tools" will be made.

Tools of Estate Planning

The essential resource tools are as follows:

1. Personal information sheet (Exhibit 2-6)
2. Balance sheet (Exhibits 1-4 and 12-2)
3. Property inventory (Exhibit 2-6)
4. Financial records file (Exhibit 2-3)
5. Witnessed will (Exhibit 13-2)
6. Living will (Exhibit 13-4)
7. Letter of last instructions (Exhibit 13-3)
8. Other documents (Chapter 2)

As was stated earlier, everyone should have a designated area at home to serve as a financial records center. In this way those who must settle your estate are less likely to overlook assets that might eventually be considered abandoned and revert to the state under the *escheat* laws. Life and accidental death insurance policies should be readily available so that the settlement process with the companies concerned can be started. The witnessed will, living will, and letter of last instructions should provide the executor or executrix with information to carry out your wishes quickly and with the least amount of confusion and cost. Each of these basic documents is discussed in detail.

THE WITNESSED WILL

Basically, a *will* is a written legal document through which a person expresses the manner in which his or her estate is to be disposed of upon death. A will is also called a "testament." To make this written document legal, the *probate* or *surrogate* courts in each state require the signing of a written will to be witnessed by competent adults.

The will should have two witnesses' signatures affixed at the bottom of the will. Some states might require three witnesses and a notary public's signature, date, and seal on the document. The witnesses' role is to *attest* that the maker of the will actually signed the will in their presence and did so of his or her own free will.

Witnesses for a will should be of majority age and competent. Witnesses a little younger than the maker of the will and permanently residing in the community obviate the time and cost associated with search.

The witness section of a will can take various forms. Exhibit 13-1 conveys the notion of the witnesses' role.

In addition to the witnessed will, there are two others: the *oral* will and the *handwritten,* or *holographic,* will. Few courts recognize them.

The witnessed will is usually in typed form, having been drafted and finalized in the office of a lawyer. Other witnessed wills may be in preprinted form, such as those sold in office supply stores, with the blanks completed either with a typewriter or in pen and ink by hand. No matter how the document is written, the witnesses to the signing and their attesting to this fact is the key point.

Who Has a Will?

Estimates from several groups indicate that as many as 60 to 70 percent of Americans die without preparing a formal will. In other words, only 30 to 40 percent undertake the task of drawing up this important document.

EXHIBIT 13-1   Witness Section of a Will

_____, in soundness of mind and under no pressure or duress, asked us to appear as witness to observe the signing of this last will and testament consisting of _____ pages. The will was signed in our presence on this _____ day of the month of _____ in the year _____.

_____ witness

Residing at _____

_____

_____ witness

Residing at _____

_____

There are probably several reasons why many people do not have wills at the time of death. Many of the younger people have accumulated little in the way of assets and do not see the need of the document. The laws of *intestate,* dying without a will, may provide a satisfactory form of distributing assets. The succession of distribution might be as follows: (1) to the spouse, (2) to the children, (3) to the grandchildren, (4) to the parents of the deceased, (5) to the grandparents of the deceased, (6) to brothers and sisters of the deceased, and so on.

At the other end of the age scale, many elderly persons will have exhausted all their major assets or have long since passed them on to their children. They have given away the small heirlooms and other mementos. Therefore, these people may feel no need to write a will.

Finally, many consider writing a will to be a most unpleasant task, akin to signing their own death warrant. And many have just put off the task.

Who Should Have a Will?

Today, all adults should have a will when they have taken on major responsibilities or have assets that they wish to go to specific persons. The financial problems relating to premature death are somewhat lessened when the person who died had life insurance that designated a beneficiary. A witnessed will simply establishes a succession of "beneficiaries" for other assets.

Major Elements in a Witnessed Will

Most basic wills should include the following information. If you have considerable property, heavy responsibilities as a head of a household, handicapped children or other family members requiring special care, many material things such as family heirlooms that should be passed along to specific people, and so on, then you will necessarily add these sections into your basic will.

Heading of Document. The title might be written as follows: The Last Will and Testament of John Howard Doe.

Declaration Statement. A statement of declaration should state that this is the last will and testament of John Howard Doe. Include the full address (street, city, county, state, and zip code). There is usually a statement indicating soundness of mind at this point.

Administration. A sentence or paragraph is written naming the executor or executrix to take charge of the estate and settle the necessary affairs. List three possible names in priority that should take on this responsibility; for example, names of your spouse, attorney, bank, son or daughter, and so on could serve in this position. The person selected must be of majority age and have the ability to serve in this capacity.

Bonding. A statement should be made declaring that the provisions of bonding be waived in the case of the executor. A similar statement should be made and permission granted to name guardians and the waiver of bonding requirements. "The posting of bond shall be waived in the case of my executrix . . .".

Marital Status. If you are married, a statement should be made declaring that you are married including the full name of your spouse. A woman's maiden name may also be written in this section. Include the address of your spouse for clarification.

Children. A statement is made listing the names of your living and legally adopted children. List all living children's names even if they are not to receive any assets.

Guardians. Names of guardians are listed in order of priority to take care of your children in the event that both parents die at the same time. A single parent should do the same. A declaratory statement on this topic of guardianship is to be written in the will. A list of guardians for incapacitated parents or handicapped or retarded children is to be considered in the will document.

Debts. A statement is made that all debts that you have incurred are liquidated. This statement might include words granting authority that the debts are to be paid by the executor or executrix.

Bequests, Legacies, and Devises. A section in the will should provide for a listing of specific gifts to be made. The list might start with *bequests* or *legacies* (personal property items). Examples are silverware, a gold pocket watch, cash, a photo album, and so on. The will should clearly identify the person's name, the address and relationship, and the item given. "I give my brother, George Leroy Doe of Helena, Montana, my gold pocket watch with hunter's case." "I give $500 cash to our city library in Middletown . . .". Another list might include *devises* (real property) if any. Examples are land and/or structures. This is likely to be an unusual gift for most estates, as most land and structures (such as the house and land) would go to a surviving spouse as part of the bulk or remainder of the estate.

Trusts. A separate section or paragraph for testamentary trusts might have to be established. Here would be included the size of the trust, the purpose, the name of beneficiary, the name of the trustee, authority of the trustee over the principal and income, disposition of the trust at the end of its need, and so on.

Common Disaster Clause. A separate paragraph is included in the event that a husband and wife are killed in the same accident or in the event that one spouse survives the other by only a few hours or days. The statement establishes how the assets are to be distributed, trust funds to be set up for minor children, who the guardians will be, and so on. When there are no remaindermen, there should be procedures for disposing of all assets and distribution to specific people or groups.

A Hold Harmless or Exculpatory Clause. A statement is made in the will to absolve from blame minor errors or omissions on the part of executor or executrix.

Disposition of Residual Assets. A statement is made that all other assets, both real and personal, are to be given to a specific person or persons. Allocating residual assets to two or more persons should not result in complicating the survivors. Giving the house and land to adults and minor children could prevent the home from being sold until the youngest person reaches majority age. The will reduces these possibilities by spelling out clearly the steps to be taken.

Dating of the Will. A sentence is entered that indicates that the above page(s) and space is provided for placing the month, date, and year. The month should be written out (e.g., March, September, April); this will be done at the signing and witnessing of the will.

Signing of the Will. There is a sentence stating that you are signing the will in the presence of competent witnesses. A space in this sentence should allow the signature of the maker of the will to be entered.

Witnesses' Attestation Clause and Signatures. For all intents and purposes, wills are usually not recognized by the probate courts unless the maker of the will signs his or her name to the will in the presence of at least two or maybe three competent witnesses. The witnesses will also sign the will and enter the date and their residence as part of an attestation statement. This attestation statement of the witnesses reaffirms that the maker of the will is of sound mind and has made the testament of his or her own free will. In addition to the signing and witnesses' signatures, observation of a notary public with his or her signature, dating, and seal affixed to the document might be required.

Other Features. Because of legal requirements, the will is to be free of errors and without eraser marks, smudges, or crossed-out words. The will is written on very-high-quality paper so as not to deteriorate.

After Making a Will . . .

For the 30 to 40 percent of the people who prepare wills, two concerns should be reviewed: (1) keeping the will up to date and (2) possible challenges to the will when it is probated.

When should a will be revised? Major changes in earnings and marital status, children being born, death of a family member, the need to establish trust funds, and so on can be reasons for revising a will. Since many of these very situations are legal matters, it is best to consult an attorney. Minor revisions to a will can be made with an amendment called a *codicil.* Other events may require writing a new will.

Occasionally, one will read that a will of a well-known personality is being challenged. Lots of money or real estate will always provide incentive to bring challenges whether or not there is merit. A nonwitnessed will is a good reason to instigate a challenge. Other challenges might be based on fraud, undue influence, concern about a witness's age, competence, or the disinheritance of a spouse or child. These potential problems can be reduced by using the services of a lawyer and careful homework on the will maker's part.

A sample witnessed will is shown in Exhibit 13-2.

"Being of sound mind, I never worked hard enough to have anything to leave."

From *The Wall Street Journal*—
Permission, Cartoon Features Syndicate.

EXHIBIT 13-2 Sample Will

THE LAST WILL AND TESTAMENT OF
JOHN LEE MAY

I.

I, John Lee May, of 4321 Third Street, Anytown, Iowa, be of sound mind and over 21 years of age, do hereby publish this my last will and testament.

II.

I am married to Mary Ann (Smith) May. We have no children.

III.

I appoint my wife, Mary Ann May, to serve as my executrix. If she does not survive me, I appoint my brother, Mark Allen May, of Route 3, Neartown, Iowa. If he does not survive me or cannot serve in this capacity, I appoint the Second National Bank of Anytown, Iowa, to serve as executor. I declare that my wife or other executors serve independently and the requirements for bonding be waived.

IV.

I direct that all of my just debts be paid.

V.

I hereby make the following bequest:

Gold pocket watch with hunter's case which was my father's is to be given to my brother, Mark Allen May.

VI.

Should my wife survive me, I give all of remaining property to her. If my wife does not survive me, I ask that my brother to sell publicly or privately and at fair prices, the residual assets that I shall own at that time. I direct that Ten Thousand Dollars ($10,000) of the proceeds be given to my brother, Mark Allen May, and I further direct that an additional Ten Thousand Dollars ($10,000) be given to my wife's sister, Ruth Cora Smith, who resides at 300 Main Street, Midtown, Iowa. If neither my brother Mark Allen May nor Ruth Cora Smith survive me, I direct that my executors place their portions and any residual assets in my estate be given to the Trustees of Anytown College for the purpose of establishing the John Lee and Mary Ann May Scholarship Fund, with the principal of the fund to remain intact and the earnings be made available for students in financial need based upon the College's standards.

VII.

In the presence of witnesses and in a sound and disposing mind and of my own free will and under no undue influence, I declare this to be my last will and testament on November 15, 19X1.

John Lee May

John Lee May, in soundness of mind and under no pressure or duress, and of his own free will, asked us to appear as witnesses to observe the signing of this last will and testament consisting of one page. The will was signed in our presence on this 15th day of the month of November of the year 19X1.

Richard A. Roe witness, residing at 231 10th Street
Anytown, Iowa

Nancy C. Bock witness, residing at 450 Main Street #10
Anytown, Iowa

A LETTER OF LAST INSTRUCTIONS

The sudden death of someone is a traumatic event. But, besides the grief and confusion that may accompany the experience, death can cause needless arguing among family members.

Some of the dispute can be eliminated in a *letter of last instructions*. This letter may include the names of those who need to be contacted as well as how they should be reached. It could include instructions about anatomical bequests, honorariums, budget limitations, and the disposition of small personal effects and clothing. The letter might include where the will is located as well as other important documents and advisors and indicate the decedent's wishes for funeral and burial arrangements.

There is no set format in which this letter is to be prepared. However, it does serve to complement the will because the will is probably not the best place to include funeral details. The next of kin should have flexibility with funeral arrangements. Whatever is placed in a will has to be carried out under the auspices of the court. Exhibit 13-3 could serve as a worksheet to jotting down your thoughts and directions. A last letter of considerable merit and courage may then be developed.

THE LIVING WILL

A new document emerging as part of the estate planning tools is the living will. Its purpose is to inform others of your wishes regarding being kept alive by artificial means or other "heroic measures." When there is an expectation that physical or mental recovery is extremely remote, it is a request that one be allowed to die.

This document does not have legal status in many states at this time. However, knowledge of this document by family friends and attending doctor may serve to guide physicians and family with difficult decisions. Information about this living will document can be obtained from the Concern for Dying, 250 West 57th Street, New York, N.Y. 10019. A sample of the living will appears in Exhibit 13-4.

FUNERALS, ALTERNATIVE SERVICES, AND BURIAL

The 15,000-plus funeral homes in the United States constitute a $6.4-billion-a-year industry. The average cost of a funeral in recent years has been $2,150. However, in some states, where options have been greater, it may average $900 to $1,100. And alternative low-cost plans may be investigated by first reviewing the ads in the Yellow Pages of the telephone directory.

EXHIBIT 13-3 Letter of Last Instructions Planning Sheet

I. General Information:

  A. The person to be in charge of all arrangements: _____

    Address:_____ Telephone: _____

    Alternant:_____ Telephone: _____

II. Funeral and burial service or Alternative People's Memorial service:

  A. Funeral service and burial special requests

    Name of director:_____ Telephone:_____

    Embalmment:_____ Type of casket:_____

    Open or closed casket service:_____ Specific clothing or jewelery to be

    worn and removed: _____

    Flowers:_____

    Specific memorial service (special music, songs, etc.): _____

    _____

    _____

    _____

    Person to deliver eulogy:_____

    Address:_____ Telephone: _____

    Alternant:_____ Telephone: _____

    Specific honorarium to those who performed extra work $_____per person.

    Maximum budget to be spent on my funeral director's services: $_____

    Memorial Service only:_____ Location:_____

    _____ Speaker: _____

    Address:_____ Telephone: _____

    Refreshments to be served:_____

  B. Alternative People's Memorial type of service (a simple service, no elaborate casket, cremation and ashes, simple burial plan, burial with service, etc.)

    Service Group:_____ Telephone:_____

    Type of Plan: _____

    Estimated cost of specific plan: $_____

III. Burial Service:

  Location of cemetery:_____

  Burial plot:_____

  Headstone: Inscription: _____

       Type:_____ Budget: $_____

  Names of pallbearers: _____

  _____

  Honorary pallbearers:_____

EXHIBIT 13-3 *(continued)*

Grave side services:_____ Specifics:_____

_____ Honor guard:_____

Cost questions needed on coach, limousine, police escort, printing:_____

IV. Special budget for special travel and lodging of parents: $_____

Provisions, if any, on any meals before or after funeral:_____

V. Notification of specific people, and how they are to be notified:

    1. Immediate relatives:

        _____ by_____

        _____ by_____

        _____ by_____

        _____ by_____

        _____ by_____

    2. Employer:_____ by_____

    3. Fraternal, clubs, alumni, newspaper, etc. to be notified:

        _____

        _____

        _____

        _____

VI. Information for drafting obituary:

Birthday:_____ birth place:_____ schools attended:_____

_____

_____

Cities and towns lived:_____

Government and military service, awards, etc.:_____

_____

Companies worked and chief skill or profession:_____

_____

Special achievements:_____

Community service activities:_____

_____

VII. Miscellaneous Information:

Cremation authorization:_____ Anatomical gifts:_____

Location of will: _____ Location of living will:_____

Location of insurance policies:_____ Charity donation by friends:____

_____

EXHIBIT 13-4 Living Will Sample

My Living Will
To My Family, My Physician, My Lawyer and All Others Whom It May Concern

Death is as much a reality as birth, growth, maturity and old age—it is the one certainty of life. If the time comes when I can no longer take part in decisions for my own future, let this statement stand as an expression of my wishes and directions, while I am still of sound mind.

If at such a time the situation should arise in which there is no reasonable expectation of my recovery from extreme physical or mental disability, I direct that I be allowed to die and not be kept alive by medications, artificial means or "heroic measures". I do, however, ask that medication be mercifully administered to me to alleviate suffering even though this may shorten my remaining life.

This statement is made after careful consideration and is in accordance with my strong convictions and beliefs. I want the wishes and directions here expressed carried out to the extent permitted by law. Insofar as they are not legally enforceable, I hope that those to whom this Will is addressed will regard themselves as morally bound by these provisions.

(Optional specific provisions to be made in this space — see other side)

DURABLE POWER OF ATTORNEY (optional)

I hereby designate _____ to serve as my attorney-in-fact for the purpose of making medical treatment decisions. This power of attorney shall remain effective in the event that I become incompetent or otherwise unable to make such decisions for myself.

Optional Notarization:

"Sworn and subscribed to

before me this _____ day

of _____, 19_____."

_____
Notary Public
(seal)

Signed_____

Date _____

Witness _____

_____
Address

Witness _____

_____
Address

Copies of this request have been given to _____

_____   _____

(Optional)   My Living Will is registered with Concern for Dying (No. _____)

Reprinted with the permission of Concern for Dying, 250 West 57 Street, New York, NY 10019.

TRUSTS

A *trust* is a legal contract for the management and control of certain assets held by one person for the benefit of another. An *inter vivos,* or living, trust is created during the lifetime of the grantor. A *testmentary* trust is a trust established under the terms of a will to administer property *after* death of the person who made the will. One normally thinks of trusts as being set up for children in the event that both parents die or to provide for a widow or a son or daughter.

However, there is almost an unlimited number of ways in which a trust can be used. Trusts can do about the same thing as wills. Trusts can consist of almost any kind of income-producing property. Trusts set up for a specific goal will be allowed to stand, whereas wills established for identical purposes could be challenged. A will must be probated; a trust will bypass the probate process.

Trusts are sometimes identified by their degree of flexibility. A *revocable* trust is established to accomplish certain goals, but it allows the grantor to cancel the trust at any time. An *irrevocable* trust is considered similar to a delayed gift to a specific receiver. The grantor cannot change his or her mind once the trust is established. A *reversionary* trust is designed for a specific time period to benefit a certain person. At the end of the time, the assets revert back to the grantor.

The reversionary trust is used by families to lower their federal income taxes. The parents may have bonds and stocks transferred to a trust with the interest and dividend income directed to the children. The children, having a lower income base, will receive the income and pay the income taxes on it. The tax rate is usually lower than that of the parents, and therefore the income taxes paid by the family will be lower. For the family to receive this tax benefit potential, the trust must be established for a period of 10 years and 1 day.

There are many books written on the topic of trusts as well as periodicals directed at people who are in the estate planning business. The commerce section of your public library can provide you with a variety of fascinating literature on the subject. The IRS has booklets on the latest income tax requirements related to trusts. Even if you do not use a trust, it can add another dimension in your thinking when it comes to personal money management.

COMMUNITY PROPERTY LAWS

If you live in the state of Arizona, California, Idaho, Louisiana, Nevada, New Mexico, Texas, or Washington, your estate planning is governed by community property laws. Generally, in all community property states, the community property goes to the surviving spouse to the exclusion of children and other heirs. That is, the property accumulated *during* the marriage is owned equally and goes to the surviving spouse, regardless of which spouse earned it. In some states property owned individually prior to marriage and property received by gift or inheritance during marriage remain separate property.

For clarification, suppose that two young people get married and during their lifetime together accumulate land, a house, furniture, stocks and bonds, and so on. Three children are born to this marriage. In year 15 of the marriage, the husband dies in a car accident. There is no will. In a community property state, all the assets go to the widow; none go to the children.

In noncommunity property states, on the other hand, the widow might only receive an equal sharing with the children, in this case a fourth of the assets; in other noncommunity property states, she may receive a third. The house and land might not be able to be sold since an adult and minor children jointly hold title. In a noncommunity property state, a will must be written to assure that the widow in this case receives the house and land.

As stated earlier, in most community property states, property accumulated before the marriage remains separate as does that received by gift or inheritance. For separate property to belong to the couple jointly, a *community property agreement* must be prepared and signed by both husband and wife. If the property is to be kept separate, it must not be allowed to become commingled with the joint or community-acquired property.

In summary, the objective of the community property agreement is to benefit the surviving spouse. This agreement brings into the marriage the previous separate properties and declares them to be jointly owned. Without the agreement, the separate property would have passed to other heirs in accordance with the state's succession laws.

In a community property state, when a community property agreement is being prepared, a will is likely to be prepared also by each party. These two documents help to bring all the properties in to be passed on to the survivor. The maker of the will can still direct that certain piece of property be given to a specific individual. The maker can also set up provisions for guardians, name executors, waive bonding requirements, and so on as was discussed earlier in the chapter.

If a widow or widower, each with considerable assets, plan to marry, they need to consider whether to maintain separate estates or to merge their assets. They will need to consider the state law, wills, community property agreements, marital agreements, estate taxes, and so on in their planning.

ESTATE, GIFT, AND INHERITANCE TAXES

The Tax Reform Act of 1976 brought about major changes in laws regulating federal estate and gift taxes. This complex area of study is well beyond the scope of this text, so we will consider only some of the basics as they may affect own estate planning in general.

A key point in time now in estate planning is December 31, 1976. Assets owned and held on this date can be raised from their original cost (actual price paid) to their fair market value on December 31, 1976, whichever was higher.

For example, if you purchased land valued at $4,000 in 1962 and still held it on December 31, 1976, when it was valued at $9,000, you may value the property for estate purposes at $9,000. If you still owned the property today and it is valued at $15,000, the gain, if it were sold, only will be taxed on the difference between the $15,000 and $9,000. That is, the tax rate would be applied to a $6,000 gain.

The government recognizes that much of the increase in the value of property is largely a result of inflation (cheaper dollars). Therefore, this December 31, 1976 benchmark is a simple technique to wipe out some of the taxes on inflation.

Another provision in the act allows estate taxes to be paid over a period of up to 15 years so as to avoid forced sales, particularly of small businesses and farms. Old laws required payment in nine months after the death of the estate owner.

Another feature of the 1976 Tax Reform Act unifies estate and gift tax rates. In the exemption or tax credit exemption on gift and estate taxes in Tables 13-1 and 13-2, note the gradual upward movement on the size of the exemption. This again eliminates taxing an estate that is growing mainly as a result of inflation.

The act also increased the marital deduction for inheritances to surviving spouses to the greater of $250,000 or 50 percent of the adjusted gross value of the estate.

You can give up to $10,000 a year, or $20,000 if it comes from a husband and wife, to a person without having to report the gift for tax purposes.

State inheritance laws vary throughout the 50 states, and no attempt will be made at reviewing them. All that can be done here is to set forth the expected tax rates in this area and the groups or classification in which heirs might find themselves.

TABLE 13-1   Taxable Inheritances
According to the 1976 Tax Reform Act,
1982–1987 and Beyond

For the Year	Exemption from taxes
1982	$225,000
1983	275,000
1984	375,000
1985	400,000
1986	500,000
1987 and thereafter	600,000

TABLE 13-2 Unified Federal Estate and Gift Tax Rates, 1988 and Beyond

Taxable Estate or Gift			
More Than (1)	But Not More Than (2)	Tax on (1)	Rate on Excess (1)
0	$ 10,000	0	18%
$ 10,000	20,000	$ 1,800	20
20,000	40,000	3,800	22
40,000	60,000	8,200	24
60,000	80,000	13,000	26
80,000	100,000	18,200	28
100,000	150,000	23,800	30
150,000	250,000	38,800	32
250,000	500,000	70,800	34
500,000	750,000	155,800	37
750,000	1,000,000	248,300	39
1,000,000	1,250,000	345,800	41
1,250,000	1,500,000	448,300	43
1,500,000	2,000,000	555,800	45
2,000,000	2,500,000	780,800	49
2,500,000	—	1,025,800	50

Heirs might be grouped in classes A, B, or C, for example, with group A representing the immediate family (spouse, lineal children, and grandchildren), group B including brothers and sisters, and group C including nonrelated people and nieces and nephews. State estate tax exemptions and percentage rates will vary according to class of relative. Immediate family exemptions are the largest; group C heirs may not receive any exemptions and the percentage rates are high.

A state inheritance tax on an estate going to group A (immediate family) might be taxed on the rates shown in Table 13-3 over and above the total exemptions.

TABLE 13-3 Sample State Inheritance Tax Rates

Amount	Percentage Rate
$1– 25,000	1%
25,001– 50,000	2
50,001– 75,000	3
75,001–100,000	4
100,001–200,000	7
200,001–500,000	9
500,001 and over	10

AVOIDING PROBATE

The state surrogate or probate court will act on the estate of a deceased person. This is true whether a person dies intestate or has a will. Some state laws are very conservative with bank accounts immediately frozen and safe deposit boxes sealed, so that the family has to depend on other resources until the probate is completed. Other states are more liberal.

The probate court reads and proves the signatures of the will maker and witnesses. The court also notifies any creditors and makes an accounting of all the assets owned by the decedent. The notification of heirs and defending the will against challenges are activities performed by the probate court.

Because of the time and delay in certain states, ownership arrangements have emerged to bypass the probate process. The best example is the life insurance policy. The beneficiary receives the proceeds directly. Separate bank accounts in each spouse's name will continue to keep cash available to the spouse.

How can other property such as savings accounts, stocks, bonds, and so on avoid the probate process? In a family, the assets can be owned jointly in the form *tenants by the entireties*. This tenancy is limited to a husband and wife.

Holding title as *joint tenants with right of survivorship* provides that, when one of the tenants dies, the title of his or her share of the assets usually can be transferred to the survivor without going through probate court proceedings. This form of joint tenancy can apply to any two or more people. While there may be several ways in which to avoid probate, one should hold a perspective as to whether it meets stated objectives and does not aggravate other favorable estate tax possibilities.

SUMMARY

Estate planning is a complex and technical subject because of 50 sets of state laws, federal and state taxes, and individuals' need to do a certain amount of homework.

An estate is property that is governed by a will and passes through it to other people. Abandoned property will revert to the state under escheat laws. A will is a written legal document through which a person expresses the manner in which his or her estate is to be disposed of upon death. Most probate courts require that a will be witnessed by two or more competent adults. Only 30 to 40 percent of the U.S. population prepare wills. A person who dies without a will is said to die intestate.

Information about an individual's funeral requests should be placed in a letter of last instructions rather than in a will. The living will is a document that the individual not be kept alive by artificial means.

There are over 15,000 funeral homes in the United States and the average funeral has cost $2,150. The Federal Trade Commission requires specific consumer information be made. Alternative associations are attempting to provide lower-cost funerals.

A trust is a legal contract for the management and control of certain assets held by one person for the benefit of another. There are eight community property states in the United States. The objective of a community property agreement is to benefit the surviving spouse.

The Tax Reform Act of 1976 brought about major changes in federal estate and gift tax laws. December 31, 1976 is an important date for evaluating assets for estate and gift tax purposes. Activities of a probate court include proving signatures of the deceased and witnesses, notifying creditors, making an accounting of assets, locating heirs, distributing assets, and so on.

TIPS

1. Build a file of notes and news clippings relating to your estate planning. This can be a source for modifying your goals, raising questions with your attorney, changing investment, and so on.

2. Life insurance proceeds to a beneficiary are not subject to the laws of probate; the beneficiary receives the assets without probate delays.

3. Allow your survivors flexibility in funeral and burial arrangements, particularly if your estate is not large.

4. Appraisal of antiques and works of art may be helpful in valuing your estate. Expect to pay a professional's hourly fee.

5. Throw out old letters and correspondence that you do not want others to see. Conducting a good thorough house cleaning periodically is in itself good estate planning.

6. Even if you never get around to writing a will, write out requests for what you would like to see done with some of your assets. Some of your requests may be honored, particularly on token items that you want to give away.

ADDITIONAL READINGS

"The ABC's of Making a Will," *U.S. News & World Reports*, May 7, 1984, pp. 67–70.
"Estate Tax Law Is Changing Again," *Business Week*, May 7, 1984, pp. 156–60.
Kubler-Ross, Elisabeth, *On Death and Dying*. New York: Macmillan, 1979.
"The Limits to a Do-It-Yourself Will," *Changing Times*, November 1984, p. 82.
Reiter, Mark, "Drafting an Heir-Tight Will," *Money*, June 1984, pp. 133–36.

"When It's All in the Family," *Changing Times*, January 1986, pp. 62–68.
"You Don't Have to Be a Ford to Start a Foundation," *Business Week*, November 23, 1987, p. 140.

GLOSSARY OF USEFUL TERMS

Administrator   One who administers a decedent's estate during probate. An administrator is appointed by the judge of a probate court when no executor or executrix is named in the will.

Attestation   The witnessing of a document's execution and a signed statement to that effect.

Bequeath   A gift of property by means of a will.

Bequest   A gift of personal property (such as a gold watch) or money under a will.

Codicils   Writings executed subsequent to a will and forming a part of the will.

Community Property   Property held jointly by husband and wife and accumulated during a marriage that belongs equally to each spouse in certain states.

Curtesy   The right of a widower, provided that he had a child by his wife, to a lifetime interest in all her real property at the time of her death.

Custodial Care   A type of retirement care given when a person is no longer able to take care of himself or herself.

Death Tax   Inheritance tax levied by state.

Decedent   A deceased person.

Devise   A gift of real property (land and/or structures) by the last will and testament of the donor.

Disability   Inability to engage in a substantially gainful activity because of an illness that can be expected to be of a long and indefinite duration or will result in death.

Donee   The recipient of a gift.

Escheat Laws   State laws that provide for abandoned property, assets, money, unclaimed wages, and the like to revert to the state.

Estate   Interest in property. The property owned by a decedent before the property is distributed according to the terms of a will or by the laws of inheritance if the owner died without a will (intestate).

Estate Tax   A tax levied on the transfer of rights to property in an estate.

Euthanasia   A painless death, the act of causing death; advocated by some in cases of incurable diseases.

Executor (Executrix)   The personal representative of a testator appointed by the testator and approved by the judge of a probate court. The executor takes charge of the decedent's estate, pays the debts, and distributes the balance of the property to beneficiaries of the will pursuant to the order of the probate court.

Exculpatory Clause   Absolution from blame. Usually included in trusts and wills to absolve trustees or executors from minor omissions in the documents.

Gift Tax   Tax levied by federal and state governments on the transfer of financial assets as gifts.

Guardian   A person appointed by a will or court to care for minor children or an incompetent adult.

Heir One who is entitled to receive or inherit property.

Holographic Will A will written entirely by the testator in his or her own hand.

Hospice A place for dying when further medical treatment is considered pointless. It implies a warm secure place and friends and family.

Inter Vivos While living.

Inter Vivos Trust A trust created during the lifetime of the grantor. Also called a living trust.

Intestate Having no will at death.

Irrevocable Trust A trust that cannot be changed later by the person who created the trust.

Joint Tenancy with Right of Survivorship Two or more persons owning the same land and having the same unity of interest, time, title, and possession with right of survivorship.

Legacy A gift of personal property, generally a specific item of value mentioned in a will. The legatee is the recipient.

Letter of Last Instructions A document written by a person to his or her survivors relating to locations of property, records, funeral and burial arrangements, persons to notify, and so on. Not a will.

Marital Deduction The transferring to one's spouse by will, free of federal estate and gift taxation, up to 50 percent of one's adjusted gross estate.

Medicaid A state-administered program that provides medical, health care, nursing care, and so on to those whose assets have been exhausted by illness.

Oral Will A will given orally by a person contemplating imminent death. This will is usually not valid: called nuncupative will.

Power of Attorney An agent's written authorization from his or her principal.

Probate The procedure of proving a will before a probate or surrogate court having jurisdiction over the administration of the deceased person.

Skilled Care A type of retirement care given in an infirmary for most medical problems except surgery, broken bones, and acute diseases.

Skilled Services An important term in insurance coverage in Medicaid and extended medical insurance coverage. Some coverages will make payments in cash for up to 365 days for skilled services.

SSI (Supplemental Security Income) A federal income maintenance program for the aged, blind, and disabled.

Testamentary Trust A trust established under the terms of a will to administer property after the death of the person who made the will.

Testator The person who has made a will or the decedent who left a will.

Testatrix A female person who makes a will.

Tenancy in Common Ownership of real property in which each owner has title to an undivided share of the property. If one owner dies, his or her interest passes to heirs and not to the surviving owner or owners of the estate.

Tenants by the Entireties A type of joint tenancy in which the co-owners are husband and wife. Neither can sell without the other's consent, and, upon death of either, the survivor gets the title.

Thanatology The study of death.

Trust A legal contract for the management and control of certain assets held by one person for the benefit of another.

Trust Companies   Companies that receive money and invest it for the benefit of a third party.

Trustee   A person in whom property is vested in trust for another.

Trustor   One who gives something (grantor).

Uniform Anatomical Gift Act   Legislation that permits a U.S. citizen in any state to donate his or her entire body or only certain organs.

Will   A written legal document through which a person expresses the manner in which his or her estate is to be disposed of upon that individual's death. Also called a testament.

Appendix A

Annuity and Compound Interest Tables

TABLE A.1 Future Value of $1

Year	5%	6%	7%	8%	10%	12%
1	1.05000	1.06000	1.07000	1.08000	1.10000	1.12000
2	1.10250	1.12360	1.14490	1.16640	1.21000	1.25440
3	1.15763	1.19102	1.22504	1.25971	1.33100	1.40493
4	1.21551	1.26248	1.31080	1.36049	1.46410	1.57352
5	1.27628	1.33823	1.40255	1.46933	1.61051	1.76234
6	1.34010	1.41852	1.50073	1.58687	1.77156	1.97382
7	1.40710	1.50363	1.60578	1.71382	1.94872	1.21068
8	1.47746	1.59385	1.71819	1.85093	2.14359	2.47596
9	1.55133	1.68948	1.83846	1.99900	2.35795	2.77308
10	1.62889	1.79085	1.96715	2.15892	2.59374	3.10585
11	1.71034	1.89830	2.10485	2.33164	2.85312	3.47855
12	1.79586	2.01220	2.25219	2.51817	3.13843	3.89598
13	1.88565	2.13293	2.40985	2.71962	3.45227	4.36349
14	1.97993	2.26090	2.57853	2.93719	3.79750	4.88711
15	2.07893	2.39656	2.75903	3.17217	4.17725	5.47357
16	2.18287	2.54035	2.95216	2.42594	4.59497	6.13039
17	2.29202	2.69277	3.15882	3.70002	5.05447	6.86604
18	2.40662	2.85434	3.37993	3.99602	5.55992	7.68997
19	2.52695	3.02560	3.61653	4.31570	6.11591	8.61276
20	2.65330	3.20714	3.86968	4.66096	6.72750	9.64629
22	2.92526	3.60354	4.43040	5.43654	8.14027	12.10031
24	3.22510	4.04893	5.07237	6.34118	9.84973	15.17863
26	3.55567	4.54938	5.80735	7.39635	11.91818	19.04007
28	3.92013	5.11169	6.64884	8.62711	14.42099	23.88387
30	4.32194	5.74349	7.61226	10.06266	17.44940	29.95992
32	4.76494	6.15339	8.71527	11.73708	21.11378	37.58173
34	5.25335	7.25103	9.97811	13.69013	25.54767	47.14252
36	5.79182	8.14725	11.42394	15.96817	30.91268	59.13557
38	6.38548	9.15425	13.07927	18.62528	37.40434	74.17966
40	7.03999	10.28572	14.97446	21.72452	45.25926	93.05097
45	8.98501	13.76461	21.00245	31.92045	72.89048	163.9876
50	11.46740	18.42015	29.45703	46.90161	117.3909	289.0022

TABLE A.2 Present Value of $1

Years	5%	6%	7%	8%	10%	12%
1	.95238	.94340	.93458	.92593	.90909	.89286
2	.90703	.89000	.87344	.85734	.82645	.79719
3	.86384	.83962	.81630	.79383	.75131	.71178
4	.82270	.79209	.76290	.73503	.68301	.63552
5	.78353	.74726	.71299	.68058	.62092	.56743
6	.74622	.70496	.66634	.63017	.56447	.50663
7	.71068	.66506	.62275	.58349	.51316	.45235
8	.67684	.62741	.58201	.54027	.46651	.40388
9	.64461	.59190	.54393	.50025	.42410	.36061
10	.61391	.55839	.50835	.46319	.38554	.32197
11	.58468	.52679	.47509	.42888	.35049	.28748
12	.55684	.49697	.44401	.39711	.31863	.25668
13	.53032	.46884	.41496	.36770	.28966	.22917
14	.50507	.44230	.38782	.34046	.26333	.20462
15	.48102	.41727	.36245	.31524	.23939	.18270
16	.45811	.39365	.33873	.29189	.21763	.16312
17	.43630	.37136	.31657	.27027	.19784	.14564
18	.41552	.35034	.29586	.25025	.17986	.13004
19	.39573	.33051	.27651	.23171	.16351	.11611
20	.37689	.31180	.25842	.21455	.14864	.10367
22	.34185	.27751	.22571	.18394	.12285	.08264
24	.31007	.24698	.19715	.15770	.10153	.16588
26	.28124	.21981	.17220	.13520	.08391	.05252
28	.25509	.19563	.15040	.11591	.06934	.04187
30	.23138	.17411	.13137	.09938	.05731	.03338
32	.20987	.15496	.11474	.08520	.04736	.02661
34	.19035	.13791	.10022	.07305	.03914	.02121
36	.17266	.12274	.08754	.06262	.03235	.01691
38	.15661	.10924	.07646	.05369	.02673	.01348
40	.14205	.09722	.06678	.04603	.02209	.01075
45	.11130	.07265	.04761	.03133	.01372	.00610
50	.08720	.05429	.03395	.02132	.00852	.00346

TABLE A.3   Future Value of Annuity of $1 in Arrears*

No. of payments	5%	6%	7%	8%	10%	12%
1	1.00000	1.00000	1.00000	1.00000	1.00000	1.00000
2	2.05000	2.06000	2.07000	2.08000	2.10000	2.12000
3	3.15250	3.18360	3.21490	3.24640	3.31000	3.37440
4	4.31013	4.37462	4.43994	4.50611	4.64100	4.77933
5	5.52563	5.63709	5.75074	5.86660	6.10510	6.35285
6	6.80191	6.97532	7.15329	7.33593	7.71561	8.11519
7	8.14201	8.39384	8.65402	8.92280	9.48717	10.08901
8	9.54911	9.89747	10.25980	10.63663	11.43589	12.29969
9	11.02656	11.49132	11.97799	12.48756	13.57948	14.77566
10	12.57789	13.18079	13.81645	14.48656	15.93742	17.54874
11	14.20679	14.97164	15.78360	16.64549	18.53117	20.65458
12	15.91713	16.86994	17.88845	18.97713	21.38428	24.13313
13	17.71298	18.88214	20.14064	21.49530	24.52271	28.02911
14	19.59863	21.01507	22.55049	24.21492	27.97498	32.39260
15	21.57856	23.27597	25.12902	27.15211	31.77248	37.27971
16	23.65749	25.67253	27.88805	30.32428	35.94973	42.75328
17	25.84037	28.21288	30.84022	33.75023	40.54470	48.88367
18	28.13238	30.90565	33.99903	37.45024	45.59917	55.74971
19	30.53900	33.75999	37.37896	41.44626	51.15909	63.43968
20	33.06595	36.78559	40.99549	45.76196	57.27500	72.05244
22	38.50521	43.39229	49.00574	55.45676	71.40275	92.50258
24	44.50200	50.81558	58.17667	66.76476	88.49733	118.1552
26	51.11345	59.15638	68.67647	79.95442	109.1818	150.3339
28	58.40258	68.52811	80.69769	95.33883	134.2099	190.6989
30	66.43885	79.05819	94.46079	113.2832	164.4940	241.3327
32	75.29883	90.88978	110.2181	134.2135	201.1378	304.8477
34	85.06696	104.1838	128.2588	158.6267	245.4767	384.5210
36	95.83632	119.1209	148.9135	187.1022	299.1268	484.4631
38	107.7095	135.9042	172.5610	220.3159	364.0434	609.8305
40	120.7998	154.7620	199.6351	259.0565	442.5926	767.0914
45	159.7002	212.7435	285.7493	386.5056	718.9048	1358.230
50	209.3480	290.3359	406.5289	573.7702	1163.909	2400.018

* To convert from this table to values of an annuity in advance, determine the annuity in arrears above for one more period and subtract 1.00000.

TABLE A.4   Present Value of Annuity of $1 in Arrears*

No. of payments	5%	6%	7%	8%	10%	12%
1	.95238	.94340	.93458	.92593	.90909	.89286
2	1.85941	1.83339	1.80802	1.78326	1.73554	1.69005
3	2.72325	2.67301	2.62432	2.57710	2.48685	2.40183
4	3.54595	3.46511	3.38721	3.31213	3.16987	3.03735
5	4.32948	4.21236	4.10020	3.99271	3.79079	3.60478
6	5.07569	4.91732	4.76654	4.62288	4.35526	4.11141
7	5.78637	5.58238	5.38929	5.20637	4.86842	4.56376
8	6.46321	6.20979	5.97130	5.74664	5.33493	4.96764
9	7.10782	6.80169	6.51523	6.24689	5.75902	5.32825
10	7.72173	7.36009	7.02358	6.71008	6.14457	5.65022
11	8.30641	7.88687	7.49867	7.13896	6.49506	5.93770
12	8.86325	8.38384	7.94269	7.53608	6.81369	6.19437
13	9.39357	8.85268	8.35765	7.90378	7.10336	6.42355
14	9.89864	9.29498	8.74547	8.24424	7.36669	6.62817
15	10.37966	9.71225	9.10791	8.55948	7.60608	6.81086
16	10.83777	10.10590	9.44665	8.85137	7.82371	6.97399
17	11.27407	10.47726	9.76322	9.12164	8.02155	7.11963
18	11.68959	10.82760	10.05909	9.37189	8.20141	7.24967
19	12.08532	11.15812	10.33560	9.60360	8.36492	7.36578
20	12.46221	11.46992	10.59401	9.81815	8.51356	7.46944
22	13.16300	12.04158	11.06124	10.20074	8.77154	7.64465
24	13.79684	12.55036	11.46933	10.52876	8.98474	7.78432
26	14.37519	13.00317	11.82578	10.80998	9.16095	7.89566
28	14.89813	13.40616	12.13711	11.05108	9.30657	7.98442
30	15.37245	13.76483	12.40904	11.25778	9.42691	8.05518
32	15.80268	14.08404	12.64656	11.43500	9.52638	8.11159
34	16.19290	14.36814	12.85401	11.58693	9.60857	8.15656
36	16.54685	14.62099	13.03521	11.71719	9.67651	8.19241
38	16.86789	14.84602	13.19347	11.82887	9.73265	8.22099
40	17.15909	15.04630	13.33171	11.92461	9.77905	8.24378
45	17.77407	15.45583	13.60552	12.10840	9.86281	8.28252
50	18.25593	15.76186	13.80075	12.23348	9.91481	8.30450

* To convert from this table to values of an annuity in advance, determine the annuity in arrears above for one less period and add 1.00000.

Appendix B

Glossary, Alphabetical Reference List

For the definitions of the following terms, consult the glossary of the chapters indicated by the numbers in parentheses.

A

Abstract (8)
Acceleration Clause (6)
Accounting Period (11)
Acid-Test Ratio (10)
Add-On Clause (6)
Adjustable-Rate Mortgage (8)
Adjusted Gross Income (11)
Administrator (13)
Aliens (11)
Alimony (11)
AMEX (10)
Amortization (8)
Annuity (5)
Appraisal (4) (8)
Appreciation (8)
Arm's-Length Transaction (11)
As Is (9)
Asking Price (10)
Assets (1)
Assigned Risk (4)

Assumed Liability (4)
Attestation (13)

B

Baby Bonds (5)
Bait (6)
Bait and Switch (9)
Balance Sheet (1)
Balloon Contract (6)
Bank Deposit Slip (5)
Bankruptcy (6)
Bank Statement (5)
Bear (10)
Bear Market (10)
Bearer Bonds (5)
Beneficiary (4)
Bequeath (13)
Bequest (13)
Bid Price (10)
Big Board (10)
Binder (4)

Index